PHILOSOPHY'S ARTFUL CONVERSATION

PHILOSOPHY'S ARTFUL CONVERSATION

D. N. Rodowick

HARVARD UNIVERSITY PRESS

Cambridge, Massachusetts
London, England
2015

Library of Congress Cataloging-in-Publication Data

Rodowick, David Norman.
  Philosophy's artful conversation / D. N. Rodowick.
     pages cm
  Includes bibliographical references and index.
  ISBN 978-0-674-41667-3 (alk. paper)
  1. Theory (Philosophy)   2. Philosophy, Modern—21st century.   I. Title.
  B842.R58 2014
  101—dc23
                                                      2014007448

. . . and for Stanley Cavell,
whose example steered me through the middle,
in hope that I find my own way in the end.

CONTENTS

In Place of Beginning Again . . .

He sent thither his Theôry, or solemn legation for sacrifice,
decked in the richest garments.

—George Grote, *A History of Greece* (1862)

Philosophy's Artful Conversation brings to a close a project encompassing three volumes in which I discuss the fate of cinema studies as a field of humanistic inquiry in the twenty-first century. The first book, *The Virtual Life of Film* (2007), explored the philosophical consequences of the disappearance of a photographic ontology for the art of film and the future of cinema studies as the creative process of filmmaking becomes overtaken by digital technologies. *Elegy for Theory* (2014) surveys critically the place and function of the idea of theory in the humanities as we have lived and still live it today. *The Virtual Life of Film* concludes by reaffirming the importance of theory in that every discipline sustains itself "in theory"—a discipline's coherence derives not from the objects it examines but rather from the concepts and methods it mobilizes to generate critical thought. *Elegy for Theory* continues this argument through a critical and historical examination of what theory means for the arts and humanities, and why and how it has become a contested concept over the past thirty years.

Philosophy's Artful Conversation also takes the fate of theory in cinema studies as exemplary of the more general contestation of theory in the humanities. Where *Elegy for Theory* presented a genealogical perspective on theory's contested life, *Philosophy's Artful Conversation* marks a turn in my larger argument whereby the problematic existence of theory becomes the possibility of philosophy, especially what I call a philosophy of the humanities. My picture of a possible philosophy of the humanities takes inspiration from the later philosophical works of Ludwig Wittgenstein and their influence on figures as diverse as G. H. von Wright, P. M. S. Hacker, Charles Taylor, Richard Rorty, and Stanley Cavell. The book then concludes with an extensive discussion of Gilles Deleuze and Stanley Cavell as contemporary philosophers with distinctly original conceptions of the specificity of philosophy and of philosophical expression in relation to film and the arts. In reading these two thinkers together, I want to deepen and clarify their original contributions to our understanding of film and of contemporary philosophical problems of ontology and ethics, and interpretation and evaluation.

In *Elegy for Theory*, I expressed my hope that the book would be read and thought about as a whole composed of many interconnected parts and voicings, where a sympathetic ear attends to the unfolding of themes and variations, harmony and counterpoint, refrains, returns, and improvisations, as different lines of thought depart from and return to one another in new contexts. *Philosophy's Artful Conversation* deepens and expands this composition. Or, similar to its companion volume, perhaps *Philosophy's Artful Conversation* is less a musical score than newly unfolded pages of a topographic map, revealing yet larger and little-known horizons and landscapes, featuring plateaus with uneven elevations.

Ideally, readers will approach the two books as an interconnected whole. Yet similar to *Elegy for Theory*, many readers will justifiably approach this book in sections or parts, and not necessarily in the order I myself have conceived. Indeed, the two books may be read separately and independently of one another. Nonetheless, there are natural continuities between the two works, and they do comprise a single project. *Philosophy's Artful Conversation* picks up where *Elegy for Theory* leaves off. In the earlier book, I argue that our contemporary tendency to characterize "Theory" as a genre of discourse in the humanities is a fairly recent phenomenon, appearing gradually only after World War II. To the extent that a concept of "film theory" emerges in a common framework with ideas of literary or art theory, and that all three have comparable conceptual commitments forged in the shifting discursive contexts of aesthetics, Russian formalism, structuralism, and poststructuralism, the study of film study provides an admirably clear case for describing transformations and debates on theory in general. By the same token, the post-Theory debate launched by David Bordwell and Noël Carroll in film studies in the 1990s, with which I begin this book, offers a fascinating and clarifying context for investigating the conceptual claims of the various efforts to critique, overturn, or forget "Theory" more generally in the humanities.

The plateaus of *Philosophy's Artful Conversation* thus mark off several interconnected territories where philosophy tests its difference from and frontiers with theory. My guiding idea is that while philosophy is linked to theory in many inescapable ways, it still remains distinct from theory as a practice.

These plateaus are in turn divided by a valley that passes from further exami-
nations of theory's contested life to a more constructive vision of or for philosophy, or what I will call a philosophy of the humanities.

In our contemporary moment, philosophy has many rivals, many from
within philosophy itself, who seek to transform it or even to do away with it by
projecting a single standard of rationality for all forms of thought. This attitude is exemplified in contemporary attacks on theory in the humanities and
in the prestige currently enjoyed by cognitive science and evolutionary psychology. David Bordwell's critique of interpretation and his promotion of historical poetics are formidable examples of this trend. In these sections my intention is not to question Bordwell's influential and admirable work on
problems of history, style, and poetics, but rather to respond to his rather acid
critique of and disdain for the humanities. Bordwell's work on historical poetics is guided by a concept that I call, somewhat ironically, "'good' theory." As
a rival to what both Bordwell and Noël Carroll call Grand Theory, good theory aims to anchor analysis and history in the epistemological ideals of rational and empirical inquiry proximate to the natural sciences. I use the example
of good theory to question whether this standard of rationality is any more
stable than the positions it opposes, and to introduce my critique of what P.
M. S. Hacker calls the tendency to "scientism," or the illicit extension of the
methods and concepts of experimental science into areas of human expression and culture where they do not apply.

Bordwell's critique of interpretation and his promotion of historical poetics
marks one phase in contemporary contestations of theory, where the turn to
cognitivism and evolutionary psychology have provided new opportunities to
replace theory with methods and approaches inspired by analytical philosophies of science. Another phase subjects the association of theory with science
to philosophical critique. Deeply influenced by Ludwig Wittgenstein's purported critique of theory in the *Philosophical Investigations,* this perspective
calls for a new orientation in the examination of culture and the arts through
a philosophy of the humanities.

No doubt the appeal of good theory is very great, especially for those who
seek certainty and stable grounds for knowledge. The open questions remain,
however, of what counts as knowing, and whether or not there is a single standard of knowledge applicable in all cases, or whether there are justifiable
forms of knowledge that are both contingent and context dependent and that
are to be valued for their contingency and context dependency. In my view,
the logical frameworks of cognitivism and historical poetics, on the one hand,

and the strain of analytic philosophy of science proximate to and critical of the humanities, on the other, overreach in projecting their particular view of rationality as a single standard of explanation. The interest of the later Wittgenstein for my book, and for the humanities in general, begins with his attack on the identification of philosophy with science. This leads to another critical challenge to theory as laid out in the introduction to Richard Allen and Malcolm Turvey's important collection, *Wittgenstein, Theory and the Arts*. In reading Allen and Turvey, I examine and reassess Wittgenstein's purported rejection of theory as a method inappropriate for philosophical investigation of thought and culture. My aim here is to ask whether the conceptual investigation and evaluation of theory in all its historical varieties and differences can be preserved within the framework of philosophy as Wittgenstein conceived it, which also means asking whether the borders between philosophy and theory must really be strictly marked.

The turn to the later Wittgenstein introduces one of the major arguments of the present volume, which is to sketch out an idea of a philosophy of the humanities inspired by G. H. von Wright's assertion that the humanities study phenomena of culture or expression—call these forms of human life—that may and should be distinguished logically from methods and objects of study in the natural sciences. A primary task of a philosophy of the humanities is to assess the limits of scientific explanation, and in turn to describe and defend the sui generis character of humanistic understanding. Questions of interpretation, aesthetic judgment, and ethical evaluation are of central concern to the humanities, and here I set out the layered and multifaceted connections between these activities and Wittgenstein's more prominent philosophical attention to problems of language and psychology.

One of the principal trends of twentieth-century philosophy, which von Wright justly criticized, is an excessive concern with epistemology that leads to a kind of conceptual poverty and value nihilism. The goal of a philosophy of the humanities is to redress this imbalance between epistemology and ethics, and to understand how the particular form of the will to truth expressed by scientism not only excludes ways of knowing and interpreting that may be of great value but also willfully tries to make the humanities disappear behind the mask of science. The line of thought that weaves from the later Wittgenstein through the work of von Wright, Hacker, Stanley Cavell, Richard Rorty, and Charles Taylor, among others, can then be understood as motivated by the desire to assert and defend the autonomy of humanistic investigation and understanding.

The idea that a philosophy of the humanities derives from the sui generis character of humanistic understanding takes inspiration from Charles Taylor's account of humans as self-interpreting animals. Taylor's fascinating claim is that our knowledge of reality and the reality of our selves are inseparable from our experience of reality in terms of both knowledge and value, and of what we value in our ways of knowing ourselves and in the modes of existence we construct and inhabit. To interpret and to understand necessarily require a reflexive turn in acts of self-interpretation where problems of knowing are inextricably intertwined with questions of import and value. Therefore, ethics and reason, evaluation and interpretation, are intertwined activities because to claim to know is always to value certain ways of knowing, and to value is to project a world commensurate with the forms of reason one aspires to define and develop in conceptual expression. To project a world also means that philosophy is concerned with the expansion and conceptual renovation of our expressive resources as avenues toward possible transformations of our terms of existence. Philosophy must be imagined as a practice of change and invention, of augmenting, enlarging, and enhancing our conceptual schemes, of creating new styles of thought, and of projecting future states of self and society to which we aspire.

Along these lines of thought, the remainder of *Philosophy's Artful Conversation* is devoted to discussing two philosophers as exemplars of the twinned projects of ethical and epistemological evaluation: Gilles Deleuze and Stanley Cavell. Deleuze and Cavell are two contemporary philosophers with distinctly original conceptions of the specificity of philosophy and of philosophical expression in relation to film and the arts. In reading these two thinkers together, I want to deepen and clarify their original contributions to our understanding of film and of contemporary philosophical problems of ontology and ethics, and of interpretation and evaluation. Here my argument is guided by three primary questions: What are Deleuze and Cavell's particular conceptions of philosophy, and why is art or film so central to those conceptions? How do Deleuze and Cavell conceive philosophical practice as being immanent to artistic or cinematographic expression? And finally, what conception of ethics informs these two prior questions?

Despite their apparent differences of approach and style, the philosophical work of Deleuze and Cavell is linked by many common themes: the relation of philosophy to art or science; the necessary role of the friend in philosophy; the critique of the *cogito* as an image of thought and existence; and dedication to an image of time or change as force, becoming, and recurrence deeply influenced by Nietzsche and Kierkegaard. Another obvious way of linking Deleuze and Cavell is that in their own unique ways both share a picture of philosophy as inherently problematic; that is, as posing its own existence as a problem that must continually be revisited, rethought, and reassessed. The problematic nature of philosophy often takes the form of ethical questioning—what is the good of philosophy?—and in both philosophers the ethical relation is inseparable from our relationship to thought. For how we think, and whether we sustain a relation to thought or not, is bound up with our choice of a mode of existence and our relations with others and to the world. Odd as it may seem, there is a profound connecting thread that runs through Wittgenstein, Deleuze, and Cavell in the idea of restlessness and homelessness as the condition of thought, and that what matters most to philosophy can only be shown, and not possessed or expressed. And if it could be expressed, it is likely to be misunderstood. In this perspective, philosophy is not a state to be attained but a condition always to be discovered.

My account of Deleuze's possible contributions to (film) philosophy follow upon my sketch of the elements or grammar of a possible philosophy of the humanities, with its emphases on activities of interpretation and ethical evaluation. A key criterion for linking and contrasting Deleuze and Cavell is their common articulation of dilemmas of skepticism and the problem of belief. Here the path from Deleuze to Cavell takes an interesting turn. While Deleuze's Spinozan ontology presents a universe or plane of immanence where skepticism should be made irrelevant, in *Cinema 2: The Time-Image* his ethical picture of humanity's broken link with the world demonstrates Deleuze's difficulty in accounting for the human dimensions of this dilemma and the possible range of responses to it. A deep though not immediately apparent connection between Cavell and Deleuze might be located precisely at this point. There is a sinuous line where Cavell's and Deleuze's accounts of ontology complement one another, like two pieces of a puzzle whose pictures portray different worlds that nonetheless fit precisely at their joins. Along this line, Deleuze's ethical demand to restore belief in this world finds itself paired with Cavell's career-long examination of the grammar of acknowledgement and the logic of moral perfectionism. In turn, Cavell's work is exemplary of a philosophy of and for the humanities, particularly in his original attempt to rebalance the concerns of epistemology and ethics.

The common denominator between Deleuze and Cavell occurs in a grammar of worlding or worldliness: to acknowledge our connection to the world as a moral connection to the world and to others; to believe again not in a transcendent world but in this world with its reticence or recalcitrance, and also with its powers of change. Deleuze and Cavell are therefore both concerned with a similar problem: how does the subject undergo or experience change? However, unlike Deleuze, in Cavell time does not operate as a metaphysical constant but rather as an ethical will that must be continually reenacted because it is continually forgotten. One might say, then, that moral perfectionism is to Cavell's philosophy what becoming is to Deleuze's. Both concepts require new attention to the force of time in relation to qualities of change and transformation rooted in new and original approaches to Nietzsche's thought. I call this discovering a passion for time. For both philosophers, the moving image is a privileged medium for exploring this passion for time, but in a special way. Filmic expression does not exemplify concepts or provide examples for philosophy; as artful *expression* it *is* philosophy, or rather, a becoming-philosophy tending toward conceptual formation. As expression, one of art's many happy occupations is to be a friend to philosophy, and to aid in philosophical becoming.

1. A Permanent State of Suspension or Deferment

> Theory is essentially a scientific discourse, which is not only an abstract, generalizing, or foundational discourse, but also—and this is its distinctive trait—one that turns back on itself. A language that turns back on itself.
>
> —Roland Barthes, "On Theory"

In 1970, Roland Barthes gave an interview, "On Theory," to the French magazine, *VH*. What is most extraordinary about his remarks is his clarity about the stakes of theory in 1970 and the structure of theory as it would unfold so complexly over the next two decades. Barthes begins by signaling a contemporary disruption in the senses of theory that separate it from the discursive context of the nineteenth century, whose residues, one might add, were still to be found in the multiple origins of the discourse of structure. Barthes insists that theory not be opposed to the concrete nor confused with abstraction; this is his way of distinguishing two discursive formations of theory. Dominated by the kind of rationalism and empiricism associated with positivism and the rise of experimental science, the nineteenth century hesitates before theory, or searches for definitions of science distinguishable from theory. By the same token, positivism begins to turn from philosophy, or to seek a new place for philosophy as a helpmeet to science. This was one of the principal lessons of my *Elegy for Theory*.

In this turning point of 1970, Barthes also asserts that theory has taken on a new sense, which also withdraws from the practice of philosophy and the abstractions of metaphysics and now finds a new mode of concrete expression in the immanent analysis of texts. Theory passes through the text in an activity of fragmentation and discontinuity whose exemplary practice is Barthes's reading of Balzac's "Sarrasine" in *S/Z*. And here there is another disruption with an even older sense of theory. Etymologically, theory indicates a practice of observation, contemplation, meditation, or speculation, leading to a disinterested knowing independent of application. Through his interest in semiology and textual analysis, and through the influence of Levi-Strauss and Lacan,

Barthes opposes these characterizations of theory and projects instead a third sense, one that is clearly indebted to Julia Kristeva's account of theory as I described it in *Elegy for Theory*. "Theory is essentially a scientific discourse," Barthes offers, "which is not only an abstract, generalizing, or foundational discourse, but also—and this is its distinctive trait—one which turns back on itself. A language which turns back on itself."[1]

Theory in this sense does not seek to complete itself in a system of thought, but rather engages in an ongoing practice of reflexive critique—Barthes says that it inhabits a permanent state of suspension or deferment. This reflexivity is neither circular nor closed; it does not seek to enclose truth within theory. Rather, Barthes seeks a concept of theory through a discourse that thinks itself in terms of its material organization of meaning while engaging in a continuous autocritique that evades the lures of abstraction, continuity, and closure. Barthes wonders, then, whether the new sense of theory is not simply writing, or *écriture* in the then current vocabulary. "Writing," says Barthes, "in the contemporary sense of this word, is a theory. It has a theoretical dimension, and theory must not refuse writing or mobilize itself within a pure *écrivance*, which is to say, a purely instrumental view of the language that it uses" ("On Theory" 690–691).

One might smile at this kind of language today, recognizing its proximity to *Tel Quel*'s nearly forgotten language of literary modernism and the discourses of Theory of the 1980s and 1990s. Note, however, that Barthes is not promoting a political modernism (nor did he ever, I believe), but rather a close critical and analytical attention to the relation between discourse and theory, as well as to the discourse of theory; or better, that theory is produced through discourse and is never separate from it, materially or historically. On the one hand, Barthes's statements bring into sharp focus one of the persistent and unifying characteristics of the multiple, dissenting, and contradictory discourses of contemporary theory—its resolute reflexivity and self-criticism, which is always probing the axiological and epistemological borders of discourse, refusing to let it stand still or close within itself. On the other, Barthes is careful to avoid any claims of identity, for either the text or the subject, and this pushes him back from the center to the edges of contemporary theory. Theory seeks knowledge. It might even seek "scientific" knowledge. But to do

1. "Sur la théorie," *VH* 101 (Summer 1970); reprinted in Roland Barthes, *Oeuvres completes*, ed. Éric Marty, vol. 2, *1968–1971* (Paris: Éditions du Seuil, 2002), 690, my translations.

so is never to find the truth of a text, a subject, or a body, but rather to continually test how we approach or assert the question of knowledge in discourse, and what we value or not in that knowledge and the discursive forms it takes.

In *Elegy for Theory*, I suggested that we think of the problem of the history of film theory not as fixed and successive periods, or conceptual schemes overturning and replacing one another, but rather as overlapping and intersecting genres of discourse full of retentions, returns, and unexpected extensions, as well as ellipses and omissions. Nevertheless, the emergence or unfolding of discursive genres, one out of the other, occurs neither progressively nor continuously, but rather in series of disruptions and discontinuities that mark real differences between what I have called the aesthetic discourse, the discourse of signification, and that of ideology or culture, each of which involve turnings and remappings of concepts of theory. Moreover, I hinted at the end of *Elegy for Theory* that in film study, and perhaps the arts and humanities in general, a moment has arrived where contemporary theory reaches its end, which leads to some deep and disturbing questions: What comes after the contemporary? And what comes after Theory? In this context, certain key works anticipate a rupture that occurs between 1985 and 1995. I am thinking here of the unlikely pairing of David Bordwell's *Narration in the Fiction Film* and Gilles Deleuze's *Cinema 2: The Time-Image,* both of which were published in 1985. Neither book is a work of Theory or even "theory," and indeed both lead toward the controversial moment of "post-Theory" in the late 1990s, which in turn opens onto new competing yet tangentially related approaches to film philosophy. Stanley Cavell's work on film, beginning with *The World Viewed* in 1971 and continuing with major statements like *Pursuits of Happiness, Contesting Tears,* and *Cities of Words,* forges another path, which like Deleuze touches film theory along many of its edges without really interacting with it. In the same way that Jean-François Lyotard claimed that the postmodern is always what comes before the modern, it might be said that in their projections of film philosophy, Cavell and Deleuze stand outside or to one side of theory, marking out philosophy as an alternative path or a possible path to come. And if there is something that still challenges us in the critiques of post-Theory, it may not be exactly that theory has come to an end, though certainly the discursive period often called "contemporary" theory is drawing to a close, and it may even be said that contemporary *film* theory is in a moment of upheaval and transition. The stakes of our contemporaneity have changed, such that the response to what comes after theory is, often, philosophy. But what is philosophy? The paradox of this turning is its initial detour through history.

2. How Theory Became History

> Even though we may show our theory to be true, in some sense, we may be challenged to show that it is significant.
>
> —Charles Taylor, "Understanding and Ethnocentricity"

In *The Virtual Life of Film,* I argue that the evolution of cinema studies since the early 1980s has been marked both by a decentering of film with respect to media and visual studies and by a retreat from theory. No doubt this retreat had a number of salutary effects: a reinvigoration of historical research, more sociologically rigorous reconceptualizations of spectatorship and the film audience, and the placement of film in the broader context of visual culture and electronic media. But not all of these innovations were equally welcome. In 1996, David Bordwell and Noël Carroll argued in their edited collection *Post-Theory* (University of Wisconsin Press) for the rejection of 1970s "Grand Theory" as incoherent. Equally suspicious of cultural and media studies, Bordwell and Carroll insisted on anchoring the discipline in film as an empirical object subject to investigations methodologically allied to the natural sciences. Almost simultaneously, other philosophical challenges to Theory came from film scholars influenced by analytic philosophy and the later philosophy of Ludwig Wittgenstein. These debates emerged against the vexed backgrounds both of the culture wars of the 1990s and the rise of identity politics and cultural studies. Confusing "theory" with Theory, often lost in these debates is the acknowledgment that no judgments can be advanced—in history, criticism, or philosophy—in the absence of an axiological examination of our epistemological commitments. Put simply, theory has a critical dimension that promotes, evaluates, and adjudicates these commitments in an open-ended dialogue. To want to relinquish theory or to overcome it is more than a debate over epistemological standards; it is a retreat from reflection on the ethical commitments behind our styles of knowing. With this claim in mind, this book argues not for a return to the 1970s concept of theory, but rather for a vigorous debate on what should constitute a philosophy of the humanities critically and reflexively attentive to its epistemological and ethical commitments. I will return to this argument in later sections.

In *Elegy for Theory* I characterized the history of contemporary theory as being marked by distinctive conceptual divisions and conflicts. The Marxist and psychoanalytic theory of the subject inaugurated by *Tel Quel* in literature and by *Screen* in film studies was quickly challenged by new approaches and rhetorical stances including cultural studies, reception theory, feminist, postcolonial, and queer theory, and finally, new historicism and cognitivism. At the same time, within these divisions there are certain key conceptual commitments that wind through all the discourses like Ariadne's thread, linking various concepts of subjectivity and identity to often-unacknowledged problems of epistemology. In his introduction to *Post-Theory* Bordwell observes, in some cases convincingly, that there are deep continuities of doctrine and practice between the discourses of ideology and culturalism despite the debates that arise between them. If one is attentive to history as a pattern of discontinuities, both minor and major, contemporary theory is defined less by a break or division between, say, psychoanalysis and cognitivism than by a set of family resemblances linking the quarrelsome family of contemporary thought axially around questions of spectatorship, meaning, and cultural value, as well as the stakes of "theory." The problem of how to examine the activities of spectatorship, defining and assessing their range of subjective effects, is as important to cognitivism as it is to psychoanalytical or culturalist models. While the conceptual domain of contemporary film theory lacks unity, it is still defined by a powerful horizon of regularities where certain deep patterns of logic and discourse thread through the period. One of these involves how the problem of identity is fueled by the dialectic of negativity and the reflexive critical force of theory. The other has to do with the epistemological standpoints of claims to theory, which sustain all its processes of critique, debate, evaluation, and judgment, and which has only been rarely examined as such. Post-Theory and the cognitivist critique can be understood as one more branching of the second problem, extending the metatheoretical attitude in new directions.

By the mid-1990s film theory and indeed the concept of "theory" itself were challenged from a number of perspectives. This contestation occurred in three overlapping phases. The first phase is marked by David Bordwell's call throughout the 1980s for a "historical poetics" of film, and culminates in the debates engendered by his *Making Meaning: Inference and Rhetoric in the Interpretation of Cinema* (Harvard University Press) and by the special issue of *iris* titled "Cinema and Cognitive Psychology," both published in 1989. The keystone of the second phase is the 1996 publication of *Post-Theory*. Subtitled *Reconstructing Film Studies,* the book represents an attempt to establish film studies as a discipline modeled on cognitivist science and historical poetics, and to re-anchor practices of theory in the epistemological ideals of rational and empirical inquiry proximate to the natural sciences. While the second phase attempts to return theory to a model of "scientific" investigation and explanation, the third phase subjects the association of theory with science to philosophical critique. Deeply influenced by Ludwig Wittgenstein's purported critique of theory in the *Philosophical Investigations,* this perspective calls for a new orientation in the examination of culture and the arts through a philosophy of the humanities.

Throughout the 1980s and 1990s, then, theory is subjected to a triple displacement—by history, science, and finally by philosophy. At the same time, another salutary effect of post-Theory was its call for greater conceptual clarity in the stakes and structure of theory itself. In a contribution to the *Encyclopedia of Aesthetics,* Bordwell offers one of the clearest and most focused definitions: "Film theories offer systematic, general explanations of aspects of the nature, functions, and effects of cinema."[2] This well-considered and generous formulation would seem to cover a great variety of different types and styles of aesthetic writing on cinema. However, not all kinds of explanations are equal. Just as Althusser asked that we distinguish between true and false ideas, Bordwell will ask that clear lines be drawn between what I will characterize as bad and good theory.

As suggested at the end of *Elegy for Theory,* developments in cinema studies in the 1980s were marked by a historical and a cultural turn echoing the influence of the new historicism in literary studies. The renewed interest in history was no doubt responsible for some of the most influential publications of the decade, including *The Classical Hollywood Cinema: Film Style and Mode of Production to 1960* (Columbia University Press, 1985), coauthored by Bordwell with Kristin Thompson and Janet Staiger, and Bordwell's own *Narration in the Fiction Film* (University of Wisconsin Press, 1985). Both books were received as major contributions and interventions in contemporary film study, which at the height of its age of Theory was already confronting a number of impasses. It cannot and should not be said that either project was against

2. "Film Theory," in *Encyclopedia of Aesthetics,* ed. Michael Kelly, vol. 2 (Oxford: Oxford University Press, 1998), 197.

theory. Both books argued implicitly for a reconceptualization and re-orientation of theory, focusing and reducing its epistemological ambitions. This line of thought becomes clearer in Bordwell's subsequent work on cognitivism and film theory. From the mid-1980s, Bordwell has been making a much-needed case for revising the methods and concepts of historical research, and for re-balancing the relationship between history and theory in film study. In retrospect, I believe Bordwell was neither rejecting, revising, nor extending "theory" in the 1980s, but rather trying to invent a new path between history and theory, which he called "neoformalism" or "historical poetics," a path which he hoped would reform and remodel the discipline of film studies itself.

Bordwell's work is equally exemplary of a recasting of theory for the field of cinema studies. It is important to appreciate Bordwell's contribution to what I have characterized as the metatheoretical attitude. Among his generation, Bordwell was one of the first to exhibit a fascination with the history of film study itself, and to focus attention on problems of methodology with respect to questions of historical research and the critical analysis of form and style. Throughout the 1980s, Bordwell produced a number of influential methodological essays promoting a historical poetics of cinema. From *Narration in the Fiction Film* to *Making Meaning,* the broad outlines of his approach are made apparent. One cannot accuse Bordwell of a retreat from theory—no one's commitment to good theory building is greater or more admirable. Rather, he wants to recast theory as *history,* or rather, to ground theory in the context of empirical historical research. In this way, Bordwell responds to what are perceived to be the twin threats of cultural and media studies. On the one hand, there is a risk of methodological incoherence for a field whose interdisciplinary commitments have become too broad; on the other, the risk of diffusing, in the context of media studies, cinema studies' fundamental ground—film as a formal object delimiting specifiable effects. One aim of historical poetics, then, is to project a vision of methodological coherence onto a field of study perceived to be losing its center, and to restore an idea of film as a specifiable form to that center; in other words, poetics is searching for grounds to anchor and stabilize conceptually film's virtual life, both formally and historically. *Poetics* concerns questions of form and style. It deals with concrete problems of aesthetic practice and describes the specificity of film's aesthetic function while recognizing the importance of social convention in what a culture may define as a work of art. In *Narration in the Fiction Film,* the historical side of poetics addresses the proliferation of distinct modes of narration (classical Hollywood, Soviet or dialectical materialist, postwar European art cinema, parametric narration) as delimitable in time and sensitive to national and/or cultural contexts. Here Bordwell makes his best case for basing the analysis of individual works upon sound historical investigation and explicit theoretical principles in a way that avoids arbitrary boundaries between history, analysis, and theory.

By 1989 Bordwell's attack on interpretation and his promotion of cognitivism as a model of "middle-level research" recast theory with respect to three proposals. First, his appeal to middle-level research calls for pulling back from broader concerns of ideology and culture to refocus attention on film's intrinsic structure and functions. Second, he promotes a comparable turn from psychoanalytic theories of the subject to the study of filmic comprehension as grounded in, ideally, empirically constrained investigations of mental and perceptual structures. Finally, his renewed emphasis on history also signals a withdrawal from high-level conceptual concerns to refocus research on the fundamental data of films themselves and the primary documentation generated from their production contexts. Bordwell accuses interpretation of reaching too high in grasping for abstract concepts to map semantically onto its objects. Here the film-object itself disappears in its particularity, becoming little more than the illustration of concepts. Moreover, interpreters are reflexively insensitive to the cognitive operations they execute. They produce no new knowledge, but rather only repetitively invoke the same heuristics to model different films; in other words, interpretation is understood as a process of repeating and perpetuating the same heuristic models, not for accumulating new data and explanatory frameworks.

The sometimes unruly responses to *Making Meaning* and *Cinema and Cognitive Psychology* demonstrate that Bordwell's criticisms touched a nerve, and there is little doubt that his work in this period is a genuine and important response to the impasse in theory that cinema studies began to confront by the end of the 1980s.[3] In the critique of so-called Grand Theory, what is most interesting here is the implicit alliance of historical poetics and cognitivism with analytically inclined philosophies of science, above all as exemplars of what Bordwell calls rational and empirical inquiry. In the two introductions to *Post-Theory,* both Bordwell and Carroll promote strong views of what constitutes good theory building, in stark contrast to the then-current state of

3. See in particular *Film Criticism* 17, no. 2–3 (1993), a special issue devoted to critical discussion of *Making Meaning,* as well as Bordwell's debate with Dudley Andrew on cognitivism in *iris* 11 (Summer 1990).

contemporary film and cultural theory. Ironically, one consequence of this appeal, strongly implicit in Carroll's contribution, "Prospects for Film Theory: A Personal Assessment," is that film *theory* does not yet exist, an implication that strongly recalls Christian Metz's position in the 1960s and early 1970s. Carroll criticizes both classical and contemporary film theories according to three basic arguments: they are essentialist or foundationalist, taking films as examples of a priori conditions; they are doctrine driven rather than data driven, meaning not susceptible to empirical examination and verification; and finally, they deviate too widely from *film*-based problems; that is, the concrete particularity of filmic problems disappears when they are taken up to illustrate broader concepts of ideology, subjectivity, or culture. Alternatively, characterized by "ordinary standards of truth" as a regulative ideal, good theory seeks causal reasoning, deduces generalities by tracking regularities and the norm, is dialectical and requires maximally free and open debate, and, finally, is fallibilistic. In this sense, good theory is historical in being open to revision through the successive elimination of error. Middle-level research presents the provisional ground for a theory or theories of film projected forward in a process of debate, falsification, and revision.[4] The "post" in "postTheory" is a curious misnomer, then, for what has been characterized as Theory is epistemologically invalid, and, ironically, what comes after may only appear after a period of long debate and revision. A legitimate film theory remains to be constructed, the product of an indefinite future.

Hesitancy before "theory" will be a familiar theme for those who have already read *Elegy for Theory*. Sometimes theory hovers in an indefinite future as a desired though as yet unattained or unattainable state of knowledge; alternatively, Boris Eikhenbaum exemplified the tendency to temper theory with method in order to avoid the abstractions of philosophy and to bring poetics closer to nomothetic reasoning. In insisting that poetics is neither a doctrine nor a method, Bordwell projects a view not dissimilar from Eikhenbaum's, which is unsurprising considering the influence of Russian formalism on historical poetics. However, in the nearly twenty years since *Post-Theory* was published it is surprising how little the stakes of the debate have changed;

---

4. Succinct accounts of Carroll's commitment to theorizing as a provisional process motored by fallibilism and marked by a competitive multiplicity of theories of different levels of generality, are also found in his introduction to *Theorizing the Moving Image* (Cambridge: Cambridge University Press, 1996), xiii–xix, and his essay "Cognitivism, Contemporary Film Theory and Method: A Response to Warren Buckland" in the same volume, 321–335; see also David Bordwell's foreword to the volume, ix–xii.

in many senses, Theory has not been transcended or overcome, though it has continued unraveling and branching into diversely intertwining series of "field studies," to invoke Francesco Casetti's terminology. By the same token, historical poetics and cognitivism have taken firm root in cinema studies, producing many interesting offshoots and spreading for more widely and diversely than Bordwell or Carroll have often been ready to admit.

Why, then, has the post-Theory moment not fully arrived? In the introduction and first chapter of *Poetics of Cinema* (Routledge, 2008), Bordwell suggests that the reasons are largely institutional, which motivates him not only to deepen and clarify his methodological commitments to poetics but also to extend his criticisms of Theory, his notions of theorizing, and his conception of the relation of poetics and theory to empirical research. One ongoing and curious feature of Bordwell's defense of film poetics is not only his hesitancy before theory, but also his association of Theory with literary study, academic research, and the Modern Language Association (as a hegemonic institution promoting Theory). So admirably committed to concreteness, detail, and clarity in other domains, Bordwell constructs Theory, whether in his 1996 introduction to *Post-Theory* or his 2008 introduction to *Poetics of Cinema*, in ways that only thinly disguise an ethical critique in the form of epistemological objections. This pitting of poetics against Theory requires a rhetoric forged in agon, conflict, and opposition in order to identify and identify with a domain of reason from which others seem to have withdrawn or have never aspired to. From "A Case for Cognitivism" to *Poetics of Cinema*, what I have always found most striking about Bordwell's critiques of Theory, the humanities, and indeed most of academic film study is that little is added and nothing subtracted from his own worthy and productive vision of historical poetics, in either its results or its methodological clarity and conviction, by these criticisms. The open questions, then, are why do they return and what do they hope to achieve.[5] Though the idea may seem paradoxical to most, in a strong

5. In an early review of Carroll's *Mystifying Movies,* Warren Buckland notes that an effect of this polarizing rhetoric is to limit meaningful debate in advance through a binary logic that "reformulates, transforms, misrepresents, and systematically distorts the values and norms of the scheme or the theory that has been translated or interpreted, for such an interpretation is carried out on the outside, not the inside, of the theory under interpretation." See Buckland's "Critique of Poor Reason," *Screen* 30, no. 4 (1989): 84. I could also add that in the two introductory essays to *Post-Theory,* few ideas apart from the "grand Theorists" are engaged directly through their authors. Carroll's introduction is without footnotes, and in Bordwell's essay the footnotes maintain a sort of running dialogue with the main text to two purposes: first, to show that the database is large and that this is indeed a complete and not one-sided account of "film theory"; second, to lay out a bibliography of alternative texts for the opposing philosophical and

sense Bordwell's rhetorical strategies express a deep commitment to the fundamental questions of philosophy as I defined them in *Elegy for Theory*: to evaluate (in this case critically and skeptically) the limits of reason or knowledge in a domain in order to project another mode of existence or form of life with its own community sustained by other discursive commitments and reasoning protocols. Critical evaluation of the logical and discursive limits of knowledge and attentiveness to the historical forms of discontinuity of our relationship to knowledge are key components of my conception of philosophical practice. Most striking in the discourse of post-Theory, however, is that criticism does not seek to change the world of "academic humanities," as it were, but rather to leave it behind for a better and more reasonable community. In fact, one of the goals of criticism is to define or project that future community, or to rediscover it as a path not taken.

Equally striking in the identification of Theory with the humanities is the implicit placement of the method and practice of poetics as another domain to one side or outside of the humanities. It is as if Bordwell believes that the humanities have relinquished all interest or commitment to artworks in their immanence, as well as the analysis of form and style in well-defined historical frameworks. However, even if I find this near blanket condemnation of the humanities to be logically and historically flawed, my goal here is not to challenge it further, nor am I concerned to criticize Bordwell's unique and considerable accomplishments in constructing a poetics of cinema. (Indeed, in most contexts I spend my time defending them.) My interest is rather to uncover and make conceptually precise the concept of "good theory" in relation to my larger account of the vicissitudes of theory in relation to philosophy, on the one hand, and science on the other.

---

cognitivist account as a site of potential truth. One feels strongly that this rhetoric is less about providing a full and adequate picture of theory as it is to draw tendentiously its limits, the better to foreground why the competing cognitivist account is better. The two introductions also ignore the presence of substantial criticism and debate within the framework of so-called Grand Theory. Or worse, the presence of such debate is read as being inconsistent and contradictory, and thus assumes that the imagined grand Theory is homogenous and unified. Both subject-position and culturalist theory are presented as a sort of anonymous collective (the realm of "theoretical" common sense or consensus), which is then represented as misleading, false, or subject to poor reasoning. On the alliance of cognitivism with social science and its opposition to the "humanities," see also Bryan Vescio, "Reading in the Dark: Cognitivism, Film Theory, and Radical Interpretation," *Style* 35, no. 4 (Winter 2001): 572–591. On conflict and disunity in post-Theory and film theory in general, see Casey Haskins, "The Disunity of Film Theory and the Disunity of Aesthetics," in *European Film Theory*, ed. Temenuga Trifonova (New York: Routledge, 2009), 32–46.

In his 2008 introduction to *Poetics of Cinema,* Bordwell largely restates without modification his objections to Grand Theory: it is doctrine driven and aims too high, often presuming "that all human activity can be subsumed within some master conceptual scheme."[6] Moreover, its reasoning protocols are marred by argument from authority, unjustified associative leaps, vagueness and obfuscation, and avoidance of empirical evidence. Bordwell does not ignore or deny that Theory is itself a contentious domain with many competing perspectives. But he also asserts that what unites these positions under the grand umbrella of Theory is "the idea that any program propelled by doctrines can be applied, via imaginative extrapolation, to one phenomenon or another. The cluster of doctrines isn't questioned skeptically; the effort goes into diligent application" (2). "We have lived with this writing for 30 years," Bordwell continues. "Its limping cadences, convulsive syntax, and strategic confusions have dulled our senses. Very likely, no one in the history of English ever published prose as incomprehensible as that signed by Theorists" (2). Has there ever been a clearer expression of the longing for a different world? In the bipolar world that Bordwell constructs, the commitment to historical poetics and good theory aims at nothing less than a transformation of the field of film studies, and one that will distance it from the humanities.

In contradistinction, good theory has a goal as simple as it is direct: "producing knowledge that is reliable and approximately true" (3). Moreover, this knowledge is historical in quite specific ways. Its concepts are corrigible—it is continually revisable in the light of new evidence, whether derived from documentary and archival research or innovative analysis of the form and style of specific artworks. In addition, I also believe that Bordwell accepts that concepts themselves are open to invention and innovation, as long as they stay close to evidence and are ideally empirically constrained. All of this is noncontroversial.

However, if good theory distances itself from the humanities, to what alternative domain does it gravitate? One likely candidate is "science." The problem here is that both Bordwell's and Carroll's appeals to science, when they occur, are as vague and overly general as their critical view of the "humanities."[7]

6. (New York: Routledge, 2008), 2.

7. In footnotes, Bordwell often reproduces enormous bibliographies of research in cognitivism and in evolutionary criticism. However, despite his attention to and criticism of reasoning protocols, he gives little sense of what positions he adheres to in either logic or the philosophy of science. In most cases his position seems largely and simply Aristotelian. (By the same token, Carroll's conception of "dialectics" is Platonic rather than Hegelian.) The situation is even more

Nonetheless, Bordwell is very clear, especially in later work, that in his view poetics is not a science nor does it want to become one. For example, there is no commitment to covering laws as a necessary condition for producing knowledge. However, to the extent that theory is a component of poetics, it serves a now-familiar transitional or intermediate function: methodologically, it makes poetics proximate to reasoning protocols that are closely associated with science. For the moment, though, good theory is not quite equivalent to science but rather involves a broader tradition of rational and empirical inquiry, which, as Bordwell puts it, is committed to historical research and a mix of inductive and deductive reasoning. "By rational inquiry," Bordwell clarifies,

> I mean probing concepts for their adequacy as descriptions and as expla-
> nations of problems. Problems are stated as questions to be answered; the
> more concrete, the better. Empirical inquiry—not "empiricism," as hu-
> manists have to be told over and over—involves checking our ideas against
> evidence that exists independent of our beliefs and wishes—not evidence
> delivered in pristine innocence, without conceptual commitments on
> the part of the seeker, and not facts that "speak for themselves." What is
> evidence? It's what is corrigible in the light of further information. And
> to those who believe that facts are inevitably relative to your standpoint,
> I'd reply that both concepts and evidence can cut across different re-
> search frameworks. . . . Rational-empirical research programs have been

---

obscure in Carroll's critical essays and responses to criticism. While Carroll often evokes "post-positivist" philosophies of science, gesturing toward patterns of agreement and disagreement with Thomas Kuhn, or appealing to "ordinary standards of truth and error," the varieties of history or philosophy of science that he adheres to are almost invisible in his writings and must be extrapolated conceptually from his arguments. Still, certain general commitments appear. In *Making Meaning*, Bordwell critiques interpretation because it "does not on the whole produce scientific knowledge" (257), and further, that it should be pressed "to produce knowledge in [something] like the sense applicable to the natural and the social sciences" (263). In his introduction to *Post-Theory*, Carroll complains that "one reason we have reached this impasse is that film scholars generally have little, if any, background in the actual practices of theory building, since most of them have exclusively hermeneutical training, as opposed to education in theoretical disciplines such as the natural or social sciences, or philosophy" (42). Or further: "What I am saying is: let us take advantage of the insights derived from reflection on the scientific enterprise in order to think about what the structure of our own practice might be" (59). In a so-far-unpublished essay, "Film Theory and the Philosophy of Science," Meraj Dhir has presented an excellent defense of Carroll's position with respect to contemporary debates on the history and philosophy of science.

undertaken by many other film scholars, perhaps more by historians than by critics and theorists, but I try to answer questions from a distinctive angle. That angle I call the poetics of cinema (3–4).

Key criteria of rational and empirical inquiry include being categorically explicit and open to criticism on conceptual grounds. Concrete evidence must be invoked in a way that is equally open to critical appraisal and correction. Another aspect of poetics that associates it with good theory is that it "appeals to intersubjectively available data that are in principle amenable to alternative explanation."[8] Intersubjectivity here indicates that described events and explanations are universally observable and communicable. Finally, as theory poetics is proximate to science in another way—it is willing to make appropriate best use of biological and neurological, psychological, social scientific, and evolutionary accounts as components of causal explanations. In this it is also distinct from the humanities, which Bordwell feels distrusts science.

Poetics is presented, then, as both an alternative path to theory and as a rival to the dominant hermeneutic strategies of the humanities. In the humanities, method is synonymous with adherence to an interpretive school, which means for Bordwell that the writer must "master a semantic field informed by particular theoretical concepts and then to note certain features of films that fit that field" ("Poetics" 12). Here Bordwell recapitulates arguments from his concluding chapter to Making Meaning, "Why Not to Read a Film," which is fundamentally a defense of two positions: that interpretation is not equal to theory, and that historical poetics is not so much a theory as a theoretical activity driven by a certain functionalism. The question here is not who makes meaning (the culturalist view point), but rather where and how meaning is made. This shift defines all the epistemological stakes of the argument.

In Making Meaning, Bordwell offers a rich and complex account of interpretation as an institutionally structured craft activity, governed by conventional knowledge structures (schemata), inductive inferential procedures (heuristics), and standard rhetorical forms. The interpretive act ascribes im-

8. "Poetics of Cinema," in Poetics of Cinema, 15. In his new introduction to Ozu and the Poetics of Cinema (Ann Arbor: Center for Japanese Studies Publications, University of Michigan), Bordwell also explains, in a statement that uncannily echoes my account of Eikhenbaum in Elegy for Theory, that "I try to provide only as much 'theory' as is necessary to solve the midrange problems I've tackled. The fewer theoretical presuppositions you hold, and the more you appeal to intersubjectively accessible evidence, the stronger your argument gets." Available online at https://www.cjspubs.lsa.umich.edu/electronic/michclassics/online/books/ozu.php.

plicit or symptomatic meanings to a text through the application of one or
more semantic fields or conceptual structures that organize potential meanings relationally. To refer to a locus classicus of contemporary theory, semantic fields can be exemplified as ordered sets of distinctions such as active/pas-
sive, masculine/feminine, and voyeurism/fetishism. Operating from broad
assumptions and hypotheses, the interpretive critic maps pertinent semantic
fields onto appropriate cues identified in the text, and through inferential procedures translates different kinds of schemata into an action that allows "the
critic to show the film *enacting* the pertinent semantic values."[9] My paraphrasing here is rather abstract, though Bordwell himself offers many astute
and clarifying examples. From the point of view of the functionalism of historical poetics, one problem with interpretation is that while it may be based
on fairly close readings from textual evidence, it draws meaning from the
"outside," as it were, and too abstractly. There is no such thing as a strictly intrinsic interpretation, then, and the act of interpretation itself violates what
Russian formalism already identified as a principle of immanence.

However, the issue before us is the picture of "good theory" expressed
through Bordwell's critique of interpretation. In "Why Not to Read a Film,"
Bordwell is careful to distinguish interpretive from theoretical writing, especially since the former often masquerades as the latter. This is one of the car-
dinal sins of interpretation. In Bordwell's conception, a theory consists of a
systematic propositional explanation of the nature and function of phenomena, say the cinema, and theoretical writing differs from interpretive writing
in that it proposes, analyzes, and criticizes theoretical claims. One might say
that theories are explanatory, critical, and conceptually based; they explain
through constructing and invoking apposite concepts, which are open to revision or falsification through critique. A critic does not need theory to produce interpretations. "If theory as a body of doctrine consists of propositional
knowledge," Bordwell writes, "critical interpretation is principally a matter of
procedural knowledge, or know-how. Producing an interpretation is a skill,
like throwing a pot. The potter need not be a chemist, a minerologist, or a
professor of pottery. In some cases, learning 'theory' may help people acquire
certain interpretive skills, but it cannot replace those skills" (*Making Meaning*
250). Interestingly, one might say the same thing about the procedural skills
for producing artworks, as indeed Bordwell does in later articles and books.

9. *Making Meaning: Inference and Rhetoric in the Interpretation of Cinema* (Cambridge, MA:
Harvard University Press, 1991), 249.

The production of theories may also be considered a practice, of course, with its own institutional contexts, reasoning protocols, and rhetorical strategies. (Here, somewhat surprisingly, Bordwell is not so far from Althusserian epistemology, nor are Bordwell or Carroll necessarily vulnerable to Althusserian critiques of "empiricism.") However, for Bordwell interpretation is not often conducted in a "theoretically perspicuous" (251) way, meaning it is not usually open to conceptual self-interrogation, *pace* Barthes. When theory is "applied" through interpretation, it is usually done in "a piecemeal, ad hoc, and expansionist manner. . . . While the constraints on 'pure' theorizing are logical and broadly empirical, the constraints on using theory in interpretation arise from the needs of the immediate task. . . . 'Theory' will be selectively assimilated by the normalized routines of interpretation" (250–251). For Bordwell, this is an unjustified restriction and reduction of theoretical activity, and in many cases I grant he is correct.

The objectives and stakes of interpretation and theory should be epistemologically distinguishable, then, first because interpretive heuristics are not open to counterexample. Once a semantic field, heuristic, or schema is put into play, apposite examples are assumed to be equally interpretable. In contrast to theory construction, interpretation refuses "to stipulate when something will *not* count as a valid interpretive move or as an instance of meaning. Let me be clear: *within the interpretive institution*," Bordwell insists, "such conceptual moves do not count as errors. They help produce interpretations that are judged to be novel and persuasive. But this shows that the criteria governing *this* practice ill-accord with the conventions of another one, that called theorizing" (*Making Meaning* 252). Good theory must have the potential to be in error, that is, it should be falsifiable and open to counterexample. But appeals to theory in interpretation are pragmatic and rhetorical rather than demonstrative. Thus, interpretive arguments are not fallible in the strict sense, nor can theory assure an interpretation, whether inductively or deductively. Interpretation, then, usually evokes theory to frame and define evidence in a text, or as a warrant or authority to support a reading.

Critics are rational agents to the extent that they seek to apply the tools and procedures of their craft to produce novel interpretations. But in Bordwell's view, interpretive procedures stand and fall on novelty and persuasiveness, not standards of truth and error. What are the general criteria, then, according to which good theory is produced? In a now thoroughly familiar argument, Bordwell suggests that theoretical arguments must be governed by clear principles of pertinence, setting out what the theory will and will not explain.

By the same token, these explanatory accounts must possess degrees of generality distinguishing broad concepts from middle range and fine-grained ones, and should be reasonably counterintuitive in terms of producing surprising perspectives or results. Quotidian assumptions should be specifiable and open to interrogation. Most importantly, a theory must be corrigible, empirically falsifiable, and conceptually coherent. "All these criteria—broad but not unlimited scope, internal coherence, empirical adequacy, the ability to be disconfirmed—are ones by which a theoretical argument ought to be judged." (*Making Meaning* 253).

Are there any virtues to interpretation? In fairness Bordwell believes there are. Many exemplars of interpretation, Bordwell writes, "deserve praise because they have introduced conceptual schemes that reorient our understanding. They have activated neglected cues, offered new categories, suggested fresh semantic fields, and widened our rhetorical resources. Innovative frames of reference have heightened our awareness of what can be noticed and appreciated in artworks" (*Making Meaning* 256). Interpretation might also serve what is conventionally understood as one of the main concerns of the humanities in that it "answers to a widely felt interest in motives, intentions, and ethical responsibility by showing that artworks which do not offer explicit guides for behavior can raise significant issues of thought, feeling, and action" (258). Yielding to Dilthey's concept of *Verstehen* or understanding, Bordwell also suggests that interpretation may offer reasoned speculation on the possibilities of meaning, and become an occasion "to explore a theory's semantic implications and affinities" (258).

At the same time, interpretation is for the most part incapable of producing scientific knowledge in the sense of explaining processes that underlie external phenomena, and in this it falls short of theory. "Neither causal nor functional explanation is the aim of film interpretation," Bordwell explains. "Indeed, in a certain sense, knowledge of the text is not the most salient effect of the interpretive enterprise. It may be that interpretation's greatest achievement is its ability to encourage, albeit somewhat indirectly, reflections upon our conceptual schemes. By taming the new and sharpening the known, the interpretive institution reactivates and revises common frameworks of understanding. Interpretation takes as its basic subject our perceptual, cognitive, and affective processes, but it does so in a roundabout way—by attributing their 'output' to the text 'out there.' To understand a film interpretively is to subsume it to our conceptual schemes, and thus to master them more fully, if only tacitly" (*Making Meaning* 257).

To the committed humanist, these activities may not seem so unreasonable or undesirable, but for Bordwell interpretation's sins outweigh its virtues. In contrast to some of the great exemplars of pre-1968 film theory, such as Rudolf Arnheim, Lev Kuleshov, Sergei Eisenstein, André Bazin, and Noël Burch, what Bordwell calls the contemporary interpretive project has not produced or extended the conceptual resources for understanding film style, form, or structure. Poetics follows these exemplars of classical film theory in avoiding interpretation by constraining analysis to questions of composition, effects, and functions. Historical poetics also draws inspiration from another genealogical line stretching from Aristotle to the Russian formalist *Poetika Kino* and Todorov's *Poetics of Prose*. In this way, historical poetics connects back to a modified structuralism on my cartography of theory as drawn in *Elegy for Theory*, but without the commitment to language as an object. The concept of signification is thus displaced by comprehension, but to the extent that comprehension is also concerned with problems of meaning and spectatorship, the cognitivist turn may be more a variation on the discourse of signification than a complete break from it. In addition, many of these predecessors were also concerned to make method proximate to reasoning protocols in the natural sciences.[10]

Nevertheless, despite finding some value in the early work of Christian Metz and the semiological analysis of film, on the whole the project of historical poetics seeks to define a break or point of epistemological rupture and discontinuity with contemporary Theory, and in a familiar move frames itself in a retrojecting alternative lineage. Thus in the history of film theory, it becomes possible to imagine a postcontemporary moment once "contemporary" film theory is circumscribed as a particular discourse that has completed itself and condemned itself to repetition. This is one of the generative contexts of post-Theory and the "end" of the contemporary. The retrojecting movements

10. Poetics also takes inspiration from earlier models of film criticism (Manny Farber is a particular favorite) in attending complexly to the surface of a work according to principles of immanence. Bordwell also finds exemplary criticism in the pages of reviews like *Movie* and *Monogram,* and even gives some credit to semiotically oriented textual analysis. Here a "sensuous criticism" attends to phenomenal qualities of texts to the extent to which they begin to organize meaning, or are directed towards meaning, but from within the text. Precise description may then be complemented by historical study of particular films to account for what processes brought them into being and what forces—aesthetic, institutional, economic, or political—have mobilized them for specific purposes. Drawing on all these examples, Bordwell then argues that "a theoretically rigorous historical scholarship is at present a strong candidate for reinvigorating film study." *Making Meaning,* 266.

of post-Theory thus seek to circumvent those phases in the history of theory forged in the problematics of signification, psychoanalysis, and ideology, and to characterize them as deviations from the main line of theory. At the same time, while historical poetics opposes itself to the discourses of signification and ideology, it has many points of contact not only with structuralism but also with filmology, especially in the version offered by Étienne Souriau. (See, for example, section 14 of *Elegy for Theory*, "An Uncertain and Irrational Art.") If Bordwell has some sympathy for the early Metz, might this derive partially from Metz's own hesitations before the overly scientific ambitions of hard structuralism? The strongest continuity, however, is perhaps the most delicate yet complex one, which is a certain hesitation before "theory" and the ways in which the meanings and values of theory in relation to poetics hover uncertainly between science and philosophy, in ways analogous to Souriau's conception of aesthetics. Bordwell and Carroll's demand for good theory and for a stable framework for pursuing research and dialectical criticism also share with filmology the desire to find a common theoretical framework and vocabulary in which data and results can be shared across a variety of analytic and experimental approaches.

Here Carroll's professed adherence to "post-positivist" philosophies of science may diverge from logical positivism, but there are still many ways in which both Bordwell and Carroll hover close to a version of positivism that passes through formalism, filmology, and structuralism. While Bordwell and Carroll demonstrate no obvious commitments to positivism, and justifiably decline to characterize their enterprise as "scientific," the ideal of good theory is clearly open to charges of "scientism," a tendency that P. M. S. Hacker has described as "the *illicit* extension of the methods and forms of explanation of the natural sciences."[11] (Hacker's defense of the humanities and his reasons for calling such extensions illicit will be taken up in Section 3.) Not all such extensions are misconceived, but many are, and the goal is to avoid applying the positivistic doctrine of methodological monism across scientific and humanistic epistemology—especially since contemporary scientific methods are themselves badly characterized as striving for methodological monism and indeed may be open to a variety of heterogeneous explanation schemes.[12] In

11. "Wittgenstein and the Autonomy of Humanistic Understanding," in *Wittgenstein, Theory and the Arts,* ed. Richard Allen and Malcolm Turvey (New York: Routledge, 2001), 42.

12. Methodological monism insists on the unity of scientific method as a theory type, regardless of the research domain to which it is applied. A key tenet of positivism, methodological monism is closely tied to a second doctrine sometimes called the subsumption-theoretic model

particular, Bordwell and Carroll's position is aptly described by what Hacker calls "non-reductive methodological scientism." In this view, even if one accepts that social and psychological phenomena are not logically or ontologically reducible to physical processes or functions, "the logical structure of explanation in humanistic studies, in particular the explanation of human thought and action, is the same as that of typical explanations in the natural sciences" ("Wittgenstein and the Autonomy of Humanistic Understanding" 43). A fully scientific explanation of human behavior requires knowledge of causes and of underlying causal laws that may determine it. Often these causal laws are taken to describe regularities of neural or abstract functional computational mechanisms. The assumption here is that all rational explanation must have the same general form, exemplified by forms of explanation in the natural sciences. Beyond the commitments to empiricism and a principle of immanence, one could also point to other affinities with positivism, including a fairly unified conception of scientific method, the ideal of promoting general understanding through discovery of necessary and sufficient conditions for phenomena, the idea that investigation should be supported by corrigible and confirmable empirical research whose results have the potential to be surprising, and the conviction that the ultimate goal of research is to produce knowledge in a way that aspires to be value free and universally applicable. In addition, Bordwell and Carroll share a view, commonplace since Comte, "acknowledging that the tradition of rational and empirical inquiry, however subject to error, is our most reliable path to knowledge, which can be used for progressive ends" ("Introduction" 5). In other words, adherence to a subsumption-theoretic model is the best available framework for guiding and assuring social as well as scientific progress.

Poetics, then, has a long and distinguished genealogy, and Bordwell suggests that poetics has maintained a persistent aim across the span of centuries: "The poetics of any artistic medium studies the finished work as the result of a process of construction—a process that includes a craft component (such as rules of thumb), the more general principles according to which the work is composed, and its functions, effects, and uses" ("Poetics of Cinema" 12). In addition, poetics has further critical dimensions, which may be analytical (the study of a device or devices in a single work or group of works), theoretical

---

of explanation, which seeks to subsume all individual cases to causally bound general laws of nature, including, one assumes hypothetically, presumed laws of human nature. See *Elegy for Theory*, section 5.

(setting out conditions for a class or genre of work), and/or historical (understanding how artworks assume given forms within and across time periods). Historical, analytical, and theoretical activities are combined in historical poetics to explain the principles through which artworks are constructed, how they produce well-defined effects, and how they emerge historically and evolve in particular empirical circumstances.

In each of these cases good theory is deeply concerned with problems of causality and intentionality. Take the question of "effects." In "Film Interpretation Revisited," Bordwell explains that "I take 'effects' to include all possible responses we can ascribe to the film viewer, and propose to treat meanings as one (large) class of effects. There are non-meaningful effects: the perception of color or pattern, 'hard-wired' responses to certain cues (e.g., the phi phenomenon, or the startle response evoked by sudden blasts of music or noise in a thriller). There are also effects which involve the ascription of non-interpretive meanings (referential and explicit, on the typology under discussion)."[13] What is most interesting here is how the problem of meaning is produced through a conceptual continuum grounded ultimately in the body, or rather, physiological and neurological processes; in this, Bordwell is not so far from Claude Levi-Strauss or Roman Jakobson. I will return to this idea in discussing Bordwell's commitment to good naturalization and rational agent theory. Poetics is also open to a variety of models of causation and change, including teleological, intentionalist, and functional. In this same paragraph is found once again the disclaimer that poetics need not claim to offer scientific explanations, yet it remains proximate to scientific reasoning protocols. It has "the explanatory value of any empirical undertaking, which always involves a degree of tentativeness about conclusions" ("Poetics of Cinema" 16). Moreover, poetics is perhaps similar to other scientific disciplines, such as geography and archaeology, "which fall short of predictive accuracy but have good records of ex post facto explanatory power. It's probably best to say that poetics joins the overarching tradition of rational and empirical inquiry to which science and kindred disciplines belong" (16).

In a section titled "One Poetics of Film," Bordwell offers, again with admirable clarity, an account of the role theory plays in poetics and the nature of the reasoning he adheres to. Bordwell situates himself in a tradition of dealing with the singularity or particularity of artworks. One line is art historical in the sense of systematically tracking forms and styles in the visual arts and

13. *Film Criticism* 17, no. 2–3 (Winter/Spring 1993): 117, n. 16.

explaining change causally. The key figures here are Heinrich Wölfflin, Alois Riegl, Erwin Panofsky, and E. H. Gombrich. In literary theory, the genealogy passes through Russian formalism and Prague School structuralism, which are valued for their concrete analysis of works and how they function in historical contexts. Bordwell locates an equally rich tradition in music theory. However, here again, just as poetics hovers close to science without being scientific, it aims at theory without being theoretical, at least in a specific sense: "If we take a film theory to consist of a set of propositions explaining the fundamental nature and function of all cinematic phenomena, the poetics I'm setting out doesn't amount to a theory in that sense. It's best described as a set of assumptions, a heuristic perspective, and a way of asking questions. It's frankly empirical and tries to discover facts and truths about films" ("Poetics of Cinema" 20).

Bordwell says much the same thing about his commitments to cognitivism. The idea that cognitivism is less a theory than a perspective, frame of reference, heuristic, or problem-solving program goes back to Bordwell's first major methodological statement, "A Case for Cognitivism." As in the later "Poetics of Cinema," Bordwell takes great care to set out cognitivism's core assumptions. In contrast to psychoanalysis, for example, cognitive explanations are concerned with normal and successful actions, such as perception, recognition, and ordinary comprehension (though in each case this will come down mostly to nonintentional and thus subnormative processes). One then moves forward to propose theories about how such processes of habitual mentation work, and to analyze and test these theories "according to canons of scientific and philosophical inquiry."[14] A key constraint is put into practice in both instances: mental representations and actions, cognitively defined, are posited as irreducible frameworks for explaining human social action.

While cognitivism may be concerned with meaning, it is not based in questions of signification or language; rather, its key concepts involve rational and intentional acts of mentation. In contrast to behaviorism, cognitivism acknowledges that within any acceptable theory of mind a gap must exist between intelligible and intentional actions, on the one hand, and the physiological mechanisms that underlie or execute them on the other. This gap is filled by mentation: active or intentional mental processes or functions, which include activities such as perception, thought, belief, desire, intention, planning, and

14. "A Case for Cognitivism," *iris* 9 (Spring 1989): 13.

feeling. These processes may be considered mental representations, though to what degree they must be grounded in fundamental neurological structures is left ambiguous. In focusing on intentional acts, cognitive research frames meaning as a mental activity that is purposive, rule-guided, and deliberately performed. These criteria are key components of Bordwell's appeal to the concept of the rational agent. In sum, a key question of cognitivism is how mental activity can be considered representational, that is, to be meaningful or to possess semantic content open to theorization.

Cognitivism is also subject to another methodological constraint, which Bordwell characterizes as "good naturalization." In its concern with mental representations and functions that occupy the gap between meaningful intentional acts and physiological processes, one might say of the cognitive frame of reference that it hovers between philosophy and science. In Bordwell's account, it is thus situated in a conception of the history of science as a process of "turning philosophical doctrines into matters for empirical investigation" ("A Case for Cognitivism" 14). Cognitivism is committed to a "naturalizing" epistemology that wishes to build upon the best empirical investigations of mind, brain, and associated sensory systems. One of the most fascinating aspects of cognitivism is how it is situated conceptually and methodologically at the frontier between body and mind, thus fueling the possibility that clinical and experimental studies will contribute to the solution of some long-standing philosophical problems. This idea further frames and focuses the concept of mentation on which cognitivism's appeals to good theory are built. The criterion of good naturalization means that the mental phenomena or actions that are most open to empirical investigation and causal or functional explanation are ones wherein mind and brain will find their closest connections. Bordwell draws from recent cognitive research the idea that if lower-level sensory mechanisms are "'informationally encapsulated,'" as Jerry Fodor puts it, and thus "impervious to conscious awareness," the mind can be studied as sets of specialized and autonomous functions or modules.[15] One might think of these modules as something like internal information processors, functioning algorithmically, or at least in rule-guided ways that favor "rapid, probabilistic extrapolation from limited samplings of data" (15). In this respect, artificial intelligence research is another major influence on cognitivism whereby "mental

15. "A Case for Cognitivism," 15. Bordwell is referring here to Jerry Fodor's *The Modularity of Mind* (Cambridge, MA: MIT Press, 1983) and J. L. Garfield's *Modularity in Knowledge Representation and Natural Language Processing* (Cambridge, MA: MIT Press, 1987).

representation is a matter of structurally comparable computational activities, not of embodiment in any one sort of material. That is, it just so happens that our brains are the hardware for the programs that they run" (15).

Bordwell appeals to cognitivism, then, as an alternative approach to film theory. Anticipating the post-Theory debate to come, he is searching for a conceptual framework to remap the concept of theory itself in relation to film study, and in so doing to transform cinema studies as a discipline. Equally anticipating the arguments of *Making Meaning,* in press at the time of this essay's publication, Bordwell argues that contemporary film theory has been too dominated by hermeneutic and interpretive approaches to films and theories. Here theories tend to be mined for their semantic cores and potential for narrativization, as it were. And if the principal appeal to theory is as an allegorical key to texts, or to texts as illustrations of theoretical concepts, then Bordwell feels that scientific aspirations can and will be ignored. But if a theory is to have epistemological value, it must *explain* rather than explicate or allegorize. Thus Bordwell argues that "the cognitive framework has a signal advantage. *It does not tell stories.* It is not a hermeneutic grid; it cannot be allegorized. Like all theorizing, it asks the Kantian question: Given certain properties of a phenomenon, what must be the conditions producing them? It then searches for causal, functional, or teleological explanations of those conditions" ("A Case for Cognitivism" 17). In its commitment to good naturalization, cognitivism perhaps diverges from many of the culturalist assumptions of contemporary theory; but it also shares with recent film theory a commitment to constructivist explanations. Here Bordwell is searching for common ground, both to place cognitivism firmly within the project of contemporary film study but also to offer it as an alternative or even a corrective concept to theory.

The concept of constructivism is meant to further characterize the active nature of cognitive functions that transform perceptual inputs through rule-guided inference-building structures. However, constructivism must be constrained by good naturalization. Under the concept of good naturalization, research questions are best answered through empirical work guided by problems and hypotheses. Good naturalization also posits that actions performed by intentional agents are minimally rational. In turn, minimal rationality implies that intentional mental actions are based on the inferential model of practical syllogisms, according to the regulative assumption that perceived means are adjusted to intended ends. On these bases, rational agent theory is promoted as an alternative to theories of spectatorship that rely on appeals to unconscious or nonintentional processes.

The concept of rationality provides a key criterion for pursuing causal accounts according to the epistemological constraints of good naturalization, and thus the connection between the two must be pursued more deeply. In its formal, historical, and psychological dimensions, poetics needs certain kinds of forms, objects, or structures to ground it epistemologically, and it further needs to acquire empirical data leading to new information. These are key conditions for the causal reasoning underlying Bordwell's version of rational and empirical inquiry. Film form, style, and convention as immanent processes anchor the first need; new historical, documentary, institutional, and contextual information fulfills the second. Similar kinds of constraints on structure and process are necessary in order to pursue the psychological question of comprehension in a rational and empirical way. Combining bottom-up and data-driven perceptual and neurological structures with more top-down conceptual ones, Bordwell's account of mentation involves a dynamic set of relationships between body, brain, and mind. On the one hand, pictorial and narrative comprehension build up from perception to recognition by invoking human physiological and cognitive capacities that have evolved over time to deal with patterns of information in the world. On the other, comprehension draws experientially on extensive domains of knowledge and skills for understanding narrative. Comprehension is then defined as grasping "the concrete significance of the perceptual material as patterns of social action. In this case, the patterns are presented in the form of a story" ("Poetics of Cinema" 43).

Understanding how filmic effects are registered in or by spectators is then a matter of modeling "the *processing* of films by viewers," and these models must build upon the best scientific findings in cognitive and evolutionary psychology to construct a plausible framework for theorizing ("Poetics of Cinema" 44). For these reasons, poetics is both mentalistic and naturalistic— mentalistic in its commitment to describing those mental representations wherein the embodied mind engages with artworks, and naturalistic in its adherence to the idea that the scientific investigation of mental life provides the most reliable knowledge of cognitive processes. This approach admittedly involves a degree of idealization of spectatorship, but so do, Bordwell is correct to say, most other accounts, whether psychoanalytic, narratological, or culturalist. Mental naturalization may not contribute much to understanding differences among spectators, but it does aspire to account for intersubjective and cross-cultural regularities, which are potentially universal in the sense that they derive from the fundamental mental structures on top of which higher-level conceptual activities are built.

The cognitivist model of dynamic interaction between bottom-up and top-down processing is exemplary of Bordwell's commitment to a naturalizing epistemology; in fact, this model goes a long way toward demonstrating the necessity of making poetics proximate to science. Dealing with high-level and potentially culturally acquired concepts, top-down processes are potentially open to self-examination. However, the closer one descends to bottom-up processes, the more they are "impervious to introspection"; in other words, to the extent that we have no prior knowledge of these mandatory and automatic physiological and neurological processes, the more open they are to scientific and causal accounts. In a complete model of comprehension, bottom-up and top-down processing are inseparable, and in this way good naturalization flows freely, as it were, back and forth across the dimensions of mental life. The commitments to mentalism and naturalization mean that to be subject to good theory, even higher-level conceptual processes, in principle open to introspective examination, take on increased epistemological value owing to their proximity to more naturalized processes and their inseparability from them—they are grounded in naturalization, as it were. Thus Bordwell emphasizes that "neurological research will eventually show that any experiential process involves complicated feedback and input-output among many mental systems," and later claims that contemporary research will ask us "to consider that many of what we take to be learned or culturally guided mental activities will turn out to be packed into our biological equipment" ("Poetics of Cinema" 45). Good theory will always and invariably be grounded in the brain.

Considering his critique of interpretation, it is interesting to note how Bordwell wants to incorporate acts of "appropriation," or the context dependency of meaning making, into his model of viewer activities. This idea follows from his earlier statement in "Why Not to Read a Film" that historical poetics will deal not only with creation and comprehension but also with protocols of reception. On the one hand, this is a strategy for enhancing the interpretative freedom and activity of spectators and demonstrating their commitment to rational, means-ends endeavors. In addition, it extends poetics in the direction of cultural studies, or at least shows that there is a potential bridge between poetics and cultural studies. On the other, Bordwell wants to include appropriation not only to extend his schema to the full spectrum of mental life—from perception to comprehension to appropriation—but also to frame culture in the conceptual context of mental naturalization, and to make culture, or some dimensions of cultural comprehension, subject to good theory.

Appropriation shows the way acts of comprehension may diverge according to different cultural contexts. However, good theory seeks to balance appropriation against other comprehension activities, and again, the theory becomes more epistemologically sound the more it focuses on convergences and cross-cultural regularities that are grounded in the body and on automatic processes that are impervious to introspection and belief. Therefore, Bordwell notes that adequate explanations of comprehension must draw upon several diverse explanatory frameworks, including "biological capacities of the human organism (for example, the mandatory perception of apparent movement), acquired but very basic perceptual processes (for example, ballistic eye movements, object recognition), acquired but culturally widespread cognitive skills (for example, means/end analysis, personification), and acquired and culturally variable processes (for example, particular notions of personal identity, historical conventions of narrative construction). It seems likely that a tenable theory of this sort will have recourse to perceptual and cognitive research in anthropology, psychology, linguistics, and aesthetics" (*Making Meaning* 272). Poetics is thus open to a variety of different research programs or theories that can constructively incorporate and debate alternative positions. And in this way, Bordwell acknowledges that he shares with both Russian formalism and cognitivism, broadly defined, "their broad theoretical ambitions and their methodological commitment to conducting rational and empirical inquiry into principles of art making within and across cultures" ("Poetics of Cinema" 54). In the ideal research community that Bordwell seeks, the conversation advances through dialectical argumentation, empirical research, and theoretical explicitness characteristic of all these approaches, and becomes the ground for their ongoing dialogue.

A naturalizing epistemology demands that the more a process is involuntary and closed to introspection, the more it gains epistemological value in good theory. However, this constraint contradicts Bordwell's commitment to rational agent theory, or at least demands further investigation of the concept. The concept of rational agents has played a key role in economics, game theory, decision theory, and especially research on artificial intelligence. In most cases, the "rationality" of the agent is defined in a specific framework: the agent is assumed to have clear preferences, to model uncertainty according to predictable values, and in confronting choice will always execute actions that optimize outcomes. Moreover, rational agents are not necessarily defined through criteria of personhood—a rational agent need only be capable of selecting from inputs and executing decisions, and this can be a person, a corporation, a machine, or software. Artificial intelligence borrowed the concept from economic theory, in fact, to describe autonomous programs capable of goal-directed activity.

In contradistinction to the discourse of ideology, above all in its conceptual commitment to psychoanalysis, Bordwell further characterizes the rational agent as engaged in active, intentional, rule-guided, and ends-directed activities, defined by means-end reasoning and practical responsiveness to institutional constraints and opportunities. Bordwell's 2008 overview of poetics puts new emphasis on the concept of rational agency, which functions not only on the side of comprehension but also that of creation. The concept is of central concern to Bordwell's characterization of good theory, first because it organizes all the criteria by which cognitivism opposes itself to psychoanalysis and, one would think, any psychological account committed to the potential intelligibility of unconscious actions. This argument is continuous from *Narration in the Fiction Film* to the more recent *Poetics of Cinema*. Second, the continuity of the concept demonstrates that it functions as the ground for Bordwell's commitments to mentalism and naturalism. However, if I am right that the epistemological stakes of this theoretical framework rely on criteria of good naturalization, as well as on processes and functions that are nonintentional and impervious to inspection, then one wonders why any concept of agency is necessary to the account. This observation is especially apposite if the criteria of good naturalization become more grounded epistemologically the closer they veer toward mandatory and automatic mental processes.

Bordwell provides fairly convincing accounts of these cognitive functions and operations in relation to narration and comprehension. I am struck, though, by Bordwell's attraction to the literature on cognitivism coming out of artificial intelligence. Moreover, despite his insistence on the value of describing these functions and operations as activities, they are neither necessarily conscious nor intentional. Automatic and bottom-up processes are certainly not intentional in any philosophical sense. Higher-level and concept-driven processes would logically be considered intentional, the more so the higher one moves up the mental hierarchy. The concept of appropriation certainly implies both the intention to remap meaning in new ways and an agency performing the semantic remapping. Yet it remains the case that Bordwell tends to describe all of these processes as anonymous, automatic, and rule guided in ways that undermine appeals to intentionality. Even the reasoning protocols of interpretation are characterized as routine or habitual. As processes they do not require agency as a necessary condition (though perhaps it is a sufficient one). What is necessary to the theoretical framework is that these operations be characterizable as "rational," which means open to a good theorization whose epistemological values depend on good naturalization.

In an astute critical essay called "Cognitive Film Theory," Richard Allen also interrogates how cognitivism attributes the quality of rationality to cognitive functions and operations, and further argues that cognitivist film theory, of which Bordwell and Greg Currie are the exemplars, projects a mistaken picture of the mind.[16] Citing Reid Hastie, one of Bordwell's authorities, Allen puts into focus how constructivist theories of perception tend both to personify presumed mental operations such as schemata, and to characterize them in specific ways. For example, in Hastie's article "Schematic Principles in Human Memory," a schema is treated as a "naive theory of some stimulus domain" and the individual using it a " 'naive scientist.' "[17] Here Hastie assumes, first, that human beings actively apply schemata, and second, in doing so this psychological action functions analogously to a "scientific theory": it discriminates between salient and unimportant inputs and then posits networks of associations believed to be characteristic of the inputted data as a way of providing rules for thinking about them.

In *Narration in the Fiction Film,* Bordwell draws a fairly similar picture of mental function in the act of narrative comprehension. The spectator approaches a film tuned and prepared "to focus energies toward story construction and to apply sets of schemata derived from context and prior experience" (34). This activity is then characterized by a given set of actions whose rationality is defined by seeking *unity,* testing information for *consistency,* and establishing patterns of *coherence.* In addition acts of comprehension involve strong degrees of *hypothesis testing:* "The viewer also finds unity by looking for relevance, testing each event for its pertinence to the action. . . . Such general criteria direct perceptual activity through anticipations and hypotheses, and they are in turn modified by the data supplied by the film" (34). One might say that for Bordwell, comprehending in general means theory making, as well

16. In *Wittgenstein, Theory and the Arts,* ed. Richard Allen and Malcolm Turvey (New York: Routledge, 2001).

17. Cited in Allen, 178. A related but shorter and more straightforward critique of Bordwell's model of comprehension is offered by Geoffrey Nowell-Smith in "How Films Mean, or, from Aesthetics to Semiotics and Half-Way Back Again," in *Reinventing Film Studies,* ed. Christine Gledhill and Linda Williams (London: Arnold, 2000), 8–17.

as revising and correcting theories in light of new information. The rational agent is first and foremost an internal theory builder, just as for Hastie comprehending means behaving like a "naïve scientist."

Two questions are immediately raised by this account. First, by what right may normal and quotidian comprehension, aesthetic or otherwise, be considered an *activity,* and who or what is carrying out this activity? For Bordwell, active construction is a characteristic of the entire system of the mental representations comprising cognitive activities. Yet it is unclear how or why one would contrast data-driven, automatic, and involuntary processes as "active" in contrast to the putatively passive accounts of other psychological theories. Moreover, to the degree that such processes are not conscious and unreflective, one must also question why and in what ways they are considered to be "rational," much less intentional. As Allen argues, "a constructivist psychology of perception does not necessarily entail an active percipient, one who is consciously seeking out cues, for it is possible for a spectator who engages in all the requisite inference-making procedures to remain entirely unaware of them. Bordwell does claim that top-down processes are more overtly based upon expectations, and speaks . . . of an 'effort toward meaning'. This may support the idea of an active spectator. But to justify the concept of the active spectator this way requires drawing a sharp distinction between bottom-up and top-down processes, a sharp distinction that Bordwell rejects" ("Cognitive Film Theory" 179).

A subtle rhetorical move takes place here, where rather than defining the activity of spectatorship, nonconscious inference-making procedures are offered as grounds for its rational basis. How does this take place? Allen makes a convincing case for how cognitivist accounts of perception as inference make unjustified leaps in presenting causal accounts of physiological processes as the logical grounds for cognitive, inferential activities. Following Anthony Kenny, Allen faults this kind of reasoning as involving an unacknowledged "homunculus fallacy." In Kenny's account, the homunculus fallacy is a pervasive error in psychological theories defined by "the reckless application of human-being predicates to insufficiently human-like objects."[18] More than a harmless heuristic device, such misapplication of psychological verbs to physiological and causal functions leads to conceptual and methodological confusion. This is another way of seeing what is at stake when the

18. "The Homunculus Fallacy," in *Investigating Psychology: Sciences of the Mind after Wittgenstein,* ed. J. Hyman (New York: Routledge, 1991), 155.

mandatory and automatic processes proposed as the good objects of naturalizing epistemology are credited with forms of reasoned and conscious agency
that one usually grants only to the normative behaviors of complete individuals. Cognitive functions are often characterized as rule-guided, inferential
procedures in this manner. But as Allen points out, "For a rule to act as a rule,
for it to function normatively, it must be capable of being followed and being
broken and be invoked by the agency that is following the rule to justify the
inference or interpretation being made. Causal processes are mechanisms and
mechanisms are not normative in character. Brains cannot infer, they cannot
justify their inferences by invoking rules, and nor can they make mistakes"
("Cognitive Film Theory" 184). Allen concludes, quite reasonably, that an inference is a form of thought, but a perception is not; therefore, the argument
that perceptions are inferences is unsustainable.

I will hold to one side here the full complexity of Allen's critique of how constructivist theories of comprehension teeter uncertainly and in a circular way
around questions of agency in relation to conscious or nonconscious mental
functions. This circularity has to do with unwarranted assumptions that lead to
applying the homunculus metaphor to automatic processes and causal mechanisms. This rhetorical move is a fallacy to the degree to which true premises
(causal mechanisms of perception) lead to false conclusions (the psychological
explanation that perception may be an active and conscious inference-guided
activity). Kenny sees such moves as unjustified extensions of human-being predicates (for example, activity, consciousness, rationality) to functions or parts of
the brain. In reference to Bordwell's account of narrative comprehension, though,
the critique applies to many other varieties and domains of cognitivism. Allen
further adds that "If these processes are not predicated of the conscious agent in
the sense that it is not the agent who actually infers, tests and forms hypotheses,
then it must be the activities of something or someone else who is the object of
knowledge, of an homunculus whose psychological processes mimic our own
but are explicable in terms of material processes. But, as we have seen, the
homuncular conception of the mind is incoherent, it involves predicating psychological capacities to a brain that can only rightfully be predicated of the
whole person" ("Cognitive Film Theory" 188).

Allen further explains how Greg Currie's version of cognitive film theory
refers outright to the homunculus metaphor. In his Fodor-influenced account
of the dynamic modularity of the brain, Currie makes explicit how the homunculus fallacy operates in Bordwell's own model of rational agency in the
interaction of bottom-up and top-down processes. In Currie's own words,

We can think of [a] person as constituted by a hierarchy (or complex of hierarchies) of intelligent creatures or homunculi. The farther down the hierarchy you go, the less intelligent is the homunculus carrying out the operations at that level, until we reach the ground floor, where intelligence bottoms out into straightforward causal interactions where notions of information, reason, evidence and inference play no role, and where everything that happens is driven by brute causal powers in accordance with natural law. The person or agent himself occupies the top level of the hierarchy and is more intelligent than any of the homunculi that operate at subpersonal levels. . . . The primary insight of the homuncular or hierarchical view is that, when an operation is conducted below the personal level, we are not driven to describe that operation in purely causal, nomological terms. We can describe it as a task carried out for a certain purpose, employing information of certain kinds, and conducted within certain constraints of efficiency, reliability and so forth. That way, we describe it as a task performed by a subpersonal homunculus.[19]

Here again we return to the way that rational agent theory is agnostic about personhood, although now armed with arguments about why the functional elements of this theory can be neither intentional agents nor rational. The concepts of artificial intelligence, with their analogies between programmable rule-guided activities and the inferential activities of thought, must carry a lot of the blame here. As Allen points out, in adhering wholesale to the homunculus fallacy,

Currie implicitly denies that there is a conceptual distinction between normative, rule-governed actions and causal mechanisms, and between persons and brains (or computers), there is just a hierarchy of more complex and less complex systems. Yet his theory depends upon the assumption that there is a conceptual distinction to draw between operations at the higher personal level and brute causal processes at the lower level. The distinction is blurred through Currie's use of the vocabulary of "purpose." It is of course possible to ascribe a purpose in the sense of a function, a telos, or a rationale to a causal system, and it may well be fruitful to conceive the interaction of parts of the brain in these terms. But the

19. *Image and Mind: Film Philosophy and Cognitive Science* (New York: Cambridge University Press, 1995), 84.

vocabulary of "purpose" does not apply to an agent in the same way as it applies to a mechanism, and its application to a mechanism does not make that mechanism person-like or intelligent creature-like: we do not explain human agency in functional terms. . . . By blurring the distinction between the functional purposiveness of an organ and the purposiveness of an agent, Currie mistakenly invites us to believe that human beings are simply highly complicated purposive (in the biological sense) organisms and that understanding the complexity of purposive human behaviour is an empirical matter awaiting the discoveries of cognitive science. ("Cognitive Film Theory" 200)

In attributing normative behavior to mechanisms, and psychological predicates to physiological and cognitivist functions, constructivist psychology is grounded in forms of tautology characteristic of the homunculus fallacy. In turn, a form of explanation that aspires to be causal and as value neutral as possible is thus found to be ruled by metaphor and an unquestioned doctrinal assumption.

However, the fault of good theory and naturalizing epistemology is not to be found in their alliance with scientific reasoning and empirical forms of inquiry, but rather in the insistence that causal accounts are the whole of reason or rationality. In taking parts for the whole, the functions of the brain are confused with reasoned behavior, and the mind becomes populated with an internal society of more or less intelligent little persons or agents. Here all the semantic values of rationality are organized around theoretical principles that Bordwell associates with "rational and empirical inquiry"—they are indeed sound theoretical principles exhibiting great coherence and internal consistency, as well as openness to empirical confirmation and disconfirmation. But if good naturalization favors operations that are anonymous, universal, and nonintentional, then there is no agent to perform or carry them out—they are automatic processes—and once intentionality is subtracted from the framework, there are no clear justifications for characterizing these operations as either rational or irrational, conscious or nonconscious. The concept of rational agency is less that of an agent than that of an internal information processor using cues to execute determinable operations, and instead of the unconscious we are faced with nonconscious and automatic functions to which certain activities or features of consciousness are attributed. Thus, the desire to ascribe rationality to these operations must come from other motivations.

The cognitivist emphasis on automatic and mandatory mental functions also leads to another important question: How do we assess and renovate our conceptual schemes? Or as importantly, how do we produce new ones? To do so requires an agency that is intentional and capable of self-examination in ways that are both epistemological and ethical. In other words, these questions lead us not only to investigate how thought is possible and by what means but also to ask: Why do I seek to think in this way? What do I value in this framework of thought? What communities of thought do I join and leave behind in so doing? Bordwell and Carroll wish to constrain value talk with truth talk by reducing epistemology to causes and functions. But indeed, among the most forceful aspects of the post-Theory critique are the ethical criticisms and desires it projects. Looking at the reverse side of Bordwell and Carroll's criticisms, I think it is also important to examine their ideal projection of good theory as the ethical appeal for a new mode of existence where, in their view, politics or ideology has not supplanted reason. Here "dialectics," as Carroll presents it, becomes the basis of an ideal research community of rational agents working on common problems and data sets with results that are falsifiable according to "ordinary standards" of truth and error. But these ideals rest on no firmer philosophical grounds than the ideological theories they critique. For example, while Grand Theory is criticized for its obsession with an irrational and unconscious subject that cannot account for its actions, Bordwell's promotion of "rational agents" as the logical ground of mental functioning is equally unstable and open to question. Indeed in supplying criteria of rationality to both the method and object of investigation, the concept is circular and seems to have no clear motivation apart from posing the subject of good theory as recognizing itself in the object it wants to examine. (Doesn't the rational agent function allegorically here?) The concept of the rational agent functions tautologically as a projection where the ideal scientific subject seeks the contours of its own image in the model of mind it wishes to construct or to discover—good theory applies admirably to theory-building homunculi and naïve scientists.

With a perspective that aspires to be free of ideological positioning and to assert an epistemology that is value neutral, the two introductions to *Post-Theory* nonetheless express the longing for a different world modeled on an idealized vision of scientific research: a community of researchers united by common epistemological standards who are striving for a universalizable and truthful picture of their object. We are closer now to understanding my assertion that debates over epistemological standards are often and equally the expression of ethical commitments that sustain or defend different styles of knowing or even, one might say, modes of existence or forms of life in theory. From this point of view, listing, defining, and refining the epistemic criteria of good theory (or in fact, any theory) thus amounts to mapping out and evaluating what Charles Taylor has called, after Elizabeth Anscombe, the "desirability characterizations" interwoven into its concepts, discourse, and practices.[20]

This observation returns us to an important dimension of the post-Theory critique. For reasons similar to the ones above, the strategy of distinguishing cognitive from psychoanalytic accounts on the basis of rational versus irrational motivation is specious and unwarranted.[21] On the one hand, to the extent that it is defined by automatic and nonintentional operations, there is no agent in rational agent theory much less one characterized by rationality or irrationality. On the other, whatever faults of argumentation may be legitimately ascribed to psychoanalytic film theory (in past work I have designated quite a few myself), psychoanalysis does offer complex accounts of agency and of intentional processes. Especially in Freud's later mental topography, there are not one but several locales of agency, as the ego, superego, and id are posited as sites of interacting and often conflicted intentions. In addition, from the very beginning a primary motivation in building the theoretical framework of psychoanalysis was to demonstrate analytically that these conflicted intentionalities are not irrational, but rather have their own reason whose logic could be ascertained and motivations clarified. The conceptual objects of classical psychoanalysis—the dream work, parapraxis, fantasy, and the etiology of neurosis—are all described and defined by their internal and self-consistent logics. Indeed Freud's great accomplishment was to demonstrate the degree to which many otherwise mysterious psychological phenomena could be characterized as rational processes in the strong sense that their reasons could be coherently explained and their intentions clarified in ways that were open to scientific description and analysis; in other words, explanations that were both corrigible and intersubjectively verifiable.

In these respects, Carroll's frequent characterizations of psychoanalysis as "a theory whose object is the irrational" are demonstrably false and misleading

20. "Understanding and Ethnocentricity," in *Philosophical Papers, vol. 2: Philosophy and the Human Sciences* (Cambridge: Cambridge University Press, 1992), 119.

21. For a more detailed and nuanced account of this issue, see Louis A. Sass, "Wittgenstein, Freud and the Nature of Psychoanalytic Explanation," in Allen and Turvey, 253–295.

("Prospects for Film Theory" 64). In building the theoretical framework of psychoanalysis on the analysis of dreams, parapraxis, the formation of sexuality, and fantasy, to a large extent Freud was attempting to show both that these processes are part of normal mental functioning and that psychological processes were open to scientific research and theoretical examination, even if they could not yet be causally located in physiological and neurological mechanisms. One place where Carroll's (and to a certain extent Bordwell's) critique of psychoanalysis is entirely specious is in the claim that even if it is granted that professional psychoanalysts can make descriptive empirical claims about "data" generated in their practices, because psychoanalytic film theorists have no therapeutic practices, they produce "confecting theories, but with no empirical constraints" and no proper access to data ("Prospects" 66). The criticism is incoherent, or if it has any grounds, those grounds are extendible to cognitive film theory and its relationship to all associated external fields of experimental psychological research. Both cognitivism and psychoanalysis have produced concepts that inspired fruitful exploration (and sometimes dead ends) in both nonclinical and perhaps nonempirical contexts such as philosophy, religion, and art. No, the bright line Carroll wants to draw lies elsewhere, and I hope to show further on that it is dim and blurry.

Good theory attains value the closer it stands to good naturalization—that is, processes open to causal explanation and functions impervious to introspection. (Carroll, and again to a certain extent Bordwell, have already yielded to the idea that humanistic disciplines can produce empirically confirmable or disconfirmable evidence.) And so I return to the implicit claim that the critique of Theory, though in many ways valuable, is an unjustified critique of the humanities in general as without method, reason, theory, or the capacity for self-criticism. Alternatively, what needs to be clarified and defended are forms of reason whose practices are founded on the very quality of being open to introspection. Even a rationalist as committed as Jürgen Habermas understood and defended psychoanalysis on these terms.[22] As a theory, psychoanalysis does not stand or fall on whether it produces causally complete cures, or can ultimately be grounded in biological and neurological mechanisms, but only to the degree that its explanations are convincing in terms of reasons examined through analytical introspection that are intersubjectively debatable

22. See for example *Theory and Practice,* trans. John Viertel (Boston: Beacon Press, 1973), especially 9–10. This idea is worked through more completely in *Knowledge and Human Interests,* trans. Jeremy J. Shapiro (Boston: Beacon Press, 1971).

and verifiable. Indeed, the fundamental measure of therapeutic progress (there is no "cure" if the examined mechanisms are part of normal mental functioning, even if they often cause suffering) is that the process of analysis that takes place between therapist and patient must be transferred to the analysand as a capacity for critical self-examination. Here I will take a great leap that I hope soon to defend. Freud considered psychoanalysis to be a developing science and not philosophy. But like philosophy, the value of psychoanalysis is that it is in principle open to all as a practice of reasoned and critical analytic introspection. Indeed its reasons can only be developed and scrutinized through introspection and dialogue in a process motivated by doubt, uncertainty, or even crisis. (Remember Wittgenstein's proposal that the form of a philosophical question is, "I cannot find my way.") Good theory wants to bring the humanities and philosophy closer to the reasoning routines of the natural sciences. Much good can come of this critical project, which should be defended for many kinds of questions. Our greater task now, however, is to understand the potential critical and conceptual power of the humanities, whose reasons are indeed logical and philosophical, and to turn philosophy not completely away from theory, but toward the humanities.

3. "Philosophy is not one of the natural sciences"

> Philosophers constantly see the method of science before their eyes, and are irresistibly tempted to ask and answer questions in the way science does. This tendency is the real source of metaphysics, and leads the philosopher into complete darkness.
>
> —Ludwig Wittgenstein, *The Blue Book and Brown Books*

In their critique of interpretation and humanistic investigation, the logical frameworks of cognitivism, historical poetics, and the analytic philosophy of science overreach in projecting their particular view of rationality as a single standard of explanation and theory as necessarily methodologically monistic. In fact, we are not dealing here with a conflict between rational and irrational explanation, or even domains of truthful explanation that could be placed on a scale of rationality and that are testable through fallibility and dialectical correction. Perhaps judgments of truth value in explanations are less applicable here than reasonableness, or rather, how we assess the value and quality of reasons given and received, and how those reasons can be built into local and contingent consensus. One could call this the search for agreement rather than the quest for certainty, which so obsessed Bertrand Russell or G. E. Moore. (To reach tacit agreement, one can certainly pass through a series of disagreements, and agreement does not have to be complete.)

This may not be a case of combating Theory with its other, or even of placing a number of theories into competition with one another to decide which one or ones "best account(s) for data." To do so would be to give the game up entirely to a position that recognizes only the power of scientific rationality and wishes to extend its domain over all forms of action, whether natural or social. Here we must turn briefly, and perhaps only in schematic form, to a very old debate in order to describe both the limits of "scientific" explanation and the sui generis character of humanistic understanding. Bordwell or Carroll's idea that a healthy debate is characterized by multiple theories competing for dominance according to criteria of falsification and the progressive elimination of error assumes that there is agreement on the proper model of theorization subject to a single standard of judgment, and that this model may turn out to be universally applicable with fairly stable reasoning protocols. But the main idea of this book and its pendant, *Elegy for Theory*, is that "theory" is an unstable concept, and that in both the history of philosophy and the philosophy of science there has been continual and conflictual debate on the conceptual parameters of theory itself. It may be that our relation to theory always has been, and perhaps always will be, contingent and historical.

The idea that there is a contrast to be struck between scientific explanation and historical understanding has a long pedigree. Readers will already recognize here Johann Gustav Droysen and Wilhelm Dilthey's critiques of positivism in trying to carve out a more or less autonomous logical space for the *Geisteswissenschaften*, the "moral" or human sciences. In his classic work, *Explanation and Understanding*, G. H. von Wright has shown that this debate has an even more ancient ancestry, which he draws in the contrast between Aristotelian and Galilean explanation types, the former favoring teleological or finalistic explanation, and the latter promoting causal or mechanistic accounts. In other words, the Galilean explanation type seeks to explain and predict phenomena, while the Aristotelian wants to make facts finalistically understandable. Lest one should think that I am defending a mode of diplomacy that Carroll and other post-Theory adherents feel is an accommodating pluralism, I will say from the outset that I agree with most of von Wright's more subtle and nuanced conclusions. One can find much to value in both forms of reasoning. But it would be foolish to believe that truth is irrevocably allied to either explanation or understanding, and equally so to assert that truth lies somewhere in the middle in the form of compromise on some types of questions. And so von Wright concludes that we should recognize and accept that despite all the potential points of intersection between the two domains of reason, "there is also a basic opposition, removed from the possibility both of reconciliation and of refutation—even, in a sense, removed from the truth. It is built into the choice of primitives, of basic concepts for the whole argumentation. This choice, one could say, is 'existential.' It is a choice of a point of view, of framework of belief, which cannot be further grounded."[23]

Although this comment does not receive further clarification, I am struck by von Wright's suggestion that adherence to a domain of reason is marked by an existential choice, indeed what in *Elegy for Theory* I called the choice of a mode of existence as both a discursive community and a form of discourse in which this choice is examined and justified. Moreover, conflict between positions seems built into the commitment to primitive concepts, which can only be asserted since they are foundational yet only elusively and allusively justified. With respect to the idea of a naturalizing epistemology characteristic of one form of theory, I have shown how its grounding in rational agents is both circular and not further justifiable within the theory itself—the concept as such can never be proven or demonstrated according to the terms of fallibility set by this form of theory.

Nevertheless, there is and often has been a historical and sometimes productive dialogue between the two positions amounting to a kind of progress. Von Wright observes that the temporary dominance of one of the two positions often follows from innovations deriving from criticism of the contrasting trend. In the case under consideration, both historical poetics and the arguments against Theory, from either a historical or culturalist perspective or that of the analytical philosophy of science, gave rise to productive arguments and criticisms in the face of the impasses of the discourses of ideology and political modernism. At the same time, von Wright adds, "What emerges after the breakthrough is never merely a restoration of something which was there before, but also bears the impress of the ideas through whose criticism it has emerged. The process illustrates what Hegel described with the words *aufgehoben* and *aufbewart,* perhaps best rendered in English as 'superseded' and

---

23. Georg Henrik von Wright, *Explanation and Understanding* (Ithaca, NY: Cornell University Press, 1971), 32.

'retained.' The position which is in process of becoming superseded usually wastes its polemical energies on fighting already outmoded features in the opposed view, and tends to see what is retained in the emerging position as only a deformed shadow of its own self" (*Explanation and Understanding* 32–33). Words of caution, then. For just as the critique of Theory often rails against arguments that have already faded in the Other it projects, we must be attentive here to what is constructive and new in searching for the possibilities of a film philosophy as both a cure for theory and a productive partner with theory.

I generally agree with Richard Allen's two main conclusions in his critical essay "Cognitive Film Theory": that Bordwell's historical poetics has produced one of the finest and most productive accounts of film style and narration in contemporary film study, but that his theory of narrative comprehension is for the most part unsustainable. Now, according to the explicit standards of good theorization to which both Bordwell and Carroll are committed, their theories remain impervious to criticism unless I can falsify or correct some aspect of their data or offer a more complete alternative explanation. I have no intention of doing this. But in this intention I hope to start down the path to showing some of the ways in which philosophy touches upon many problems of theory yet remains distinct from theory as a practice. The central problem with Bordwell and Carroll's projection of good theory, as I see it, is an overvaluation of naturalizing epistemology and of causal reasoning, especially in the framework of humanistic inquiry. (A subsidiary problem is an underdetermined and largely unexamined commitment to "rationality" as a value underwriting naturalizing epistemology.) In both cases, good theory finds itself allied with one of the principal trends of twentieth-century philosophy, which von Wright justly criticized as an excessive concern with epistemology leading to a kind of conceptual poverty and value nihilism. Instead, the two critical tasks of philosophy, in my view, are to interrogate the bases, grounds, and frameworks wherein reasons are given and defended, both to constrain them when they are unreasonable but also to expand and ramify them in the production of new frameworks, contexts, and concepts, and to evaluate the axiological commitments that frame or structure our forms of reason giving. To claim to know is always to value certain ways of knowing, and to value is to project a world commensurate with the forms of reason one aspires to define and develop in conceptual expression. Here the role of philosophy is to examine and critique the conceptual structures that frame and inform human expressiveness and action. And these concepts inform everyday discourse and thinking no less than more exotic activities of analysis and interpretation. Later, I will expand this definition to include activities of conceptual innovation as well as addressing problems of agreement and of establishing common frameworks for conversations (even conflictual conversations or debates) within which reason giving, interpretation, and evaluation all take place.

Apart from Carroll's vague references to postpositivist philosophies of science, Bordwell and Carroll make no explicit appeal to philosophy or a kind of philosophy in their introductions to *Post-Theory* and associated essays, and this is congruent with their desire to temper theory with the reasoning protocols of the natural sciences. (In many ways, philosophy falls "behind" both good theory and experimental science here.) Richard Allen and Murray Smith's critique of contemporary film theory in *Film Theory and Philosophy* (Oxford: Clarendon Press, 1997) echoes Bordwell and Carroll's perspective with the explicit aim of reorienting theory along the main lines of twentieth-century analytic philosophy. Accusing Theory of an "epistemological atheism" powered by an exaggerated ethical concern with the critique of a capitalist modernity, Allen and Smith's criticisms make clear a number of philosophical assumptions absent from the post-Theory critique. From the analytic point of view, arguments for and against "theory" take place against the background of a philosophy of science. One engages in theory building or not according to an epistemological ideal based on natural scientific models. In employing the methods and forms of scientific explanation, however, philosophy becomes indistinguishable from science, at least with respect to theory construction. Philosophy disappears into science as "theory" becomes indistinguishable from scientific methodology.

As I argue in *Elegy for Theory,* from the beginning of the twentieth century analytic philosophy was responsible for projecting an epistemological ideal of theory derived from natural scientific methods. Bertrand Russell's 1914 essay "On Scientific Method in Philosophy" presents a concise definition of this ideal: "A scientific philosophy such as I wish to recommend will be *piecemeal* and tentative like other sciences; above all, it will be able to *invent hypotheses* which, even if they are not wholly true, will yet remain fruitful after the necessary corrections have been made. This possibility of *successive approximations to the truth* is, more than anything else, the source of the triumphs of science, and to transfer this possibility to philosophy is to ensure a progress in method whose importance it would be almost impossible to exaggerate."[24] This is an admirably succinct summary of the epistemology to which Carroll and Bordwell, and Allen and Smith, subscribe. Theories are built piecemeal out of preliminary and falsifiable hypotheses, and one must establish the factual character of the parts before the whole can be understood. The theory then advances in successively closer approximations to the truth as hypotheses are further tested, refined, or rejected in light of new evidence.

Russell's ideal overturns philosophy's ancient concern for balancing epistemological inquiry with ethical evaluation. Here, "theory" disappears in two ways, at least as it is generally conceived in the humanities. Not only is the activity of theory given over to science but also philosophy itself begins to lose its autonomy and self-identity—it would seem to have no epistemological function save in the light reflected from scientific ideals. Analytic philosophy attacks theory on more than one front. First, there is the implicit tendency to delegitimate extant *film* theory to the extent that it draws on concepts and methodologies influential in the humanities that fall outside of the reigning norm of what W. V. O. Quine would call a "naturalized philosophy." Consequently, because so little aesthetic thought on film conforms to scientific models, Carroll concludes that, for the most part, a "theory" of film does not yet exist, though it might at some future date. The conflict over theory in film studies thus reproduces in microcosm a more consequential debate, one that concerns both the role of epistemology and epistemological critique in the humanities and the place of philosophy with respect to science. Analytic philosophy wants to redeem "theory" for film by placing it in the context of a philosophy of science. At the same time, this implies that the epistemologies characteristic of the humanities for a number of decades are neither philosophically nor scientifically legitimate. And so the contestation of theory becomes a de facto epistemological dismissal of the humanities.

The rise of cognitivism, evolutionary psychology, and historical poetics and the debates on post-Theory in both film studies and the humanities represent a trend where throughout the 1990s philosophy allies itself with science as a challenge to theory. In this phase of the debate, "theory" is the contested term. Very quickly, however, "science" becomes the contested term as a philosophy of the humanities gives over theory to science and opposes itself to both. Important keys to this transition are the late works of Ludwig Wittgenstein, especially his

---

24. In *Mysticism and Logic, and Other Essays* (New York: Longmans, Green and Co., 1918), 113, my emphases.

Philosophical Investigations, as well as G. H. von Wright's calls for a philosophy of the humanities in works like *The Tree of Knowledge* (E. J. Brill 1993).[25]

The interest of the later Wittgenstein for my arguments, and for the humanities in general, begins with his attack on the identification of philosophy with science. In asserting that "Philosophy is not one of the natural sciences" (*Tractatus Logico-Philosophicus* 4.111), Wittgenstein presents a formidable challenge to Bertrand Russell's conception of philosophy as allied to epistemological models drawn from the natural sciences. In contrast to Russell, Wittgenstein argues that science should not be the only model of explanation and knowledge, and so he insists on the specificity of philosophy as a practice. Von Wright echoes this assertion in writing that

> A philosophy which does not look for answers to questions, does not explain or theorize about the things which attract the philosopher's curiosity, and does not try to provide the foundations for our beliefs, is not a philosophy for which scientific thinking sets the pattern. It, on the contrary, fights the infiltration of this thinking into philosophy and makes it responsible for the confusions from which the philosopher tries to rid himself. It is not, need not be, hostile to science as such. But it may be said to take a critical or even hostile attitude to the influence of science outside its proper domain—and in particular on philosophic thought. In *this* it runs counter to an intellectual mainstream of the century.[26]

The questions lie open before us, then, of what concept of philosophy responds to these criticisms, and how philosophy can contribute to critical thought in the humanities.

Richard Allen and Malcolm Turvey's introduction to their compelling and provocative collection *Wittgenstein, Theory and the Arts,* along with P. M. S. Hacker's contribution to the volume, offer an admirably clear and useful

---

25. Following von Wright, including his logical investigation of these questions in *Explanation and Understanding,* other important contributions to the critique of scientism and the affirmation of the distinctiveness of humanistic inquiry, though often in very different ways, come from the work of P. M. S. Hacker, Charles Taylor, Richard Rorty, and of course, Stanley Cavell. Another locus classicus, though from a different philosophical tradition, is Hans-Georg Gadamer's *Truth and Method.* I will comment further on most of these thinkers in the sections to follow. Late in the writing of this book, Richard Moran also directed me to Bernard Williams's fascinating lecture, "Philosophy as a Humanistic Discipline," *Threepenny Review* 85 (Spring 2001): 8–13.

26. "Wittgenstein and the Twentieth Century," in *The Tree of Knowledge,* 97.

overview of the later Wittgenstein, especially with respect to arguments critiquing the misapplication of causal explanations and supporting the autonomy of philosophy for the humanities. As such the book is not only a timely intervention against the versions of scientism in film studies promoted by historical poetics and cognitivism, but also a productive defense of the humanities in a time where its values and forms of reasoning remain under siege.

One of the most curious aspects of Allen and Turvey's introduction, however, and in the editorial line of the volume overall, is the place of "theory" as a focusing concept, not only as an object of philosophical analysis and criticism but also as a way of addressing the central argument of the book: Wittgenstein's purported rejection of theory as a method inappropriate for philosophical investigation and inquiry. One of Allen and Turvey's principal objectives is to contest, in ways not dissimilar from Bordwell, the prestige "theory" currently enjoys in the humanities as a form of explanation. "For if the later Wittgenstein is right," they explain, "regardless of the specific conceptual confusions embedded in specific theories, theory itself is in most cases a logically inappropriate form of explanation for humanistic subject matter. In other words, humanistic subject matter is not, for the most part, amenable to theorization."[27] Theory is displaced, then, in order to follow through on von Wright's suggestion that a philosophy of the humanities should be distinguished from the philosophy of science, and that this is the most appropriate model for humanistic inquiry. To accept or reject this argument (or to know which elements of the criticism should be retained or excluded) entails knowing precisely what theory is and how it is supposed to characterize forms of explanation that are routinely deployed in the humanities. Like Bordwell and Carroll, Allen and Turvey are critical of theory as a practice within humanistic investigation, but unlike Bordwell and Carroll they wish to defend the humanities, and by recourse not to scientism but rather to philosophy, or again, a certain conception of philosophy.

Whether or not this view is too restrictive is the matter under examination, which leads again, and hopefully for the last time, to one final conceptual description of theory. Allen and Turvey provide an admirably direct and clear account of the logical criteria characterizing "theory," or at least the version of theory they target for criticism. In spite of the various forms theories take in

27. Richard Allen and Malcolm Turvey, "Wittgenstein's Later Philosophy: A Prophylaxis against Theory," in *Wittgenstein, Theory and the Arts,* ed. Richard Allen and Malcolm Turvey (London: Routledge, 2001), 2.

the humanities, in their view all theories possess two fundamental features: "First, they unify a range of apparently disparate, unconnected phenomena by postulating an underlying principle that these phenomena putatively have in common and that can explain their nature or behaviour. Second, the common, underlying principle postulated by the theory—whether it takes the form of an entity, process, force, concept, or something else—is at least initially hidden from view. It is these two features—the unification of apparently diverse phenomena, and the postulation of an underlying principle that cannot be immediately discerned—that theories typically share, despite their other differences" ("Wittgenstein's Later Philosophy" 2).

Allen and Turvey focus strategically on three primary pillars of the enterprise of contemporary Theory to exemplify these criteria and to demonstrate their operations as theory: the structuralist account of narrative in Barthes's period of methodological passion, Lacanian psychoanalysis as represented in the work of Slavoj Žižek, and Bordwell and Currie's cognitive accounts of filmic comprehension. Ironically, though significantly, all three examples have aspired to or allied themselves with a concept of science, though with often radically contradictory versions of what "science" might mean. (All three examples also exist in some tension with different notions of "philosophy.") The choice of examples is significant since structuralism and psychoanalysis have so dominated one powerful genetic line in contemporary discourses of Theory. Moreover, adding the competing example of cognitivism, putatively opposed to structuralism and psychoanalysis, is meant to demonstrate how the logical characteristics of theory are present even in starkly opposed views through criteria that unite them all in a common discourse.

Allen and Turvey's critique is fairly convincing on the surface. Structuralism, for example, must indeed postulate that in all cases meaning is produced by patterned systems of differences, and to the extent that structures are universal, collective, and asubjective they are, as it were, hidden from view. Nor can structuralism's appeal to hypothetical-deductive procedures stand as a science, "because nothing can disconfirm the structuralist axiom that there must be an underlying structure that supports and makes possible the diverse forms taken by narrative in human cultures" ("Wittgenstein's Later Philosophy" 28–29). Žižek's Hegelian and Lacanian perspective is vulnerable to analogous criticisms. Similarly, cognitivism builds its epistemological framework by demonstrating the unifying functions of cognition through cross-cultural regularities and the actions of operations that are impervious to introspection. Allen and Turvey seem to have found something like the deep structure of theory, or at least its fundamental logical characteristics. Moreover, this argument is commensurate with Bordwell's assertions of the underlying unity of so-called Grand Theory though, paradoxically, cognitivism falls within the same conceptual framework.

Our task is now twofold. Before moving further along in my elegy for theory, we need to know whether the conceptual investigation and evaluation of theory in all its historical varieties and differences can be preserved within the framework of philosophy as Wittgenstein conceived it, which means asking as well whether the borders between philosophy and theory must really be strictly marked. (Is there a variety of language games in which "theory" is deployed, or is there only one as Allen and Turvey assert?) Second, the case for the autonomy of humanistic understanding proffered by Wittgenstein's interpreters needs to be set out and evaluated in order to understand more clearly their arguments concerning the meaning and value of cultural practices and how they should be interpreted and evaluated, both critically and historically.

4. "I will teach you differences"

> The "space of reasons," therefore, is also a cultural space.
>
> —P. M. S. Hacker, "Wittgenstein and the Autonomy of
> Humanistic Understanding"

In a well-known story that recurs across the essays published in *Wittgenstein, Theory and the Arts* and in many other accounts, Wittgenstein characterized the project of his later philosophy by paraphrasing Kent's admonishment to King Lear: "I will teach you differences." This phrase exemplifies two of the fundamental guidelines for the thought of the later Wittgenstein: the appeal to particular cases and the avoidance of generalities, especially synthetic or subsumptive generalities. I believe Wittgenstein thought that only in this way could philosophy accompany us in a search for conceptual clarity by avoiding misleading philosophical friends. In adopting a genealogical perspective on theory and its variety of discordant senses, I have tried to follow this advice as a constant reminder of distinctions produced and effaced in the history of the conceptual transformations of theory, especially in relation to similar mutations in conceptions of philosophy. This reminder is important. For appealing as it might be to think that the fundamental structure of theory has been identified in two key features, and that once so identified philosophy can purge itself of theory, in point of fact there is very little warrant for this idea in the later Wittgenstein. Nor do I think that these principles offer clear guidelines for distinguishing an autonomous space for humanistic investigations by differentiating them from scientific explanations while purging theory from philosophy. To better understand these problems, the questions of what Wittgenstein meant by "theory" and whether even the so-called attack on or rejection of theory is a central component of his later philosophy must be more closely examined.

My first point is a simple one, though it may yield complex consequences. In the nearly 200 pages of the *Philosophical Investigations*, the word "theory" appears exactly once. To be sure, it appears in a crucial and often-cited passage worth revisiting in its entirety:

> It was true to say that our considerations could not be scientific ones. It was not of any possible interest to us to find out empirically "that, contrary to our preconceived ideas, it is possible to think such-and-such"— whatever that may mean. (The conception of thought as a gaseous medium (*Die pneumatische Auffassung des Denkens*).) And we may not advance any kind of theory. There must not be anything hypothetical in our considerations. We must do away with all *explanation*, and description alone must take its place. And this description gets its light, that is to say its purpose, from the philosophical problems. These are, of course, not empirical problems; they are solved, rather, by looking into the workings of our language, and that in such a way as to make us recognize those workings; *in despite of* an urge to misunderstand them. The problems are solved, not by reporting new experience, but by arranging what we have always known. Philosophy is a battle against the bewitchment of our intelligence by means of our language. (§109)[28]

---

28. All citations are from the revised fourth edition of the *Philosophical Investigations*, trans. G.E.M. Anscombe (Malden, MA: Wiley-Blackwell, 2009). For Wittgenstein to call this "die pneumatische Auffassung des Denkens" raises interesting questions of interpretation. In an alternative translation, I might offer something like "a meaningless mechanical conception of mind," though "gaseous" certainly conveys Wittgenstein's implication that the "theory" is vague, inflated, or full of hot air. In New Testament theology, the *pneuma* also means "spiritual," belonging or relating to spirit and spiritual existence, in which case Wittgenstein could be referring to those areas of experience such as religion, ethics, or aesthetics wherein we run up against the frontiers of our language. (I will comment further on this question later on.) Here there is a fascinating though perhaps unlikely connection to the Pneumatomachi, a fourth-century Macedonian sect who denied the divinity of the Holy Spirit; they believed that Jesus Christ and

Now as always the open question is, what does "theory" mean in this passage? What problem does theory present for Wittgenstein, and by what criteria is it defined and then proscribed from philosophical investigations? A good deal but not all of Wittgenstein's meaning is plainly presented in the text itself: a theoretical problem is empirical in nature, addressed through the construction of hypotheses, and takes the form of explanations seeking new and previously unknown information. In addition, as in many passages of this deeply introspective work, the subject of Wittgenstein's critical attitude is Wittgenstein himself. One signpost to the meaning of theory in this passage, then, is Wittgenstein's reminders of how to avoid the logical snares retroactively apparent in the *Tractatus,* with its belief in the possibility of reducing language to primitive signs corresponding to simple elements of reality capable of picturing the world as a bounded whole commensurate with the possible forms of all truth statements. In this the *Tractatus* presented a theory in all the senses that Wittgenstein came later to doubt: seeking underlying principles when none are needed, explaining through reference to a principle that is posited rather than observed, and building an argument out of systematically connected exceptionless theses.

While this passage is the only reference to theory in the *Philosophical Investigations,* similar arguments can be found in the *Zettel* and in the *Blue and Brown Books.* Yet it remains the case that such passages are infrequent and that theory as such may not have been a special conceptual preoccupation through which Wittgenstein's efforts to define the specificity of philosophy were defined, or if it was, the historical and conceptual targets of those efforts are quite specific. In fact, I have already laid those targets out in *Elegy for Theory;* namely, those dimensions of positivism and logical positivism that subscribe to the doctrine of methodological monism and subsumption-theoretic models of explanation. Whatever their variety or spaces of deployment, theories in this sense seek methodological unity and homogeneity, the subsumption of individual cases to generalizable laws, and they favor causal explanations. In this

---

God the Father were consubstantial, and also that the Holy Spirit was a creation of Christ the Son. The odd connection to Wittgenstein is reported in a 1930 conversation on Schlick's ethics with Friedrich Waismann, where Waismann relates that in a reply to his question, "Is the existence of the world connected to the ethical?" Wittgenstein replied, "Men have felt a connection here and have expressed it in this way: God the Father created the world, while God the Son (or the Word proceeding from God) is the ethical. That men have first divided the Godhead and then united it, points to there being a connection here." See Waismann's "Notes on Talks with Wittgenstein," *Philosophical Review* 74, no. 1 (January 1965): 16.

semantic domain a theory is considered to be a synthetic explanation of a range of facts considered to be hypothetically true. It is one influential and widespread concept or model of theory but indeed not the only one.

These models come from the domains of science and the philosophy of science; they are the principal sources of the scientism in philosophy and the humanities justly criticized by von Wright and Hacker after the example of Wittgenstein. No doubt, to the extent that conceptual residues and ideologies of positivism still inhabit formalism, structuralism, cognitivism, and perhaps even psychoanalysis, they all remain vulnerable to the definition and critique of theory offered by Allen and Turvey. However, I still feel that a number of consequences of Allen and Turvey's argument are worrisome and perhaps unearned. Foremost among them is the critique and rejection of theory, which is the unifying idea of the entire book, and which very likely has little warrant in Wittgenstein himself as I have just demonstrated.

Alternatively, what is fundamentally warranted, and crucially so, are the efforts of von Wright and Hacker, or Charles Taylor and Stanley Cavell, to define after Wittgenstein the relative autonomy of humanistic understanding with respect to science and the philosophy of science. The issues here would then be first whether theory should be absolutely identified with scientism and methodological monism, and second whether the later Wittgenstein proscribes this. At the same time, if the critique of theory is so closely associated with scientism and the subsumption-theoretic model, does it really blanket the whole of the humanities? Or is it just a way for philosophy to adjudicate a border dispute between the natural and human sciences, where frequent friendly visits may even be welcome as long as the neighbors have a clear view of the logical constraints on their activities? Theory in the strictest sense, or even what von Wright refers to in *Explanation and Understanding* as the "quasi-causal" logic of much historical research (which admits some causal explanations though without reference to covering laws), can serve humanistic investigations in many productive ways, above all in identifying and clarifying natural constraints on cultural practice and meaning in terms of perception and comprehension.

Here another important question presents itself. If a philosophy of or for the humanities is possible, and does involve other methods or modes of knowing, why does this alternative not amount to a theory in the strict sense? As Allen and Turvey argue in their introduction to *Wittgenstein, Theory and the Arts,* philosophy differs from science in that its subject matter is not empirical in nature—only nature is subject to investigation by empirical methods.

"Empirical" has a precise definition here as that of which we can have no prior knowledge. Alternatively, philosophy is concerned with problems of sense and meaning, and these problems are not empirical in the sense that language use and creative expression are already part of a commonly accessible stock of human knowledge.

This involves a second criterion: statements about empirical phenomena are, and must be, falsifiable. Philosophical investigation, however, concerns testing the limits of sense and meaning of given propositions. In this way, Wittgenstein's case for a philosophical anthropology as the best framework for investigating human behavior and creativity is based on what Hacker calls the autonomy of human understanding.[29] This concept is exemplified in the conventional distinction between reasons and causes. Simply speaking, in a causal explanation each effect is presumed to have a cause identified by a hypothesis, which may and must be rejected or revised in light of further evidence. The idea of theory presented here is no doubt associated with the semantic domain of subsumption-theoretic accounts. Causal explanations are legitimate in scientific contexts because actions have origins that derive from states of affairs of which we have no prior knowledge. Most human action and behavior, however, is ill served by causal explanation, for agents have the capacity to justify their behaviors with reasons. As Allen and Turvey explain:

> A reason for an action is identified by the fact that it can potentially be cited by the agent to justify what he did. An agent's reason is typically authoritative and complete. That is, it is not a conjecture or hypothesis on the part of an agent or others observing the agent that further evidence might prove, disprove or qualify. Since the reason for an action is not a hypothesis, it is not something that is typically unknown or hidden. An agent does not usually discover his reason for doing something by deducing a hypothesis and testing it against the available evidence. . . . Furthermore, it is also usually self-sufficient in the sense that the agent

29. Hacker describes the task of defining the relative autonomy of human understanding as the search for "forms of understanding and explanation appropriate to and dependent upon the understanding of language and its uses in the stream of human life." See "Wittgenstein and the Autonomy of Humanistic Understanding," in *Wittgenstein, Theory and the Arts*, 59. It might be added that the issue of defining the relative autonomy of humanistic understanding remains a complex and unsettled question. See for example the contributions and debates between Hubert Dreyfus, Charles Taylor, and Richard Rorty published in *The Review of Metaphysics* 34, no. 1 (September 1980).

does not have to find out any more information in order to better justify his action. ("Wittgenstein's Later Philosophy" 15–16)

In other words, reasons are not hidden from view and are thus open to inspection and introspection.

I will comment critically on these criteria later on, but before moving forward it is necessary to clarify and qualify some unexamined assumptions here. First, in this account agents are considered as being completely transparent to themselves in terms of reasons. However, frameworks of knowing can also be intuitive, unacknowledged, and incompletely accounted for. Reasoning may falter and agents may not be in full self-possession of their claims to reason. Indeed, an agent may need to find out more information to justify his reasons though this information may not be empirical in nature. There is nothing in Wittgenstein to suggest that an agent be fully in possession of self-knowledge or capable of achieving such a state, as we shall see. The important criteria here involve first acknowledging that acts of reason giving and justification are human capabilities or potentials, and then insisting that the criterion of openness to introspection defines the space of human understanding and self-understanding.

To say that reason giving is agential is also to say that it is intentional in ways foreign to the search for previously unknown data and causes. This is why Hacker says that the space of reasons is also a cultural space. Whereas causes operate in the domain of automatic, physical, natural, or subnormative processes, intentional acts operate in the realm of reasons and choices. Intentional acts thus lead to questions of purpose, and appropriate responses will take the form of giving reasons for what one intended as a form of explaining oneself (and for understanding oneself). The grammar of reason giving—for example, justification, forward-looking reasons, desirability characterizations in terms of the schemes and values of the culture of the agent, backward-looking reasons, description or redescription of the intended act—is thus clearly distinguishable from causal explanations, as Hacker well points out. Knowledge of causes is generally though not exclusively inductive, but accounts of reasons are not. Knowledge of causes is discovered because previously unknown data or information are brought to light; but one does not normally find out or uncover one's reasons for executing an intention unless they are assumed to be unconscious in the psychoanalytic sense, and even then the criteria of prior availability and openness to introspection still apply. Causes make events occur but reasons guide and justify intentional acts, and consequently, unlike causes, reasons provide the grounds for evaluating and understanding human actions. Therefore, one cannot say of reasons that they are true or false, right or wrong, but only that they are good or poor, defensible or indefensible, justifiable or unjustifiable, persuasive or doubtful. Similarly, characterization of a reason does not specify a sufficient condition for the performance of the intended act, nor can accounts of reasons in reference to intentional acts be subsumed to time-independent and generalizable laws.

To explain an action as done for a reason, for the sake of an intended goal, or in order to bring about a certain state of affairs, is thus not tantamount to giving a causal explanation. Reason giving is an expression of self-understanding and thus representative of how an agent himself understands (whether well or poorly) his intentions and actions—human behavior and cultural activity stand in need of understanding and interpretation rather than explanation. Nevertheless, while expression involves performing meaningful and intentional acts, these acts are also variegated, multilayered, and perhaps intentionally or unintentionally ambiguous or even contradictory, and thus human expressive activities refer to social conventions and institutions that vary culturally and historically, and which are irreducible to causal or subnormative functions. Therefore, the cultural practices and behaviors of human communities are time dependent in the sense that understanding the mutually imbricated horizons of intents and reasons, expressions and interpretations, requires acknowledgment of appropriate contexts and attention to the surrounding and antecedent histories of these activities.

For all these reasons, the description and interpretation of expressive acts and cultural practices require concepts different in kind from those that best serve the natural sciences; hence the Wittgensteinian insistence on a commitment to the autonomy of intents and cultural practices. (Later, I will follow Deleuze in asking whether and to what extent "concepts" are appropriate at all for scientific practice.) Autonomy now indicates that agents have the capacity for authoritative self-examination and self-justification. Therefore, a key difference between scientific and philosophical inquiry is that science tests its hypotheses against external phenomena, that is, the natural world. But philosophy admits only to internal or self-investigation. This is less a question of truth and error than judgments concerning the approximate rightness of a proposition tested against prior experience and knowledge in contexts both historical and contingent. "The phenomena of nature do not, in the requisite sense, have a meaning," Hacker explains, "are not rule-governed or intentional, are not thus embedded in customs and institutions and in specific situations, and are not actions done for reasons" ("Wittgenstein and the Autonomy of Humanistic Understanding" 70). Humanistic accounts are also evaluative in ways that causal explanations cannot be. Understanding the thoughts, expressions, and actions of others requires imagination and empathy, both an intuitive grasp of others' reasons and the possibility of projecting oneself into their perspectives and contexts. Interpreting and evaluating an intentional act therefore requires an account not only of the knowledge and beliefs guiding an action but also of the agent's goals, values, and reasons, as well as his understanding of himself and his role in the situation and his conception of others' beliefs and understanding of that role. In other words, interpretation and evaluation have strong ethical components. "Often understanding his action requires not only an explanation of the agent's reasons, but also an explanation of why those reasons weighed with him," Hacker insists,

> which can sometimes be given by references to his self-understanding, or his conception of the expectations of others, or the values which he has imbibed in the context of the society of which he is a member. Such explanations are alien to the natural sciences. They are not reducible to causal, sub-normative explanations, and are not formally homogeneous with the nomological forms of explanation characteristic of the sciences. . . . For what underlies the generalizations of the study of culture and society is not the blind movements of matter in space, but the actions and activities of man, sometimes intentional, often done for reasons, typically moved by motives and directed to ulterior goals, and only intelligible as such. (70–71)

Reviewing the distinction between reasons and causes thus helps to begin to unravel the conceptual confusions surrounding the idea of theory in cinema studies or the humanities; for example, not only why Bordwell and Carroll have been so wedded to a certain idea or ideal of science and the theoretic-subsumption model, but also why theory in its current sense, even from a culturalist or psychoanalytic perspective, remains so compelling for a great many fairly intelligent people. Perhaps these epistemological ideals present inappropriate criteria for cultural investigation. Film theories, like all humanistic investigation, concern human activities and thus presume a high degree of prior knowledge, self-knowledge, and self-examination. Like any cultural activity, cinema is a human creation and thus is embedded in practices and institutions that form the basis of our quotidian existence. We may not have fully conscious knowledge of these practices and institutions, nor any desire to construct theories about them in the form of propositions or concepts, yet we act on and through them in coherent and consistent ways. This is why cultural theories are able to solicit agreement in the absence of empirical research and experimentation. Their power and plausibility is based on the extent to which they seem to clarify for us what we already know and do on a daily basis, what we intend to do in the future, or what we have done in the past. Here we need no external examination beyond the critical investigation of our own practices as they evolve historically. However, what film studies or the humanities have called theory in its multiple and variegated guises might more appropriately be called aesthetics or philosophy. And indeed, perhaps we could achieve much methodological and conceptual clarification by setting aside "theory" provisionally in order to examine what a philosophy of the humanities, and indeed, what a film philosophy might look like.

5. An Assembling of Reminders

> Since there can be no way of circumscribing the conceptual confusions which may distort human thinking or of predicting in advance fresh sources of conceptual entanglement which may emerge from a culture, there will be no end to the need for philosophical criticism.
>
> —P. M. S. Hacker, "Wittgenstein and the Autonomy of Humanistic Understanding"

> Both statements of fact and statements of value rest upon the same capacities of human nature; that, so to speak, only a creature that can judge of value can state a fact.
>
> —Stanley Cavell, *The Claim of Reason*

In contesting the appeal of good theory to methodological monism and thus to a single standard of rationality, I suggested that within the context of humanistic understanding judgments of truth in explanations may be less applicable than applying standards of reasonableness, or rather how we assess the value and quality of reasons given and received and how those reasons can be built into local and contingent consensus.

Von Wright characterizes this attitude in a distinction between the rational and the reasonable. For example, an argument can be rational but its premises and conclusions may be unreasonable. Rationality is goal-oriented and has to do primarily with formal correctness of reasoning, efficiency of means to an end, and the confirmation and testing of beliefs. Judgments of reasonableness, however, are value-oriented and aimed at qualitative assessments of our forms of life or modes of existence. "The reasonable is, of course, also rational," von Wright explains, "but the 'merely rational' is not always reasonable."[30] This is von Wright's way of rebalancing the split between epistemology and ethics, or logical and moral reasoning, in twentieth-century philosophy. As I have already stated, perhaps one could call this the search for agreement rather than the quest for certainty, which so obsessed Russell and Moore, and in a very different way, Wittgenstein. To reach tacit agreement, one can certainly pass through a series of disagreements, and agreement does not have to be complete. However, reason giving is messy, conflictual, contentious, contingent, and often disagreeable. According to concept and context, individuals (or theories) may have conflicting accounts or justifications for the same actions, behaviors, or interpretations. And these conflicts may be in part or whole reasonable within their own contexts and frameworks for justification. Moreover, because all human activity is historically open, and conflicts of interpretation are always generated by discrepant or discordant contexts, no final consensus can be hoped for.

No doubt the appeal of good theory is very great, especially for those who seek certainty or stable grounds for knowledge and clear lines of demarcation between what is true or capable of being true, and what is not. But the key problem here is what counts as knowing; whether or not there is a single standard of knowledge, applicable in all cases, or whether there are justifiable forms of knowledge that are both contingent and context dependent, and which are to be valued for their contingency and context dependency. Such an appeal is not a defense of either perspectivism or relativism. It is, however, meant as a strong critique of scientism in the humanities, or the improper extension of the theoretic-subsumption model to domains of cultural activity to which it does not and cannot apply. It also helps us to understand how the particular form of the will to truth expressed by methodological monism not only excludes a priori ways of knowing and interpreting that may be of great value but also willfully tries to make the humanities disappear behind the mask of science. The line of thought that weaves from the later Wittgenstein through the work of von Wright, Hacker, and Charles Taylor can be understood as motivated by the desire to protect and preserve a domain of knowledge and

30. "Images of Science and Forms of Rationality" in *The Tree of Knowledge*, 173.

form of understanding from erosion and distortion by an instrumental and technological reason. To assert and defend the autonomy of humanistic investigation and understanding is also to protest the illegitimate encroachment of the natural sciences into domains where they do not apply.

Accordingly, what the humanities might need instead of a defense of Theory is more powerful conceptual resources for evaluating the value and limits of causal and quasi-causal reasoning with respect to problems of cultural creation, interpretation, and evaluation. At the same time, the criterion of the autonomy of understanding, interpretation, and reason giving as practical activities is an important component in a defense of the humanities, and in constructing a possible philosophy of the humanities. However, one must also be attentive to this criterion's limits as well as its powers. I am thus led to ask whether the Wittgensteinian hesitancy before theory and its desire "to leave language untouched" limit important possibilities and potentialities of a philosophy of the humanities.

The fact of the matter is that Wittgenstein's struggle to define the conceptual activities of philosophical investigation is neither systematic, synthetic, nor proscriptive. (One might also ask if such a form of investigation is amenable to judgments of right or wrong, correctness or incorrectness, truth or falsity. In a similar manner, the suggestion that our cultural activities are governed by "rules" rather than, say, norms or conventions, must also be considered.) A critical and humanistic philosophy should be attentive to the open, experimental, and exploratory nature of Wittgenstein's writings, in order to preserve their sense of struggle and internal conflict, of not getting one's conceptual bearings or direction quite right, and of remaining open to new paths that the investigation may eventually clear. Indeed, in spite of the value and clarity of their arguments, most worrisome in Allen and Turvey's account is their tendency to draw limits, to exclude and forbid, and in turn to give in to what Wittgenstein characterized in *The Blue and Brown Books* as the "craving for generality," or the desire to treat variegated phenomena as if they were essentially of the same type rather than doing justice to their variety and differences.[31] In avoiding generalities and seeking to account for particular cases, philosophical investigation wants to account for difference, singularity, or what makes something unique, or a new accomplishment or intuition. This teaching of differences has been, I hope, a watchword in writing my elegy for theory.

31. See *The Blue and Brown Books* (New York: Harper and Row, 1965), 18.

What elements of Wittgenstein's later philosophy point, then, toward the possibility of a conception of philosophy built on the autonomy of humanistic understanding? Hacker observes that Wittgenstein was a critical philosopher in at least two senses related to Kant's conception of *Kritik*. Both philosophers were concerned with exploring and testing the limits of reason and reason-ableness, Kant through his doctrine of the faculties and Wittgenstein through philosophical investigations of the limits of expression. "Where Kant delim-ited knowledge in order to make room for faith," Hacker notes, "Wittgenstein, in the *Tractatus*, delimited language in order to make room for ineffable metaphysics, ethics, and religion."[32] In the years following Wittgenstein's dis-appointment with the *Tractatus* and his slow construction of the *Philosophical Investigations*, his investigations into the limits of language no longer shied away from value talk as untouchable; rather he insisted that understanding the grammar of ethical or aesthetic expressions requires attention to their distinctive contexts and the roles they play in given forms of life.

Like Kant, Wittgenstein was a trenchant critic of philosophical illusions produced when the bounds of sense are transgressed. In particular, he re-jected metaphysical claims for giving access to the language-independent es-sence of things, no less than he questioned the appeal of logic for settling claims of certainty and abstract reasoning. In addition, Wittgenstein began remap-ping philosophy's concepts of the agent or subject in important ways, both denying that the subject has privileged access to his own consciousness and that subjective and mental activities are essentially better known than actions in the external world. Like Kant with his dialectical critique, Wittgenstein finds that we lose our way or are misdirected in our reasons through inexact concordances with the conditions of sense and the unfounded migration of concepts and expressions beyond their legitimate contexts. Wittgenstein's most mordant critiques are aimed at the inappropriate use of psychological concepts for logical explanations of human actions. Foremost among these concepts is the ascription of the first person pronoun to a self-identical and self-present Cartesian ego that seems both to inhabit the body and to remain distinct from it, as well as the belief that such ascription is immune to mis-identification and reference failure. Here the ego is always identical to itself as the site of a certain rationality. Consequently, Wittgenstein was as critical of the inclination to think of the mind as an inalienably possessed private

32. "Wittgenstein and the Autonomy of Humanistic Understanding," in *Wittgenstein, Theory and the Arts*, 39.

domain of subjective experience to which the subject has privileged access and self-knowledge as he was of the tendency to confuse, through criteria of numerical and qualitative identity, knowledge of objects with knowledge of persons and experience. Through such criticisms, in Hacker's view, Wittgenstein hoped to lay down guidelines for a philosophical anthropology and for building the foundation of a philosophy of the humanities that could withstand the constant and often illegitimate encroachments of scientism.

Wittgenstein's critique of the misapplication of psychological concepts hopefully derails a misunderstanding that certainly arises here—what does it mean to speak of the "human" in the humanities? To the extent that the enterprise of Theory has been identified with a philosophical antihumanism for the last fifty years it should be said that the idea of defending the autonomy of humanistic understanding does not necessarily include returning to older concepts of "humanism," as is clear in the very different Wittgenstein-influenced work of Richard Rorty, Donald Davidson, or Charles Taylor. To defend the humanities as the critical investigation and evaluation of what is distinctively human about cultural creation and interpretation implies no conceptual commitments either to an ideal of "man" as a freely acting and fully self-conscious agent, or to the *cogito* as the source and origin of meaning. No one was more aware than Wittgenstein of the limits of human understanding and potential failures of meaning, interpretation, and sense, or how our own quotidian practices of expression and interpretation often remain opaque to us.

However, Wittgenstein's implied concept of human agency in relation to potentials for expression in relation to forms of life is complex and not easily grasped. To connect intentional expression to forms of life means that our cultural activities and expressiveness are always practiced in two dimensions, as it were—both collective and individual, global and local, impersonal and personal, and public and anonymous—such that accounts of a particular expression must refer equally to the cultural context or form of life in which it is embedded. This is what is often referred to as Wittgenstein's holistic conception of meaning. Therefore, the potential for deployments of practice, both successful and unsuccessful, and opportunities for understanding and misinterpretation, as well as invention or innovation within practice, are framed by culture and the history of collective or social use. To express is to perform a singular and intentional act but also to evoke an entire social and collective framework of experience—all expression is public and social in some sense, and thus meaning and interpretation can never be constrained by or reduced to individual intents. In a similar way, misunderstanding and disagreement occur not only because of friction between cultural or idiosyncratic contexts but also because of the impossibility of fully accounting for the "rules" connecting statements to "states" of meaning. Expression as an intentional cultural activity is therefore both an action and a state, a singular active performance whose meaning and interpretability are also embedded in a cultural and impersonal grammatical context, open to innovation and historical change. Expression, then, must be thought of simultaneously as an action verb as in "to state or express" and as a historical condition or fact of existence, that is, as a framework circumscribing potentialities of sense or meaning. Therefore, whatever senses or meanings we attribute to expression are no longer "subjective" meanings or the property of individual enunciators, but rather are constitutive of a complex intersubjective social matrix that frames or conditions the potential for public communication no less powerfully than it does for violent misunderstanding and disagreements.

In this context, to be understood or to fail to understand, and to reach agreement or not, occurs through "grammatical" missteps of various kinds; not only a lack of clarity in concept or expression but also the mapping or projection of concepts into domains where they do not apply, or disconnecting them intentionally or unintentionally from contexts in which they could be better understood. Here is what Wittgenstein might mean, then, in refusing hypothetical explanations and insisting only on description. To return to clarity, to interpret efficiently, or to reach agreement thus entails grammatical descriptions or characterizations that draw out the multiple and varied relationships that connect and reconnect a singular expression or instance to its ever-evolving collective and cultural environment or context. Here philosophical investigation, as Wittgenstein conceived it, involves two principal and interconnected activities, perspicuous description and connective analysis. As described by Hacker, perspicuous description—*übersichtlichen Darstellungen* is Wittgenstein's phrase—examines "the uses of expressions, the various forms of their context dependence, the manner in which they are integrated in behaviour, the point and presupposition of their use, and their relations of implication, compatibility or incompatibility with other expressions" ("Wittgenstein and the Autonomy of Humanistic Understanding" 41). *Dartstellung* can also mean portrayal, depiction, presentation, schema, account, or statement. It thus indicates a kind of showing or demonstration. Sometimes Wittgenstein also uses the verb *beschreiben,* which implies description but also depiction, characterization, picturing, drawing, and delineating. *Übersichtlich* indicates that the account should be open, clear, and capable of being obviously and plainly understood.

Alternatively, "connective analysis" evaluates philosophically problematic concepts. Here the grammars of problematic concepts are examined by rigorously tracing out conceptual connections, which having been overlooked or forgotten, or alternatively, overstretched or misapplied, lead to conceptual confusion and philosophical perplexity. "A main source of our failure to understand," Wittgenstein wrote, "is that we do not *command a clear view* of the use of our words (*daß wir den Gebrauch unserer Wörter nicht* übersehen)— Our grammar is lacking in this sort of perspicuity" (*Philosophical Investigations* §122), and this is a persistent problem for philosophers no less than ordinary language users.

Wittgenstein's insistence on developing a clear view or overview of our expressive and conceptual practices and capacities is clearly indicated in his frequent use of verbs and qualifiers such as *übersehen* and *übersichtlichkeit,* which encourage us to have a view of or on, to look over, assess, or see more clearly something we have failed to see, overlooked, or missed. Philosophy neither explains nor deduces, formulates hypotheses, or discovers what was unknown, for to survey the expressive practice of human culture is to explore a territory where in principle nothing is hidden and everything is public and open to view. Perhaps philosophy in this sense is something like the making of grammatical maps by producing clearer descriptions of the features of our expressive activities and reminding us of expected and unexpected pathways of meaning, keeping us going in the right direction and avoiding navigational mishaps, and reminding us not to stray too far from an intended route.

Philosophical investigation thus involves not only conceptual characterization and clarification but also a restoration or reminding of absent or missed connections between things. Wittgenstein called this further activity an assembling of reminders (*ein Zusammentragen von Erinnerungen*) by making manifest and accounting for the implicit or explicit criteria underwriting reasons and interpretations. Assembling reminders is both an attractive and a strange concept in that it encourages us to recall that we often forget not only what we mean but also *how* we intend to mean. Call this a certain philosophical absentmindedness that in every one of us provokes misfires of reason: to have overlooked, to be unaware, to be subject to misdirected "perceptions" or perspectives, to look in the wrong place, to be distracted, to have insufficiently accounted for conceptual connections, to have insufficiently valued or valued for the wrong reasons, to have insufficiently accounted for what one values, to have insufficiently thought through consequences, to misunderstand or be misunderstood, to be confused or distracted, to have misapplied context or not found the right context for interpretation; in short, to have failed to explain oneself completely. And to rectify such misfires, "we remind ourselves," Wittgenstein offers in the *Philosophical Investigations,* "that is to say, of the *kind of statement* that we make about phenomena. . . . Our investigation is therefore a grammatical one" (§90). This phrase sheds new light on what it means to offer a perspicuous description of our quotidian expressive acts. The grammatical investigation of our claims to sense, meaning, agreement, or conviction is not simply an assertion of the meaningfulness of ordinary language, but rather of how language "grammatically" sets the conditions or potentialities for making sense, achieving meaningfulness, reaching agreement or sustaining conviction: "our investigation . . . is directed not towards phenomena, but, as one might say, towards the *'possibilities'* of phenomena," Wittgenstein insists (§90). And these possibilities are in plain view, or may be brought into plain view, because of our common capacity for expression. At the same time, to possess the capacity for expression does not assure that we reliably mean what we say, or even know completely how to mean what we say, or to say what we mean.

6. ". . . a complicated network of similarities overlapping and criss-crossing"

> We learn and teach words in certain contexts, and then we are expected, and expect others, to be able to project them into further contexts. Nothing insures that this projection will take place (in particular, not the grasping of universals nor the grasping of books of rules), just as nothing insures that we will make, and understand, the same projections.
>
> —Stanley Cavell, "The Availability of Wittgenstein's Later Philosophy"

We have come some way in understanding what is at stake in Wittgenstein's philosophical anthropology as the effort to delimit the autonomy of human cultural activity—its language games and forms of life—with respect to the activities of philosophical investigation and theoretical explanation. However, two obstacles lie in the path of connecting these arguments to what I want to call a film philosophy, or even more broadly, a philosophy of art and human expressiveness. Where von Wright or Hacker refer to the autonomy of human or humanistic understanding, Allen and Turvey insist upon the autonomy of *linguistic* understanding, as if the only form of human expression was speech. The second and more important obstacle has to do with evaluating the senses of ordinary or everyday expressiveness with respect to philosophical expression.

Attentive readers have already noticed or wondered about my use of expression, expressiveness, or expressivity in passages where one might ordinarily find "language." Despite all of the justifiable critiques that could be made of contemporary Theory from semiology to postmodernism, one of its fundamental accomplishments has been to open and completely transform the question, what is called "discourse"? From film semiology's attempts to overcome a purely linguistic account of language in its confrontations with the image, to Derrida's grammatological critique of the identification of speech with thought as the origin and anchor of meaning, to Foucault's archaeological and genealogical transformations of discourse and Lyotard's accounts of the figural, one signal accomplishment of the age of Theory was to critique thoroughly and completely transform the privilege of meaning and expression as being constrained exclusively by linguistic structures. Allen and Turvey are virtually unique in their own book in insisting that the autonomy of human expression and understanding be constrained to the linguistic in a strict sense—this constraint is not self-evident or widespread in other Wittgenstein-influenced accounts.

Still I am led to ask a simple question: How much would be changed in philosophy if the widely held default assumption that meaning or sense is *linguistically* constrained were renounced and the more expansive term "expression" were substituted for "language"? As even Wittgenstein well understood, human powers of expression are variegated and manifold, and every act of linguistic expression is not only embedded holistically in a variety of signifying actions (gestural, physiognomic, indicative, etc.), but also shot through with nonlinguistic elements that equally have the capacity to intend meaning and to demand interpretation. If this were not so, how would a philosophy of art be possible? Indeed, following Derrida, Foucault, Deleuze, and Lyotard, my more than twenty years of philosophical work on the figural has tried to show that our conception of discourse should be transformed in just these ways.[33] But let it just be said for the moment that nothing is changed or altered in either Wittgenstein's conception of philosophical investigation or von Wright

33. See for example the essays collected in *Reading the Figural, or, Philosophy after the New Media* (Durham, NC: Duke University Press, 2001).

and Hacker's approach to defending the autonomy of cultural practices and interpretive activities if the broader term "expression" is evoked to characterize every form of human activity that (1) is intentional in meaning or has the capacity for meaningfulness, (2) lends itself to interpretation (but also misinterpretation and ambiguity), and (3) entertains or promotes possibilities for conceptual transformation and renewal through recontextualization. (And here the fact that many ordinary expressions are often quite extraordinary must also be accounted for.)

This observation leads to the second obstacle. One of the key difficulties in the standard view of Wittgenstein is knowing how to follow his suggestion that philosophy concern itself primarily with ordinary or normative uses of language. To free language from its metaphysical uses and bring it back down to earth means in principle understanding that the procedures, conventions, or rules that govern meaning are open and available to everyone, and in turn can be explained by anyone. For example, Allen and Turvey feel that a primary feature of theory is the appeal to occult, hidden, or otherwise invisible structures of meaning or culture. This appeal was an acknowledged flaw even of the *Tractatus,* as Allen and Turvey clearly explain: "An invisible system of representation of the sort postulated by the *Tractatus,* Wittgenstein came to realize, cannot account for how users of a language actually use language themselves. Rather, the meaning of an expression must be visible to its user if he is to be able to use it correctly. And the norms, standards or rules that define its correct use in a specific context must in principle be ones that its user can appeal to in justifying his usage, or in explaining how the expression is to be used correctly to others. If they were not, how could he himself ever use language correctly, or challenge the incorrect use of language on the part of another?" ("Wittgenstein's Later Philosophy" 8).

Now the first worry in such characterizations is the criterion of visibility (and by implication, invisibility), which is often unreasonably extended to the idea that quotidian practices of language use, and justifying one's use, are self-evident and universally available. In many cases they are, but the correct sense of the argument is difficult to characterize. Justifications of this argument often appeal to another justly famous passage from the *Investigations:* "Philosophy simply puts everything before us, and neither explains nor deduces anything—Since everything lies open to view there is nothing to explain. For what is hidden, for example, is of no interest to us" (*Philosophical Investigations* §126). Allen and Turvey closely follow Wittgenstein's sense here in arguing that language use describes a public and autonomous domain that is open to view, meaning that practice is not determined by anything external to actual usage, such as deep structures of grammar, mental operations, or correspondence to a meaning-endowed world. Moreover, if these rules were unavailable they could not play a normative role. Therefore, Allen and Turvey conclude, "if meaning is visible, and if the assumption that meaning needs to be unified by being reduced to a single essential function such as describing has been rejected as mere prejudice, then theory of any kind (not just a theory that is explicitly scientific) must be an inappropriate methodology for philosophical investigations into sense and meaning. For there are no concealed, underlying principles of meaning to postulate, and no 'essence' to reduce meaning to, to unify it" (10). Allen and Turvey appeal to the criterion of visibility because it is tied so strongly to their definition and critique of "theory"—if an explanation appeals to latent, hidden, indiscernible, invisible, or otherwise nonconscious structures or forces, it is both characterizable as theory and inappropriate for accounts of humanistic investigation and understanding. However, the consequences of this "non-theoretical conception of meaning," which do indeed appear to be faithful to Wittgenstein's intended sense, are too restrictive such that philosophical investigation is now restrained only to indicating and describing: "Philosophy may in no way interfere with the actual use of language; it can in the end only describe it. For it cannot give it any foundation either. It leaves everything as it is" (*Philosophical Investigations* §124).

Now, §109 of the *Investigations* may advise against the proposal of "theories," that is, the construction of hypotheses and the search for new and previously unknown information, but it says nothing about visibility or invisibility, nor does §126 necessarily lend itself to a similar interpretation. The criterion of visibility is imposed from without by the as yet unjustified mandate that the *Philosophical Investigations* authorizes a blanket critique and rejection of theory in its broadest sense (given that we know precisely what "theory" is and in what sorts of language games it is embedded). The key question here, however, is to understand what it means to say that meaning is "open to view." Again, one might assume that Wittgenstein's meaning in such passages is fairly plain, if only one knows how to see it. At the end of the passage Wittgenstein writes, *"Denn, was etwa verborgen ist, interessiert uns nicht"*; what is hidden (*verborgen*) does not interest us. *Verborgen*, of course, does not only mean hidden, out of view, or concealed but also latent or dormant; alternatively, what is concealed may not be invisible, but like Poe's purloined letter is rather missed in plain sight like all of the potential misfires of reason I described earlier. The more slippery passage includes the phrase, *"Da alles offen daliegt"*—there everything lies open, not open to view but simply *there*, available. Here the German adjective *offen* lends itself to a range of interesting senses: open, overt, unconcealed, unsealed, clear, outright, direct, candid, active, but also, loose, raw, undetermined, undecided, and unsettled.

The criterion of visibility is deeply misleading, I believe, and too forcefully reduces the sense of Wittgenstein's recommendations or reminders. Seen plainly in such pages are Wittgenstein's objections to the kinds of theory that insist that only those functions or operations that are impervious to introspection are epistemologically valid. (Scientistic "good theory," then, is an obvious candidate for criticism whose influence must be overcome if we are to see our way clear to valuing the kinds of philosophy that frames and supports the arts and humanities.) Rather than speaking of visibility or invisibility when trying to open and map the terrain on which humanistic investigations can and should take place, perhaps it would be better to say that we are interested in those expressive and cultural activities and practices that are open to observation and introspection as capacities of human intentional creation, expression, and interpretation.

Two crucial points must be made here. As I see it, the standard view of Wittgenstein imagines the autonomy of linguistic meaning and the condition of being open to view as something like the world's largest public library. However, the latent assumption in the standard view is not only that all the books are available to every human but also that every human has read every book in the library, and perhaps having temporarily forgotten the content of this or that volume, needs a gentle reminder now and then of where the books are placed and what resides within them. But it is also unavoidably the case that the total content of this great depository can never be known, that much of what we know we forget, and that we often lose sight of the networks of association that connect, enlarge, and deepen our ideas and arguments, or in turn link them in unexpected contexts or innovative colligations. In this case a community and a form of life are required in which peers, colleagues, students, librarians, and even interfaces and databases collectively collaborate in both challenging and enlarging the web of contexts through which meaning and interpretation are pursued. It is also importantly the case that each one of us continually adds to this library by creating new contents and new contexts for it.

In addition, in spite of their considerable differences, there is a strong similarity between the standard view of the autonomy of linguistic meaning as a normative practice and the scientistic model of mind as subnormative behavior; both propose a terrain for investigation that is not open to change and in which characteristic activities must remain untouched. If we take him at his word, and I am not sure we should absolutely do so, Wittgenstein's admonitions to leave language untouched, only to describe, and to constrain our activities to perspicuous characterization hover close to similar proscriptions imposed by scientism and causal explanation. The admonition that language remain untouched presupposes a conception of our individual and collective expressive capacities as if they were geological features of an unchanging landscape, when in fact they comprise a city, which we are constantly building, extending, clearing, redesigning, and reconstructing. No single citizen can have or retain a complete mental overview of this ever-evolving space—philosophical maps are necessary, and they are open to diverse interpretations while enabling a variety of trajectories through and across the conceptual polis—yet every citizen can contribute in ways both minor and major to the expressive and cultural resources of this collective project.

In the standard view of Wittgenstein there is a third and final problem correlative to both the constraint of language to linguistic usage and to the admonition to leave language untouched—this problem concerns the status of "rules" of usage. The application of rules is one of Hacker's key criteria for asserting why the subject matter of the humanities is not generally amenable to the forms of explanation given in the natural sciences, and why humanistic reason is different in kind and irreducible to natural scientific reasoning. Some of these criteria are now familiar to us. One involves the holistic conception of expression, which characterizes language as a public, norm-governed practice partly constitutive of the form of life and culture of its speakers; another involves Wittgenstein's argument against private languages. Intentional expression is social and collective. Learning a language is part of acculturation, of belonging to a community, and one acquires behaviors alongside language acquisition. In these respects, precise distinctions and adjudications of reasoning, interpreting, and evaluating cannot take place generally and abstractly, but only through practice: "an explanation of the meaning of an expression," Hacker explains, "is internally related to instances of its correct application. The internal relation between a rule for the use of an expression and its extension is fixed by the *practice* of applying the rule, of correcting misapplications of it, of explaining the meaning of the expression by reference to the rule, by the responses (of understanding, misunderstanding and not understanding) to the expression in use, which exhibit what counts *in practice* as correct and incorrect applications" ("Wittgenstein and the Auton-omy of Humanistic Understanding" 60).

This brings us back round to the question of how the knowledge of rules of usage is open to view. All such rules must be implicitly known and under-stood within human communities. One might also say that these rules are fully deployed and embedded in our social and cultural forms of life, a quality that opposes them to the process of discovering and describing previously un-known causal relations in the natural world that are in turn subsumable to covering laws of which we can have no prior knowledge. Such rules are pres-ent, implicit, or open to view in every instance of expressive or cultural prac-tice, but they are also flexible, plastic, and open to improvisation in ways that nomological relations are not. I wonder then why "convention" is not thought the appropriate term. "Rules" seems too strict and inflexible. Are not conven-tions something like rules of thumb, applied in flexible, contingent, and context-dependent situations open to improvisation and invention? In addi-tion, "rules" imply that there is some implicit list of obligatory requirements whose violation immediately and inevitably leads to non-sense. To assume the prior existence of a relatively fixed set of rules that must be invoked to anchor our reasons may also lend support to the appeal of scientism and good theory, as if giving reasons always means returning to a bounded site of knowledge, which we mine for our reasons and which is capable of being exhausted or described completely and with certainty.

Therefore, it is important to insist with Wittgenstein that expressive and cultural activities are "not everywhere circumscribed by rules" (*Philosophical Investigations* §68), but that a grammatical analysis or comparison may show us what is entailed in "being governed by rules." As Stanley Cavell usefully explains, "The concept of a rule does not exhaust the concepts of correctness or justification ('right' and 'wrong') and indeed the former concept would have no meaning unless these latter concepts already had. Like any of the ac-tivities to which it is related, a rule can always be misinterpreted in the course, or in the name, of 'following' it."[34] Thus rules do not determine the nature of a game or how it is practiced, "And we can learn a new game without ever learning or formulating its rules ([*Philosophical investigations*] §31); not how-ever, without having mastered, we might say, the concept of a game" ("The

---

34. "The Availability of Wittgenstein's Later Philosophy," in *Must We Mean What We Say?* (Cambridge: Cambridge University Press, 2002), 49.

Availability of Wittgenstein's Later Philosophy" 49). The concept of rules in Wittgenstein refers not so much to strict constraints or limitations as much as potentialities and frameworks of practice where neither language, expression, nor games have an essence or an irreducible set of core characteristics. (And here we are reminded again of §124—philosophy offers no essence or foundation for language, and in attending only to "the actual use of language," refers to the kinds of practices or games that we expressively deploy.) Hence the importance of Wittgenstein's appeal to "intermediate" or impure cases, where rather than searching for identity or essence one seeks to discern patterns of family resemblance wherein language games are considered to be open sets. In such intermediate cases no individual member of the set may serve as a token for the whole, for there is no whole apart from the shifting pattern of relationships defining the "game," or patterns of similarity and difference between two or more games—there are only practices or uses that exhibit "a complicated network of similarities overlapping and criss-crossing" (*Philosophical Investigations* §66). An example of an intermediate case would be John Ruskin's deployment of the term "theoria," wherein the language games of theory in its classical senses and in the domain of aesthetics or nineteenth-century philosophies of art both overlap and contest one another as genres of discourse.[35] In identifying and attending to intermediate cases, philosophical investigation finds itself in situations of uncertainty where it is difficult to decide how to define and apply the conventions of proximate and contrasting games and practices. Sets overlap in intermediate cases and thus provoke the desire to understand where differences can and should apply. An intermediate case is always clarifying, then, because it might belong to more than one set or game, and thus it aids us in establishing relations of contrast and similarity, overlap and friction, between practices—in short, it helps us ascertain differences while also indicating mutations or changes in or of practice.

Intentional acts are expressed and characterized through practices that are, moreover, embedded in forms of life wherein the following of a rule has a degree of plasticity requiring improvisation, and whether a game has been played correctly is open to questions of agreement and disagreement, which in fact may not be answered with finality or certainty. For these reasons, the concept of rules should not be understood as restrictive, nor can rules be characterized as a sort of calculus of meaning: "Our ordinary use of language

35. See D. N. Rodowick, *Elegy for Theory* (Cambridge, MA: Harvard University Press, 2014), 26.

conforms to this standard of exactness only in rare cases," Wittgenstein observed. "Why then do we in philosophizing constantly compare our use of words with one following exact rules? The answer is that the puzzles which we try to remove always spring from just this attitude towards language" (*The Blue and Brown Books* 25–26). Philosophy must be something more than description, then. One needs to restore the openness and contingent quality of these constraints, as well as a sense of play in language, such that philosophy may be also considered a practice of change and invention, of augmenting, enlarging, and enhancing our conceptual schemes, of creating new styles of thought, and of projecting future states of self and society to which we aspire. Call this philosophy as experimentation.

7. *Gedankenwegen:* On Import and Interpretation

> Working in philosophy—like work in architecture in many respects—is really more a working on oneself. On one's own interpretation. On one's way of seeing things. (And what one expects of them.)
>
> —Ludwig Wittgenstein, *Culture and Value*

Wittgenstein's commitments to human activities as being generally open to anyone's inspection and to our common abilities to give accounts and reasons for our actions mean that in principle philosophy is open to everyone as a quotidian event. In addition, in contrast to the practices of experimental science philosophy is a form of noninstrumental reason, meaning that it requires no special technologies or resources apart from human capacities of thought, expression, imagination, and empathy. Alternatively, these capacities do not mean that the desire to be meaningful or to be understood commonly results in successfully executed events. To advance toward intelligibility, meaning, and agreement might also require the elaboration of new frameworks or concepts for understanding that progress and retrogress through exchanges both orderly and disorderly. And in investigating, reasoning, and reaching agreement, language does not remain untouched but rather is being continually renovated, innovated, and transformed.

Even if all our cultural and expressive activities are potentially open to view, this does not mean that they are immediately or completely intelligible or interpretable. (What is "theorizing" if not speculating, imagining, or wondering if our attempts at expression, interpretation, or reason giving are successfully executed or not? What draws us to theory other than *failures* of understanding or explanation?) To accept this principle does not require (or exclude) a concept of the unconscious in the psychoanalytic sense nor does it locate sense giving and sense making activity in the automatic and subnormative mental processes of cognitivism. We are speaking here of human capacities of expression and interpretation and our potentials for executing them, which are not only not completely available to us because they are cultural and collective but also because they are historical in the sense of being contingent and open to innovation, creation, and experimentation.

It will (or should) seem paradoxical to characterize philosophy as a quotidian event, or as something that is not a special practice or a practice of specialists, in the same way that theory often can be. As Kant already recognized, philosophy passes through or attends to "ordinary" expression because it is concerned with our common capacities for presentation, self-presentation, reasoning, interpreting, and understanding. The interests of philosophy are thus what are of interest to us all in virtue of being social and expressive beings. However, if this is so, then why is it that philosophical expression since the time of Socrates has been characterized as disorienting and difficult, provoking alarm, confusion, exasperation, and dismay? Here again Wittgenstein's deep commitment to the ordinary is illustrative, especially since his own language poses fascinating obstacles to interpretation. Wittgenstein philosophizes, and we in turn produce theories of what he might have meant, until such time as we begin philosophizing ourselves, and we all have the capacity to do so. Our satisfaction with the ordinary leads to *doxa,* but philosophical investigation and expression at their most powerful are paradoxical and critical, leading us to conceptual innovation, as well as ethical evaluation and transvaluation.

This is what I think Stanley Cavell means in "The Availability of Wittgenstein's Later Philosophy" when he proposes that Wittgenstein's appeal to ordinary language as the subject of philosophical investigation suggests new categories of criticism. Here our task is finally to understand what these kinds of critical activities might entail as practices toward a philosophy of the humanities. In investigating the friction between philosophy and the expression of ordinary beliefs Wittgenstein does not suggest that philosophy is a superior way of knowing, which must reform or "correct" language conceptually, nor is he defending ordinary beliefs against philosophical abstraction. Rather, in its excessive concern with epistemology, and in its quest to achieve certainty or shore itself up against skeptical doubt, philosophy has aimed at the wrong targets. The question of belief is only raised in fact by the problem of nonbelief; that is, when dilemmas of skepticism or certainty are raised in philosophy and put under scrutiny and critical pressure. In this way, philosophy has built *Luftgebäude,* as Wittgenstein puts it, or castles in the air, which raise questions for philosophy that interest only philosophy. Thus Cavell observes that perhaps Wittgenstein

> wishes to show that, in its conflict with "what we all believe," the philosopher has no position at all, his conclusions are not false (and not meaningless), but, one could say, not *believable*—that is, they do not create the stability of conviction expressed in propositions which are subject (grammatically) to belief. . . . For Wittgenstein, philosophy comes to grief not in denying what we all know to be true, but in its effort to escape those human forms of life which alone provide the coherence of our expression. He wishes an acknowledgment of human limitation which does not leave us chafed by our own skin, by a sense of powerlessness to penetrate beyond the human conditions of knowledge. The limitations of knowledge are no longer barriers to a more perfect apprehension, but conditions of knowledge *überhaupt,* of anything we should call "knowledge." ("The Availability of Wittgenstein's Later Philosophy" 61–62)

How to reengage philosophy, then, with our ordinary dilemmas of doubt, wonder, curiosity, discord and agreement, conflict and contradiction, understanding and misunderstanding, justice and injustice, of adjudicating promises kept and broken, of sense made or unmade? (And here "to make sense" may mean not just being sensible and rational but also *creating* meaning and new contexts for meaning.)

All of which is to say that philosophy's new critical categories are now reoriented grammatically toward the concrete practices where these activities actually take place: in our human capacities for expression and creation, knowledge and self-knowledge, which we are capable of exercising and required to exercise on a daily basis. In the rational and epistemological tradition that descends down through the Enlightenment from Bacon, Descartes, and Locke, philosophy's original sin, Cavell argues, is its lack of concern "with the knowledge of persons and in particular with self-knowledge; viz., its neglect of history as a form of human knowledge" ("The Availability of Wittgenstein's Later Philosophy" 68, note 11). Here we return to the value vacuum produced by modern philosophy's excessive concern with epistemology and knowledge of objects and matters rather than persons. Our intellectual problems, Cavell suggests, are set by the very success of instrumental knowledge, that is, "by the plain fact that the measures which soak up knowledge of the world leave us dryly ignorant of ourselves" (68).

Along these lines, Cavell approaches Wittgenstein in a deeply original way, and one that demonstrates how Wittgenstein's new categories of criticism are generated through the grammatical style of the *Investigations* itself, which endeavors not to teach or to convince, but to *show* practices of grammatical investigation and critique. (This is perhaps all that a philosopher, or a theorist, can really do.) In a move that brings us full circle back to *Elegy for Theory*, and to Pierre Hadot's account of ancient philosophy as driven by an ethical disquiet that demands a changed conception of both self and world where knowledge and self-knowledge advance through one another, Cavell concludes his essay with a convincing account of how the style of the *Investigations* displays all the hallmarks of a grammar of confession. The question here is not to understand what Wittgenstein writes, but rather to immerse oneself critically and imaginatively in the *how* of his practice, gradually approaching its method or methods through its own suggested techniques of perspicuous description, connective analysis, and the examination of intermediate cases. In a deeply original move, Wittgenstein recasts confession as dialogue, especially a dialogue with one's self. Thus the grammatical form of the *Investigations* exhibits

> what serious confessions must: the full acknowledgment of temptation ("I want to say . . ."; "I feel like saying . . ."; "Here the urge is strong . . .") and a willingness to correct them and give them up ("In the everyday use . . ."; "I impose a requirement which does not meet my real need"). (The voice of temptation and the voice of correctness are the antagonists in Wittgenstein's dialogues.) In confessing you do not explain or justify, but describe how it is with you. And confession, unlike dogma, is not to be believed but tested, and accepted or rejected. Nor is it the occasion for accusation, except of yourself, and by implication those who find themselves in you. There is exhortation ("Do not say: 'There *must* be something common . . . but *look* and *see* . . .'" (§66)) not to belief, but to self-scrutiny. And that is why there is virtually nothing in the *Investigations* which we should ordinarily call reasoning; Wittgenstein asserts nothing which could be proved, for what he asserts is either obvious (§126)—whether true or false—or else concerned with what conviction, whether by proof or evidence or authority, would consist in. . . . Belief is not enough. Either the

suggestion penetrates past assessment and becomes part of the sensibility from which assessment proceeds, or it is philosophically useless. ("The Availability of Wittgenstein's Later Philosophy" 71)

Here Cavell finds that Wittgenstein's writing is both deeply practical and critical in ways similar to Freud. Taking seriously Wittgenstein's assertion in the *Investigations* that "There is not *a* philosophical method, though there are indeed methods, like different therapies" (§133), Cavell shows that both philosophy and psychoanalysis compel forms of understanding that must be accompanied by self-transformation, and part of this self-transformation involves describing and restoring the broken links that divide us from the sense of ourselves and our relation to others. "Both of them," Cavell continues, "are intent on unmasking the defeat of our real need in the face of self-impositions which we have not assessed (§108), or fantasies ('pictures') which we cannot escape (§115). In both, such misfortune is betrayed in the incongruence between what is said and what is meant or expressed; for both, the self is concealed in assertion and action and revealed in temptation and wish" ("The Availability of Wittgenstein's Later Philosophy" 72). This is why the form of dialogue in the *Investigations* is so interesting and compelling, especially in how the competing voices of temptation and correctness cycle through stages of assertion, doubt, speculation, and self-correction. The place, voice, and thought of Wittgenstein seem so quixotic, mobile, mercurial, and unfixable in the grammar of the *Investigations* because Wittgenstein himself is projected less as a unique author or enunciator than as an "intermediate case"—a self-projected philosophical friend or conceptual persona—whose positions shift, sometimes dramatically, from section to section, and whose portrait takes form not in words but in the conceptual pattern of family resemblances that emerges from and between, not the sections or phrases themselves, but in the gaps, ellipses, and blank spaces that both separate and assemble them into the larger grammatical architecture of the work itself. In this, the *Investigations* is an exercise in both self-examination and in self-portraiture, but one that can never be finished because on close examination the subject it projects dissolves into a corona of lightly indicated images, "just as if each figure in a painting were surrounded by delicate shadowy drawings of scenes, as it were in another dimension, and in them we saw the figures in different contexts" (*Philosophical Investigations* II vi, 155e).

The "subject" of grammatical investigation thus concerns us all as human subjects in our quotidian dilemmas of interpretation, understanding, evaluation, discrimination, and consensus building. And we only advance through these dilemmas, as Cavell puts it, in confronting and assessing the self-imposed restrictions and "pictures" that block our real needs. In this, philosophy becomes an exemplary practice or repository of methods. What is thus requested through philosophy is a reflexive turn back on the conditions or possibilities of expression, or "a request for the person to say something about himself, describe what he does. So the different methods are methods for acquiring self-knowledge. . . . Perhaps more shocking, and certainly more important, than any of Freud's or Wittgenstein's particular conclusions is their discovery that knowing oneself is something for which there are methods—something, therefore, that can be taught (though not in obvious ways) and practiced" ("The Availability of Wittgenstein's Later Philosophy" 66–67).

In a fascinating footnote, Cavell also observes that in many important ways Wittgenstein thought of his methods as liberating, as when writing in §133 that "The real discovery is the one that makes me capable of stopping doing philosophy when I want to.—The one that gives philosophy peace, so that it is no longer tormented by questions which bring *itself* in question." At the same time, Cavell observes, this request for self-examination and self-overcoming can seem intolerable: "The reason why methods that make us look at what we say, and bring the forms of language (hence our forms of life) to consciousness, can present themselves to one person as confining and to another as liberating is, I think, understandable in this way: recognizing what we say, in the way that is relevant in philosophizing, is like recognizing our present commitments and their implications; to one person a sense of freedom will demand an escape from them, to another it will require their more total acceptance. Is it obvious that one of those positions must, in a given case, be right?" (57, note 7).

In Wittgenstein the question of how to know what we intended or wished to say is thus linked with the general question of self-knowledge but also with the problem of not sharing a concept or a context with proximate communities, leading to a sense of disorientation when we cannot find ourselves in others. In another passage from the *Philosophical Investigations* important to Cavell, Wittgenstein writes that "one human being can be a complete enigma to another. We learn this when we come into a strange country with entirely strange traditions; and, what is more, even given a mastery of the country's language. We do not *understand* the people. (And not because of not knowing what they are saying to themselves.) We cannot find our feet with them" (*Philosophical Investigations* II 190e). In all of these cases, we may arrive at agreement, or a consensus for a theory or theories, but even so, as Hacker asserts, there will still be no end to the need for philosophical criticism. The difficulties of philosophy are no more and no less than our daily dilemmas and hesitations before questions of doubt and certainty, deciding and procrastinating, hesitating and committing, agreeing and disagreeing. And in this hesitation or blocking, this bumping of our heads against the quotidian problems that expression and interpretation present to us, might philosophy find its own theoretical dimension?

Philosophical investigation differs from the logical quest for certainty, and in turn, as von Wright insisted, "The phenomena which the humanities study have features of their own which distinguish them logically from the typical objects of study in the natural sciences. A primary task of a philosophy of the humanities is to try to capture and do justice to those features."[36] To those who want truth from philosophy, or at least the proper conditions for truth telling, this turn in philosophy is scandalous for at least two reasons. Here the quest to enlarge our powers of reasoning takes place less through adding progressively to our knowledge of the external world than in examining the capacities and limits of human reason itself as expressed in its forms of communication and cultural practices. And further, strategies for enlarging our capacity to interpret and to understand necessarily require a reflexive turn as acts of self-interpretation where problems of knowing are inextricably intertwined with questions of import and value.

Analogous arguments are closely associated with Charles Taylor's innovative work on interpretation and his definition of humans as self-interpreting animals. Cavell notwithstanding, more than any other philosopher since Wittgenstein Taylor has consistently worked through the implications of defining the sui generis character of humanistic understanding. Humans are characteristically self-interpreting because, from a scientific or theoretical perspective, they are not just objects among other objects immersed in webs of causal relations, nor can one separate the knowledge of the subject from the object she or he investigates. In other words, there is no such thing as a structure of meaning for subjects that is independent of their interpretive and self-interpretive activities. One is woven into the other, Taylor argues, such that "the text of our interpretation is not that heterogeneous from what is interpreted; for what is interpreted is itself an interpretation; a self-interpretation which is embedded in a stream of action. It is an interpretation of experiential meaning which

---

36. "Humanism and the Humanities," in *The Tree of Knowledge,* 163–164.

contributes to the constitution of this meaning. Or to put it in another way: that of which we are trying to find the coherence is itself partly constituted by self-interpretation."[37] At the same time, the will to interpret and acts of interpretation always occur within frameworks of import ascription, which also ask for accounts of value. "This is an animal," Taylor writes, "whose emotional life incorporates a sense of what is really important to him, of the shape of his aspirations, which asks to be understood, and which is never adequately understood. His understanding is explicated at any time in the language he uses to speak about himself, his goals, what he feels, and so on; and in shaping his sense of what is important it also shapes what he feels."[38]

It is impossible to do justice to the full range and complexity of Taylor's arguments here, especially with respect to the important role that the articulation and interpretation of emotions plays in his definition of human beings as self-interpreting animals. What I would like to do is to open out and clarify some potential meanings for interpretation in the humanities in relation to the ascription of value, and thus better comprehend the distinction of understanding from explanation. In ways similar to Cavell, Taylor adopts from Heidegger the idea that *Verstehen* is a *Seinsmodus*; in other words, understanding and self-understanding are inseparable as ways of fashioning a form of life or mode of existence—here the quest for meaning is intertwined inextricably with assessments of value. This argument has been a recurring theme of this book and its pendant, *Elegy for Theory*. But this assertion also raises the question, what forms of knowledge or reason are appropriate when human beings take themselves and their cultural practices as "objects" of investigation?

The thesis that humans are self-interpreting animals—especially as a way of distinguishing the epistemological space of the humanities from that of the natural sciences—runs counter not only to our conventional sense of object-subject distinctions but also to our most tenaciously held criteria for wanting and claiming certainty in knowledge. Conventionally, to think about a thing clearly with the purpose of obtaining certain knowledge of it requires that it be thought of primarily objectively and as an object among other objects distinct from our subjective experiences and standpoints, which are considered

37. "Interpretation and the Sciences of Man" in *Philosophy and the Human Sciences*, 26. This essay offers one of Taylor's strongest critiques of scientism and one of his most interesting responses to the hostility of the verificationist perspective to the dilemmas of the hermeneutic circle.

38. "Self-Interpreting Animals" in *Philosophical Papers, vol. 1: Human Agency and Language* (Cambridge: Cambridge University Press, 1985), 74.

to be secondary. From a scientistic point of view, these secondary and experiential qualities should be excluded as much as possible because they relate to our experience of objects, or what we take to be objects, and are thus considered subjective, variable, and not amenable to intersubjective validation. As Taylor nicely puts it, "they cannot make good a claim to be independently part of the furniture of things" ("Self-Interpreting Animals" 46).

Here two difficulties are confronted. One is a version of epistemology that in aspiring to clarity, objectivity, and certainty must effectively exclude the human and the subjective from its realm of investigation, or conversely, reduce the human to properties or qualities of objects and subnormative functions or operations. I have called this, somewhat ironically, "good theory." The second difficulty, though Taylor does not pose it as such, is to know how and under what conditions the subject may investigate itself subjectively qua subject within this framework as a function of understanding. No doubt this is the key question that any possible philosophy of the humanities must address. The conventional epistemological distinction between primary and secondary qualities, or the objective and subjective, must be overturned or undermined in order to comprehend that our knowledge of reality and the reality of our selves is inseparable from our experience of reality in terms of both knowledge and value, and of what we value in our ways of knowing ourselves and the modes of existence we construct and inhabit. (This argument provides one of the closest points of contact between Taylor and Cavell, as we shall see further down the road.)

The open question here, to which Taylor and Richard Rorty have differing but also similar responses, is whether a strict distinction between objective and subjective knowledge can really be made. To put it another way, since all knowledge arises from human practices and social contexts, the desire to produce a kind of transsubjective or asubjective knowledge (to which structuralism, for example, aspired) is illusory, because the pursuit of knowledge, in whatever context or through whichever method, unavoidably involves interpretive activities. To pursue this line of thought is not only to demonstrate the overlapping and interpenetrating borders between the human and natural sciences but also to restore the maligned concept of interpretation as a central aspect of human and intentional activity in whatever domain.

Central to the activity of interpretation is the assignation of what Taylor calls import ascriptions. Explaining oneself, giving a reason, constructing and defending a concept, describing a desire or emotion, or expressing what Richard Rorty calls a sentential attitude, are all activities of justification that involve or make explicit a qualitative judgment concerning the objects under investigation, of whatever sort. Such justifications equally involve the ascription of "imports," or as Taylor puts it, providing a perspicuous description of the "way in which something can be relevant or of importance to the desires or purposes or aspirations or feelings of a subject; or otherwise put, a property of something whereby it is a matter of non-indifference to a subject" ("Self-Interpreting Animals" 48). Describing, justifying, or giving reasons involves making sense of the state of affairs so described or the actions so justified, as well as accounting for the import of the act or situation as we experience it. Philosophically, such activities involve making explicit their import ascriptions, which are less the affirmation of a judgment than grasping the sense of the situation that incorporates or leads to the judgment. Such accounts are necessarily subjective in that they are experience dependent, but this experience is also cultural, or rather, depends on accounting for one's experience of a culture or one's social existence as a subject in solidarity or in conflict with other subjects; we return here to Wittgenstein's insistence on the holistic nature of all claims to knowledge or sense. Import ascriptions are thus also accounts of the values accepted or given within a form or life, for the expressive or semantic dimension of the ascription can only be explained with reference to a subject for whom these meanings have import, and without such subjects, there would be neither import nor sense.

Since the early modern period, one of the great recurring illusions of Western science has been that culture and history may be bypassed in explanations of human actions, and that all such explanations avoid confronting the fact that they are both cultural and historical. But Taylor's rather radical claim, at least from a positivistic or scientistic point of view, is that there is no epistemology, no theory or method, from which an intending subject and its forms of life can be subtracted. All forms of describing, explaining, reasoning, or conceptualizing are unavoidably subject referring, and therefore to examine the epistemological and conceptual frameworks of a theory or a method necessarily involves a holistic investigation of their import ascriptions. To look at theorizing as a practice also means acknowledging that our ways of conceptualizing and shaping theories unavoidably incorporate elements of self-characterization or self-definition that shape knowledge practices, and thus any theory purporting to understand the intentional acts of such agents and practices cannot be considered either purely instrumental or objective.

Subject referring does not necessarily mean self-referring, however, and the class of subject-referring imports is much broader than that of self-referring or self-regarding imports. This is so for two reasons. First, explications of import ascriptions are usually not qualifiable by a single term but evoke rather a whole network of meanings for the subject. Second, even though subject-referring properties do not lend themselves to the logic of scientistic or objectivist accounts because they can only be explicated in experience-dependent terms, this does not mean that they are purely subjective. To make an import ascription is to produce a judgment about a situation—its value and meaning—that cannot be simply reduced to how we feel about it, because producing and communicating an interpretation is a public and social event open to conversation and debate, agreements and disagreements, which in turn may potentially transform the terms of debate, the language in which it is expressed, and the nature of the epistemological and axiological commitments that have been entered into. Another way of putting this is to say that we experience the world collectively before we experience it individually.

In this context, restoring the value of interpretation is more interesting than continuing to map the borders, no matter how porous, between the human and natural sciences. Moreover, seeking out knowledge of human beings, their cultures, and their creative practices may not mean overcoming and transcending the dilemma of the hermeneutic circle but rather embracing it—not as a circle but rather as an ever-expanding skein of new conceptual vocabularies and connective relations. In one of the fragments collected in the *Zettel*, Wittgenstein remarks that there is no need for interpretation when one "feel[s] at home in the present picture" (§234).[39] The need or will to interpret, then, arrives when I am subject to disagreeable situations, when I am homeless or adrift, bereft of needed conceptual resources, or when I am faced with an obstacle to thought, or I lack signposts to move further in thought or understanding. To interpret, or perhaps to theorize, means acquiring or moving toward a new conceptual framework, or as Wittgenstein puts it, stepping from one level of thought to another: *"Wenn ich deute, so schreite ich auf dem Gedankenweg von Stufe zu Stufe* (§234).

Charles Taylor's several essays examining how humans are characteristically self-interpreting animals offer some landmarks for this *Gedankenweg*—steps, levels, or passages wherein the acquiring of knowledge is both a self-examining and self-transforming process. These activities are all built upon Taylor's intuition that all knowledge is in some respects subject referring.

---

39. Ed. G. E. M. Anscombe and G. H. von Wright (Berkeley: University of California Press, 1967).

One initial step involves a process that Taylor calls growing insight. Establishing the meaning, value, or sense of people, objects, events, or states of affairs is an activity shaped by complexes of subject-referring imports of which we may only be partially aware. To develop the capacity for identifying, presenting, and perspicuously describing deeply felt but inarticulate imports is to bring potential insight into our lives as subjects, giving sense and making sense of what is important to us qua subjects. Thus Taylor writes that, "If we think of this reflexive sense of what matters to us as subjects as being distinctively human—and it is clearly central to our notion of ourselves that we are such reflexive beings; this is what underlies the traditional definition of man as a rational animal—we could say that our subject-referring feelings incorporate a sense of what it is to be human, that is, of what matters to us as human subjects" ("Self-Interpreting Animals" 60).

Because these feelings are articulable and articulated, they are in a strong sense interpretations. To examine an object, event, or situation is to express both its sense and one's feeling about it, and these expressions lead to or generate series of more expansive and finely tuned characterizations. Interpretive responses generate expression, and expression leads in turn to qualifications, extensions, and refinements in meaning and understanding. Insight is then amplified by further assessments that evaluate, weigh, and rank our import ascriptions through a process of qualitative discriminations in the context of the forms of life we inhabit, thus affirming or challenging them. Taylor calls this strong evaluation, which examines not just objects in the light of our desires but also the desires themselves in a second-order evaluation that is inherently reflexive. Strong evaluations involve subject-referring imports, and reciprocally, subject-referring feelings are or involve strong evaluations in a process of moral reasoning that is close to what Stanley Cavell calls moral perfectionism. "Implicit in this strong evaluation," Taylor writes, "is thus a placing of our different motivations relative to each other, the drawing, as it were, of a moral map of ourselves; we contrast a higher, more clairvoyant, more serene motivation, with a baser, more self-enclosed and troubled one, which we can see ourselves as potentially growing beyond, if and when we can come to experience things from the higher standpoint" (67).

The process of giving expression to our sense of things makes present to us the imports guiding our responses, defining and characterizing them, leading to further assessments and evaluations that are as much social and contextual as personal. These assessments ascribe a form to what matters to us, a logic of sense, and at the same time open us to the domain of what it is to be human.

However, like all forms of reason, this activity is not completely free of disagreeable qualities of ambiguity, mischaracterization, uncertainty, or self-
doubt; nor does strong evaluation necessarily lead to progressive improvement
in morals or moral reasoning. For

> these feelings also open the question whether this characterization is ad-
> equate, whether it is not incomplete or distortive. And so from the very
> fact of their being articulated, the question cannot but arise whether we
> have properly articulated our feelings, that is, whether we have properly
> explicated what the feeling gives us a sense of. In an important sense, this
> question once opened can never be closed. . . . The attempt to articulate
> further is potentially a life-time process. At each stage, what we feel is a
> function of what we have already articulated and evokes the puzzlement
> and perplexities which further understanding may unravel. But whether
> we want to take the challenge or not, whether we seek the truth or take
> refuge in illusion, our self-(mis)understandings shape what we feel. This
> is the sense in which man is a self-interpreting animal. ("Self-Interpreting
> Animals" 64–65)

Interpretation and self-interpretation are, in other words, interminable because
our reasons and justifications are incomplete and persistently open to question. They prevent the interpretive circle from ever completing itself and thus
fuel a hermeneutic spiral, whether virtuous or vicious.

Language shapes the reflexive experience of reasoning, assessment, and evaluation not only by giving expressive form to import ascriptions and reasons but
also by providing new conceptual vocabularies for them. When different experiences, senses, or emotions are assessed or evaluated under different concepts
they are experienced differently and potentially undergo a transvaluation. This
is a process that entails recognizing that vocabularies for describing and assessing imports themselves shape and extend or expand our assessments. One
might add that they also change the sense of the experience itself.

Taylor attributes two kinds of conceptual revolution to this process of transvaluation, one in relation to a personal stance in need of transformation, the
second of which recognizes the necessity of transformation under a new concept. Perhaps one could say that the first kind of transformation involves a
critical dialogue with oneself and the acquisition of a deeper insight into one's
import ascriptions. But the second kind of transformation and transvaluation
involves another kind of confrontation wherein one's self-understanding and

conceptual frameworks for self-understanding are challenged in the encounter with other cultures, perspectives, and points of view. It is as if we come to understand the limits and confinements of our own conceptual vocabularies for self-assessment and self-understanding in comprehending that a number of different subject-referring accounts are equally possible and desirable. In addition, we are susceptible to the necessity of (self) transformation under a new concept because the open, incomplete, and fragmentary nature of our interpretations of self and of others means that our conceptual vocabularies can never be decisively fixed because they can never be fully described in objective terms. For these reasons, the reflexive process of interpretation, assessment, and evaluation, of making and remaking qualitative distinctions, can never be definitively closed.

There is another important dimension to the process of transformation under a new concept, one that deepens our sense of understanding of how the subject may investigate itself subjectively qua subject. In his essay "Theories of Meaning," Taylor unfolds the consequences of what he terms the expressive or triple-H (Herder-Humboldt-Heidegger) account of meaning in contrast with designative and truth-conditional accounts of language, wherein language is considered a phenomenon of nature like all others, making of it a pliant and transparent instrument of thought.[40] Meaning cannot be simply treated as representation, nor can we come to understand how meaning or interpretation work from the standpoint of monological and neutral observers. Taylor's account characterizes expression not only as attempts at communication or the transmission of sense but also as acts of disclosure. Language in its broadest sense is thus defined as the site of three human activities: making articulations, and thus putting before us and making us more aware of our import ascriptions, assessments, and conceptual commitments; putting this discourse in a public space, and thereby constituting a public space for further evaluation and assessment; and finally, in this process discriminating, reworking, and refining values and concepts that are fundamental to human concerns, and thus opening us reflexively to those concerns.

If this is really to be an expansive, critical, and transformative process, interpretations must not only be partial and open to critical investigation and debate, they must be crucially out of phase with their explananda. Interpretations

40. "Theories of Meaning," in *Human Agency and Language,* 248–292. In fact, there are more broadly four H's in Taylor's account of what he calls the Romantic or expressive family of theories, which includes Johann Georg Hamann.

thus involve confrontations—with recalcitrant objects and texts as well as competing conceptual frameworks for interpretation—that not only produce new conditions of sense but also new conditions for reassessing the sense of one's self. This argument follows from Taylor's claim that there is no such thing as structures of meaning independent of our interpretations of them, and thus that all meaning is experiential in the sense that every interpretation involves a degree of self-interpretation embedded in a stream of action. This domain of experiential meaning shifts interpretive activities in a new and interesting direction, for an interpretation must not only transform its object or give it a new sense. Interpretation does not simply restore sense or coherence to an expression; it also *produces* new forms or situations of coherence. Moreover, to the extent that this is a new sense for the subject, and that the subject is embedded in the larger context of experiential meaning, the subject too is potentially transformed in interesting ways.

Taylor's essay "Understanding and Ethnocentricity" offers his most complete account of what it might mean to undergo transformation under a new concept. Taylor's principal thesis is that interpretive theories, or ways of understanding the practices of humans as self-referring animals, must be distinguished from descriptions of theories in the natural sciences, and thus that "Understanding is inseparable from criticism, but this in turn is inseparable from self-criticism."[41] Ethnography offers an interesting case for exploring the ways in which efforts to understand another society—or more broadly, intentional acts and practices that stand in need of interpretation because of a felt discontinuity with our sense of ourselves and our own forms of life—challenge us to criticize and remap our self-definitions. The problem confronted here is that one cannot achieve an adequate explanatory account of alien languages, cultures, or experiences until one's own self-definitions are understood, defined, and accepted. And further, in their difference from our own forms of life or conceptual contexts, these encounters may encourage us to expand our own language of human possibilities.

The key question here is how to make sense of others, and what happens to us when we feel compelled to make sense of others. Taylor frames his argument ethnographically or anthropologically; that is, he asks how we understand and make sense of alien cultures and practices. But we might also feel compelled to interpret any action or activity, including artful expression, which seems to resist our capacity to understand or interpret it. (A similar extension

41. "Understanding and Ethnocentricity," in *Philosophy and the Human Sciences,* 131.

can and should be made, in my opinion, to Donald Davidson's fascinating account of problems of linguistic translation in "Radical Interpretation" and other essays.)

Following out the consequences of our sympathetic responses to such alien encounters helps clarify the steps or stages guiding our will to interpret. First, to want or to be willing to interpret means accepting that an intentional act—even more so one we feel to be alien—must in principle be understandable in that it arises from common human capacities for expression and self-reference. The first move in such acts of interpretation is to try to arrive at how the agent, text, or expression may have wished to understand itself. This idea is commensurate with Davidson's account of rational accommodation, or what is sometimes called his Principle of Charity. Further, interpretive understanding does not simply arrive at meaning or come to a conclusion in finding or adopting the point of view of the subject or text which stands in need of interpretation, for simply recovering this self-description may shed no light whatsoever on the acts or make them more comprehensible. In other words, an interpretation does not complete itself simply in comprehending the agent's self-descriptions. There are several reasons for this. The given explanandum may not fully understand itself, or be subject to omission or contradiction, misinformation or illusion, or cannot or not yet have found the right language of self-characterization. Thus there is no need to frame our explanantia in the same language as the subject, nor should we do so.

Those who gravitate toward the natural sciences as a model for the social sciences or humanities will want to bypass these self-descriptions altogether as "subjective," for they cannot be intersubjectively validated in unproblematic ways—there is no hope of replicable findings. But this is to give up the game too quickly. One cannot avoid the subject-referring qualities of intentional acts—or else we have renounced the human in the human sciences. At the same time, we have not successfully interpreted by simply understanding the other's point of view or putting ourselves in their place. What Taylor calls the "interpretive view" is distinguishable from both the natural-science model and the false ally that misconceives interpretation as successfully concluded in adopting the explanandum's viewpoint. Taylor terms this the "incorrigibility thesis," meaning that interpretation must take the agent's self-account as absolutely authoritative. This view must be tempered, as I have already pointed out, by acknowledging that the agent might be mistaken or subject to the variety of misfires of reason. We all are. This acknowledgment produces a new framework for what theory should do in relation to self-description and understanding. If there is a multitude of reasons why our authoritative self-referring accounts might be incomplete or unreliable, if what passes for common sense or common knowledge may in fact be inadequate, then theory is

> very much in the business of correcting common-sense understanding. It is of very little use unless it goes beyond, unless it frequently challenges and negates what we think we are doing, saying, feeling, aiming at. But its criterion of success is that it makes us as agents more comprehensible, that it makes sense of what we feel, do, aim at. . . . And so there is no way of showing that some theory has actually explained *us* and *our* action until it can be shown to make sense of what we did under *our* description (where this emphatically does *not* mean . . . showing how what we did made sense). For otherwise, we may have an interesting, speculative rational reconstruction . . . but no way of showing that it actually *explains* anything. ("Understanding and Ethnocentricity" 124).

The incorrigibility thesis is attractive because it seems to safeguard against ethnocentrism and other forms of cultural prejudice or bias. But the interpretive view wishes both to avoid the false neutrality, objectivity, and universalism of scientism *and* to engage others' forms of self-understanding critically with a view of potentially transforming them, if necessary. If this were not done, there would be no possibility of producing new interpretations or of undergoing a change in understanding and value. For in challenging the language of self-understanding in others, we may also be challenging our own language of self-understanding. This process is generated by misunderstanding and disagreement, and thus there is value in being disagreeable because there are many instances where such acts of interpretation are transformative on both sides. "In fact," Taylor explains,

> it will almost always be the case that the adequate language in which we can understand another society is not our language of understanding, or theirs, but rather what one could call a language of perspicuous contrast. This would be a language in which we could formulate both their way of life and ours as alternative possibilities in relation to some human constants at work in both. It would be a language in which the possible human

variations would be so formulated that both our form of life and theirs could be perspicuously described as alternative such variations. Such a language of contrast might show their language of understanding to be distorted or inadequate in some respects, or it might show ours to be so (in which case, we might find that understanding them leads to an alteration of our self-understanding, and hence our form of life—a far from unknown process in history); or it might show both to be so. (125–126)

Taylor's description of coming to terms in languages of perspicuous contrast is close in spirit and logic to Davidson's concept of "passing theories" and to Gadamer's "fusion of horizons." There is neither time nor space to follow out the implications of these comparisons here. What is important is to hold on to the idea that interpretation refers equally to questions of meaning and matter, that is, import. Conflicts in interpretation often arise because different cultures, in the broadest and most varied sense of the term, are defined by different import vocabularies, and even within a given culture, people with different import vocabularies have very different experiences. Moreover, as Taylor points out, "conceptual mutations in human history can and frequently do produce conceptual webs which are incommensurable, that is, where the terms cannot be defined in relation to a common stratum of expressions" ("Interpretation and the Sciences of Man" 55). When this happens, there is no way forward in understanding or in thought without the creation of new concepts and new strata of expressions through the acknowledgment that our powers and means of expression are replete with possible extensions. However, Taylor's main point, and the connective thread between all his various accounts of interpretation, is that understanding is inseparable from ethical evaluation, and that both understanding and evaluation are potentially open to extensions, creative transformation, and transvaluation. In other words, "in the sciences of man in so far as they are hermeneutical there can be a valid response to 'I don't understand', which takes the form, not only 'develop your intuitions', but more radically, 'change yourself'. . . . A study of the science of man is inseparable from an examination of the options between which men must choose" (54).

Taylor's characterization of the need for transformation under a new concept might be further deepened and extended by comparison with Richard Rorty's pragmatist account of inquiry as recontextualization. Rorty departs from Taylor in arguing that boundaries between the natural and human sciences need not and cannot be observed. Nonetheless, there are points of contact between the two thinkers in that both more or less agree that the activities of pursuing knowledge and defining meaning are invariably subject-inflected in both the natural and human sciences (though perhaps in different ways) and that both domains seek consensus or some form of intersubjective verifiability.

In his essay "Inquiry as Recontextualization: An Anti-Dualist Account of Interpretation," Rorty begins by asking that we "think of human minds as webs of beliefs and desires, of sentential attitudes—webs which continually reweave themselves so as to accommodate new sentential attitudes."[42] We need not ask for the moment where new beliefs, attitudes, or concepts come from, nor about how one might parse the flow of information between an external and internal world. Just assume, Rorty asks, that new beliefs and desires keep appearing that challenge, contradict, or place under tension our current webs and imagine how we respond: "For example, we may simply drop an old belief or desire. Or we may create a whole host of new beliefs and desires in order to encapsulate the disturbing intruder, reducing the strain which the old beliefs and desires put on it and which it puts on them. Or we may just unstitch, and thus erase, a whole range of beliefs and desires." ("Inquiry as Recontextualization" 93).

Part of the problem here is how to think about and account for the flow of change wherein human knowledge and attitudes toward the world and society are modified and transformed, expand and deepen, or even stagnate. Rorty characterizes inquiry as a reweaving of beliefs or a process of continuing recontextualization where the "more widespread the changes, the more use we have for the notion of 'a new context.' This new context can be a new explanatory theory, a new comparison class, a new descriptive vocabulary, a new private or political purpose, the latest book one has read, the last person one has talked to; the possibilities are endless" (94). Traditionally, philosophy has sorted out this kind of contextual remapping into two kinds of classes, which might be distinguished as inferential and imaginative—Rorty compares their respective attitudes toward discourse as translation and learning a new language. Inferential processes involve the acquisition of new truth-value candidates without a corresponding transformation of discourse: "We speak

---

42. In *Philosophical Papers, vol. 1: Objectivity, Relativism, and Truth* (Cambridge: Cambridge University Press, 1991), 93.

of inference when logical space remains fixed, when no new candidates for belief are introduced. Paradigms of inference are adding up a column of figures, or running through a sorites, or down a flow-chart" (94). One might be reminded here of the inferential and inductive processes of good theory that map data into new domains without corresponding transformations of methods, concepts, or modes of expression.

Transformation through imagination, however, involves a new set of attitudes or even mutation of one's discourse repertoire through the innovative use of metaphors fallen out of use, the invention of neologisms, or the colligation of heretofore unrelated texts and concepts. In a footnote Rorty adds, "successful colligation of this sort is an example of rapid and unconscious reweaving: one lays one set of beliefs on top of another and finds that, magically, they have interpenetrated and become warp and woof of a new, vividly polychrome, fabric" (95). Rorty notes that there is a tendency to associate the concept of rationality exclusively with inference, as good theory in fact does, and before the postpositivist philosophies of science of Thomas Kuhn, Stephen Toulmin, Paul Feyerabend, or Norwood Russell Hanson the physical sciences were indeed thought to be definitive and exclusive models of rationality. The scandal now is that shifting scientific paradigms may indeed require learning a new discourse and adopting unfamiliar concepts in ways that are closer to "theory" in a broader and perhaps more humanistic sense.

Rorty's account of inquiry as recontextualization is self-characterized as an antidualist account. One dualism he hopes to undermine strictly separates the human and natural sciences into two incommensurable domains, one dealing exclusively with texts and the other exclusively with objects or matter.[43] Another has to do with a version of realism characteristic of both domains where inquiry involves and is valued for finding out the nature of something that lies beyond and outside the web of our beliefs and desires, and which only seeks a discourse commensurate with that "outside." This outside is considered to be in possession of its own intrinsically privileged context; it would also be primarily objective in the sense that Taylor challenges. However, from the perspective of Rorty's pragmatism, or even of a Wittgensteinian holism, no such dualism or distinction of the subject and object of knowledge—as if two exteriors in confrontation with one another—is in fact possible or desirable. This is first because, in an attitude that recalls Georges

43. This is the subject of another influential Rorty essay, "Texts and Lumps," in *Objectivity, Relativism, and Truth* (Cambridge: Cambridge University Press, 1991), 78–92.

Canguilhem, Gaston Bachelard, or Louis Althusser, Rorty observes that the intelligibility of an object of inquiry, whether text or lump, is always framed by context in the form of the questions asked of it, the concepts evoked for it, and the desirability characterizations that inform them both. In turn, this means that there is no simple representation of an object by a discourse external to it, for objects are always already contextualized or woven into a web of beliefs and pragmatic attitudes about them. "Once one drops the traditional opposition between context and thing contexualized," Rorty argues,

> there is no way to divide things up into those which are what they are in-
> dependent of context and those which are context-dependent—no way to
> divide the world up into hard lumps and squishy texts, for example. Or,
> to put it another way, there is no way to divide the world up into internal
> and external relations, nor into intrinsic vs. extrinsic properties—nor in-
> deed, into things that are intrinsically relations and things that are in-
> trinsically terms of relations. For once one sees inquiry as reweaving be-
> liefs rather than discovering the nature of objects, there are no candidates
> for self-subsistent, independent entities save individual beliefs—individual
> sentential attitudes. But these are very bad candidates indeed. For a be-
> lief is what it is only by virtue of its position in a web. ("Inquiry as Recon-
> textualization" 98)

Rorty notes that his attitude is characteristic of antiessentialism in both the analytic and continental traditions—there are neither essences to objects or even essences themselves wherein questions of certainty can ground themselves. However, his larger concern, in ways similar to Taylor, is with the value of interpretation or hermeneutics, but not necessarily as a way of defining and preserving the domain of human understanding in the usual ways. And in fact, Rorty is not willing to subscribe to a strict distinction between the natural and human sciences, especially one which excludes rationality from the latter and interpretation from the former—these are two sides or dimensions of any knowledge practice, which can neither be strictly separated nor serve as a ground for separating the sciences from the humanities, or vice versa. Rorty's objective, rather, is to undermine the view that the aim of inquiry is to represent objects or to translate them into an adequate representational language, and in turn to substitute the view that the goal of inquiry is to make our beliefs and desires coherent with a view toward deepening and clarifying them, or when they fail us, challenging and renovating them. The only concept of object that one needs in this perspective is what Rorty calls an intentional object: "An intentional object is what a word or description refers to. You find out what it refers to by attaching a meaning to the linguistic expressions to that word or description. That, in turn, you do by either translating or, if necessary, becoming bilingual in, the language in which the word or description occurs. Whether that is a useful language for your purpose is as irrelevant to objecthood as the question of whether the object has any causal powers" ("Inquiry as Recontextualization" 106–107). Concepts of both essence and empiricism have disappeared here, as objects cannot stand outside of descriptions, which are themselves context dependent and subject referring. Rorty's pragmatist account thus transforms the pursuit of knowledge and recasts it not as establishing the coherence or correspondence of a relation between minds and objects but rather as the ability to arrive at consensus through persuasion. Rather than opposing texts and lumps, subjects and objects, or trying to identify one with the other, both are dissolved into transitory and contingent webs of meaning, intelligibility, and significance.

In similar ways, Rorty refers to the work of Donald Davidson to break down not only the dualism between object and subject but also the frontiers between intercultural and intracultural understanding. "The difference between banally intercultural and controversial objects," he insists, "will be the difference between the objects you have to talk about to deal with the routine stimulations provided by your familiars, and the objects required to deal with the novel stimulations provided by new acquaintances (e.g. Aristotelians, Polynesians, avant-garde poets and painters, imaginative colligators of texts, etc.)" ("Inquiry as Recontextualization" 107). When confronting radical novelty in practice or expression, in whatever cultural context or domain, interpretation begins by appealing to Davidson's Principle of Charity. Here one assumes, first, that there is coherence or sense to a novel expression, if the correct context and translation protocol can be found for it, and second, that in view of the common human capacity for expression and interpretation, there are already in principle overlaps and important points of contact in the forms of life confronting one another; in other words, miscomprehension only exists in situations where some degree of understanding is nonetheless possible. As Rorty puts it, according to Davidson's Principle of Charity, in accommodating ourselves to the discourse and customs of strange beings such as the Nambikwara, poets, artists, string theorists, or humanists "we are already, automatically, for free, participant-observers, not *mere* observers" (107).

Such a principle applies to all difficulties of interpretation and understanding in whatever epistemological or cultural domain we find ourselves, and thus dissolves yet another philosophical dualism: the one that separates (causal) explanation from (interpretive) understanding. There is no longer a polarity between the two epistemological perspectives, but only a scale running in degrees from one to the other. And there is no singular or particular method appropriate to one and alien to the other, but only shifting series of pragmatic stances or contexts in which each adapts its vocabularies and methods to the problems and questions that confront it.

To the extent that it allows a distinction between the natural and human sciences, then, Rorty's version of pragmatism does not promote the idea of two methodological domains or cultures separate from and opposed to one another, but sees them rather as interpenetrating genres of discourse about the world. Each of these genres has an improvisational or experimental quality, which is less about dividing the world and culture up into subject matters or disciplines than attempting to recast pragmatically the intelligibility of objects, events, texts, or states of affairs through whatever conceptual frameworks we can mobilize, co-opt, renovate, extend, or invent in a given historical moment and context. This recasting is tantamount to creating new languages or logics of sense and significance, not ex nihilo, of course, but rather as modifications and extensions, whether slight or radical, of previous genres of discourse, which in turn will be themselves refashioned in new, future contexts. Different genres or strands of discourse may interact and intertwine, Rorty explains, as do art and the criticism of art or science and the history of science, or philosophy and criticism. However, "there are no rules for whether they should or shouldn't intertwine—no necessities lying in the nature of a subject or a method. There is nothing general and epistemological to be said about how the contributors to the various genres should conduct themselves. Nor is there any ranking of these disciplines according to degrees or kinds of truth. There is, in short, nothing to be said about the relation of these genres to the world, only things to be said about their relations to each other. Further, there are no ahistorical things to be said about the latter sort of relations" ("Texts and Lumps" 91–92).

While Rorty is less committed than von Wright or Taylor to mapping differences between the human and natural sciences, nonetheless he shares their criticisms of instrumental and technological reason and their resistance to a scientism that reduces what is rational and true only to those functions or processes that can be characterized as subnormative, automatic, and blindly causal. But what Rorty hopes to gain by such a critique is perhaps both a humanization of science and a theoretization of interpretation. "Viewing inquiry as recontextualization," Rorty concludes,

> makes it impossible to take seriously the notion of some contexts being intrinsically privileged, as opposed to being useful for some particular purpose. By getting rid of the idea of "different methods appropriate to the natures of different objects" (e.g., one for language-constituted and another for non-language-constituted objects), one switches attention from "the demands of the object" to the demands of the purpose which a particular inquiry is supposed to serve. The effect is to modulate philosophical debate from a methodologico-ontological key into an ethico-political key. For now one is debating what purposes are worth bothering to fulfill, which are more worthwhile than others, rather than which purposes the nature of humanity or of reality obliges us to have. For antiessentialists, all possible purposes compete with one another on equal terms, since none are more "essentially human" than any others. ("Inquiry as Recontextualization" 110)

This modulation of perspective is very close to what Taylor calls assessment or second-order evaluation. However, Rorty turns his arguments in another direction. The desire to know or to seek understanding and the tendency to enlarge one's interpretive context through recontextualizing may be thought of as characteristically human, but perhaps no more so (and no less) Rorty insists, than the capacity to use opposable thumbs: "We have little choice but to use that thumb, and little choice but to employ our ability to recontextualize. We are going to find ourselves doing both, whatever happens. From an ethico-political angle, however, one can say that what is characteristic, not of the human species but merely of its most advanced, sophisticated subspecies— the well-read, tolerant, conversable inhabitant of a free society—is the desire to dream up as many new contexts as possible. This is the desire to be as polymorphous in our adjustments as possible, to recontextualize for the hell of it" (110). Perhaps this is a new motto for the humanities.

8. "Of which we cannot speak . . .": Philosophy and the Humanities

> In certain cases, as the saying suggests, one *remains* a philosopher only
> by—being silent.
>
> —Friedrich Nietzsche, *Human, All Too Human*

In the preceding pages, I have often examined the debate on theory from the point of view of competing epistemological stakes. Accused of "epistemological atheism," the very concept of theory is wrested from the Continent to be returned semantically to the shores of science and the terrain of British and American analytical philosophy. Initially, this debate was posed as a conflict between Theory and philosophy. But the later Wittgenstein took this argument in another direction, one that also questions "theory" but as a way of turning philosophy from science to restore it to the humanities. In so doing, Wittgenstein was less concerned with the epistemological perfectibility of philosophical language than with reclaiming philosophy's ancient task of *theoria*. Where Rorty concludes his discussion of inquiry as recontextualization in a somewhat elitist key with an appeal to the most advanced and sophisticated subspecies of humanity, Wittgenstein placed his hopes in the acknowledgment that we are all subject to "grammatical" confusion. Therefore, the only way to free ourselves for other steps toward thinking is through an instinctive revolt against the conceptual restraints that bind us, which in turn leads to something like a wholesale rearrangement of our language—that is, of the conceptual and expressive repertoires available for our interpretations and our self-descriptions and self-assessments.[44] Rorty calls this recontextualization or learning a new language; Taylor calls it transformation under a new concept. In either case, the path toward knowledge requires a reflexive turn through assessments of the terms for self-knowledge in which critical evaluations of ways of knowing are linked to the preservation or transformation of

---

44. In the "Big Typescript," Wittgenstein writes: "Human beings are deeply embedded in philosophical, *i.e.* grammatical confusions. Freeing them from these *presupposes* tearing them away from the enormous number of connecting links that hold them fast. A sort of rearrangement of the whole of their language is needed. ('Man muss sozusagen ihre ganze Sprache umgruppieren.')—But of course that language has developed the way it has because some human beings felt—and still feel—inclined to think that way. So the tearing away will succeed only with those in whose life there already is an instinctive revolt against the language in question and not with those whose instinct is for the very herd which created that language as its proper expression." Cited in von Wright's own translation in *The Tree of Knowledge*, 97.

a mode of existence or form of life. If the politics and epistemology of Theory have been subject to much soul searching and epistemological critique, it is important nonetheless to find and retain in theory the distant echo of its connection to philosophy, or to *theoria,* as restoring an ethical dimension to epistemological self-examination; or as Rorty put it, to modulate philosophical debate from a methodologico-ontological key into an ethico-political key. As Wittgenstein tried to teach us, what we need after theory is not science, but a renewed dialogue between philosophy and the humanities wherein both refashion themselves in original ways.

Georg Henrik von Wright remains a fascinating figure for me, not only as one of Wittgenstein's most devoted students but also as a key figure in the history of logic and twentieth-century analytic philosophy who, like Wittgenstein, suffered an ethical crisis in the course of his long career that led him to reassess and transform his conception of philosophy. In his late collection of texts, *The Tree of Knowledge,* von Wright writes movingly of his disappointment with the overreaching ambitions of behaviorism, positivism, and logical positivism that ultimately failed, on the one hand, to make of philosophy an epistemological handmaiden to science, and on the other, to provide a secure or even satisfactory philosophical foundation for the humanities. No one, I think, would consider von Wright an epistemological atheist, yet he remains a powerful opponent of the instrumental rationality through which philosophy kept its distance from the humanities in the twentieth century. Von Wright insists that two general problems frame the failures of twentieth-century philosophy, especially with respect to the humanities. One has to do with the conceptual poverty of naturalizing epistemologies; the other with the value vacuum produced by this attitude. The conceptual poverty produced by an excessive concern with epistemology is fueled by an unwavering commitment to the legacies of positivism that inform all the varieties of scientism in theory, whether in formalism, structuralism, cognitivism, or logic, but also with their common desire to make of language or expression an instrument of thought and analysis. This attitude, so characteristic of logical positivism, expresses the impulse of logic progressively to refine language in hopes of making it the grounds for certainty and a perfect instrument of thought.

Throughout the essays collected in *The Tree of Knowledge,* whose original dates of publication range from 1957 to 1991, von Wright links the history of twentieth-century analytic philosophy to an ever-widening and deepening instrumentalization of language and thought fueled by the steadily increasing prestige of science and technology in the twentieth century. "The form of rational thought which I used to regard as the highest in our culture," von Wright explains, "was becoming increasingly problematic because of the repercussions it had on life as a whole" (3). Indeed, as I have already suggested, throughout his book von Wright is calling for a complete reassessment of the terms or grammar of a certain concept of rationality, which has led not only to the domination of culture by technology and scientism but also a miscomprehension and devaluation of culture in its human dimensions of invention and expressivity.

This is why von Wright seeks a new valuation of the humanities, and a new emphasis on philosophy's diagnostic and critical role for contemporary culture. Taking inspiration from Wittgenstein's philosophical anthropology, a philosophy of the humanities would be concerned with the analysis of conceptual structures in everyday discourse and thinking that relate to human actions, norms, and valuations. In its many variants, the ideology of positivism was driven by a utopian vision of liberal-democratic consensus wherein perfect understanding and communication could be progressively achieved through logical refinements of language. But Wittgenstein's philosophical anthropology presents a very different vision of the embeddedness of human life in language and culture, one which enables possibilities for community and creation, but which also divides and separates us into discordant webs of beliefs and destructive attitudes leading to doubt, confusion, and uncertainty. The conceptual poverty of a positivistic or scientistic version of rationality relates not only to the scarcity of concepts, which are malformed or inapplicable to our current needs, but also to their ethical poverty, or their incapacity or disinterest in presenting useful frameworks for defining, interpreting, understanding, and passing through or beyond the dilemmas that block us from a better life. Like Nietzsche, and sometimes Wittgenstein, von Wright appeals to philosophy as a diagnosis of values, which is another way of understanding Rorty's appeal to rebalancing the methodologico-ontological mode of philosophy with an ethico-political one. The instrumental rationality of scientism and logic considers itself exempt from moral reasoning and evaluation. To question instrumental rationality does not mean ignoring or rejecting the enormous achievements of modern science but rather counterbalancing them with a critical rationality that acknowledges and investigates the value of the human "striving for knowledge as a *form or way of life,* i.e., as a striving to know and understand for the sake of knowing and understanding in themselves and for no other purpose" ("The Tree of Knowledge" 151). This is a different vision for the evaluation of progress in philosophy, which is less concerned with adding to our stock of knowledge, as if layering bricks to complete an ever more complex and unassailable structure, than with continually turning the earth and surveying the terrain that nourishes thinking and makes it possible. Or, as Wittgenstein put it in 1930, "I am not interested in constructing a building, so much as having a perspicuous view of the foundation of possible buildings. So I am not aiming at the same target as the scientists and my way of thinking is different from theirs."[45]

What can be said, then, about the province of a philosophy of or for the humanities? At the conclusion to the *Tractatus,* Wittgenstein famously asserted that "What we cannot speak about we must pass over in silence." Often bypassed in this context is the preceding statement: "My propositions are elucidatory in this way: he who understands me finally recognizes them as senseless [*unsinnig*], when he has climbed out through them, on them, over them. (He must so to speak throw away the ladder, after he has climbed up on it.) He must surmount these propositions, and then he will see the world aright."[46] Often taken as an admonition to remain silent in the face of what propositional logic cannot express or contain, Wittgenstein's later philosophical investigations give evidence of the importance to philosophy of those domains of experience that are *unsinnlich*—non-sensical, or perhaps, contrary to ordinary or common sense—where no final consensus can be achieved nor one single standard of rationality apply; these domains are "super-natural" (though not irrational) in the sense that naturalizing epistemologies can account neither for their conditions of sense nor their value to us. Most prominently, these are domains of aesthetic or ethical experience where understanding is grasped, intuited, or brought close to intelligibility through insight or intuition before it can be clearly expressed, much less linguistically encapsulated.

Philosophy's inheritance from logical positivism in the twentieth century was twofold. One aspect was the desire to exclude "unanswerable" questions of ethics and aesthetics from philosophy, or at least to reframe them in potentially more limited ways. The other was the desire to make philosophy disappear into science. These two tendencies are related in that what excludes questions of art

45. *Culture and Value,* ed. G. H. von Wright in collaboration with Heikki Nyman, trans. Peter Winch (Chicago: University of Chicago Press, 1980), 7e.

46. *Tractatus Logico-Philosophicus* (London: Routledge and Kegan Paul, 1974), §6.54. The German text reads, "Meine Sätze erläutern dadurch, dass sie der, welcher mich versteht, am Ende als unsinnig erkennt, wenn er durch sie—auf ihnen—über sie hinausgestiegen ist. (Er muss sozusagen die Leiter wegwerfen, nachdem er auf ihr hinaufgestiegen ist.) Er muss diese Sätze überwinden, dann sieht er die Welt richtig."

or ethics, and what makes philosophy disappear into science, is the commit-ment to subsumption-theoretic models of explanation and the assumption that these models are universally applicable. The last line of the *Tractatus* meant to indicate that these unanswerable questions may well instead be the most central concerns of philosophical investigation, and the remainder of Wittgenstein's philosophical life was devoted to finding and giving reasons for why this may be so.

In the "Lecture on Ethics," prepared for delivery in Cambridge sometime between September 1929 and December 1930 though unpublished in his life-time, Wittgenstein suggests that final and conclusive agreements on such ques-tions cannot be hoped for. But this does not mean that ethical or aesthetic experiences are incommunicable or incomprehensible; hence Wittgenstein's long fascination with intermediate and impure cases as occasions for investi-gating these experiences philosophically, though often indirectly. Ethical and aesthetic judgments present cases where humanity expresses its urge to run up against the limits of language. The failure to find an adequate concept or expression may indeed lead us to silence, but it is just as likely to produce in series a variety of different statements or forms of expression, all of which fail to convey these experiences adequately to ourselves or to others, but which nonetheless bring forth the blurred outlines of the experience in our repeated attempts to convey it, like lines in a sketch that create the impression of a pic-ture or idea as compelling as it is incomplete. ("A thinker is very much like a draughtsman whose aim it is to represent all the interrelations between things," writes Wittgenstein in 1931 [*Culture and Value* 12e].) Through the assembly of related intermediate cases and perspicuous grammatical investigation, a la-tent image develops that nowhere lies fully in the expressions themselves, but rather emerges in patterns of similarity and difference perceived among or between the expressions so produced. This is perhaps a case of finding or see-ing patterns in the differences between things that are brought to light in dif-ferent ways through different framings or contextualizations, through con-nective analysis rather than direct descriptions.

Consider these images or features expressions, then. But what we want to communicate, convey, apprehend, or understand lies nowhere in the image, but rather is only graspable in a pattern of relationships that is itself neither pictured nor expressed, yet becomes "visible," as it were, if only in an intuited way. Wittgenstein's "Lecture on Ethics" offers by example procedures for de-veloping or drawing out these pictures through language in a process of com-paring a number of more or less synonymous expressions of the defining characteristics of ethics. Though each expression differs slightly from the others, it is nonetheless possible to assemble patterns of difference and commonality in ways similar to the construction of a composite photograph. The effect thus produced is neither a consensual definition of ethics nor a complete understanding of the concept. Rather, as Wittgenstein might put it later on, definitions and concepts of ethics are deployed in a variety of language games in order to produce a pattern of family resemblances where different but overlapping conceptual senses can be "seen": "so if you look through the row of synonyms which I will put before you, you will, I hope, be able to see the characteristic features they all have in common and these are the characteristic features of Ethics."[47] This is what Wittgenstein might have meant earlier in asserting that the world is "seen" correctly, not through propositions but only when propositional thought has been transcended, overcome, quelled, or outgrown, all of which are senses appropriate to the German word, *überwinden*. Moreover, the two fundamental domains where expression and thought enter into such difficult but potentially expansive relationships are also the two areas of primary concern to a philosophy of the humanities, aesthetics and ethics.

In sorting through our expressive and conceptual difficulties in these domains, Wittgenstein also advises that we distinguish the trivial or relative from the absolute senses of concepts. If as G. E. Moore put it, "Ethics is the general inquiry into what is good," "good" might be characterized in a relative sense as progressively approaching a certain predetermined standard. Judgments of relative value stand close in form to scientific propositions in that they can be posed as statements of fact adjudicated according to fairly quantitative measures. Potentially, they possess a certain logical necessity and are open to procedures for reaching agreement through the falsification and elimination of competing accounts. One could perhaps forge a science of relative good, but it would say nothing about what concerns us in judgments of absolute value, or what Taylor calls import ascriptions and assessments, for "no state of affairs," Wittgenstein offers, "has, in itself, what I would like to call the coercive power of an absolute judge" ("Lecture on Ethics" 7). In such situations, Wittgenstein continues, "I can only describe my feeling by the metaphor, that, if a man could write a book on Ethics which really was a book on Ethics, this book would, with an explosion, destroy all the other books in the world. Our words used as we use them in science, are vessels capable

47. "A Lecture on Ethics," *Philosophical Review* 74, no. 1 (January 1965): 5.

only of containing and conveying meaning and sense, *natural* meaning and sense. Ethics, if it is anything, is supernatural and our words will only express facts." (7).

Make no mistake, Wittgenstein's distinction between factual discourse and "supernatural" concepts is not a lapse into either mysticism or metaphysics. Or rather, perhaps it is a recasting of metaphysics in a way that brings it down to earth, that is, to the level of our quotidian experiences and statements. In any case, such concepts can provoke no compelling agreement through logical necessity, meaning they cannot be factually explained but only conveyed and understood in special ways wherein language may be both transcended and transformed, if it does not instead lead us astray. Wittgenstein states that he can only offer a metaphor, or perhaps an analogy, simile, or even allegory—all of which are forms wherein the experience can only be indirectly related or which require the invention of new forms of expression.

In Wittgenstein's account, then, the apprehension of absolute value, whether ethical or aesthetic, is less a matter of objective statements of fact than subject-referring descriptions of experiences and beliefs, which are necessarily open and contingent. (As will be seen in pages to come, one of these will later provide an unexpected and striking connection to the philosophy of Gilles Deleuze.) Wittgenstein says that his own best way of describing the experience of absolute value "is to say that when I have it *I wonder at the existence of the world*. And I am then inclined to use such phrases as 'how extraordinary that anything should exist' or 'how extraordinary that the world should exist'" ("Lecture on Ethics" 8).

The paradox of expressions of absolute value is not only that they are descriptions of super-natural experience but also that they are non-sensical. But if Wittgenstein here calls them "nonsense," it is also important to account for how the character and meaning of the word are transformed. These semantic transformations tend in several directions. From one point of view it is nonsense to wonder at the existence of the world because we cannot imagine the world as *not* existing; there is a certain ineluctable self-evidence to existence. But this is not to say that we have lapsed into tautology or have thus disarmed and dispelled the experience, for to follow Rorty's previous analogy, to question these experiences skeptically is no more or less sensible than questioning why we have opposable thumbs. We will inevitably undergo these experiences and entertain these questions—they are characteristics or potentials of experience that are best investigated by other means.

Another point of view notes that such experiences never take the form of factual or propositional statements, but rather are most often expressed in the form of similes or allegories. The paradox has now been compounded. Its domain of reference is both self-evident (I cannot imagine the world as not existing) and super-natural (I wonder at the existence of the world), and additionally it eludes ostensive definition—all descriptions of the experience must approach it indirectly or at a tangent. From a logical point of view such experiences are disturbing because as experiences they should have factual dimensions, and to leave them unaccounted for in scientific explanation only means that they have yet to be defined as scientific problems, or that the correct means of logical analysis of what we mean by ethical or aesthetic expressions has not yet been found. But this is not what Wittgenstein means by "nonsense." And here we circle back to the final statements of the *Tractatus* where Wittgenstein implicitly distinguishes the power of language to describe from its powers of showing or demonstration. For when confronted with the argument that what should be searched for are correct logical analyses of absolute value, Wittgenstein responds that

I at once see clearly, as it were in a flash of light, not only that no description that I can think of would do to describe what I mean by absolute value, but that I would reject every significant description that anybody could possibly suggest, *ab initio,* on the ground of its significance. That is to say: I see now that these nonsensical expressions were not nonsensical because I had not yet found the correct expressions, but that their nonsensicality was their very essence. For all I wanted to do with them was just *to go beyond* the world and that is to say beyond significant language. My whole tendency and I believe the tendency of all men who ever tried to write or talk Ethics or Religion was to run against the boundaries of language. This running against the walls of our cage is perfectly, absolutely hopeless. Ethics so far as it springs from the desire to say something about the ultimate meaning of life, the absolute good, the absolute valuable, can be no science. What it says does not add to our knowledge in any sense. But it is a document of a tendency in the human mind which I personally cannot help respecting deeply and I would not for my life ridicule it. ("Lecture on Ethics" 11–12)

In a conversation held in the same time period of the preparation of the "Lecture on Ethics," Friedrich Waismann reports similar thoughts, where

Wittgenstein describes this human drive to run up or against the confining borders of language as characteristically ethical: "This thrust against the limits of language is *ethics*. . . . In ethics, one constantly tries to say something that does not concern and can never concern the essence of the matter. It is a priori certain that, whatever definition one may give of the Good, it is always a misunderstanding to suppose that the formulation corresponds to what one really means. (Moore). But the tendency, the thrust, *points to something*."[48]

Humanity feels compelled to run along or against the frontiers of language. In other words, we struggle constantly against the confinement of thought in or by language. And if this struggle is ethical, it is less about achieving a consistent or universal definition of the Good or the Beautiful than expressing a desire to transform the terms of our existence. Moreover, if this drive "points to something," the experience is assumed to be real or significant, and not something illusory or irrational. Ethics is a matter of deep concern for philosophy, then, even if it cannot be expressed in the form of a question and there is no answer to it. At the same time, for Wittgenstein philosophy has no resources for investigating these experiences apart from those that can be applied to and through language. What Cavell, Taylor, or Rorty add to Wittgenstein, then, are strong arguments for reconsidering this drive. Rather than understanding it as examining our confinements in language and attempting to describe and correct lapses in sense, philosophical investigation becomes equally or more concerned with the expansion and conceptual renovation of our expressive resources as avenues toward possible transformations of our terms of existence.

Questions of interpretation, aesthetic judgment, and ethical evaluation are of central concern to the humanities, and what I have hoped to show in the preceding pages are the layered and multifaceted connections between these concerns and Wittgenstein's more prominent philosophical attention to problems of language and psychology. For example, in comments reported in the *Lectures and Conversations on Aesthetics, Psychology and Religious Belief* Wittgenstein observes that the field of aesthetics is very large but also full of grammatical confusion. The scale or pervasiveness of aesthetic questions is such that they touch upon many different domains of philosophical investigation and at the same time refuse to be reduced to a single or unified theory or method. In addition, the reach and significance of the aesthetic in human experience and culture is far greater than that of artistic expression; in other

48. "Notes on Talks with Wittgenstein," *Philosophical Review* 74, no. 1 (January 1965): 13.

words, our forms of life are deeply engaged at multiple and daily levels with aesthetic sensations and interests, indeed much more so than our routine encounters with intended works of art.

Grammatical confusion in our interpretations and evaluations of aesthetic experience arises from two common tendencies. The first tendency, common in the language games of good theory, blinds us to the fact that aesthetic judgments involve or evoke types of concepts that are ill served by empirical investigation, and similarly, that the kinds of conceptual satisfaction we seek in aesthetic questions will not be found through empirical evidence or experimentation. In particular, Wittgenstein's hostility to the empirical psychological commitments of *Kunstwissenschaft* is undisguised. "The sort of explanation one is looking for when one is puzzled by an aesthetic impression," Wittgenstein writes, "is not a causal explanation, not one corroborated by experience or by statistics as to how people react. . . . This is not what one means or what one is driving at by an investigation into aesthetics."[49] Under the influence of explanatory models misappropriated from science, it is all too easy to discount or disparage the many and varied kinds of things that happen when we undergo aesthetic experience and make aesthetic judgments.

In like manner, the long historical tendency of aesthetics to seek to classify ontologically genres or media of art, as well as art itself, conceals more than it reveals about the varieties of aesthetic experience and their importance to us. Wittgenstein's recommendations for sorting out our grammatical and conceptual confusions here are now familiar. Generalities should be avoided and deep attention applied to the concrete case, accompanied by perspicuous description of the particular artworks and experiences themselves, as well as the judgments we offer about them. One should also strive to see connections through the assembly, examination, and comparison of intermediate cases within their cultural context, in order to understand what role they play in the communally unfolding language games of their time and place. These activities, among others, broaden and deepen our knowledge of aesthetic matters and enhance our capacities not only for perception and description but also for formulating and sharing our judgments with others. This is a mutually amplifying process of learning to see and learning to value, whereby achieving versatility in aesthetic judgment is guided by entry into what Wittgenstein called a "special conceptual world" (*Zettel* §165). One might say that this special

---

49. *Lectures and Conversations on Aesthetics, Psychology and Religious Belief,* ed. Cyril Barrett (Berkeley: University of California Press, 1966), 21.

conceptual world is guided by rules but only if one accepts that these rules are historically contingent and highly sensitive to context. Moreover, in practical experience they are deployed irregularly along a continuum of expression from the cognitively explicit and linguistically encapsulated to implicit, intuitive, and only behaviorally manifested rules of thumb. Generally speaking, then, learning to see and learning to value is a question of adding to one's cognitive stock, amplifying one's perceptual sensitivity and openness to new experience, acquiring new frameworks or contexts for judgment, and developing the potential for imaginatively applying or creating concepts.

Within the framework of a philosophy of the humanities, then, activities of interpreting, locating meaning, and engaging in ethical evaluation deploy a variety of overlapping tasks, including conceptual clarification and enlargement, imaginative colligation and the creation of new connections between elements, creating more detailed interpretations and new frameworks for interpretive understanding, restoring overlooked connections or making them newly apparent, and finally, contextualizing and recontextualizing "for the hell of it." Paradoxically, David Bordwell's sympathetic account of interpretation's (limited) activities and virtues is now reframed in a new context. In ways similar to aesthetic expression itself, the many language games deployed through interpretive activity may introduce new conceptual schemes that reorient understanding by making neglected or overlooked traits apparent, offering new categories of intelligibility and comprehension, creating fresh semantic fields and innovative frames of reference, and broadening our rhetorical resources. Interpretation might also respond to our ethical need to explore important concerns of thought, feeling, and action through art and aesthetic judgment. Our varied activities of interpretation, judgment, and evaluation thus offer occasions for criticizing but perhaps also renewing and transforming possibilities of meaning and value. Call these activities, if you like, theory.

I have argued that Wittgenstein's purported attack on theory is both too broad and too restrictive, and that it is more important to foreground what the later Wittgenstein brings to a philosophy of the humanities. The humanities are centrally concerned with the interpretation and evaluation of cultural expressions, and with placing these expressions in historical and social contexts. There are, of course, many competing and often conflicting methods and theories for defining what interpretation and evaluation may mean as activities, and how they are carried out in a variety of language games. This is because philosophy and the humanities, a philosophy of the humanities, are concerned with special kinds of often unanswerable or undecidable questions such as: What is art? What is the value of art? or What does this work mean? Perhaps theoretical answers (at least of the subsumptive sort) are indeed inappropriate for these kinds of questions. We are limited rather to giving reasons while evaluating both the form and axiology informing those reasons. No theory will ever completely answer these questions for us, although there have certainly been psychological—and more recently, evolutionary psychological—attempts to frame and answer these questions. Thus, the simple reason for the openness and undecidability of the language games of theory is that no causal explanation is adequate to these questions—they are not subject to the test of fallibility, nor is it possible to reach final agreement for the reasons we may give.

In liberating humanistic inquiry from the bonds of empirical and causal explanation a philosophy of the humanities may make propositional claims, but these claims need not be fallible—they only require suasion and clear, authoritative self-justification. This is because humanistic theories are subject referring and framed by culture. Unlike the investigation of natural and automatic or subnormative phenomena, philosophical investigations examine what human beings already know and do, and this knowledge is in principle public and accessible to all. In Bordwell's sense of the term, "naturalization," whether good or bad, has little relevance here, as humanistic (self) inquiry does not necessarily require finding new information but rather only clarifying and evaluating what we already know and do, or know how to do, and understanding why it is of value to us. Indeed, in contrast to scientism what interests the humanities is precisely those cultural activities, both creative and interpretive, that are open to introspection.

In their descriptive emphasis, Wittgenstein's philosophical investigations do support one important aspect of historical poetics strongly—the analysis of the internal norms of cultural objects and of our everyday sense-making activities in relation to those objects. Nonetheless, a "nonempirical" notion of history is wanted here, and for specific philosophical reasons. Natural laws are time independent, at least in a human context, and thus are appropriately explored through falsifiable causal explanations. Alternatively, cultural knowledge is historical in a particular sense. It emerges and evolves in the context of multiple, diverse, and conflictual webs of social interactions that require constant reevaluation on a human time scale. Von Wright puts the case directly: "The use of theory in the human as well as in the natural sciences is for explaining and making us better understand the world in which we live. But since the world men build for themselves, i.e. social reality, changes as they go on building it, its explanatory principles—and not only our knowledge of them—will change too in the course of this process" ("Humanism and the Humanities" 170). Therefore, the senses of history deployed in the humanities and in the course of philosophical investigations should be guided by knowledge "that man's place in the world-order is not *fixed,* if by 'fixed' we mean determined by factors which are extraneous to human action" (170), and therefore, I might add, covered by nomothetic principles. Human history and natural history may not be investigated by the same means, even if their domains may overlap with respect to certain problems. Unlike scientists, humanists must examine phenomena that may be shifting before their very eyes. They must account for change in the course of its becoming, while they themselves might be in a process of self-transformation.

Clearly, one of the obvious limits of both the cognitive critique of "interpretation" and analytic accounts of art or cultural creativity is their incapacity to account for the new. One of the most beautiful accomplishments of the later Wittgenstein was to restore to all of humanity the capacity for philosophizing, to make of us all philosophers of ordinary language in our quotidian practices of expressing ourselves, interpreting the intentions and meanings of others, giving reasons, and negotiating matters of accord and disagreement. But Wittgenstein's sense that philosophy should leave language "untouched," which would be one way of restraining ourselves pragmatically from relying too heavily on generalities and metaphysical justifications, may also block investigation of one of its most powerful ordinary uses—creation. Means of expression and interpretation are being continually renewed and innovated, and thus must also be continually reinterpreted and reevaluated. And once a new usage or a new work of art is created, it is not frozen into an object to be mined for meaning; it is always open to new contexts for interpretation and sense making, for gaining and losing value for us, and regaining value in new historical situations.

To what extent, then, is the enterprise of theory still possible? And how might we return the specificity of its activity to philosophy? The two questions are different yet related, and both are linked to the fate of the humanities in the twenty-first century and the place of art and moving images in the future of the humanities. Possible answers begin in recognizing that epistemological atheism does not follow from an ethical critique of modernity. And indeed what links philosophy today to its most ancient origins are the intertwining projects of evaluating our styles of knowing and the examination of our modes of existence and their possibilities of transformation. Within this very large and general domain, many forms of thought and life are possible. Perhaps they form "theories" in the sense of local, contingent, and malleable accounts of human cultural activity, and perhaps they even compete (and should compete) in some senses with respect to strategies for accounting for, epistemologically and evaluatively, our various and ever-changing strategies for interacting with the world and with others. Moreover, there are many ways that these theories may be considered rational and even empirical, without assuming a form of eliminative competition that requires unification in subsumptive-theoretic accounts or insists on standards of methodological monism.

I want to continue, then, and eventually conclude my elegy for theory by exploring these questions in discussion of two contemporary philosophers as exemplars of the twinned projects of ethical and epistemological evaluation: Gilles Deleuze and Stanley Cavell. Neither Deleuze nor Cavell offers answers to these questions or solutions to these problems. Rather they offer different and original frameworks for how these questions may be posed and investigated in relation to film and forms of artistic or cultural expression. Deleuze and Cavell are the two contemporary philosophers with the strongest commitment to cinema, yet with distinctly original conceptions of the specificity of philosophy and of philosophical expression in relation to film, literature, and the other arts. Though an unlikely pairing, reading these two philosophers together can deepen and clarify their original contributions to our understanding of film and of contemporary philosophy. Here I want to make the case that a (film) philosophy may and should be distinguished from theory. At the same time, I want to distinguish for the humanities a fluid metacritical space of epistemological and ethical self-examination that we may continue to call theory should we wish to do so.

9. What is (Film) Philosophy?

> Compare a concept with a style of painting. . . .
>
> —Ludwig Wittgenstein, *Philosophical Investigations*

Nineteen seventy is one fascinating turning point for the genealogy of Theory in the senses closest to us; 1985 is another. In this year Gilles Deleuze published in France the second volume of his cinema series, *Cinema 2: The Time-Image*. Whether Deleuze's cinema books are works of film theory, film philosophy, or even just philosophy is a question that must remain open and suspended for the moment. However, it can be said that quickly in France, and slowly but surely in other countries, the two books were received as major yet somewhat controversial interventions in the field of film studies. Deleuze's cinema books confronted an impasse in film theory head-on by infusing film theory with a new and disorienting vocabulary, recharacterizing cinema history, and restoring pride of place to the power of the concept in relation to the image.

One of the great paradoxes of these books, equally apparent in both the French and Anglophone contexts, is how they seemed to emerge out of time. In nearly 700 pages of philosophical and conceptual analysis, *Cinema 1: The Movement-Image* and *Cinema 2: The Time-Image* are works that appear as if from another dimension. (Frankly, both Kracauer's *Theory of Film* and Cavell's *The World Viewed* probably had the same effect in their own time. Is untimeliness a characteristic of works of film philosophy?) There are very few points of contact in Deleuze's cinema books with the discourse of ideology and the subject, psychoanalysis, or even the narratology dominant in academic French film study in the 1970s and 1980s. It as if the era of *Tel Quel,* of Jean-Louis Baudry and Christian Metz's turn to psychoanalysis, or even of the predominance of "*Screen* theory" had never existed. At the same time, the books have many points of contact with modern film theory and the discourse of signification, even if they pull conceptual series alternative to Metz's first film semiology from it, especially in Deleuze's return to and recontextualization of figures like André Bazin, Pier Paolo Pasolini, Noël Burch, and Pascal Bonitzer, and his provocative remapping of Charles Sanders Peirce in relation to Henri Bergson to produce a new classification of images and signs, one more indebted to logic than linguistics. No doubt, there is also a certain French cinephilism in the books that roots them in other attitudes of the 1960s wherein thought about the cinema was in close contact with the new modern cinemas of Italy, France, Japan, Germany, and other countries.

However, the cinema books return to the 1960s and 1970s in another important way. They are Deleuze's first major project after his important collaborations with Félix Guattari, including *Anti-Oedipus, Kafka: For a Minor Literature,* and *A Thousand Plateaus.* Nonetheless, the concepts and arguments of schizoanalysis make only infrequent and minor appearances in Deleuze's film studies.[50] Rather, as I argue in *Gilles Deleuze's Time Machine,* the film

50. For a fascinating discussion of how concepts from schizoanalysis nonetheless thread through the cinema books, see Ian Buchanan, "Is a Schizoanalysis of Cinema Possible?" in

books are best understood as a complex series of folds where Deleuze returns to the major concepts and concerns that inform his greatest philosophical works, in particular *Difference and Repetition* and *Logic of Sense,* both published in 1969. Indeed, I have often quipped that one should read *The Movement-Image* and *The Time-Image* as a 700-page-long footnote to *Difference and Repetition,* or more seriously, as a rethinking of Deleuze's principal works of the 1960s through a new account of images and signs in the cinema.

At the same time, the two cinema books anticipate concepts and arguments taken up later in Deleuze and Guattari's *What Is Philosophy?,* which marks the return of the concept after its artful expression in the Image. In this framework, Deleuze's cinema books and occasional essays and interviews present two pairs of elements that show what a film philosophy might look like. These elements recur throughout Deleuze's philosophical work. On the one hand, there is the relation of Concept to Image. Here the creation of concepts defines the autonomy of philosophical activity while the Image becomes the key to understanding the profoundly immanent relation of subjectivity to the world. (Later, I will discuss this principle of immanence as a commitment to Spinoza's doctrine of the univocity of Being.) The second set involves Deleuze's original reconsideration of Nietzsche's presentation of ethical activity as philosophical interpretation and evaluation. Ethics, interpretation, and evaluation are in fact key points of contact between a philosophy of the humanities and that domain of the philosophy of art that might be called film philosophy.

Deleuze ends *The Time-Image* with a curious plaint for theory. Already in 1985, he argues, theory had lost its pride of place in thought about cinema, seeming abstract and unrelated to practical creation. But theory is not separate from the practice of cinema, for it is itself a practice or a constructivism of concepts. "For theory too is something which is made, no less than its object," Deleuze writes.

> A theory of cinema is not "about" cinema, but about the concepts that cinema gives rise to and which are themselves related to other concepts corresponding to other practices. . . . The theory of cinema does not bear on the cinema, but on the concepts of the cinema, which are no less practical, effective or existent than cinema itself. . . . Cinema's concepts are

Afterimages of Gilles Deleuze's Film Philosophy, ed. D. N. Rodowick (Minneapolis: University of Minnesota Press, 2010), 135–156.

not given in cinema. And yet they are cinema's concepts, not theories about cinema. So that there is always a time, midday-midnight, when we must no longer ask ourselves, 'What is cinema?' but 'What is philosophy?' Cinema itself is a new practice of images and signs, whose theory philosophy must produce as conceptual practice.[51]

A slippage is obvious here, with theory standing in for philosophy. But that being said, what does Deleuze wish to imply in complaining that the contemporary moment is weak with respect to creation and concepts, and that concepts themselves are not found "in" artistic expression but rather that expression gives rise to concepts, which must be further refined or crafted in philosophy itself? The most complete response comes from the most obvious successor to the problems raised in the cinema books—Deleuze and Guattari's *What Is Philosophy?*

What Is Philosophy? is a strange book, bathed in fatigue and pathos in ways consistent with its existence as a last book—a final act of combat in a long battle where philosophy struggles to hold onto and reassert its place and function with respect to a series of rivals, and to defend itself against charges of obsolescence, which have often come from within philosophy itself. (Recall again the insistence of logical positivism and its successors that philosophy should disappear into science or theory.) The human sciences, sociology, epistemology, linguistics, psychoanalysis, and symbolic logic, indeed theory in all its variegated forms, have presented themselves as rivals to philosophy in the twentieth century. And in the contemporary moment, the situation worsens with challenges from information science, marketing, advertising, and all the mass arts of communication that fancy themselves as creators and "conceptualists." "It is certainly painful to learn that 'Concept' designates a culture of service and information engineering," write Deleuze and Guattari. "But the more philosophy clashes with its impudent and inane rivals, the more it meets them on its own terrain, the more it feels its enthusiasm for the task—to create concepts that are aerolites rather than commodities. Philosophy has a mad laugh that brings it to tears. Therefore, the question of philosophy is the singular point where concept and creation rely most upon one another."[52] In an

---

51. *Cinema 2: The Time-Image*, trans. Hugh Tomlinson and Robert Galeta (Minneapolis: University of Minnesota Press, 1989), 280.

52. Gilles Deleuze and Félix Guattari, *What Is Philosophy?*, trans. Hugh Tomlinson and Graham Burchell (New York: Columbia University Press, 1994), 11, *16*; trans. modified. Originally

environment where thought is pervaded by capital at even the most capillary levels, and where creation is continually degraded by the commodity form, philosophy must more than ever rediscover and refine its creative and critical capacities.

If the question of philosophy is the singular point where concept and creation are brought together in an act of immanence, then perhaps philosophy owes more to art than it does to science. The question of film philosophy turns on how the philosophical act is related to creative acts and expressiveness, with their own special spaces, times, scenographies, and dramaturgies. The desire to ask the question, what is philosophy? issues from a special place with its own characteristic temporality, one commensurate with last stands, or better, bifurcation points in history where the descent into chaos may yet produce unanticipated utopian forces. Deleuze and Guattari suggest that such questions come late in life, or perhaps late to thought, in moments of "quiet restlessness, at midnight, when there is no longer anything left to ask" (*What Is Philosophy?* 1). In order to think, or to move thought forward, one suggests theories all of one's life and in the linear course of life's happening. But in order to ask what is philosophy, or in what consists the activity or powers of philosophy, one does not present one idea or argument after another, but reaches toward that place, that time, which make thinking in all its rarity possible. One seeks to answer this question not in a statement, description, or argument but rather in a doing within the time of the act itself.

What Is Philosophy?'s account of this activity amounts to a kind of dramaturgy, or perhaps a scenography or cartography of thought. If Wittgenstein's style of philosophy is confession, Deleuze's style is rather a theater or cinema of thought, but also a geography of thought, where in seeking out the place and time from which thought becomes possible, one frames a landscape or a geography as the mise-en-scène of philosophy. (The philosophical act is a moving cartography of images, as my friend Tom Conley might put it, and this is a clear link between the geographic and cinematographic dimensions of what Deleuze and Guattari call geophilosophy.) In spite of the wildness and unrestrained character of its vocabulary, style, and concepts, one of the most extraordinary aspects of *What Is Philosophy?* is that it is almost entirely *descriptive*. It offers no method and presents no theories; it neither proscribes nor explains. Moreover, this descriptive approach to the philosophical act endows

published as *Qu'est-ce que la philosophie?* (Paris: Les Éditions de Minuit, 1991). Original French page numbers appear in italics wherever I have modified the English translation.

it with space, time, style, and indeed a sort of figurability, as if sketching out a portrait of thought's genesis and movements. These are the two sides, then, to the book's characterization of philosophy—a creative act very close to artistic creation, and a mapping or geography framing and composing the territories and geological features of thought. One can begin to see here how, for Deleuze, of all the arts the cinema is closest to philosophy as a space and time where thought is immanent to the movements and substance of life.

Deleuze and Guattari call this "geophilosophy," but the philosophical act is equally well characterized as a scenography or dramaturgy; or more simply, the construction of an Image. The key questions, then, are how to characterize philosophical expression or enunciation, and what are the characteristic components and activities that make philosophy distinct from neighboring modalities of expression, investigation, creation, and knowing in science or in art. At the same time, how can philosophy's constructions enter into complex arrangements, combinations, or compounds with art and science in ways that blur their frontiers and multiply their points of contact, influence, and exchange? One feels the need to ask the question in French—what is *agencement philosophique?*—to evoke the multiple senses of *agencer*: to make happen, to combine or construct, to organize or arrange. Still, many ambiguities arise in Deleuze and Guattari's various deployments of this *agencement,* which seems to operate simultaneously as an intransitive and transitive verb, a strange combination of activity and passivity, where creative acts or expressions both presume a singular subject but also connect this subject to a collective space or framework that conditions these acts and expressions.

In the introduction to *What Is Philosophy?*, Deleuze and Guattari write that their response to this question has never varied. Regardless of whether one speaks of Aristotle's substance, Descartes's *cogito*, Leibniz's monads, or Bergson's duration, philosophy acts through the creation of concepts: "philosophy is the art of forming, inventing, or fabricating concepts. But it was not only necessary that the response took account of the question, but also that it determined a time, an occasion, the circumstances, landscapes and characters, the conditions and unknowns of the question" (*What Is Philosophy?* 2, 8). Later, Deleuze and Guattari characterize this terrain as philosophy's particular plane of immanence. But for the moment note only that the landscape of philosophical potentiality is populated and swarming with figural and dramatic activity. And on this terrain there is also *agon* and *agape*—challenges from adversaries and encounters with friends—whose sites and moments of conflict block or slow thought, but also enable it as a power or potentiality.

Through *agon* thought turns back on itself in a reflexive gesture whose uncertainty or hesitancy interrupts its movements. As I relate in *Elegy for Theory,* one classic adversary to philosophy is the sage. But the sage is only wise in theory, and philosophy requires something else, a friend or an intercessor.

To love wisdom (*philo-sophia*) is not to possess it but to pursue it without finality, and the only finality known to humankind is death—the rest is creation. This is why, according to Deleuze and Guattari, the Greeks invented philosophy by affirming the death of the sage. Philosophy does not need disciples, and indeed to be disciple to a sage is to eliminate the possibility of thought and to enter the dead time of repetition. But what is the function of the philosophical friend, or why does philosophy need friends? The act of philosophy, the desire that makes of philosophy a potentiality of or for thought, emerges in moments of existential crisis expressed as the ethical longing for a different way of thinking and a different community of thought. No doubt philosophy has sought a home in schools and academies. But these communities are as much virtual as actual—in fact, they must be virtual before becoming actual. The philosophical friend is not an actual or historical person or character, then, but rather "a presence intrinsic to thought, a condition even of the possibility of thought, a living category, a lived transcendental" (*What Is Philosophy?* 3, 9); as Deleuze and Guattari put it, a conceptual character or persona (*personnage conceptuel*). The friend is a conceptual persona deployed in the theater of philosophy—the emerging image of a thought and a community to come that draws thought forward toward the concept and that community as an image of philosophy's characteristic activity. The conceptual persona is therefore both a condition for the exercise of thought and a stage in the creation of concepts. An intermediary in every sense of the term, the friend introduces into thought a particular kind of material intimacy as "a vital relation with the Other that one had thought excluded from pure thought. . . . The friend, the lover, the suitor, the rival are transcendental determinations, who as such never lose their intense and animated existence in one or several characters" (4, 9–10). Nor is the friend a unified or self-sufficient function—there are as many conceptual personae in the history of philosophy as there are creators of concepts.

Paradoxically, it is not the philosopher who enunciates his or her concepts, but rather the conceptual persona who embodies as a virtual force the becoming of a new form and style of thought to which the philosopher aspires. Deleuze and Guattari themselves refer to conceptual personae as *"embrayeurs,"* Émile Benveniste's term for "shifters" or deictic indicators of location in time and space, as well as designations of grammatical person. Conceptual personae thus affect particular kinds of movements or transitional states. Deleuze and Guattari describe them as having a mysterious, intermediate, and fluctuating existence, hovering between the formed concept and the preformal or preconceptual plane of immanence, going from one to the other, and in turns figuring the subjective presuppositions that characterize the plane and marking out a place for concepts to be constructed. The conceptual persona gives life and character to philosophy, and there is no becoming of a concept without the mediation of a conceptual shifter. The conceptual persona is neither myth, allegory, nor symbol, however. Its function is neither imaginary nor abstract but rather immanent to acts of philosophical creation. Nor does the conceptual persona represent the philosopher. Rather, as Deleuze and Guattari put it, "the philosopher is only the envelope of his principal conceptual persona and of all the other personae who are the intercessors, the real subjects of his philosophy. Conceptual personae are the philosopher's 'heteronyms,' and the philosopher's name is the simple pseudonym of his personae. I am no longer myself but thought's aptitude for manifesting and deploying itself across a plane that passes through me at several places. . . . The conceptual persona is the becoming or the subject of a philosophy, on a par with the philosopher." (*What Is Philosophy?* 64, 62–63).

Later, I will connect the role of conceptual personae to that of psychological and spiritual automata in the cinema books. There are also many instances where Deleuze figures cinematic *auteurs* as if they were philosophical companions. In philosophical discourse, the conceptual persona may appear outright as a dramatic character—Socrates in Plato's dialogues, or Nietzsche's Zarathustra and Kierkegaard's Don Juan—or as something like a philosophical friend who seems to be a constant companion of philosophical invention, like the examples of Emerson and Wittgenstein in Cavell. Nevertheless, it is rarely the case that the conceptual persona is explicitly figured. More often than not, it appears only indirectly or hovers phantom-like behind the philosophical act. Unnamed and subterranean, it is usually only invoked or reconstructed by an attentive reader. Thus the division between philosophers and their conceptual personae can also be thought in another way—there is the public persona of the philosopher (Deleuze or Cavell), and there is the more intimate and private thinker within the philosophical act, a kind of implied thought or spiritual automaton at the heart of every philosophical phrase, which is in principle distinguishable from the author. In any case, there is a sort of conceptual perfectionism here analogous to Cavell's moral perfectionism as an ideal or imagined trajectory toward which thought aims, and which it likely misses or falls short of, yet which holds it in a play of forces and a continuous recurrent becoming. In this way, conceptual personae set loose the movements that define the philosopher's plane of immanence and intervene directly in the creation of his concepts. The philosopher is less a biographical life than another function in the philosophical act—a medium for philosophical creation; or better, a subjective component in the abstract machine of conceptual creation and enunciation. The conceptual persona is the subjective condition of the philosophical act, displacing the philosopher toward other states of being both grammatically and in thought—for example, Nietzsche becoming "the Antichrist" or "Dionysus Crucified." "In philosophical enunciation, one does not do something by saying it," according to Deleuze and Guattari; "rather one makes movement by thinking it through the intermediary of a conceptual persona. Are not conceptual personae thus the true agents of enunciation? Who is I? It is always a third person" (*What Is Philosophy?* 64–65, 63). The conceptual persona is the becoming-philosopher of those who will to think by creating concepts.[53]

Again, there is a whole dramaturgy of the philosophical act. And yet conceptual personae should not be confused with what Deleuze and Guattari call aesthetic figures or psychosocial types; they thus remain relatively distinct from both artistic creation and sociological analysis. Within their own domains aesthetic figures and psychosocial types serve analogous functions; through art, for example, the aesthetic figure expresses a power of affects and percepts rather than concepts, a becoming-image or sensation rather than becoming-thought. These figures present different powers of creation in different abstract machines. However, this does not mean that there are no points of intersection or exchange between art and philosophy, or that they cannot enter into complex intensive constructions or assemblages capable of transforming

---

53. I should note here that the role of Guattari in the composition of *What Is Philosophy?* is controversial. In informal conversation, Eric Alliez has expressed the opinion to me that Guattari played almost no role in writing the book, and that Deleuze retained his name as a sign of friendship or homage. But one wonders if there is something more to this double enunciation than a simple act of solidarity. If Deleuze is the philosophical author of the book, and if the book's concepts are his creations, there is still no doubt that Guattari's influence is strong, and in more ways than one. Perhaps Guattari is the coauthor of *What Is Philosophy?* not literally but structurally as intercessor, conceptual persona or shifter, or spiritual automaton, slipping within the discourse, populating the plane, and affecting the medium for the creation of concepts. Even if Guattari did not coauthor the book, there is a becoming-Guattari (his concepts, discourse, planes of immanence) that slides into the deployment of Deleuze's thought.

them together: the musical and theatrical figure of Don Juan becomes a conceptual persona for Kierkegaard, just as Deleuze's cinema books are populated with a multitude of conceptual intercessors from Sergei Eisenstein to Alain Resnais, no less than Orson Welles himself, both director and aesthetic figure, as the exemplar of a kind of cinematographic Nietzscheanism. In these situations, aesthetic figures do not present a synthesis of art and philosophy, but rather hybrid acts where two kinds of creation encounter and affect one another without losing their distinctiveness, sliding across or into one another in new stratigraphic combinations, where the compositional figures of art and the conceptual territory of philosophy encounter one another, mix, and then branch out again onto their own planes.

To assert that the aim of philosophy is the creation of concepts does not mean that concepts are forms or products, whether found or forged. This is another way in which the temporality of philosophy, like that of the humanities, differs from that of scientific advance. The pursuit of the unknown in philosophy does not amount to discovering or retrieving information that lies dormant in nature or in thought, as if digging out and refining the riches of the past, nor does it mean realizing the unrealized. The unknown in philosophy emerges out of a different kind of potentiality, a turmoil or chaos, wherein the unseen is not hidden in the earth or unnoticed in the heavens, which no technical instrument will unearth or bring to light. The unknown in philosophy is the blindness of Tiresias, aimed toward the future and not the past—it is the struggle to bring the new and the unforeseen into existence. Wittgenstein's idea that philosophical investigation must leave language untouched is at best half the story. Philosophy is also experimentation. And the struggle with language, so present in both Wittgenstein and Deleuze in their very different ways, is also for Deleuze the struggle to create or to give birth to sense in ways not yet anticipated on the terrain of thought.

Another link to Wittgenstein (and later to Cavell) is the relation of philosophy to nonphilosophy. Thought is not only the province of the philosopher; the activities of philosophy—call them for the moment interpretation and evaluation—are in principle open to everyone in all domains of daily life. But thinking is rare, even for the philosopher, and is often mistaken for other kinds of activities, such as contemplation, reflection, or dialectical communication, all of which may be considered "theoretical" in some sense. For example, even if the object of philosophy is to create concepts, philosophy itself has no object, and thus nothing to observe or to contemplate. (This is one certain way of distinguishing it from theory. In what sense could one call a concept an object?)

Moreover, if philosophy's activity consists in *creating* concepts, how could one contemplate or consider an entity that has not yet been brought into existence? To reflect, to consider calmly or meditatively in dialogue with oneself, or to mentally reproduce and examine phenomena are equally foreign to philosophy's activities, nor does thought emerge and perfect itself in a reasoned dialogue or dialectic of rivals. In contrast to contemplation, reflection, and communication, which run after universals in the forms of objective, subjective, or intersubjective idealism, concepts are singular acts of creation. Philosophy's rivals appeal to a universally apprehensible and transmittable reason. But in a phrase that strangely echoes Wittgenstein, Deleuze and Guattari insist that the appeal to universals explains nothing; they themselves must be explained. "All creation is singular, and the concept as purely philosophical creation is always a singularity" (*What Is Philosophy?* 7, *12*).

Another way to characterize philosophical activity is as a constructivism whose activity consists in "knowledge [*connaissance*] through pure concepts" (*What Is Philosophy?* 7, *12*). Here Deleuze and Guattari follow Nietzsche in asserting that you will never know anything through concepts if you have not first constructed them, that is "constructed them from within an intuition that belongs to them: a field, a plane, and a ground that must not be confused with them but rather shelters their seeds and the people [*personnages*] who cultivate them. Constructivism requires that all creation shall be construction on a plane that gives it an autonomous existence" (7, *12*). This is Deleuze and Guattari's most direct expression of the idea that concepts must be constructed from their own plane of immanence, where the French word, *plan,* variously indicates a plane, map, ground, area, staging area, or blueprint. At the same time, this "knowledge" is a *connaissance* and not a *savoir*—it is neither certain nor a point of arrival. One is always rather "on the way," even if the path is blocked or unclear. The construction of concepts is often a strange process inspired by alienation and disorientation ("I cannot find my way") such that encountering a concept, even one's own concepts, is like becoming acquainted with or getting to know a stranger, or a new friend. There is always something unsettling about the emergence of a concept, even if it robes itself in familiar terminology. The construction and baptism of a concept often follows from a peculiar necessity where concepts assume names in a variety of forms:

Some require an extraordinary word, sometimes barbarous or shocking, which must designate them, whereas others are content with a familiar and quite ordinary word that swells with such remote harmonics that they risk being inaudible to a non-philosophical ear. Some solicit archaisms, others neologisms crossed with nearly mad etymological exercises: etymology as a peculiarly philosophical sport.... The baptism of the concept solicits a specific philosophical *taste* that proceeds through violence or insinuation, and which constitutes within language a language of philosophy, not only a vocabulary but also a syntax reaching for the sublime or great beauty" (7–8, *13*).

Philosophy also has a peculiar kind of history in which strong concepts almost never disappear, but rather recur and mutate through new phases of replacement, renewal, and recontextualization "that give philosophy a history as well as a turbulent geography, each moment and place of which is preserved (but in time) and that passes (but outside time)" (8).

One way of characterizing a film philosophy, then, may be to consider Deleuze's concept of the direct image of time as a moving portrait of philosophy, and eternal recurrence as the measure of philosophical history and the time of creation. But first, we must inquire more deeply into the concept's relation to both science and art.

10. Order Out of Chaos

> When you are philosophizing you have to descend into primeval chaos and
> feel at home there.
>
> —Ludwig Wittgenstein, *Culture and Value*

Following Deleuze and Guattari, I have taken as given that philosophical activity is defined by the creation of concepts. Yet several questions remain unanswered. How are concepts related philosophically to Ideas? And what is the relation of philosophy to science or to art, each of which possesses its own creative acts and Ideas, its own histories and styles of becoming, and its own networks of influence and exchange, both between themselves and with philosophy?

For Deleuze and Guattari, the three great territories of human creation are art, philosophy, and science. These are relatively autonomous domains each of which involves acts of creation based on different modes of expression—perceptual, conceptual, or functional. Deleuze and Guattari insist at many points that while the creation of concepts defines the specificity of philosophical constructivism, this does not give philosophy a special or preeminent status with respect to other means of ideation, expression, thinking, or creating. The problem confronted in *What Is Philosophy?* is knowing how philosophical expression differs from artistic or scientific expression, yet remains in dialogue with them. Percepts, concepts, and functions are different expressive modalities, yet each may influence the other (but not in a way that affects the autonomy of their productive activity). An artist or scientist no doubt profoundly engages in conceptual activity, and so is influenced by philosophy. Yet the outputs of that activity—percepts, functions—retain their autonomy and specificity.

The question here is not whether art or films think, but rather how, where, or even whether thinking takes place and by what means. Nor is philosophy in the business of contemplating or explaining art or film as if from an external or transcendent perspective. Philosophy neither supplies concepts to art nor does it extract concepts from art. To comprehend the originality of Deleuze and Guattari's perspective, the principle of immanence must be fully grasped—here thought is no longer the property of a subject but rather a relation of intimate contact and exchange with the world where Being and world are singular expressions of a unique substance.

In the conclusion to *What Is Philosophy?,* Deleuze and Guattari write that all we ask from art, science, or philosophy is a bit of order to protect us from chaos. Chaos is one of the central concepts of the book, or perhaps it is better to say that chaos is the world or environment wherein questions of art, philosophy, and science must be staged. The role chaos plays in these arguments must be approached with delicacy and complexity. Chaos is neither disorganization nor anarchy. On the one hand, it is a global concept referring to what Deleuze in *The Movement-Image* calls a regime of universal variation or constant self-differing movement—a cosmos of fluid matter and radiating energy mutually interacting at all scales and on all points of contact in a creatively evolving open Whole. Deleuze and Guattari call this the plane of immanence, where there is neither transcendence nor externality, and no substantial division between mind and body, but only a qualitative and self-organizing process of self-differentiation in a ceaseless state of becoming. The plane of immanence is thus the expression of a radical empiricism where "Subject and object give a poor approximation of thought. Thinking is neither a line extended between subject and object nor one orbiting around the other. Thinking takes place, rather, in the relationship between territory and the earth" (*What Is Philosophy?* 85, 82). The distinction between territory and earth is meant, perhaps, to bring the plane of immanence down to a human scale. Conceived in this way, the earth is not a foundation or stable surface but rather continuous stratigraphic movement at uneven rhythms. In its movements, the earth never stops provoking deterritorializations; Deleuze and Guattari say it is deterritorializing and deterritorialized. Like the plane of immanence, or itself an instance of the plane, it is not one element among others but that which gathers all elements onto a common plane while making use of them to displace territories into series and overlapping movements of deterritorialization.

Should one take Deleuze and Guattari at their word here, or is the relationship of earth to territory only an allegorical or poetic one? Indeed the relationship is intrinsic to all existence and thought, but relative to two perspectives that shift planes like two variations of "aspect seeing." One may speak of physical geographies as much as social or psychological ones, and thus mark historical relations with the environment and the earth, whether cultural, geological, or cosmological, in the waxing and waning of cities, states, and peoples interacting with the evolving global organic whole of which they are always a part. Deleuze and Guattari call this relative deterritorialization. But there is also an absolute deterritorialization that relates to Spinoza's monistic ontology of mind, body, and nature as aspects or modes of a single expressive Substance. To be fully conscious of such an absolute deterritorialization would be to achieve an absolute Being-Thought moving at infinite speeds, something impossible or humanly unbearable. Yet such thought moves into or out of us, unless we accept the tragedy of skepticism where we are forever walled off from the external world by barriers of perception and consciousness.

The movements of territorialization and deterritorialization, absolute and relative, are meant to bypass or "forget" the dialectic and all negativity, as well as to do away with all subject-object distinctions. Instead we confront two variations, dimensions, or perspectives on a single unique substance, or thought-movement, in which our present potentials for thinking are framed or conditioned by relative historical circumstances—whether cultural, geographical, or cosmological—as territories anchoring or nourishing thought, and from which new thought must deterritorialize itself. (Later, I will explain that in its own way, and through artistic means, for Deleuze cinema expresses these two variations in the elaboration of two cinematographic planes of immanence—the movement-image and the time-image—each of which describes a different set of relationships of space to movement and time, as well as differing relations to a Whole which changes, and each of which expresses a different relationship to thought.) Put in its purest or most absolute form, one can say of pure immanence that is a Life and nothing more. In his last published text, "Immanence: a Life," Deleuze writes that *"A life* is everywhere, in every moment which a living subject traverses and which is measured by the objects that have been experienced, an immanent life carrying along the events or singularities that are merely actualized in subject and objects. This indefinite life does not itself have moments, however close they may be, but only between-times [*entre-temps*], between-moments. It does not arrive, it does not come after, but presents the immensity of an empty time where one sees the event to come and already past, in the absolute of an immediate consciousness."[54] This, in fact, is what Deleuze in the cinema books calls the pure time-image.

The plane of immanence is a radically inhuman or nonhuman environment in the sense that human perceptual capacities fall far short of forming an adequate image of or from it. Its scale and complexity overwhelm human comprehension. At the same time, bodies, minds, selves, perceptions are no more or less of this material plane and this life than the organic and nonorganic forces and matters of the universe at whatever scale; hence the need of science to isolate and compartmentalize these forces and matters into manageable fragments and to express them in terms of functions, or of art to render them apprehendable in sensations and livable in affects. Human perception and comprehension are not separate from this cosmological complexity but rather one with it as part of a single expressive substance. There is not only photography in things, as Bergson might say, but also thought. And like all things, thought is subject to entropy: "Nothing is more painful or distressing," Deleuze and Guattari observe, "than a thought escaping itself, ideas that flee, that disappear hardly formed, already eroded by forgetfulness or precipitated into others that we no longer master. . . . We lose our ideas incessantly" (*What Is Philosophy?* 201, *189*). Because thought is movement, or is never without movement, it risks fleeing from itself in all directions; at each moment thought confronts bifurcation points where it might reorganize itself at higher levels of complexity, or fall into dissipative energy. To form a relationship to thought or to hold onto it means reordering its movements—slowing it or changing its rhythms, framing or composing it, mapping it and giving it a finite coordinate space as sections or variations on infinite universal movement.

54. "Immanence: a Life," in *Two Regimes of Madness,* ed. David Lapoujade, trans. Ames Hodges and Mike Taormina (Cambridge, MA: Semiotext(e)/MIT Press, 2006), 387.

There are many different kinds of images of thought, then, and in each one there is a danger of arresting thought in fixed positions or opinions. We feel the need to furnish ourselves with a minimum of consistent and protective rules so as to order the succession of ideas in space and in time with principles of identity, resemblance, contiguity, or causality. *Doxa* shields us from chaotic thought, but it also might impede us in creative thought. In Deleuze and Guattari's perspective, art, science, and philosophy are all strategies for descending into and returning from chaos to preserve the creative movements and openness of thought. Each confronts chaos by sectioning and framing it, congealing it into an Image, no matter how fragile or ephemeral—each composes chaos in a way that makes thought happen, as event or concept in philosophy, as functions in science, or as sensation or affect in art. "The three disciplines advance by crises or shocks in different ways," Deleuze and Guattari conclude, "and in each case it is their succession that makes it possible to speak of 'progress.' It is as if the *struggle against chaos* does not take place without an affinity with the enemy, because another struggle takes on more importance— the struggle *against opinion,* which claims to protect us from chaos itself" (*What Is Philosophy?* 203). We need an image or images of thought. Yet the question remains, how is thought kept in creative movement?

As expressive modalities relating to a single plane of immanence, perhaps one might say that science, philosophy, and art form qualitatively distinct images, or emit distinctive types of signs. The aim of science is to create functions describing states of affairs, of art to create percepts through sensuous aggregates, and of philosophy to create concepts in relation to events, but the devil is in the details. In art, percepts refer to the creation of affective experience through constructions of sensuous materials. In painting, these expressive materials may be composed of blocks of lines and colors, whether figurative or abstract; in cinema, combinations of movements, durations, rhythms, and sounds. Alternatively, the role of functions helps clarify the relation of philosophy to theory in the scientific sense. There is a function, Deleuze explains, as soon as two wholes are put into a fixed correspondence.[55] Newton's inverse square law provides an apposite example. A function is a mathematical expression orienting thought (first whole) to a natural phenomenon (the

---

55. See "Having an Idea in Cinema," trans. Eleanor Kaufman, in *Deleuze and Guattari: New Mappings in Politics, Philosophy, and Culture,* ed. Eleanor Kaufman and Kevin Jon Heller (Minneapolis: University of Minnesota Press, 1998), 14–20. For an alternate version, see "What Is the Creative Act?" in *Two Regimes of Madness,* 317–329.

propagation of energy). As expression, the function is not the specific phenomenon, of course, nor is it analogous to thinking. The function is a descriptor or algorithm, close in spirit to what information science calls an abstract machine. Its descriptiveness of behaviors in the natural world is important, but this is not the key to its specificity. It is abstract and general, and its generality derives from its time independence. It produces descriptions, and these descriptions are valid for all times and all places—thus, the proposal of a second whole. In its predictiveness of future behaviors, then, the function is exemplary of what science calls "theory," and when this predictiveness becomes regular, functions become "laws."

In a similar way, in *What Is Philosophy?* Deleuze and Guattari distinguish between the three modalities of thought according to the distinctiveness of their planes, their expressive modes, and their subjective presuppositions: artistic creation takes place on a plane of composition that gives expression to the force of sensation mediated through percepts or aesthetic figures; philosophy forms concepts on a plane of immanence as expressed through or in relation to conceptual personae; and science creates functions with respect to a plane of reference in relation to partial observers.

There are interesting sets of commonalities and differences in all three definitions. Functions take the form of propositions in a discursive system that serves as the medium or grammar of scientific thought. Alternatively, art and philosophy neither refer nor represent. The powers of philosophy and art are both nonrepresentational and nonreferential even when they are profoundly figural or formal, whereas scientific prospects are propositional and referential or ostensive, expressing functions as operations of actualized states of affairs observed in given experimental frameworks. Like a good algorithm, a function will produce the same state of affairs ad infinitum without variation; its prime component is the independent variable. Functions are also expressed as logical propositions that relate to individuated forms, bodies, or things.

But there are also lived functions whose arguments are produced as perceptions and affections expressed as *doxa* or opinion; call this what is publicly known or accepted as known. An opinion is not a subjective expression, however. Humans have opinions on everything that we perceive and that affects us, but things themselves, no matter how vast or molecular, are also "opinionated" to the extent that they receive and give information in specific contexts, act and react in networks of movement, relation, and causality that pass between the virtual and the actual. In creating and describing functions, science ascends from a chaotic virtuality to actualized states of things and bodies—a function describes processes or powers through which the virtual is actualized or comes to actualization. Concepts and percepts do not travel on these lines of interaction, however. And if one descends from actualized states of affairs back toward the virtual, one discovers another kind of virtuality or power of the virtual:

> The virtual is no longer the chaotic virtual, but rather virtuality that has become consistent, an entity forming on a plane of immanence that sections the chaos. Call this the Event, or the part that escapes its own actualization in everything that happens. The event is not at all a state of things; it is actualized in a state of things, in a body, in a lived, but it has a shadowy and secret part that is continually added or subtracted to its actualization. In contrast to a state of affairs, it neither begins nor ends, but has gained or kept the infinite movement to which it gives consistency. It is the virtual distinguished from the actual, but a virtual that is no longer chaotic, having become consistent or real on the plane of immanence that wrests it from chaos. Real without being actual; ideal without being abstract" (*What Is Philosophy?* 156, *147–148*).

This virtual has the power to restore infinite movement to thought, but not as a transcendental perspective. Its consistency thus relates to its capacity to survey itself in itself as "pure immanence of what does not actualize or which remains indifferent to actualization because its reality does not depend on actualization. The event is immaterial, incorporeal, unlivable—pure *reserve*" (156, *148*). In stark contrast to the infinite difference in repetition expressed as function, as pure immanence the event is repetition of infinite differentiation: "that which starts again without having begun or ended—the immanent aternal [*l'internel immanent*]" (157)—in other words, eternal recurrence.

Philosophy and art are thus distinguished from science by their differing attitudes to chaos and through the qualities of time they express. Each expresses two different relationships to the virtual, or two ways of drawing upon and giving expression to the virtual as a temporal force. Philosophy seeks to give consistency to the virtual while preserving its powers of infinite speed. Philosophy frames or constructs a plane of immanence through a sectioning of chaotic forces, selecting the infinite movements of thought and furnishing the plane with concepts moving at thought's own velocity. Science seeks points of reference that actualize the virtual and realize it in functional states of affairs. Rather than increasing the amplitude of movement toward the infinite, science seeks to localize movement in a frame of reference by slowing down or congealing time, and expressing it in terms of functions. Functions manage chaos in forming an object of reference whose mode of existence is defined by submission to finite conditions—variables of position, movement, force, or energy—that are quantitatively determined and spatially located, whether in an actual or calculated space. These functions are not identical to the "objects" themselves. Their mode of existence is a coordinate system comprising at least two independent variables in relation to formed matter—reference as propositional form and the relation between systems and states of affairs.[56]

Philosophy, science, and art interrelate from or across a given plane of immanence in their unique ways of giving expression to it—organizing chaos, managing relations between the virtual and actual, and drawing out points of subjectivation or enunciation (conceptual personae, aesthetic figures, partial observers). Science manages chaos in expressing a function as an independent variable framed by a partial observer; philosophy gives consistency to chaos through the concept, enunciated by a conceptual persona who preserves its virtual and infinite powers of thought. What art produces is a figure or Image through organizing sensations, lifting them out of the flow and flux of the *durée;* hence art's special relationship to time. The aim of art is to create a new "existent" separate from the stream of lived time, such that Deleuze and Guattari write that "Art preserves, and it is the only thing in the world that is preserved. It preserves and is preserved in itself." (*What Is Philosophy?* 163). No

---

56. In his lecture "Science and Reflection," Heidegger offers a remarkably similar perspective, and one that characterizes the modern conception of theory as distinct from philosophy: "Theory makes secure at any given time a region of the real as its object-area. The area-character of objectness is shown in the fact that it specifically maps out in advance the possibilities for the posing of questions. Every new phenomenon emerging within an area of science is refined to such a point that it fits into the normative objective coherence of the theory. That normative coherence itself is thereby changed from time to time. But objectness as such remains unchanged in its fundamental characteristics. That which is represented in advance as the determining basis for a strategy and procedure is, in the strict sense of the word, the essence of what is called 'end' or 'purpose.' When something is in itself determined by an end, then it is pure theory. It is determined by the objectness of what presences. Were objectness to be surrendered, the essence of science would be denied. This is the meaning, for example, of the assertion that modern atomic physics by no means invalidates the classical physics of Galileo and Newton but only narrows its realm of validity. But this narrowing is simultaneously a confirmation of the objectness normative for the theory of nature, in accordance with which nature presents itself for representation as a spatiotemporal coherence of motion calculable in some way or other in advance." Heidegger calls this a "trapping-securing procedure." See "Science and Reflection," in *The Question Concerning Technology, and Other Essays,* trans. William Lovitt (New York: Harper and Row, 1977), 169.

art is eternal, of course, and all of art's materials are subject to the laws of entropy—it is only a matter of time before they return to chaos and disorganization. Nonetheless, as an autonomous act of creation, art extracts an Image from chaos and forms it as a percept, but not as a way of conserving the material or medium of the figure; rather as the action of perpetuating or maintaining its immanent and creative relations with virtual forces. This is another way of asking what an Image is in relation to the image of thought in art or philosophy. In Deleuze and Guattari's perspective, artistic expression is less a matter of forming than enduring, of giving time a thickness or consistency, making it present as a durative force. Here a figure or image is formed from an expressive material or medium, yet there is always something else created within the medium that eludes it as an incorporeal sensation or percept.

Percepts differ fundamentally from functions in that they are based on no system of reference apart from what is immanent to sensation and one's encounter with the percepts and affects produced in such "sensational" encounters. A percept is not a perception, then, but rather a relation of immanence flooding both subject and object, if this distinction is still relevant. In the acts of becoming that produce aesthetic experience, in the creation of aesthetic things or existents, percepts become something more than the perceptions of those who experience an artwork, and affect something more than the responses of emotion, boredom, or incredulity incited by aesthetic experience, or not. An affect is not an effect, and the viewer has no more and no less being than the work itself. To experience a work of art means entering into a complex series of relations with it, to become another complexly composed component in a network of sensations, perceptions, and affections. In this perspective, the viewer is less a self-identical subject than a molecular component in a new virtual community where "sensations, percepts, and affects are *beings,* valid in themselves and exceeding experience as lived. . . . The work of art is a being of sensation and nothing else—it exists in itself" (*What Is Philosophy?* 164, *154–155*). In the complex of immanent relations comprising aesthetic sensations, "We are not in the world," Deleuze and Guattari conclude, "we become with the world; we become by contemplating it. Everything is vision, becoming" (169).

Deleuze and Guattari thus reverse the usual causality through which we believe sensations are produced—it is not colors, sounds, or movements that produce effects: rather, aesthetic material or art invades or is absorbed into sensations and becomes indistinguishable from them. The materials become indistinguishable from the sensation, yet sensations are conserved or preserved as independent entities or existents, percepts, and affects. "Even if the material lasts for only a few seconds," Deleuze and Guattari write, "it will give to sensation the power to exist and to be preserved itself, *in the eternity that co-exists with this short durée.* So long as the material lasts, the sensation enjoys an eternity in those very moments. Sensation is not realized in the material without the material passing completely in to the sensation, into the percept or affect. All the material becomes expressive" (*What Is Philosophy?* 166–167, 157). Art is not a "representation," neither of reality nor of inner states; it is not a representation at all. Art expresses its own reality. The goal of art is not to represent, but rather to give existence or independent life to sensations in the form of percepts and affects, to release percepts from the perception of objects and affects from emotions as the passage from one qualitative state to another in ways that draw their powers from the creative self-differentiation of the plane of immanence, though in a human framework.

Percepts and affects are experienced as autonomous and self-sufficient existents, continuously present to themselves without fixed reference to a historical past or future, which are, in principle, completely independent of and co-equal to the beings that experience them. The expressive forms of art, or what the creative act produces, are "monuments," though characteristically Deleuze and Guattari construct a special sense for the term. Monuments are not memorials (perhaps they are im-memorials?) and their relation to temporality is not that of producing a memory-image or reinvoking the past. To be released from lived perception in a percept is to occupy an event where the Image is without anchor or reference to past memory; nor is it evoked in a stream of involuntary memory flooding from the archives of past experience. Art does not commemorate the past, but rather endows the event with composed sensations that celebrate it with their own expressive force. Art thus endures not as memory, but as fabulation. This term will be familiar to every reader of Deleuze's cinema books. Creative fabulation as an expressive act is about art's creation of its own immanent and sensory reality by releasing sensations from quotidian events, but first one must be able to envision or apprehend them.[57] This act is neither the deployment of memory nor the expression of fantasy but rather the giving of existence to something virtually present and immanent in given life itself. What Deleuze and Guattari require here is something close to the aesthetic figure of the *voyant* of modern cinema—a seer giving

57. See, for example, my chapter on "Series and Fabulation" in Rodowick, *Gilles Deleuze's Time Machine* (Durham, NC: Duke University Press, 1997), 139–169.

birth to pure optical and acoustical situations, percepts, and affects that over-flow everyday life—where artistic perception is framed by a certain philo-sophical attitude.

To understand the relation between philosophy and art, then, is to com-prehend how the figural consistency of the concept relates to the durative capacity of the percept. One of the most striking features of *What Is Philoso-phy?* is how it presents an art or aesthetics of the concept. There is an extreme sensitivity to the concept, not as something to be analyzed or accounted for, but only described in its complexity as a figure, which may effect itself through space, time, and action, but which is only experienced as thought and the movements of thought. (This in fact is the claim that Deleuze makes for the direct image of time as something like the purest form of a thought without image, or what I refer to in *Gilles Deleuze's Time Machine* as a nonspatial per-ception. We will soon return to this description of the direct image of time as Deleuze's most complete account of the concept's relation to images.)

Concepts relate to percepts through their creative force as well as their lack of referentiality. Concepts must be constructed and their form is never simple; nor can they be reduced to a singular form, sign, or proposition. Every con-cept is a multiplicity comprising a figure with variable components whose nature is to multiply—the concept is additive and constructive, entering into ever-growing *agencements* or assemblages, actively combining, constructing, assembling, linking to or connecting with to form ever more elaborate net-works. This poses an interesting question of beginnings, because concepts are never created ex nihilo. There are no absolute beginnings free of context and prior discursive frameworks, such that one always starts up from the middle, as it were; one is already in the movement of becoming, and working within or trying to force a deviation in the history of philosophy and its concepts. At the same time, concepts form a fragmentary or open whole that is simultane-ously forming and de-forming. Concepts seek to unify their components, or at least to bring them into a Figure or Image, but in the same movement the nature of conceptual creation is to articulate, to express, to cut up, and to re-arrange, giving the concept an irregular contour defined by the number of its components, with branches seeking connections to other units. The concept is a mobile figure and a moving Image, and indeed what Deleuze hoped to ac-complish in the cinema books, among other things, was to do justice to the plastic complexity and creativity of the concept as a philosophical figure.

The will to create concepts often responds to a problem that has been mis-understood or badly presented, without which it would have no sense or potential for sense. Moreover, these problems are difficult to isolate or to characterize until such time as conceptual series emerge that trace out possible solutions. Concepts do not so much respond to problems, then, as picture them or make them present. Here an interesting distinction might be made. With its emphases on witnessing, observation, and spectating, theory relates to problems through concept formation as a kind of picturing. But in its virtual force the concept itself has a nonspatial dimension. What Deleuze calls the image of thought is a theoretic image, but philosophy is concerned with something else—the genesis of thought without image.

This idea provides an immediate bridge to the cinema books as two interrelated responses to the questions, What is the relationship of movement, time, and image to thought? How can thought be put into movement, or persist and insist as movement? And in each book, both movement and time become "problematic" in relation to thought in different ways; or rather, the concept of movement itself becomes problematized. For example, in the four commentaries on Bergson extending across the two books, our common-sense notions of movement as physical change in space, elapsed trajectory, chronology, or the quantitative addition of spatial sections is soon complicated and deepened through Deleuze's original readings of Bergson's *Matter and Memory* and *Creative Evolution*. Through the signs and sensations of cinema, our quotidian sense of movement unravels onto other dimensions: the plane of immanence as universal variation, or the essential equivalence of matter and light; movement as creative evolution and change through time, the unpredictable appearance of the new and unforeseen; and finally, what Deleuze calls thought from the outside, pitched into movement by the virtual force of the Event. But there will also be a second problem, itself threading through the cinema books in a closely woven skein, where the shift from the movement-image to the time-image presents a shift in the nature of belief, and raises the ethical question of how to restore belief in this life and this world, and their possibilities for change. But these are matters for later sections.

Concepts are marked by temporal as well as spatial complexity. In fact, there are something like four temporal dimensions or rhythms to every concept. One of these is *historical*—how the creation of a concept draws on prior histories, foraging, gleaning, displacing, and adapting material from different contexts and planes of immanence. Another relates to the emergence or *becoming* of a new concept from within its own plane of immanence and its present combination and connection of elements from that plane. The third dimension establishes not the unity but rather the *consistency* of a concept, both within itself and in its relation to neighboring concepts. Deleuze and Guattari add that every concept has an endoconsistency and an exoconsistency. The components of the concept, no matter how distinct and heterogeneous, must form an open whole (this is the fourth dimension), wherein the elements are both woven together yet open on to new forms and relations of connectivity. However, the passage from a concept to or through its neighbor can often be indistinct or the two indistinguishable because they may share components, or comparable components may occupy a zone of proximity wherein concepts overlap on their frontiers.

Most of these dimensions encourage us to imagine concepts as open and mobile entities with a strong degree of plasticity, susceptible to entering into new lines of development and larger sets or ensembles. But the consistency of a concept, what gives it its particular physiognomy, is how it becomes the site of intersection of its components—a point of condensation around a strange attractor. The concept waxes and wanes, expands or contracts, in a state of continual flux that passes between and among its components, which serve in this sense as intensive traits—lines or figures that give the concept its singularity. Components occupy or territorialize the concept in series of condensation and displacement as a force of *differentiation*. But the concept also emerges distinctly from its components through forces of *integration* as a kind of transcendental synthesis or overview. However, these movements of integration and differentiation, of forming intensive traits and unfolding into expansive series, are never realized into a completed picture of a self-contained whole.

One might say, then, that concepts are fuzzy or indistinct, in the same way that Wittgenstein gravitates toward blurred or indistinct concepts that evade our attempts to pin them to language, but which become visible, apprehendable, or intelligible by assembling and comparing the language games in which they are deployed. Because the concept does not occupy or fill up a stable moment in time, space, or a particular state of affairs, one might ask, What is its location? Where is its place in language or thought? A concept is an Image, but a deterritorializing one, where the components of concepts territorialize or populate the field or ground against which the concept might show itself. This is why Deleuze and Guattari say that the concept is an "incorporeal" or pure Event, a haecceity "real without being actual, ideal without being abstract" (*What Is Philosophy?* 22). The concept shares mobility across two dimensions or perspectives with the absolute plane of immanence: "The concept is therefore both absolute and relative: it is relative to its own components, to other concepts, to the plane on which it is defined, and to the problems it is supposed to resolve; but it is absolute through the condensation it carries out, the site it occupies on the plane, and the conditions it assigns to the problem. As whole it is absolute, but insofar as it is fragmentary it is relative" (*What Is Philosophy?* 21). The mobility or movements of the concept traverse two planes, then. There are finite or singular movements that trace the contour of its components, giving them a physiognomy or drawing an Image through them. But the concept itself consists of infinite movements, a *tour d'horizon* or conspectus, a mental survey or overview that, one wants to say, is theoric.

Thinking through concepts is therefore a continuous process of construction and reconstruction. "A philosopher never stops reworking or even changing his concepts," Deleuze and Guattari write, a phrase more true of Deleuze than any other twentieth-century philosopher (*What Is Philosophy?* 21, 26–27). The philosophical act is intrinsically syntagmatic, pragmatic, and constructive—the making, unmaking, and remaking of constructions through relative and absolute series. Concepts evolve in series according to proximate connections or combinations, whether internal or external. The internal consistency of the concept is measured by the connections of its components in zones of proximity and indiscernible transitions, like variations of intensity and frequency in an analog image. Its exoconsistency, its displacement or deterritorialization into new series, occurs through bridging two or more neighboring concepts, whose components may be exhausted or incapable of further transformation (in other words, imaginative colligation). And so, Deleuze and Guattari write, this is what it means to create concepts: "to connect internal, inseparable components to the point of closure or saturation so that we can no longer add or withdraw a component without changing the nature of the concept; to connect the concept with another in such a way that other connections change their nature" (*What Is Philosophy?* 90, 87).

There is a virtual power in each concept, then, a polyvalency or plurivocity, dependent only on its zones of proximity, internal or external—this force of the virtual makes of it a fragmentary whole open to continuous modulation and change. When it is well made the morphology of the concept is viral. But rather than attacking a host to assure its mutations, it moves through chains of neighboring concepts through processes of attachment, penetration, disintegration and reintegration, self-replication and self-mediated assembly, releasing its components into neighboring assemblages: "The concept is not paradigmatic but *syntagmatic;* not projective but *connective;* not hierarchical but *arterial* [vicinal]; not referential but consistent. That being so, it is inevitable that philosophy, science, and art are no longer organized as levels of a single projection and are not even differentiated according to a common matrix but are immediately posited and reconstituted in a respective independence, in a division of labor that sustains connective relations between them" (91, 87).

Philosophical constructivism thus entails subtracting, adding, expanding, or recombining conceptual components to construct new series and points of condensation in acts of imagination, intuition, or even forgetfulness. Philosophy initiates its movements of thought through concepts, with their finite and infinite speeds, and is also often carried away by them. In a phrase Deleuze frequently cites from Leibniz, "I thought I had come home to harbor, but was thrown out again to open sea." In its combination of movements, the concept integrates its components and forms its endoconsistency but also gives rise to new series out of its exoconsistency, yet it has no reference apart from the movements of thought itself: "it is self-referential; it posits itself and its object at the same time as it is created" (What Is Philosophy? 22). And so much so that Deleuze and Guattari characterize the philosophical act as a kind of perpetual digression or digressiveness.

This is why, finally, Deleuze and Guattari assert that concepts are neither discursive nor propositional, thus providing another unexpected link to the late Wittgenstein. Where is the truth of the concept, or how is its truth to be judged? What is the nature of criticism in philosophy, and is there such a thing as progress in the history of philosophy? Deleuze and Guattari's response is to assert that a concept has no other truth than that which is shaped by its own conditions of creation. Our concepts must surely respond to problems of our own time and our own situation of thought; they arise in relation to "our history, and, above all, to our becomings" (What Is Philosophy? 27). Concepts are judged not in relation to some abstract value or criterion of knowledge, but rather only with respect to how they make present or intelligible new directions or contexts for thought emerging out of a present problematical situation; they are immanent to the problems that presently concern and derail us. "If a concept is 'better' than its predecessor," Deleuze and Guattari offer, "it is because it makes us hear new variations and unknown resonances; it executes unfamiliar constructions/assemblages [découpages] and brings forth an Event that overtakes and passes through us [qui nous survole]" (28, 32). And if we still refer to, adapt, or recontextualize concepts from earlier philosophies, this is because concepts can always be reactivated or remade in relation to new problems. Components may be extracted from them to create new series or combinations, giving rise to new concepts or novel meanings for old concepts. Philosophy advances neither through succession, subsumption, dialectical critique, nor by evoking the powers of its ancestors, but rather by performing a particular kind of work: always creating new concepts for the ever-changing problematics in which we find ourselves.

Philosophical critique does not advance through negation or refutation, then, but only in remarking that a concept has become exhausted or fatigued, that it has lost components or has been transformed in a new situation where it acquires new components or responds to new problems. The scourge of philosophy, Deleuze and Guattari observe, is philosophers who criticize without creating, or defend tired or exhausted concepts without knowing how to return them to life. Nor does philosophy desire to discuss concepts, for while every new concept finds expression on a plane of immanence that gives it an Image, there is also something intransmissable in the concept that holds it open, that remains unthought, or that confronts thought as the unthought that still resides within it. Here Socrates remains the first philosopher, or the conceptual persona that haunts all of philosophy, not because he represents philosophy as a free discussion among friends, but rather because he is a figure of disturbance and disconcertment who impedes discussion, a figure for the restlessness of conceptual creation and a thought without rest.

11. Idea, Image, and Intuition

> To think is to create—there is no other creation—but to create is first of all to engender "thinking" in thought.
>
> —Gilles Deleuze, *Difference and Repetition*

One might say that the percept is formal or formative in singular acts of creation, whereas the concept is singular yet abstract in that it relates to thought in its own temporal immanence. The expressiveness of art finds its instantiation in the sensuous products of art and its human affects, and the expressiveness of science finds its confirmation in the predicted behaviors of natural phenomena. But concepts express only thought and acts of thinking. Does this mean that thinking is purely an interior activity cut off from the sensuous and material world? Art provides important answers to this question in relating concepts to Ideas, signs, and images.

Cinema 1: The Movement-Image and *Cinema 2: The Time-Image* are rife with concepts: the plane of immanence; the movement or time image; rational and irrational connections or divisions; integration, specification, and differentiation; relative and absolute relations of sets to wholes or the Whole; the powers of the false; psychological and spiritual automata; thought of the Outside; and indeed many, many more. In a strong sense, these are concepts restored to cinema by philosophy. Yet they remain fully immanent to the cinematic image as expressive forces within cinema itself, a series of moving images. At the same time, the immanence of movement—as becoming, change, openness of the whole, or force of the Outside—is a characteristic shared by both Image and concept, so much so that there is a kind of logical reversibility or complex system of exchange between the cinema books and *What Is Philosophy?*

The philosophical act is constructive, but a construction that occurs on two complementary yet distinct dimensions: to create concepts but also to lay out or figure a scenography, mise-en-scène, cartography, territory, or plateau that delimits the consistency of concepts in their emergence and in the network of relations they establish across planes of immanence. Concepts are fragmentary wholes distributed across the plane like a casting of seeds, or the spread of planets, moons, and asteroids in a solar system, but the plane is the earth or the environment that receives the seeds and conditions their growth, or the forces of gravity and distribution of energy that holds elements in their orbits—an unlimited open Whole. As in *The Movement-Image* and *The Time-Image,* there is something here like an absolute and relative relation to the plane of immanence. The plane of immanence is absolute when related to the Whole—the regime of universal variation on a cosmological scale and the intuition of the univocity of Being as a single expressive substance. In its relative dimension, the plane of immanence is more like an expansive frame or frontier that expresses a horizon that delimits complex sets while also setting their internal consistency. Both the movement and time-image comprise or contain a multiplicity of signs and images; they are two fragmentary wholes as it were, yet each one has a consistency internal to itself comprising something like a world, which is nonetheless open to multiple hybrid configurations.

This is another way of looking not only at the history of philosophy but also at the history of art. How does ideational creation take place, or how does movement occur from one image of thought to another as in, for example, the complex transition between the movement-image and the time-image? Across the history of philosophy, and the history of art, there are a multiplicity of planes of immanence, each with their own internal conceptual consistency, their own lines and degrees of force, strata, and rhythms. However, change does not take place as a simple succession of planes, but rather as a folding and interleaving, deposits of sediment and strata in an ever-flowing stream, where planes are in flux with respect to one another, and also pass into and out of one another in impure and unexpected mixtures. Unlike the partiality of scientific theories or the fragmentariness of concepts, each plane is a singular immanent whole, carrying out selections of components and elements that vary from one plane to another.

Another question arises here: is there a point of transition, bridge, or meeting point that connects movements between plane and concept? Similar to Bergson's notion of the intermediate image as a "perception" (percept is perhaps the better term) falling between the material and the mental, the tangible and the intangible, this would be a thought consistent enough to be "sensible," but unformed enough to not yet be conceptual. The plane of immanence is distinct from concepts and their creation as force is distinguishable from matter, or the virtual from the actual. Concepts are conditioned by the plane, emerging from it and passing back into it indiscernibly, and varying constantly with respect to it. Similarly, if conceptual creation is the characteristic act of philosophy, the movements and rhythms of the plane must be considered as prephilosophical or nonconceptual in ways similar to how philosophy itself refers to intuitive or nonconceptual understanding. The force and nature of intuition thus defined, however, varies with the cartography of the plane and its characteristic features, geography, and landmarks. On the one hand, the presuppositions and intuitions forming on the plane are not extrinsic to concepts, but rather the framework or horizon setting their particular internal conditions. Immanent to philosophy, yet not wholly commensurate with it, they are the engine or energetic heart of philosophy and also its principal links to nonphilosophy, that is, to other forms of (nonconceptual) understanding in everyday life, science, or art. The plane of immanence is therefore a kind of membrane through which philosophy's productive relations with other modalities of creating and understanding resonate: Ideas, percepts, affects, functions. We are close here to what Hegel called "theory." In *Creative Mind,* Bergson calls this philosophical intuition; Deleuze calls it having an Idea.

In 1991, Deleuze gave an important lecture at the FEMIS, the French national film and television school, an excerpt of which was published as "Having an Idea in Cinema." What does it mean to have an Idea in art and how do

Ideas differ from concepts? Ideas are specific to a domain, a milieu, or a material, and so Deleuze writes that "Ideas must be treated as potentials that are already engaged in this or that mode of expression and inseparable from it, so much so that I cannot say I have an idea in general. According to the techniques that I know, I can have an idea in a given domain, an idea in cinema or rather an idea in philosophy" ("Having an Idea" 14). This argument relates to Deleuze and Guattari's insistence that concepts must be created from an intuition that belongs to them, where intuition means giving expression to the virtual forces and potentials of a given plane of immanence. Composed from variations and zones of indiscernibility in the passage between plane and concept, the concept is itinerant, wandering, vague, and without clear outlines, including those that would render it as figures of discourse—it is intensive and modular, in constant displacement on a plane of immanence. As form or force, the concept is an event whose logic of sense expresses neither whole nor fractional numbers for counting things or quantitatively presenting their qualities. There is no measure, data, or fixed outline to a concept, meaning it is completely other to scientific functions. Nonetheless, ideas in philosophy are oriented by a certain kind of figure or image, what Deleuze calls the "image of thought," and so a connection or relation must link them. In *What Is Philosophy?* the image of thought is defined as the specific terrain or plane of immanence from which Ideas emerge as preconceptual expression as "the image thought gives itself of what it means to think, to use thought, to orient one's self in thought" (*What Is Philosophy?* 37). Just as the plane is not a concept, nor the concept of concepts, it is also neither thought nor the thinkable.

This observation suggests that that there is a special connection between image and thought that is not a representation of thought; rather it is what Kant characterized as a heautonomous relation of two wholes external to one another, an interstice or disjunctive synthesis where thought is the outside of the image, and the image the outside of thought, just as in the direct image of time, space and time are incommensurable and thought is given as a nonspatial perception. We return here to the nonvisibility or nongivenness of the concept as an absolute value, of which Wittgenstein himself was equally aware. Thus, the image of thought does not comprise sets of rules or methods that can be followed, nor is it an algorithm that can be executed. It is neither a brain state imageable on screens nor a cultural expression of thought's means, ends, and forms. There is no sign or representation commensurable with thought's movements to which it can be fixed or reduced. For these reasons, Deleuze and Guattari say that what thought claims by right is infinite movement, and the only image appropriate to thought is that of infinite movement. Yet what art might accomplish for philosophy is to provide figures of thought—formative and signifying components—setting finite conditions for thought's movements. Deleuze's term for this in the cinema books is noosigns, and we will return to these signs in a moment.

Where does philosophy locate itself? From which dimension does it act, the concept or the plane? (One could ask as well, where does sensation occur, in the Idea or the Image?) In fact the possibilities of philosophy, or philosophizing, emerge in the movements from one to the other in the folds or meshes that intercalate or weave together the two sides without ever confusing them. Philosophy cannot create concepts without mapping the plane, thus setting out its different components and activities. The cartographic elements of the plane are diagrammatic lines, whereas concepts populate the plane as intensive features. On one side there is infinite movement, no matter how slow or sudden—the immeasurable rhythms of geological change or unexpected quakes and eruptions. On the other, there are intensive and ordered series of movements producing fragmentary and open segments of space, or variable framings or perspectives, that vary the rhythm of the infinite movements of the plane, "each of which constitutes a surface or a volume, an irregular contour marking a halt in the degree of proliferation" (*What Is Philosophy?* 40). This is not to say that concepts as intensive figurations are derived from diagrammatic lines, the lines sketching the contours of the figure, for example, nor are intensive series deduced from the movements of the plane. Rather, crossings between plane and concept are transitions between intuitions and intensities, a passage from the prephilosophical or extraphilosophical to philosophy.

Perhaps one of the values of art (but also all kinds of creative media or expressive materials) is to embody or make sensate the intuitive force of the concept in its moving figural intensity. Perhaps artistic construction is one kind of cartography of the concept, sketching out its intensive features in ways similar to philosophical constructivism. *The Movement-Image* and *The Time-Image* are Deleuze's concrete responses to these questions before *What Is Philosophy?* comes about to ask them more abstractly. One of the most striking features of *What Is Philosophy?* in this respect is how the figural force of the concept and its intensive features reprise the semiotic vocabulary of the cinema books. There is no reference, of course, to Deleuze's vertiginous elaboration of perception, affection, action, or relation-images, nor to opsigns, sonsigns, or crystal-images. Rather, the genesis of cinematographic signs and the figural force of concepts are related through common principles of construction: absolute and relative dimensions of a plane of immanence, formation and expansion through specification, integration, and differentiation, the open relation of intervals or interstices to a Whole that changes, determined relations between intervals and wholes. To have an Idea, then, is to express thought through particular constructions, combinations, or linkages—what Deleuze calls signs. As Spinoza insisted, signs are neither representational nor an expression of thought; rather, they are expressions of our *powers* of thinking. Ideas are not separable from an autonomous sequence or sequencing of ideas in thought, what Spinoza calls *concatenatio*. This concatenation of signs unites form and material, constituting thought as a spiritual automaton whose *potentia* expresses our powers of thinking, action, or creation. And indeed the movement- and time-images lay out their own points of thought and subjectivation in psychological and spiritual automata. We will return to all these terms and arguments momentarily.

The importance of Deleuze's cinema books is that they present his most complete account of a philosophical semiotic modeled on movement and time, and of how images and signs in movement or time are conceptually innovative; that is, how they renew our powers of thinking. The cinema books do not exemplify the abstract arguments in *What Is Philosophy?* Rather, in their own way and through their own means they are making the same case for the immanence of thought to image as a virtual and temporal force. Art relates to philosophy in that images and signs involve preconceptual expression in the same way that the image of thought involves a protoconceptual expression—they prepare the terrain for new concepts to emerge. The cinema may be best able to picture thought and to call for thinking because like thought its Ideas consist of movements, both spatial and temporal, characterized by connections and conjunctions of particular kinds. Every instance of art is expressive of an Idea that implies a concept, and what philosophy does with respect to art is to produce new constructions or assemblages that express or give form to the concepts implicated in art's Ideas. Philosophy renders perspicuous in conceptual form the automatisms that make a necessity of art's generative ideas.

The key to grasping this relation in Deleuze is to understand the originality of his characterization of the Image as both an ontological and ethical concept. Especially in the cinema books, the Image is not the product of cinematic creation but rather its raw material, the worldly substance that it forms and to which it gives expression. Hence the key place of Bergson's assertion from *Matter and Memory* that there is already photography in things. Like energy, images can neither be created nor destroyed—they are a state of the universe, an asubjective universal perception or luminosity that evolves and varies continuously. Human perception is therefore largely a process of subtraction. Because we must orient ourselves in this vast regime of universal change according to our limited perceptual context, we extract and form special Images or perceptions according to our physiological limits and human needs. This Image is the very form of our subjectivity, and persists in the crossroads between our internal states and our external relations with the world.[58]

The image is thus in relation with ourselves (interiority) and in relation with the world (exteriority) in an intimately interactive way. It is absurd to refer to subjectivity as pure interiority, because it is ceaselessly engaged with matter and with the world. By the same token, thought is not interiority but our way of engaging with the world, orienting ourselves there and creating from the materials it offers us. Thus, another way of considering the autonomy of art, philosophy, and science is to evaluate the different though related images of thought they offer us. The percept is visually and acoustically sensuous, provoking affects or emotions in us. Concepts and functions are more indirect. What the function is to scientific expression, the sign is to aesthetic expression. Art's relation to thought, then, lies not in the substance of images but in the logic of their combination and connectivity (or division and disconnectivity). No doubt every artistic image is an image of thought, a physical tracing and expression of thought given sensual form, no matter how incoherent or inelegant. However, while the aesthetic sign may imply a precise concept, it is nonetheless entirely affective and preconceptual. Yet there is a philosophical power in images. The artist's Idea is not necessarily the philosopher's. But images not only trace thoughts and produce affects; they may also provoke thinking or create new powers of thinking. In their doing so, we are thrown from sensuous to abstract thought, from an image of thought to a thought without image—this is the domain of philosophy. And in moving from one to the other, art may inspire philosophy to give form to a concept.

What does philosophy value in art? To ask this question is to ask what forces expressed in art, in images and signs, call for thinking. Philosophy parts ways

58. I review these arguments more completely in "Movement and Image," chapter 2 of *Gilles Deleuze's Time Machine.*

with science to the extent that time is taken as an independent variable—in fact, the simplest way of describing Deleuze's (or Bergson's) philosophical project is as the will to reintroduce time and change to philosophy's image of thought. Philosophy finds inspiration in art because there the will to create is brought to its highest powers. Here, as in many other ways, Deleuze goes against the grain of contemporary philosophy. While, happily, science has never renounced its powers of creation, it has become less and less conceptual. And of course, it does not need concepts as philosophy does. Contrariwise, philosophy has moved closer and closer to art, and vice versa. This is the great untold story of twentieth-century philosophy that the twenty-first century must recount; that philosophy's greatest innovations were not made with respect to science, but rather in dialogue with art—and further, that the modern arts came closer and closer to philosophical expression while nonetheless amplifying their aesthetic powers.

The Movement-Image and *The Time-Image* are books of philosophy. Yet they are also philosophy's way of acknowledging the noetic force of nonphilosophy, especially art, and of art's powers of restoring or reinvigorating conceptual creation. There is a becoming-concept in cinematographic expression that belongs only to cinema and thought's relation to cinema, which exists and persists whether philosophy recognizes its powers or not—these powers are fully immanent to cinema and its semiotic history. Indeed, for Deleuze that semiotic history is distributed across two distinct aesthetic or cinematographic planes of immanence as two great regimes of signs, the movement-image and the time-image, which in turn are variations on the plane of immanence as the cosmological regime of universal variation as self-differentiating movement. Of all the arts, cinema seems to draw the maximum of its formative and energetic resources from the universal plane. Both aesthetic regimes are variations on this universal movement-image, or perhaps two perspectives on how thought emerges in relation to it, one of which privileges the commensurability of space and time, the other of which expresses their incommensurability. In their generality and in their conditioning of signs and images, the cinematographic movement-image and time-image express two fundamental Ideas responding to a critical question or problem: how does cinema transmit the modern image of thought? While cinema's own varied answers to this question are intuitive and preconceptual, they are nonetheless singular, material, and concrete. What Deleuze calls the great cinematic *auteurs* are thus certainly thinkers. But in undertaking his cartography of the two regimes of signs, these *auteurs* become something else for Deleuze, intercessors or conceptual personae. As such, they have laid out the subjective presuppositions of the respective planes through the expressive force of their distinct and protoconceptual Ideas, which philosophy in turn makes perspicuous by describing the planes of immanence from which those Ideas emerge, the abstract machines or diagrams that condition them, the logic of intervals or relations between intervals and wholes through which they are figured along well-defined planes of consistency, the noosigns and spiritual automata that render them thoughtful, and finally their ethical modalities and regimes of belief.

Cinema presents a special case for considering the relation of philosophy to art, or concept to Image, because it is in movement and can only be considered as movement or continual becoming. But that being said, the relations between movement, image, and thought also change definition depending on their logic and relations of spatial and temporal consistency. Time can be expressed as a formed or formal relation commensurate with space (the indirect time-image), or time may recur as a force incommensurable with space (the direct image of time). Each case figures our modern image of thought differently, and activates the figurability of the concept differently.

A concept is not a percept or an image, nor is it a function or a proposition. Indeed concepts are difficult to grasp or to fix in thought for two reasons. First, they are in movement or a continual state of becoming. A concept achieves consistency or a kind of presence to thought only by relating to a plane of immanence wherein it is sustained. When concepts are forceful and well constructed, they generate thought or organize movements of thought, but they are never completely present to thought. They may be named and mapped, or even related to points of enunciation through conceptual personae, but at no point is a concept identical to or representative of thought, or expressible as a proposition. Second, a concept is never finished, whole, complete—it cannot exist or persist as a sign or representation positioned in space and frozen in time. It is neither self-sufficient nor self-identical, but rather draws all its powers from its virtuality, its self-differentiation, its becoming. We can speak of an image of thought or a thought without image, but in neither case is thought identical to the image. Rather, thought is something that when present is always in movement ahead, behind, or alongside of the image . . . or all at the same time. The key questions here, then, are: How do creative expression and philosophical expression coincide? How do we apprehend concepts if they are given neither in propositions nor percepts? What is the rapport between concept and Image?

All of the formal concepts of the cinema books are something like what Stanley Cavell, after Wittgenstein, might call "pictures" as humanly necessary yet inherently inadequate presentations of the multiple variations in which we might hold (or lose) our relationships to thought. This is why I have distinguished between images as formed presentations and an idea of Image as a set of automatisms or genetic relations expressed not as presentations, but rather as powers or potentials incompletely realized in images. This is more or less what Deleuze means by the movement-image in an absolute sense. If there is a visibility or perceptibility to this Image, however, it is given as force not form, as virtual not actual, as a logic unfolding in, around, or outside of images, or holding images in variable combinations, and these are all qualities that Images share with concepts.

Now, in spite of the multiplicity and complexity of Deleuze's vocabulary, and his wild account of the genesis and typology of movement- and time-images, his characterization of immanent moving pictures of thought is organized by a limited set of parameters. The whole history of cinema is thus organized by two fundamental Ideas—the movement-image and the time-image—as two moving images of thought emerging on their own planes of immanence. The consistency of these planes is maintained by two singular abstract machines, each of which conditions the formative force of movement in relation to the image or images: on the one hand, there is an automation of movement in the image or a self-movement of the image that generates indirect images of time; on the other, an autotemporalization of the image provoking direct images of time. The automatisms of each image, as I will explain further in a moment, are fueled by asymmetrical relations between wholes and sets forming images and their components. Yet in both cases there is the possibility of thinking in or through the deepest powers of time and the virtual—the infinite speed of chaosmos, or of constant universal variation, creative evolution, and the unexpected emergence of the new. Moreover, direct time-images are genetically related to what Deleuze calls the passive synthesis or impersonal form of time, whose variable dimensions include the splitting of the present into three incommensurable points (a passing present, conservation of the past, and an indeterminate protention of the future); the preservation of all of the past as virtual nonchronological strata; and finally, the pure form of time as expressed, on the one hand, by Kant's remapping of the *cogito* as divided within itself by the form of time, and on the other, by Nietzsche's doctrine of the eternal return as the Being of Becoming, or the fact of returning of that which differs.

To recapitulate, from a formal perspective the philosophical powers immanent to cinema are organized by two fundamental Ideas expressed across two
distinct (though interrelating) planes of immanence, each characterized or
made consistent by abstract machines generating two fundamental regimes of
signs. Here I am less concerned with describing the kinds of signs emitted
than with characterizing the abstract machines that (in)form them. Philosophy performs this task through interpretation. In Deleuze's Nietzschean perspective, to interpret is not to fix or draw out the meaning of a sign or image,
but rather to characterize the will to power that fuels its conditions of sense,
what gives it its consistency or rarity (in Foucault's sense), sets its horizons of
emergence, and accounts for how and why it is valued. I will return to and
deepen this thought in Section 12. But let it be said for the moment that there
are not only two fundamental cinematic Ideas, but also two fundamental values, each of which characterizes a given logic of sense—the dialectical and
Hegelian will to truth of the cinematic movement-image and the Nietzschean
powers of the false of the cinematic time-image. For the moment, I am only
concerned by the formal conditions or conditioning of these two powers as
ways of demonstrating how, as preconceptual or protoconceptual forces, they
condition the endoconsistency and exoconsistency of images—their logics of
formation, figurability, interconnectivity, and expansion in succession or series.
In each case, there is a logic to images expressive of these powers, which are in
every case immanent to images themselves. In both cases we begin again with
two abstract machines, one which regulates all the variations where time is
rendered as commensurable with space through movement, the other in which
the very condition of movement changes as time is expressed directly through
its incommensurability with space.

One of the conceptual difficulties in Deleuze (and part of the formal genius
of Sergei Eisenstein) is that he asks us to think of the Image simultaneously in
two dimensions as it were, as if two interlacing diagrammatic lines that condition the ongoing formation of images. One line takes the form of self-contained
sets or framings succeeding one another, or displacing or replacing one another in space; the other considers the image as an expansive whole, which is
continuously regrouping or reframing sets into larger and more complex mobile pictures. Within the context of cinematic movement-images, Eisenstein
referred to this logic as the relation between horizontal and vertical montage.
At the same time, these two dimensions of the moving image provide the
basis for beginning to comprehend how the movement-image in its deepest
sense presents four variations of thought's relation to movement: as infinite

speed on the absolute plane of immanence, or the whole aggregate of images as a universal regime of acentered variation (the Image); movement in relation to a perspective or framing relative to singular bodies or objects as the opening of intervals forming contingent, spatial sets (perception of movement); as a succession of spatialized self-contained segments (empirical and chronological form of time); and finally, as intuition of the force of the virtual as becoming, change, self-differentiation, or creative evolution.

As Deleuze encourages us to think of these logics as formal relationships between sets or ensembles, questions arise about the nature of what links sets together, or how they unfold one from the other in self-generated successive series, what separates them or holds them together, and how they may be grouped into larger ensembles at various scales (frame, shot, fragment, segment, figure, acts, or even complete textual systems, genres, and so forth). *What Is Philosophy?* links directly to the cinema books in that the figurability of the concept as a fragmentary and complex whole—forming, deforming, unraveling, and evolving in open series, the conditioning of both its endo- and exoconsistency—equally describes the formal logic relating Idea to Image in cinema. The problem of thought in relation to movement, then, is expressed differently, and takes on different values, to the extent to which one considers the nature of sets and the relation between sets as a logic of (commensurable) intervals, or whether instead formal relations are governed by (incommensurable) interstices between images, sets, or series of images, and between images and sounds.

The problem of interpreting images, then, is not one of reading or establishing meaning, but rather of describing the abstract machines, or setting out the logic of sense, that comprehend the force or will to power that generates formal relationships within and between images. Here we encounter a new set of parameters expressed by the logic of intervals and the relationship between intervals and wholes, or the Whole. An interval is basically a spatial figure with a given, indeed quantifiable, duration. (Think of Eisenstein's notion of metrical montage.) The compositional elements of intervals fill up space as elapsed time in shots, sequences, and larger montage figures. These are figures of succession and expansion establishing what Deleuze calls the empirical form of time—a linear and chronological succession-expansion in space directed by the arrow of time in the continuous elaboration of a sequential past, present, and future. However, the presentation of time in the cinematic movement-image does not reside in simple succession or the present flow of images, but rather in the montage figures that the empirical form of time conditions. Another way of putting this is that the Idea of an indirect presentation of time means that time is not given in an image or images but only in the continual elaboration of relationships within and between sets. We do not apprehend time in the image, or in the suite of images, but rather in the logical system of relationships that govern the formation, succession, and expansion of sets at variable scales. These can be figures of montage, where formal and metrical relations govern the expansion or contractions of movements, their quantitative sampling and combination of mobile sections in smaller or larger units, or noosigns that direct and regulate logical combinations of sets as expressive figures.

As two distinct planes of immanence, the cinematic movement-image and the cinematic time-image relate to or separate from one another according to how each relates to absolute movement. What makes the two planes differ, or gives them their consistency, are the different logics with which relative and absolute movement are expressed in relationships between sets and wholes. On the one hand, Deleuze asks us to consider the mobile relation between wholes and sets as a relationship between differentiation and specification. Differentiation indicates a process where a whole divides into both objects and bodies as (actual-spatial) components of a set while reintegrating these components into a (virtual-temporal) whole that passes between them as continuous duration. Specification forms specific kinds of images as spatial sets by framing space in a given perspective and delimiting space as a measurable interval. The modulation between wholes and sets, on the one hand, and between differentiation and specification, on the other, defines the two basic articulations of the movement-image as a mobile section of duration; it equally governs relations between frame, shot, and montage in the cinema. Moreover, to apprehend the Image as a mobile section of duration means comprehending it as a fundamentally deterritorializing figure whose relative and absolute dimensions are two perspectives on movement, inseparable yet quite different in their genetic relation to images. Movement is not a quality produced in the succession of images as spatial sections, but rather in the complex and indistinguishable points of passage between framing as the delimitation of a spatial set, the shot in relation to a movement it expresses, and montage as expressing a change in the whole.

Here I can do no better than to reconsider arguments (though in a fundamentally new context) that I have already set out in *Gilles Deleuze's Time Machine*. Relative movement expresses relations between the parts of a set while absolute movement defines change in the state of the whole. Relative movement involves immobile segmentations of space, which includes changes within and between the parts of a set—sectionings of space as lines, planes, or volumes. Absolute movement, however, refers to the mobility of a whole that changes as an absolute temporal and relational quality. Deleuze explains that the shot always presents this bipolar movement,

> in relation to the sets in space where it introduces relative modifications between elements or sub-sets; in relation to a whole whose absolute change in duration it expresses. This whole is never content to be elliptical, nor narrative, though it can be. But the shot, of whatever kind, always has these two aspects: it presents modifications of relative position in a set or some sets. It expresses absolute changes in a whole or in the whole. The shot in general has one face turned towards the set, the modifications of whose parts it translates, and another face turned towards the whole, of which it expresses the—or at least a—change. Hence the situation of the shot, which can be defined abstractly as the intermediary between the framing of the set and the montage of the whole, sometimes tending towards the pole of framing, sometimes tending towards the pole of montage. The shot is movement considered from this dual point of view: the translation of the parts of a set which spreads out in space, the change of a whole which is transformed in duration.[59]

Deterritorialization is another name for the bipolar quality of the image in relation to movement. Relative movement presents a tendency toward closure and the formation of spatial sets. Alternatively, absolute movement is temporal, presenting a deterritorialization of the image: whatever tries to close becomes open; whatever falls into parts or sets will return to a continuous whole; whatever congeals into space also unravels in time in a continual passage between the actual and the virtual.

In this conception, framing is less a compositional act than an exercise in aspect seeing, which asks us to apprehend the continuous alternation between two dimensions of movement that differ in nature. Framing is less the action of selecting and stabilizing a visible space or a mobile section of the world than an apperception of relations that continually occur outside of the image (the French term is *hors-champ*, or out-of-field). This is how differentiation and

---

59. *Cinema 1: The Movement-Image*, trans. Hugh Tomlinson and Barbara Habberjam (Minneapolis: University of Minnesota Press, 1986), 19–20.

specification relate to relative and absolute movement. Because relative movement is inherently spatial, the implied out-of-field is additive: the unfolding of space in camera movement, the succession of shots in editing, or the subsumption of shots or sequences into larger parts. In any case, movement is defined by physical space as content, a geometry of spatial segments that can be added, divided, or multiplied in various combinations. Here the out-of-field is by definition actual and actualizable: it serves continually to produce new visible spaces. But the Whole is neither spatial nor actual; it is temporal and virtual. It is the dimension of change itself in the form of becoming. The absolute aspect of the out-of-field relates to duration as the Open, which is no longer a set and does not belong to the order of the spatial and the actual. The movement-image only gives an indirect image of time because time and change are always measured as the division or addition of spatial segments. The direct image of time attests to another power, however. "In one case," Deleuze writes, "the out-of-field designates that which exists elsewhere, to one side or around; in the other case, the out-of field testifies to a more disturbing presence, one which cannot even be said to exist, but rather to 'insist' or 'subsist', a more radical Elsewhere, outside homogenous space and time" (*The Movement-Image* 17).

The concept of the out-of-field provides new criteria for defining the planes of consistency of cinematic movement- and time-images, and in turn, the images of thought they express. The cinematic movement-image presents an indirect image of time as exteriority or extensiveness in space; the cinematic time-image presents a direct image—anteriority of time as creative evolution, the pure form of time as change or Becoming. But how in fact can we understand logically that liminal zone where thought passes from one to the other as an unending oscillation between the virtual and actual? The passage between sets and wholes asks us to consider framing as a bipolar movement of succession and expansion, horizontal and vertical montage. But there is also a logic that associates, combines, links, and disconnects sets. In Deleuze's account, this logic is expressed in noosigns, whose different logics transform both the quality of sets and that of the out-of-field as the expression of two powers of thought that differ in nature. Adapting terms from set theory in mathematics, Deleuze says that sets are defined in the cinematic movement-image by rational divisions (*coupures rationnels*), in which the end of one set is continuous with the beginning of the one that follows. In this manner, images are linked or extended according to principles of association and contiguity, and associated images are integrated into a conceptual whole and differentiated into more extensive sets.

Here the movement-image's plane of consistency—and thus what defines its Idea, or the immanence of thought in the image—is organized fundamentally by two kinds of noosigns, one forming through a logic of association, the other through differentiation and integration. The plane of consistency is the surface of the map, noosigns are the coordinates that orient the movements of thought, and from plane to coordinates a mental cartography is drawn out. One noosign defines the linking of images by rational intervals into sequences forming an extendible world; the other assures "the integration of the sequences into a whole (self-awareness as internal representation), but also the differentiation of the whole into extended sequences (belief in the external world)" (*The Time-Image* 277). Thus the potential infinity of movement-images is governed by a horizon of thought whereby the commensurability of the interval and the whole represent time indirectly as succession in space. The commensurability of interval and whole also presents the identity of image and concept in the movement-image as its particular expression of how thought is immanent in the image. Deleuze calls the logic of association through rational links the law of the image, since it governs the sequencing of images through principles of contiguity or similitude. Integration and differentiation are the law of the concept, since together they define the relations of the whole. Movement expresses change in the whole as the integration of images into extendible sets; differentiation expresses the division of the whole into sets whose movement passes between sequences and their extensions. Together, these two "laws" define the classical image of thought, in which the plane of consistency of the cinematic movement-image is expressed as an open totality in movement whose will to power yields a model of the True as totalization. In this classical image we pass "naturally" from image to concept and back again; thought is commensurate with the dialectical expansion of the whole in a Hegelian vision of the rational unity of mind, world, and Image.

To say that the whole is the outside implies a different organization of images. Appealing as it does to the nonrepresentational and nonreferential powers of the concept, call this the force of the simulacral. In its primary definition, this outside is the force of time, whose incommensurability with space changes the function of the interval. There is no longer a rational interval assuring continuity in space and succession in time. Rather, the force of time produces a serialism organized by irrational divisions (*coupures irrationnels*) that force dissociation rather than an association of images—the division functions as a limit wherein the interval dividing sets or segments becomes autonomous, irreducible, and singular. It is interstitial and no longer forms part of any segment as the beginning of one or the end of another. In the transition to the time-image—no matter how gradual, rare, or indistinct—the definition of movement changes, as does the relation between image and thought. The plane of consistency of the time-image is best characterized by seriality: irrational divisions assure the incommensurability of interval and whole. Succession gives way to series because the interstice is a dissociative force; it "strings" images together only as disconnected spaces. The rational interval is a spatial conjunction since it belongs simultaneously to the end of one set and the beginning of the one that follows, but the irrational interstice is not spatial, nor does it form part of an image. Rather, it presents the force that unhinges images and sounds into disconnected series, which can no longer form a whole. The Idea of a direct image of time is a paradoxical construction, then. What the interstice gives is a nonspatial perception—not space but force, the force of time as change interrupting repetition with difference and parceling succession into series.

The plane of consistency of the time-image is marked by the "reign of incommensurables," and in this manner the movements of thought and the mental cartographies that trace them are fundamentally transformed and revalued. Time asserts its autonomy in the interstice with several consequences. Images, and images and sounds, are no longer conjoined by rational intervals but rather "relinked on to irrational cuts" (ré-enchaînent sur coupures irrationnelles) (The Time-Image 277); this is one of the noosigns of the time-image. Not that one image succeeds or is added to another. This montage construction might better be characterized as "differential," since sequences are formed not through linear succession in space and chronological succession in time but through the incommensurability of space and time reasserted in every irrational division. By the same token, the movements of thought are no longer represented "in" the movement of images, through either the commensurability of intervals and wholes or the open totality in movement. There is neither the integration of sequences into a whole, which promotes the representation of thought as an internal self-representation (memory, dream, fantasy), nor differentiation of the whole into a diegesis or believable world. Rather, the whole is the "outside." There is movement in the image, of course, which is given as an actual perception in space. But the differential relations "between" images and sounds are furrowed by a pure virtuality—the force of time. Time is always outside the image. It recedes from the image toward an absolute horizon, since it is incommensurable with space. Thought, too, "moves" only in incommensurable relations that recede toward an interiority deeper than the I can reach. For this reason, Deleuze writes,

There are no longer grounds for talking about a real or possible extension capable of constituting an external world: we have ceased to believe
in it, and the image is cut off from the external world. But the internalization or integration in a whole as consciousness of self has no less
disappeared. . . . This is why thought, as power which has not always existed, is born from an outside more distant than any external world, and,
as power which does not yet exist, confronts an inside, an unthinkable or
unthought, deeper than any internal world. . . . [There] is no longer any
movement of internalization or externalization, integration or differentiation, but a confrontation of an outside and an inside independent of
distance, this thought outside itself and this unthought within thought.
(*The Time-Image* 277–278, 362–363)

This is the second noosign of the time-image, whereby instead of commensurable relations between sets and wholes, or frame, shot, and montage, the
interstice produces nontotalizable and asymmetrical relations between the
inside and the outside. Logically, the outside is posited through any two incommensurable terms that come into contact independent of space. This is
the logic of the irrational interval, which is not a spatial figure since it does
not belong to any set nor can it be incorporated as part of a whole. By contrast,
in the cinematic movement-image the outside is the referent: a space with
which the image has both iconic and indexical relations and against which it
measures itself. The value of the interval is measured by a spatial commensurability where the whole is the open—a web unfolding horizontally through
relations of contiguity and continuity, and vertically through relations of differentiation followed by integration. Here the world is constituted as image,
since the image can expand to encompass any world with all the subjects and
objects in it. However, the time-image does not represent in this sense. As a
simulacral force, it neither presents an imaginary world complete unto itself
in which we are asked to believe, nor give us a transcendent perspective from
which the world should be judged as false or true, lacking or full. The outside is not space or the actual, but rather the virtual, which acts "from the
outside"—on another plane or in another dimension—as force or differentiation.
Irrational divisions are not spatial, nor are they images in the usual sense.
They open onto what is outside of space yet immanent to it: the anteriority of
time to space, or virtuality, becoming, the fact of returning for that which differs. Virtuality, or difference in itself as force, defines time as the Outside. This
force opens a line of variation in any image, sign, idea, or concept that attempts

to express it. Only on this basis can the cinema express not an image of thought, but rather, what Deleuze calls for in *Difference and Repetition*—thought without image.

The irrational division expresses the simulacral will to power of the direct image of time, where "thought has no other reason to function than its own birth, always the repetition of its own birth, secret and profound. . . . [The] image thus has as object the functioning of thought, and . . . the functioning of thought is also the real subject which brings us back to the images" (*The Time-Image* 165). The irrational division relates here to one last problem—how and in what ways thought is determinable with respect to the form or force of time—and thus to Deleuze's innovative reading of Kant and Kant's critique of the *cogito*. Kant's solution, according to Deleuze, is to define time as the immutable Form of everything that changes and moves. All that moves or changes is in time, but time itself neither changes nor moves. This does not mean that time is eternity. If so, we would be caught in the tautology of defining time by time. Rather it is "the form of that which is *not* eternal, the immutable form of change and movement."[60] Time is change, or the fact that the universe never stops moving, changing, and evolving.

Therefore, there are two perspectives on time: one which passively witnesses change without finality, the other which understands, through a transcendental synthesis, that what does not change is change itself. The form of time presumes a division of the subject into a passive Ego (*Moi*) that is in time and constantly changing, and an I (*Je*) that actively carries out a synthesis of time by continually dividing up the present, past, and future. When Deleuze asserts that "I am separated from myself by the form of time," he is arguing that the ego cannot constitute itself as a unique and active subject. Rather, it is a "passive ego which represents to itself only the activity of its own thought; that is to say, the *I*, as an Other which affects it" (*Kant's Critical Philosophy* ix). In Deleuze's reading of Kant, the form of time modulates continually between the synthetic act of the I and the ego to which this act is attributed such that

the only subjectivity is time, non-chronological time grasped in its foundation, and it is we who are internal to time, not the other way round. That we are in time looks like a commonplace, yet it is the highest paradox. Time is not the interior in us, but just the opposite, the interiority in

60. *Kant's Critical Philosophy*, trans. Hugh Tomlinson and Barbara Habberjam (Minneapolis: University of Minnesota Press, 1984), viii.

which we are, in which we move, live and change. . . . Subjectivity is never ours, it is time, that is, the soul or the spirit, the virtual. The actual is always objective, but the virtual is subjective: it was initially the affect, that which we experience in time; then time itself, pure virtuality which divides itself in two as affector and affected, 'the affection of self by self' as definition of time. (*The Time-Image* 82–83)

This is how Kant undermines Descartes's *cogito,* replacing it with a differential and simulacral force. Instead of thinking in the form of identity where *I* = *I*, Kant presents an *I* fractured by the multiple internal divisions of the passive syntheses of time. Descartes disingenuously conceals these divisions, as does most Western philosophy. While the *cogito* must assume it is present to itself in thought, what it predicates, the object of its thinking, must nevertheless always be divided from it by the form of time. This is why time cannot be known in itself. Once intuited it divides, branches, and slips away, the present falling back into the virtual space of memory, or giving way to a projected nondetermined future. This is the impersonal form of time in which the *cogito* can only place itself as a kind of quantum uncertainty. I contemplate thought, but within my self-reflection thought changes and keeps on changing; its movements are nonlocalizable. Is my thought in the ego or the I? It is, rather, in the division that constitutes them both in the impersonal form of time.

This division in the subject has profound epistemological consequences represented by what Deleuze calls the impower of thought (*l'impouvoir de la pensée*). Kant considered judgment as a power (*Kraft*), the ability to do work or to prepare the way for a synthesis, rather than as a mental faculty or capability (*Vermögen*). If the direct image of time is figured in the form of temporal paradox, the True can no longer be thought under the forms of the changeless, the self-identical, or the self-same. What used to be called the "laws" of thought (the principles of identity, of contradiction, and of the excluded middle) are effectively overthrown. Kant shrunk away from the consequences of his discovery in making judgment teleological. Later Nietzsche seized the opportunity. If the forms of truth are temporal, then we are freed from the reactive or passive position of "discovering" a preexisting truth. Instead, we are active and creative, inventing our world as we move through it. What Deleuze finds so attractive in the paradoxes of time is simultaneously Kantian and critical, and Nietzschean and inventive. What is most true and most immutable is that thought in relation to time is always changing. If we are willing to see truth in its historical and embattled forms, we are in the position of actively willing it.

The Kantian intuition of a *cogito* divided from itself by the impersonal form of time is also a picture of the time-image's expression of nontotalizable and asymmetrical relations between the inside and the outside. If there is no self-identical subject who could speak for the image or interpret it as a whole, if the complexity of the image itself can neither be reduced nor represented as a whole that could be contained in memory, then what does the time-image present in sensation? Only time, the impersonal form of time that divides the ego from the I and disjoins all forms of identity, in the subject or in the image, as a force of becoming. This is the ineluctable return of that which differs— difference in itself that returns from beyond any absolute horizon or from deeper than any interiority.

Here the psychological or dialectical automaton of the classical image of thought is displaced by a spiritual automaton, which is no longer an inferential machine where thoughts are deduced one from the other, or a physical force that renders thought identical with an image or Image. What the time-image contributes to the history of thought then is a powerlessness—in fact, a dispossession of thought in relation to the image—that is equivalent to the division of the subject by the pure form of time. The idea of movement is again subtly transformed here. Dispossession becomes a primary force rather than an effect, separate from a totality that would judge it as a simple lack. Cinema's harshest enemies have always disparaged this force in the image. Nonetheless, this is a power in the philosophical sense, where cinema confronts us with the highest problem. Cinema's most profound task is to unveil "this difficulty of being, this powerlessness at the heart of thought" (*The Time-Image* 166).

Deleuze's concept of the impower of thought is deeply influenced by Maurice Blanchot's reading of Antonin Artaud in *Le Livre à venir*. In Blanchot's reading, Artaud's idea is that cinema must rejoin the brain's most innermost reality. But this reality is not dialectical nor is it a whole, as Eisenstein believes, but rather a crack, a fissure, or a splitting. The cinema does not have the power to make us think the whole. Instead, it is a dissociative force producing a "figure of nothingness" or a "hole in appearances." Artaud's dissociative force is an unlinking of images, of images in relation to sound, of bodies in relation to voice, and of thought in relation to image. "In short," Deleuze writes, "it is the totality of cinema-thought relations that Artaud overturns: on the one hand there is no longer a whole thinkable through montage, on the other hand there is no longer an internal monologue utterable through image. . . . [If] it is true that thought depends on a shock which gives birth to it . . . it can only think one thing, *the fact that we are not yet thinking,* the powerlessness to think the whole and to think oneself, thought which is always fossilized, dislocated, collapsed. A being of thought which is always to come." (*The Time-Image* 167). This dissociative force is "a little time in the pure state," the impersonal form of time splitting the present in dissymmetrical jets between the past and future, whose noosigns are directed by the interstice or irrational division. Neither space nor the perception of space can show us this force in the image. Instead, we encounter a time anterior to space: an emptiness, a pure virtuality rendered by the incommensurability of perception in space and thought in time. This is the highest power of the false that cinema can express. Blanchot articulates most clearly a Heideggerianism that expresses the spiritual automaton of the time-image. What forces us to think is the impower of thought, emptiness, the nonpresence of a whole that could be thought.

Here we return to an earlier theme—of what inextricably unites plane and concepts, yet also separates them as the motor of thought's movements. The plane of immanence is to the concept as the unthought in thought, thought's *energeia* and blind spot, what moves or motivates its ceaseless search yet can never grant it calm harbor. The unthought within thought is the molten bedrock of every plane, the molecular and energetic movements trembling every substance. There is a fracture or division within thought that separates it from itself and holds it open, such that it will find no rest within any claim of identity, representation, or final reason. Following Foucault, Deleuze and Guattari call this immanence the intimacy of the Outside—"an outside more distant than any external world because it is an inside deeper than any internal world" (*What Is Philosophy?* 59)—neither object nor subject, but the continuous enfolding of one by the other as expressions of a single substance. "Perhaps this is the supreme act of philosophy," write Deleuze and Guattari, "not so much to think *THE* plane of immanence as to show that it is there, unthought in every plane, and to think it in this way as the outside and inside of thought, as the not-external outside and the not-internal inside—that which cannot be thought and yet must be thought. . . ." (59–60).

If the modern image of thought is fueled less by the model of the True than by the powers of the false or the impowers of thought, the question arises, how to evaluate a philosophy and its attendant concepts? If it were possible, evaluating planes of immanence would require attention to something like a philosophical environmentalism—the air one breathes, the water one drinks, the quality of the earth one stands upon. However, to experience the plane without concepts would incur a sort of philosophical madness, where one feels the earth's rotation and the vibrations of matter or flashes of energy rather than enjoying the stability, no matter how illusory, of a fixed perspective. And so how does one yield a perspective, experience crisis, or become homeless on a plane of immanence, and so commence to construct a philosophy?

An image of thought, or better, thought without image, is neither home nor harbor, but rather emerges in points of crisis and moments of anxiety and doubt. Philosophy is not a quest for certainty, but rather the improvisation and perfection of necessary navigational instruments through the creation of concepts, because the movements of thought always submit us to a certain violence with unpredictable changes of direction, or moments of delusion and unconsciousness where we wake to find ourselves on strange still-undiscovered islands. Unlike science, allied to a portrait of referential truth whose face emerges through the accumulation of data and the acquisition of instruments of ever greater resolution, creation in philosophy is inspired by a variety of different crises, many of which were recognized by Wittgenstein: self-doubt marked by the incessant acknowledgment of error, agitation inspired by the sudden recognition that one is drowning in the calm waters of illusion or self-delusion, or the daily confrontation with human folly. In each case, one realizes that philosophy has relinquished its critical force to give itself over to the forces of transcendence or lassitude—ideology, habit, religion, nihilism, or despair.

That the plane of immanence is characterized by infinite movement means that the relationship of thought to truth is full of ambiguity and mobile points of perspective. For this reason, what Deleuze and Guattari call the modern image of thought embraces a certain Nietzscheanism where philosophy is guided less by the will to truth than by an image of creation or self-creation. Call this the performativity of philosophy, but also a pragmatism in the sense that Richard Rorty avers that truth is always contextual, created and expressed from a singular plane of immanence that frames or sets the horizon for its presuppositions through a web of positive and negative features, welcoming certain components, problems, or questions and blocking others. Perhaps it is only after we have moved to another plane or projected a new context that we can evaluate which positive features have enabled thought to move forward, and which negative ones have detoured it into illusion or error (acknowledging here that the criteria and conditions of error are set by the plane and context as well), or blocked it outright. Nor is there a simple or unambiguous subject of truth in the modern image of thought. In place of the will to truth, Deleuze and Guattari write, "thought constitutes a simple 'possibility' of thinking without yet defining a thinker 'capable' of it and able to say 'I'" (*What Is*

Philosophy? 54–55). Neither a deictic marker nor point of enunciation, but rather a power or potential for thought on a presubjective plane, an empty space but not a void, waiting for concepts to occupy it.

And there are further hazards for our habitual image of a subject of knowledge, and they are intrinsic to our powers of thinking. Within the infinite movements of the plane of immanence, the possibility of having and expressing thought appears like eddies or pools out of whose regular rhythms and even contours concepts emerge as intensive, ordered series. But at any moment these pools may dissolve in new and powerful currents or be overwhelmed by tidal swells. Here we find an image common to Deleuze, Heidegger, and Blanchot in which our powers of thinking are both enabled and overwhelmed by violence or shock, which at one and the same time gives us the possibility of having and expressing thoughts, but which also undermines and disperses our power to say "I" and return us to the presubjective plane of infinite movements. After the acknowledgment that truth is created, and that thought is conditioned as presubjective potential on a plane of immanence before becoming the expression of an Idea or the acquisition of a concept, there still remains the impower or incapacity of thought, confronting us with the fact that we are still not yet thinking. To have thoughts, or to keep thought moving beyond the constraining rhythms of habit or stupidity while remaining open and receptive to the pure virtuality of the Event therefore requires a constant confrontation with a violence, of the unthought within thought that blocks it or leads it to madness, where thought advances only in fits and starts with cries and stuttering.

Here the task of the work of art is to open a line of flight that passes from the actual to the virtual by interrupting repetition with difference. Simulacra do not represent. Thought cannot confirm itself in an initiating image there. Rather, it forces us to think, if we are able, through the construction of Events. Events are immanent to every moment of time's passing yet remain both outside and in between the passage of time. Simulacra are better understood as heterocosmic forces rather than utopian worlds. Between each measure of time there is an infinite movement, so many possible worlds and immanent modes of existence, that we must recover from time's passing. The noosigns of the time-image are time's concepts in this respect. Time's direct image is not time in itself, but rather the force of virtuality and becoming, or what remains both outside of, yet in reserve and immanent to, our contemporary modes of existence.

The power of the Image is to express force, or the play of forces both flowing over and overflowing every figure or diagram, returning to us a sense of nonstratified life. The powers of becoming immanent to art also mean that there is a profound ethical component to every creative act, for every creative act is also a remapping of the world, a remaking of the world differently as well as an *agencement* creating new possibilities of Being. Interpretation and evaluation are not the only acts founding a philosophy of art and the humanities—there is also creation and experimentation. Every creative act, whether of art or the interpretation and evaluation of art, begins in a protest against routine, habit, and repetition, in dissatisfaction with a world as lived and in the present means for giving expression to existence. The creation or invention of a style, then, is always a deformation or deviation in the norms of expression, "creating a syntax that makes them pass into sensation, and which makes standard language stammer, tremble, cry out, or even sing—this is the style or 'tone,' the language of sensations, or a foreign language within language that summons forth a people to come. . . . The [artist] twists language, makes it vibrate, seizes and tears it in order to wrest the percept from perceptions, the affect from affections, and sensation from opinion—in view, one hopes, of the still missing people" (*What Is Philosophy?* 176, *166–167*).

Creation is thus fundamentally a heterocosmic force. Artists do not create for a community or a public; in the becoming of creative acts, they also create new powers of becoming, new possible modes of existence, for themselves and for that virtual community. The work of art is the midwife of a coming community, with no guarantees, of course, that a people will ever answer the call. If works of art are monuments in Deleuze's sense, events that conserve or preserve sensations in a *durée* no matter how long or short, they must interrupt or overflow repetition, not by reinvoking the past but by amplifying attentiveness to the infinite reserve of new becomings in the present, confiding "to the ear of the future the persistent sensations that embody the event: the constantly renewed suffering of men and women, their re-created protestations, their constantly renewed struggle. Will this all be in vain because suffering is eternal and revolutions do not survive their victory? . . . The victory of a revolution is immanent and consists in the new bonds it installs between people, even if these bonds last no longer than the revolution's fused material and quickly give way to division and betrayal" (*What Is Philosophy?* 176–177).

Philosophy and art share powers of becoming in ways that invite comparisons between conceptual personae and aesthetic figures. *What Is Philosophy?* is itself a testament to an inherent aesthetic dimension in philosophy, of philosophical style modeled in spatial and temporal figures as well as the figural force of language. And concepts take form, no doubt, in relation to Ideas and ways of seeing and apprehending embodied in aesthetic figures. The networks of passage between philosophy and art are a closely interwoven skein, yet Deleuze insists that their powers of becoming are distinct. Sensory becoming defines acts of becoming-other, where one thing becomes another in series of qualitative differentiations and associations; conceptual becoming is an act where the ordinary event feigns or camouflages its powers. The event that lies dormant, the sleeping giant in every passing present, is a heterogeneity embodied in an absolute form, while sensation is an alterity engaged in expressive matter. If and when art expresses or sustains a sensory event, it engages the virtual in ways distinct from the absolute Event. Art does not actualize the Event, but rather incorporates or incarnates it—it gives the Event flesh or makes of it a world. The Event in itself is the reality of the virtual, of the deepest forms of time as eternal recurrence and of nature as a universal Whole in a state of continuous becoming—a thought of time and of change before expression, reference, or sensory apprehension. Aesthetic universes, however, are reserves of the possible, the alternative, or the undetermined event. In this respect, they are deeply ethical as preserves of nondetermined choice. Through art we reassert not only the possibility of a new mode of existence but also experience the multiplicity of possible worlds, of divagations, forking paths, and unthought alternatives lying dormant in our present perception and lived duration.

Here, without any reference to the earlier books, *What Is Philosophy?* gives one of the best and most thought-provoking accounts of the time-image in its purest form. Any measurable succession in a state of affairs can be expressed as a suite of instants, like measured steps following one from the other, and these steps may be expressed in a function. To the extent that the cinematic movement-image is formed from an idea of time as empirical succession, and thus forms an image of time as a suite of instants in space, it is expressed as the functional equivalent of science's quantitative view of time. But what occurs between each step, no matter how small or rapid, is a time or duration that no process of actualization can completely absorb. This is why Deleuze and Guattari characterize the virtual as an *"entre-temps,"* or between-time. This is something that art or philosophy can apprehend better than science. The entire project of Deleuze's cinema books unfolds from this fundamental intuition of two dimensions of time, though one is deeper, more profound than the other. One sort of time unfolds in a succession of actualized, spatial instants, but the other expresses a peculiar kind of virtuality—that of becoming, or the infinite reserve of nondetermined change. This distinction between the movement-image and the time-image is a direct expression of the relation between time and *entre-temps*. This is not an allegory or example, homology or metaphor, but rather pure expression actualized in different though related forms—the percepts and affects of art, the concepts of philosophy. Filmic expression does not exemplify concepts or provide examples for philosophy; as artful *expression* it *is* philosophy, or rather, a becoming-philosophy tending toward conceptual formation. As expression, one of art's many happy occupations is to be a friend to philosophy, and to aid in philosophical becoming. The cinema books do not present a theory of cinema, where philosophy serves to form a new context, framework, or vocabulary for explaining cinema; rather, they give expression to an active philosophy immanent to the Image—a philosophy of the Image given in or through images.

Spiritual automata are thus the expression of a power, both a power of thinking and of a preconceptual subject (conceptual persona) capable (or not) of having thoughts. And this is why Deleuze and Guattari write that "it is possible that the problem now concerns the one who believes in the world, and not even in the existence of the world but in its possibilities of movements and intensities, so as once again to give birth to new modes of existence, closer to animals and rocks. It may be that believing in this world, in this life, becomes our most difficult task, or the task of a mode of existence still to be discovered on our plane of immanence today." (*What Is Philosophy?* 74–75). That thinker within me that is the unthought of my thought is also a power of transformation, indeed the power to transform life by revealing new lines of variation in our current ways of thinking and modes of existence. To believe again in life is to believe again in the transformative powers of life and the possibility of creating new modes of existence. However, we could neither invent nor choose new modes of existence if the force of time as eternal recurrence, becoming, or change did not undermine identity with difference. Differentiation maintains an opening to the future from which we derive our powers to affect life and to be affected by it. The goal of the direct time-image and other forms of art, whether successful or not, is to awaken these powers in us. To become-other, we need an image to awake the other in us as what yet remains unthought. There is no higher task for philosophy, or art.

12. The World, Time

> I want to fix my mind on what I mean by absolute or ethical value. And there,
> in my case, it always happens that the idea of one particular experience
> presents itself to me which therefore is, in a sense, my experience *par*
> *excellence*. . . . I believe the best way of describing it is to say that when I have it
> *I wonder at the existence of the world.* And I am then inclined to use such
> phrases as "how extraordinary that anything should exist" or "how
> extraordinary that the world should exist."
>
> —Ludwig Wittgenstein, "Lecture on Ethics"

The figural force of the concept is complimented by an ethical component wherein the multiplicity of the concept as a fragmentary open whole raises complex questions of time and of our relations with the Other. If Kant's critique of the *cogito* discovers that "I is an other," that the *cogito* is incapable of self-representation apart from its internal division by the pure form of time, then another important question or problem presents itself. The impower of thought may be considered a positive and creative force, but it also initiates moments of profound ethical crisis that potentially shatter our adherence to habitual modes of existence. In the relation of Concept to Image, how do we negotiate these crises, which are less epistemological than ethical?

Through the concept, we seek relief from a mental chaos or homelessness that continually threatens, stalks, or tries to reabsorb it. There is a kind of narration or dramaturgy of the concept that emerges in scenes of puzzlement, conflict, terror, anxiety, or surprise. The components of this drama are drawn from worlds both actual and possible. One begins from a field of experience taken to be a real world, not from the standpoint of a subject, but rather as a simple condition of existence and designation—there is or that is. But from within this simple field of experience, which may be the unacknowledged background of routine or quotidian experience, difference may erupt with sudden violence. The Other that emerges to shatter this calm surface is neither a subject nor an object, but rather the apprehension of a possible world, terrifying because unknown and unexpected. This possible world is virtual, which does not make it unreal, but rather more like something on the way to actualization, a potentiality for existence seeking expression: "The Other," write Deleuze and Guattari, "is, first of all, this existence of a possible world" (*What Is Philosophy?* 17, 22). And this possible world is also a self-positing reality with its own terms of existence conditioned by its virtuality as the expression of an Event, the impowers of thought, or contact with an Outside that cannot be thought; this is "a vital relation with the Other that one had thought excluded from pure thought." (4, 9).

Wittgenstein and Deleuze: no two philosophers could be further apart in style. Yet there is a profound connection that runs between them in the ideas that restlessness and homelessness are the condition of thought, and that what matters most to philosophy can only be shown, not possessed or expressed. And if it could be expressed, it would be likely to be misunderstood.

At the same time, what makes the other alien to me, or the world strange to me, also presents the possibility of what Charles Taylor calls transforming myself under a new concept. Here Deleuze emits a phrase that might come equally from Wittgenstein or Taylor: "we speak the same language, and yet I do not understand you" (*What Is Philosophy?* 110). In turn, one of the characteristic philosophical acts is self-estrangement; another is to invite one's language to become infected or deflected and transformed by alien vocabularies. When philosophy takes on the appearance of "nonsense," whether in Wittgenstein's sense or Deleuze's, this is often the sign of the emergence of a new style, syntax, or concept, which may be taken as unfathomable or perplexing. A common element of all of the language games of theory has been an initiating experience of disorientation, conflict, and existential crisis. It may yet be that the will to theory is expressed always as a problem—of a condition, world, or existence that has become, in all senses of the term, problematic. (Perhaps what so dismayed Herder, Kant, or Hegel in the genre of German aesthetic "theories" exemplified by Sulzer, Riedel, and others was the orderliness and calm of their pedagogy, their blissful ignorance of the violence of thought that philosophy contends with.) But philosophy does not respond by offering concepts as solutions to a problem, for philosophical problems are never completely resolved, but rather only expressed in new ways. This is another way of thinking of theory as an intermediate term or process—it is always in the middle or in the midst of becoming—and at the same time, the laying out of a concept through its components is something like surveying a terrain and laying out guide markers to orient thought, to keep it moving in certain directions rather than finding a point of rest.

Deleuze and Guattari characterize the apprehension of a possible world as a face surging out of the darkness and the mental chaos of thought. But is it not better characterized, more generally and simply, as an Image? All I have been trying to say in the previous pages is that for all of its abstraction, Deleuze's characterization of the image in the cinema books exemplifies conceptual creation in often-striking ways. The borders between philosophy and art are extremely porous in that the movement and creation of concepts is immanent to the image and its creativeness, and not something separate. If Deleuze sees conceptual creation in the movement- and time-images, this is not simple analogy. Rather, in turning to cinema Deleuze wants to show the ways in which conceptual creation is immanent to image and movement in all their luminescence and materiality, but at the same time the dramaturgy of the concept, and the powerlessness of thought to which conceptual creation responds, is also the expression of an ethical desire to create new modes of existence.

Every concept takes form, then, in expressions that sketch an image of a possible world. (This assertion is related to Wittgenstein's version of the limits of language, and of moving forward in relation to those limits in recognizing the capacity of language for showing and designating, or of moving in series from one "picture" to another as those pictures draw us to them, or fail us.) The emergence of the Other, or of the Image, always assumes as its precondition the determination of a sensate world, an actual world of possible experience given in perceptions, behaviors, and forces both active and reactive. The Other is a possible world emerging in an Image capable of expressing it, through the medium, as it were, of a language that could give form and contour to that Image while establishing the movement and links that enable it to form expressions by connecting to other images. The three fundamental components of the concept, then, are a possible world, a sensible Figure or image, and actual language or expression. Within and across all three components there is a constant passage between the actual and the virtual, the existent and the possible, commensurate with the concept's figurability, multiplicity, openness, and fragmentation, as well as a kind of sensation of the concept from multiple temporal perspectives: first, the apprehension of a future anterior as potential or possibility; second, a contour or figure that gives a present Image to that future in terms of its forms, powers, and possibilities of expression; and finally, a real or actual language through which the concept is expressed and into which it passes before returning to renew itself.

The problem raised here is how to evaluate the ethical powers of the Image. At the beginning of the epilogue to his *Theory of Film,* Siegfried Kracauer asks: "What is the good of film experience?"[61] The phrasing of the question clarifies what it means to bring ethics and cinema together as a philosophical problem. Kracauer does not want to know if a particular film or filmmaker is "ethical," nor is the question the basis for making moral judgments of art works and their makers. He asks, rather, how do we evaluate our *experience* of

61. (New York: Oxford University Press, 1960), 285.

the movies, meaning in what ways do the movies offer themselves as a medium for an interrogation of ourselves, of our relationship to the world and to other beings? In other words, how do moving images and other forms of art solicit and sustain the possibility of ethical thought?

Aesthetics and ethics do not make an obvious pairing, much less film and moral reasoning. In 1960 Kracauer is among the first to offer an explicitly ethical question to film theory. In so doing, he places the study of film along some of the most ancient lines of philosophical reasoning, which bring us back around to arguments I first set out at the beginning of *Elegy for Theory*. From at least the fourth century BCE, the activity of philosophy has been characterized by two fundamental questions: How do I know, and how shall I live? The latter is the most self-evidently ethical question. Yet how can the quality of one's thought be separated from the choice of a mode of existence? Both questions demand a reflexive examination of self, in its possibility of knowing itself and others, and in its openness or lack of openness to change. What links philosophy today to its most ancient origins are the intertwining projects of evaluating our styles of knowing and examining our modes of existence and their possibilities of transformation. In this way, an ethics is distinct from the usual sense of morality. Morals refer ordinarily to a transcendental system of values to which we conform, or against which we are found lacking. An ethics is an immanent set of reasoned choices. In ethical expression, we evaluate our current mode of existence, seeking to expand, change, or abandon it in the effort to achieve another way of living and another form of community. Inspiring an individual to choose a mode of existence embodied in a community, real or imagined, philosophy thus entails the expression and justification of this existential choice and its representation of the world. Therefore, *philosophein* is, simultaneously, expression and existential choice—the medium and idiom of a life.

Gilles Deleuze never devoted a book exclusively to ethics. Yet the two philosophers with whom he felt the closest allegiances, Baruch Spinoza and Friedrich Nietzsche, are importantly connected to the history of moral reasoning, and his books and repeated references to these philosophers mark his frequent examination of ethical questions. Deleuze's most provocative comments on ethics, however, appear late in his work, specifically in *The Movement-Image* and *The Time-Image*.[62]

62. The ethical arguments of *The Time-Image* in particular are also taken up in interesting ways in *What Is Philosophy?* I comment further on this relation in the concluding chapter of *Gilles Deleuze's Time Machine*, 194–210.

Here an interesting question detours our path. Why is film so important as the companion or exemplification for ethical self-examination? Indeed, the idea that art should inspire ethical inquiry marks the greatest distance between ourselves and the philosopher-citizens of Periclean Athens. At the same time, it is also one of the clearest signposts of philosophical modernity. In twentieth-century philosophy, especially in its Anglo-American and analytic incarnations, ethics has taken a back seat, indeed has been sent to the back of the bus by the more strident emphasis on logic and epistemology, an attitude forcefully summarized in Quine's insistence that the philosophy of science is philosophy enough.

The turn to film as an important site of ethical interrogation is thus doubly curious. And if there is something that can be called film philosophy today, moral reasoning persists as one of its most powerful defining activities. Undoubtedly, this is due to the influence of Stanley Cavell as the contemporary philosopher most centrally concerned with the problem of ethics in film and philosophy, above all through his examination of philosophical responses to the dilemmas of skepticism and his characterization of an Emersonian moral perfectionism. However, in Cavell's Emersonian ethics there are also curious and powerful echoes of Deleuze's Nietzschean and Bergsonian perspectives on cinema, wherein concepts of movement and time are related as the expression of belief in the world and its powers of transformation. This may appear to be an odd couple. But I am haunted by the idea of a dialogue, as if in a real conversation but between partners who seem only dimly aware of one another, in which Deleuze's cinema books, published in 1983 and 1985, respond to Cavell's *The World Viewed* (1971) and *Pursuits of Happiness* (1981), and where *Contesting Tears* (1996) and *Cities of Words* (2004) echo some of the most provocative thinking in *The Movement-Image* and *The Time-Image*.

Both space and time are lacking here to develop all the implications of this missed philosophical friendship. It is worth noting, however, that one important bridge between Deleuze's and Cavell's thought on cinema and moral reasoning is their mutual interest in Nietzsche. Another is their original way of asking ethical questions in ontological contexts. Though Cavell uses the word frequently and Deleuze rarely, both evaluate ontology as a particular approach to Being. This is not the being or identity of film or what identifies film as art, but rather the ways of being that art provokes in us—or more deeply, how film and other forms of art express for us or return to us our past, current, and future states of being. Also, in both philosophers the ethical relation is inseparable from our relationship to thought. For how we think, and whether we sustain a relation to thought or not, is bound up with our choice of a mode of existence and our relations with others and to the world.

There is also an important contrast with Cavell. Part of the difficulty of Deleuze's thought has to do with his choice to ignore or circumvent the dilemmas of skepticism and its characterizations of the self in relation to being, the world, and to others. These are central features of the philosophical culture most familiar to us, and it is disarming to consider seriously a thinker for whom the great difficulties of relating subject and object seem to have been completely dispelled or overcome. Indeed, throughout his career Deleuze turned consistently to philosophers for whom the division of the thinking subject from the world was ontologically irrelevant; hence, his recovery of a path alternative to Descartes, leading from Spinoza and Nietzsche to Henri Bergson.

In Deleuze the fundamental ethical choice is to believe in this world and its powers of transformation. How does his avoidance or circumvention of the history of skepticism and Cartesian rationalism inform this question? Although Deleuze was not known for his love of philosophical systems, Alberto Gualandi has astutely recognized his commitment to two principles, which may be considered the basis of his ethics as well as his more general philosophy. The first is Spinoza's pure ontology, or doctrine of the univocity of Being. For Spinoza, there is no division between humanity and nature, but only one absolute and unique substance for all that exists—all attributes and identities are only different manners of being for this substance, or different modalities of its expressiveness. As Gualandi explains, "The principle of univocal Being affirms the absolute *immanence* of thought in the world as it exists, as well as the categorical refusal of any form of thought *transcending* the Being of things in whatever form of the supersensible. For Deleuze as well as Spinoza, the intuition of the univocity of being is the highest intellectual expression of love for all that exists."[63] This doctrine of a single expressive substance inspires a first ethical principle: the choice to believe in *this* world, the world in which we exist now, alive and changing, and not some transcendent or ideal world. This is also an affirmation of thought's relation to the world, as the movements of thought in relation to those of matter differ only in their ways of expressing a common being or substance.

The second principle is that of Becoming, wherein the univocity of Being is characterized by its relation to movement, time, and change. Here substance

---

63. *Deleuze* (Paris: Les Belles Lettres, 1998), 18–19, my translation. See also Alain Badiou, *Deleuze: La clameur de l'Être* (Paris: Hachette, 1997).

is connected to force as self-differentiation, producing a universe of continual metamorphosis characterized by Bergson as creative evolution. Becoming is the principle of time as force, and time is the expressive form of change: the fact that the universe never stops moving, changing, and evolving, and that no static picture could ever be adequate to this flux of universal self-differentiation. In this, time is something like a metaphysical constant in Deleuze. The highest expression of this force is not Kantian, however, but what Nietzsche called eternal recurrence.

Deleuze offers an original reading of the concept of eternal recurrence. In fact, it is the key element of his philosophy of difference, as well as his ethics, linking the univocity of Being and the force of Becoming. In *Nietzsche and Philosophy* Deleuze asks, "What is the being of that which becomes, of that which neither starts nor finishes becoming? *Returning is the being of that which becomes.*"[64] What does Being speak of in one voice? It does not sing of identity, but rather of recurrence as change and differentiation, of a "returning itself that constitutes being insofar as it is affirmed of becoming and of that which passes. It is not some one thing which returns but rather returning itself is the one thing which is affirmed of diversity or multiplicity. In other words, identity in the eternal return does not describe the nature of that which returns but, on the contrary, the fact of returning for that which differs" (48). What returns eternally is not the identity of the same, but the force of difference or differentiation. What Being speaks of recurrently is difference from itself.

The ethical stance in the cinema books is fundamentally Nietzschean. (The ontological passes through Spinoza and Bergson.) Deleuze characterizes a Nietzschean ethics as encompassing two related activities, which are now familiar to us: interpretation and evaluation. "To interpret," Deleuze wrote earlier, "is to determine the force which gives sense to a thing. To evaluate is to determine the will to power which gives value to a thing" (*Nietzsche and Philosophy* 54). "Interpretation" would relate here to Deleuze's theory of film semiotics, to the logical relations between sets and wholes, and to the question of noosigns and spiritual automata. It also relates back, of course, to his idea of art as preconceptual expression. In turn, evaluation is central to the ethical project of Deleuze's cinema books. What philosophy must evaluate in any expression, including aesthetic expression, is its possibilities for life and experimentation in life. This is another important link between Nietzsche, Spinoza, and Bergson in Deleuze's account. Both Spinoza and Nietzsche distinguish

64. Trans. Hugh Tomlinson (New York: Columbia University Press, 1983), 48.

between morality and ethics. Morality involves sets of constraining rules that judge actions and intentions against transcendent or universal values. An ethics evaluates expression according to the immanent mode of existence or possibilities of life it implies. The ethical choice for Deleuze, then, is whether the powers of change are affirmed and harnessed in ways that value life and its openness to change, or whether we disparage life in *this* world in fealty to moral absolutes. Do we affirm life and remain open to its powers of continuous, qualitative self-transformation, or do we maintain an image of thought whose movements are stopped or frozen?

To evaluate modes of existence—in which we choose to believe, or on which we place our bets—does not mean comparing them qualitatively or judging them with respect to abstract values or criteria. Criteria for evaluation must remain immanent to the life examined, with respect to its own possibilities for producing new movements or intensities. "A mode of existence is good or bad," write Deleuze and Guattari, "noble or vulgar, complete or empty, independently of Good and Evil or any transcendent value: there are never any criteria other than the tenor of existence, the intensification of life" (*What Is Philosophy?* 74).

To evaluate is to ask, What mode of existence is willed in a given expression? One must go beyond the transcendent moral opposition of good and evil, but this does not mean relinquishing judgments of good and bad as ethical distinctions. Life should not be judged. But the will to power that informs or characterizes a mode of existence may be evaluated as good or bad, noble or base. From Nietzsche's vitalist perspective, all is a question of force, and ethics involves characterizing forces by evaluating the qualities of their will to power. For example, there are fatigued or exhausted forces that can be quantitatively powerful, but which no longer know how to transform themselves through the variations they can affect or receive. Deleuze finds this will to power often expressed in the films of Orson Welles—Nietzschean filmmaker par excellence—where characters such as Bannister in *Lady from Shanghai* or Hank Quinlan in *Touch of Evil* are the bodily expressions of a certain impotence: "that is, that precise point where the 'will to power' is nothing but a will-to-dominate, a being for death, which thirsts for its own death, as long as it can pass through that of others" (*The Time-Image* 140, 183).

Here force finds a center that coincides with death. These are characters who only know how to destroy or kill, before destroying themselves. This is the mode of existence of *ressentiment,* characteristic of the men of vengeance. And no matter how great the forces these characters exercise or represent, they are exhausted and incapable of transformation. This spirit of revenge is often paired in Welles's films with a blind will to truth as transcendent moral judgment. Thus Quinlan is paired with Vargas, or Iago with Othello. The latter are "truthful men" who judge life in the name of higher values:

> They . . . take themselves to be *higher men*, these are higher men who claim to judge life by their own standards, by their own authority. But is this not the same spirit of revenge in two forms: Vargas, the truthful man who invokes the laws for judging; but also his double, Quinlan, who gives himself the right to judge without law; Othello, the man of duty and virtue, but also his double, Iago, who takes revenge by nature and perversion? This is what Nietzsche called the stages of nihilism, the spirit of revenge embodied in various figures. Behind the truthful man, who judges life from the perspective of supposedly higher values, there is the sick man, "the man sick with himself," who judges life from the perspective of his sickness, his degeneration and his exhaustion. And this is perhaps better than the truthful man, because a life of sickness is still life, it contrasts life with death, rather than contrasting it with "higher values" . . . Nietzsche said: behind the truthful man, who judges life, there is the sick man, sick of life itself. . . . The first is an idiot and the second is a bastard. They are, however, complementary as two figures of nihilism, two figures of the will to power. (*The Time-Image* 140–141, *184*)

Ethics, however, is not a question of passing judgment on these figures as if from some higher moral ground. Following Nietzsche, Deleuze (and Welles) want, rather, to do away with the system of judgment to evaluate modes of existence in their relation to life. "[It] is not a matter of judging life in the name of a higher authority," Deleuze writes, "which would be the good, the true; it is a matter, on the contrary, of evaluating every being, every action and passion, even every value, in relation to the life which they involve. Affect as immanent evaluation, instead of judgment as transcendent value." (*The Time-Image* 141).

Going "beyond good and evil" does not mean renouncing ideas of good and bad, or in Nietzsche's parlance, noble and base. What is base is an exhausted, descendent, and degenerating life, especially when it seeks to propagate itself. But the noble is expressed in a blossoming, ascendant life, capable of transforming itself in cooperation with the forces it encounters, composing with them an ever-growing power, "always increasing the power to live, always opening new 'possibilities'" (*The Time-Image* 141). There is no more "truth" in one life than the other: there is only becoming, descendent or ascendant, and life's becoming is the power of the false, a noble will to power. "False" here is not opposed to the "true," but rather allied to an aesthetic or artistic will, the will to create. The base will to power is the degenerative becoming of an exhausted life with its destructive and dominating will. But the noble will to power is characterized by a certain generosity and openness; it is an artistic will, the becoming of an ascendant life that creates new possibilities and experiments with new modes of existence. If becoming is the power of the false, then the good, the generous, or the noble is what raises the false to its highest creative or transformative powers—a becoming-artist. If there is exhaustion in this aesthetic life, it is put in service to what is reborn from life through metamorphosis and creation. "It makes of becoming a protean Being," Deleuze writes, "rather than hastening it, from the height of a uniform and fixed identity, towards non-being. These are two states of life, opposed at the heart of an immanent becoming, and not an authority that would pose itself as superior to becoming in order to judge or dominate life, thus exhausting it. What Welles sees in Falstaff and Don Quixote is the 'goodness' of life in itself, a strange goodness that carries the living toward creation. It is in this sense that one can speak of an authentic or spontaneous Nietzscheanism in Welles" (*The Time-Image* 142, 185–186).

The Nietzschean moral universe defines an ontology of descent and ascent, destruction and creation, a base will to power fueled by *ressentiment* and the will to truth, and a creative or artistic will that affirms life and its powers of transformation while seeking out possibilities for enhancing these powers and this life. Between these two wills lies the deepest ethical problem: the problem of choosing a mode of existence defined by the possibility of choice.[65]

The problem of the choice of a mode of existence first occurs in the pages of *The Movement-Image* devoted to "lyrical abstraction," a style found principally in the films of Robert Bresson and Carl Theodor Dreyer. Deleuze is writing here, first, of the qualities and powers of affect in the image, especially in the treatment of light. This affection-image is distinguished from other types of cinematic movement-images through its virtuality or potentiality. In this, the affection-image is unlike action-images. The latter are caught up in chains of causality—or what Deleuze calls "real connections"—and are always expressively related to succession, as well as sets of actions and

65. This problem is explored in depth in Ronald Bogue's superb essay, "To Choose to Choose—To Believe in This World," in *Afterimages of Gilles Deleuze's Film Philosophy*, ed. D. N. Rodowick (Minneapolis: University of Minnesota Press, 2009), 115–132.

reactions rebounding between objects and persons. The action-image is thus characterized as a sensorimotor whole, bound up in an organic representation that believes in the representability of the world for a perceiving subject, as well as the unity of subject and world. Related to C. S. Peirce's category of "First-ness," or pure presignifying quality, affection-images instead present "virtual conjunctions": "There one finds pure qualities or singular potentialities—pure 'possibles,' as it were" (*The Movement-Image* 102, *145*). These qualities are lu-minescent and affective. They are possibilities for meaning and emotion ex-pressed not in a determined and meaning-laden space, but in an "any-space-whatever" (*espace quelconque*). They are ready to act or to signify, but one does not yet know in what direction or with what meaning. They are the virtual expression of choices yet to be accomplished.

How does the expression of choice correspond to the compositional logic of lyrical abstraction? Deleuze contrasts this style with German expressionism, whose approach to chiaroscuro defines a gothic world where the struggle of shadow and light submerges the contours of things in a nonorganic life. Light and darkness collude here, prolonging the anticipation of a universal dread. But in lyrical abstraction, light and darkness alternate, thus expressing "an alternative between a given state of things and a possibility or virtuality that overtakes them. . . . In effect, what seems to us essential to lyrical abstraction is that the spirit is not caught up in a struggle, but rather is beset by an alterna-tive" (*The Movement-Image* 112–113, *158–159*).

What lyrical abstraction exemplifies in the construction of any-space-whatevers is scenarios of undetermined choice. Deleuze turns here to Pascal and Kierkegaard as emblematic of a new approach to ethics in modern phi-losophy, where moral dilemmas are less a matter of selecting from a limited set of alternatives—the lesser evil or the greater good—than the expression of the mode of existence of the one who chooses. The first case means persuad-ing oneself of the absence of choice or remaining in ignorance of the power to choose, either because one believes that one course of action is morally neces-sary (this is my duty, or this confirms to an ideal of the Good), or that the situa-tion presents no viable alternatives, or that one is condemned by an inescapable drive or desire. What Deleuze calls "spiritual determination," however, presents the possibility of choosing a way of life along with the philosophical reasoning that accompanies it. Here the essence of moral reasoning is awareness of the choice between choosing or not choosing. Deleuze characterizes this aware-ness as an extreme moralism that opposes morality, and a faith that opposes religion, exemplified by Pascal's wager:

If I am conscious of choosing, there are, therefore, already choices I can no longer make and modes of existence I can no longer pursue, which are all of those I followed in convincing myself that "there was no choice." Pascal's wager says nothing else: the alternation of terms is indeed the affirmation of the existence of God, its denial, and its suspension (doubt, uncertainty). But the spiritual alternative is something else—it is between the mode of existence of one who "wagers" that God exists and the mode of existence of one who gambles on non-existence or who does not want to bet. According to Pascal, only the first is conscious of the possibility of choosing; the others are only able to choose in ignorance of the choices confronting them. In sum, choice as spiritual determination has no other object than itself: I choose to choose, and in this act I exclude every choice made in the mode of not having a choice. (*The Movement-Image* 114, *161*)

From Pascal to Bresson, and Kierkegaard to Dreyer, Deleuze identifies an ethical typology of characters whose moral choices typify different modes of existence that swing from belief in the inescapability of a moral path to those who choose the possibility of choice. Of the former, Deleuze describes three types of characters and modes of existence. First there are the "white" men of moral absolutes, of God and Virtue—the perhaps tyrannical or hypocritical guardians of religious or moral order, such as the priest-judges of Dreyer's *La Passion de Jeanne d'Arc*. There are then the grey men of uncertainty or vacillation, like the protagonists of Dreyer's *Vampyr* or Bresson's *Lancelot du lac* or *Pickpocket*. Third, there are creatures of evil and the blackness of drives: Hélène's vengefulness in *Les Dames du bois de Boulogne;* Gérard's wickedness in *Au Hasard Balthazar;* the thievery of *Pickpocket* and Yvonne's crimes in *L'Argent*. These are all instances of false choice or decisions made from denying that there is or may still be a choice.

Here, Deleuze's reading of lyrical abstraction is close to the ethical interpretation of Nietzsche's eternal return. We are not caught by the absolute values of darkness and light, or even the indecisiveness of grey. Rather, the possibility of spiritual determination, indeed what Cavell might call moral perfectionism, is a choice not to be defined by what is chosen, "but by the power choosing possesses of being able to start again at each instant, to restart itself, and to affirm itself of itself, by putting all the stakes back into play each time. And even if this choice means sacrificing the character, this is a sacrifice made in full knowledge that it will recur each time, and for all times" (*The Movement-Image* 115, *162*).

This is an image figuring an authentic choice in and of consciousness of the power to choose. To each character and image there corresponds an affect. For the white, the dark, and the grey, affects are actualized in an established order or disorder (moral absolutism, indecisiveness, or tragic destiny). But authentic choice "raises affect to its pure power or potential, as in Lancelot's courtly love, but also embodies and carries out this potential so powerfully as to release in it that which will not let itself be actualized, and which overwhelms its realization (eternal recurrence)" (115–116, *163*). (And there is yet a fifth type: the innocent embodied by the donkey in *Au Hasard Balthazar*: the holy fool who is not in a state of choosing, and who cannot know the effect of humanity's choosing, or not choosing.)

The problem of choice is presented in the affection-image by a certain relationship to light, a fluctuation of light. It is an image that solicits thought and draws us to a space of moral reasoning. Expressionism thus conveys, for Deleuze, a space determined by the alternation of terms, each of which compels an inescapable choice, in fact, a nonchoice. White-Black-Grey:

> white marks our duty or power; black, our impotence or thirst for evil; grey, our uncertainty, restlessness, or indifference. . . . [But] only one other implied that we choose to choose, or that we were conscience of choice. . . . We have reached a philosophical space [*espace spirituel*] where what we choose is no longer distinct from choice itself. Lyrical abstraction is defined by the adventure of light and white. But the episodes of this adventure mean, first, that the white that imprisons light alternates with the black where it stops, and then light is liberated in an alternative, which restores to us the white *and* the black. We have traveled, without moving, from one space to another, from a physical to a philosophical space of experimentation (or metaphysics). (*The Movement-Image* 117, *164–165*)

This passage already anticipates the problems raised by modern cinema in *The Time-Image*. The organic representation of the movement-image is based on connections that are rational as well as real. The term "rational," as I have already explained, indicates a formal relation that assures the continuity of shots within each segment, the spatial contiguity of one segment to another, and the dialectical unity of parts within the whole of the film. But these rational connections also have an ethical dimension—they are expressive of a will to truth. They express belief in the possibility and coherence of a complete and truthful representation of the world in images, and of the world in relation to thought, that is extendible in a dialectical unity encompassing image, world, and subject—hence Sergei Eisenstein's belief in the utopia of an intellectual cinema and of a direct relation between image and thought.

In Deleuze's account, however, modern cinema is inaugurated by a crisis in the action-image, and a corresponding crisis in belief. This crisis is profoundly related to the dilemma of skepticism, though Deleuze's conception of the history of cinema in relation to ontological and moral reasoning differs significantly from Cavell's. In its purest form, the movement-image, or the absolute plane of immanence, defines a world where skepticism is absent or irrelevant. This is a world defined by Spinoza's pure ontology of one unique substance, or Bergson's world of universal change and variation based on the equivalence of matter and light, and memory and matter, in a world of open creation. But from this world there emerges the *cinematic* movement-image, which, in believing itself to have overcome skepticism in the form of an identity between image and thought, nonetheless perpetuates the division of subject and object as a problem. Thus the organic form of the cinematic movement-image believes in the representability of the world for a knowing subject, but in the form of a will to truth—a separation and rejoining of subject and object. Sergei Eisenstein's theories remain the most powerful visions of a cinematic movement-image that forges a dialectical unity of subject and world through cinematic representation—the utopia of a truthful representation founded on the laws of a nonindifferent nature.[66] And indeed this is a "white" theory where all is subsumed to the dialectics of nature, and choice is no longer a possibility.

It is important to emphasize here that the purest form of the cinematic movement-image is rare. The logic of affection-images and the expressiveness of any-space-whatevers demonstrate that the action-image is, rather, in a continuous state of crisis or struggle with the essential movements of the world and of cinema, where time is defined not as space, but rather as force, the Open, or the virtual—the eternally recurring potentiality for new creation in each passing present. Similarly, there is no clear historical break between the movement-image and the time-image, for the direct image of time is an ever-renewable possibility recurring throughout the history of cinema, like an un-

---

66. See Eisenstein, *Nonindifferent Nature,* trans. Herbert Marshall (Cambridge: Cambridge University Press, 1987).

derground river that swells and recedes unpredictably, gushing up in springs
or receding still and hidden beneath deserts.[67]

Therefore, the recurrence of Bresson and Dreyer in the second volume
demonstrates a deep connection across the two cinema books. There is less a
break between the modern and classic cinema than a shift in the concept of
belief, where the direct image of time restores or gives new expression to a
potentiality always present, always renewable, within film's expressive movements. If the ethical stance of the cinematic movement-image is expressive of
a will to truth, then that of the direct image of time is given in powers of the
false that challenge the coherence and unity of organic representation. Indeed, for Deleuze modern cinema emerges from a profound and global crisis
of belief, experienced as a traumatic gulf between humanity and the world.
With neither causality nor teleology directing the unfolding of images, without a given totality in which they can be comprehended as a Whole, the powers
of nondetermined choice anticipated by affection-images are raised here to a
new power. Consequently, there arises within the universe of modern cinema
a new moral type defined by sensitivity to pure optical and acoustical situations and susceptibility to "wandering forms" *(la forme-balade)*—affective
situations where characters stroll or stray without obvious goals, destinations,
or motivation. Best exemplified by Ingrid Bergman in Rossellini's great postwar trilogy—*Voyage in Italy, Europa 51,* and *Stromboli*—the protagonists of
modern cinema wander and observe. They transmit sights rather than moti-
vating movements and actions: "The character becomes a kind of spectator.
She may move, run, or stir restlessly, but the situation in which she finds herself overflows her motor capacities on all sides, making her see and hear what
no longer justifies a response or an action. She registers more than reacts. She
surrenders to a vision, which she pursues or which pursues her, rather than
engaging in an action" (*The Time-Image* 3, 9).

Finally, this modern cinema is subject to a generalized paranoia, sensitive
to conspiracy and suspicious of all forms of totality. What Deleuze calls pure
optical and acoustical situations neither derive from presented actions nor extend into them. Rather, they confront us with situations that are so intolerable, unbearable, and unjust, but also sometimes so beautiful and overwhelm-
ing, that our capacities for reaction are arrested. In this way, the time-image

---

67. On the historical relation between the cinematic movement and time-images, see D. N.
Rodowick, "A Genealogy of Time," in *Reading the Figural, or, Philosophy after the New Media*
(Durham, NC: Duke University Press, 2001), 170–202.

produces characters and affective situations marked by a perceptual sensitivity to the intolerability of a world where faith and confidence in representation have disappeared, and where we are consumed by "the idea of one single misery, internal and external, in the world and in consciousness." (*The Movement-Image* 209). Or as Ingrid Bergman exclaims in *Europa 51:* "Something possible, otherwise I will suffocate."

Both Cavell and Deleuze assert a special connection between cinema and the concept of belief. The movement-image as plane of immanence is the most direct expression of a link between being and the world, or matter becoming luminescent, and thought emerging in relation to the movements of the world. The *cinematic* movement-image and time-image, however, appear as two ethical directions across this plane of immanence: one a transformation of the world by humanity, or the Eisensteinian belief that one can construct an image that makes thought happen; the other Antonin Artaud's intuition of an interior, deeper world "before man" as it were, produced from a shock to thought or by thought's confrontation with what is unthinkable. This is a confrontation with a time which is not that of Being, identity, or teleology, but rather an anticipatory time—of contingency, the purely conditional, the non-determined or not-yet.

The dilemma of modern cinema is in many respects that of skepticism as Cavell describes it. But as we shall soon see, Cavell describes belief in the mode of credibility and a potential overcoming of skepticism. In contrast, a European pessimism pervades Deleuze's account. As in Kracauer's late theory, the confrontation with postwar destruction, genocide, and the collapse of the grand narratives of ideology and utopia marks the decline of belief, expressed as a crisis in the action-image and the collapse of the sensorimotor schema. For Deleuze, modernity is experienced as a kind of traumatism. The break in the sensorimotor whole and the emergence of pure optical and acoustical situations

> makes man a seer who finds himself struck by something intolerable in the world, and confronted by something unthinkable in thought. Between the two, thought undergoes a strange fossilization, which is as it were its powerlessness to function, to be, its dispossession of itself and the world. For it is not in the name of a better or truer world that thought captures the intolerable in this world, but, on the contrary, it is because this world is intolerable that it can no longer think a world or think itself. The intolerable is no longer a serious injustice, but the permanent state of

daily banality. Man *is not himself* a world other than the one in which he experiences the intolerable and feels himself trapped." (*The Time-Image* 169–170, *220–221*)

The problem then becomes how to restore belief in a world of universal pessimism, where we have no more faith in images than we do in the world.

In the pure optical situation, the seer is alienated both within herself and from the world, but she also sees farther, better, and deeper than she can react or think. This augmentation of the powers of sight and of sensitivity to the injustices of the world may give the appearance of passivity or of an impotence of thought before that which is intolerable to consider. But for Deleuze the solution is not to quail before the thought that there is no alternative to this or any other situation. What Deleuze calls the impowers of thought demand a revaluation of our perceptual disjunction from the world that makes of this disconnection the possibility for a new faith, and a new thought. The problem of skepticism is here radically reconfigured. It is not that we are perceptually disjoined from the world, but rather that self, sight, and thought are divided from within and from each other by time, or by the force of time's passing. What is outside of thought that thought must confront as the unthought is our existential and ethical relationship to time as an infinite reservoir of nondetermined choice, which is also an ontology where life and thought are inseparable.

What Deleuze calls the "subtle way out" of this dilemma has already been introduced through the concept of lyrical abstraction—to commit to a mode of existence in which one chooses out of faith in the link between world, thought, and life. An arc must be drawn between *The Movement-Image* and *The Time-Image,* which together account for how new thought is generated by experiencing the powerlessness to think, just as new alternatives emerge in confrontation with the inability to choose:

Which, then, is the subtle way out? To believe, not in a different world, but in a link between man and the world, in love or life, to believe in this as in the impossible, the unthinkable, which none the less cannot but be thought: "something possible, otherwise I will suffocate." It is this belief that makes the unthought the specific power of thought, through the absurd, by virtue of the absurd. Artaud never understood powerlessness to think as a simple inferiority which would strike us in relation to thought. It is part of thought, so that we should make our way of thinking from it, without claiming to be restoring an all-powerful thought. We should rather make use of this powerlessness to believe in life, and to discover the identity of thought and life. (*The Time-Image* 170).

For Deleuze, the basic fact of modernity is that "we no longer believe in this world." However, much is explained by emphasizing that "we no longer believe in *this* world," that is, the world present to us, in which we are present, and which comprises the present time we occupy as a constant becoming.

We no longer even believe in the events that happen to us, love or death, as if they hardly concern us. We do not make cinema; rather, the world looks to us like a bad film. . . . It is the link between man and the world that has been broken. Henceforth, this link must become an object of belief, as the impossible that can only be given back in faith. Belief is no longer addressed to another world, or a transformed world. Man is in the world as if in a pure optical or acoustical situation. The reaction of which man is dispossessed can only be replaced by belief. Only belief in the world can reconnect man to what he sees and hears. Cinema must not film the world, but rather belief in this world, our only link. One often questions the nature of cinematographic illusion. To give us back belief in the world—this is the power of modern cinema (when it stops being shoddy). Christians or atheists, in our universal schizophrenia *we need reasons to believe in this world.* (*The Time-Image* 171–172, *223*)

For Deleuze, from Eisenstein to Artaud, the ethical problem is to understand that the traumatic unlinking of being from the world is yet more powerfully a leap toward faith in life, in *this* life or this world and its powers of self-transformation. The time-image's powers of the false do not show that the image is an illusion, nor do they replace a false perception with a true one. Rather, the powers of the false release the image from the form of identity and restore to it the potential for Becoming or eternal recurrence. From the cinematic movement-image to the time-image, from Pascal to Nietzsche, and in the cinema of Rossellini and Dreyer, a great shift occurs in philosophy, replacing the model of knowledge with that of belief as if in a conversion from piety to atheism, and moralism to morality—thus the turning points represented in the history of moral reasoning by Deleuze's pairing of Pascal and Hume, Kant and Fichte, or Kierkegaard and Nietzsche. One should emphasize that knowledge is based on faith no less than belief; namely, the will to truth and a belief in humanity's technological domination of nature. But even among the "pious" philosophers here, belief no longer turns toward another, transcendent world, but is directed rather to *this* world, the one in which we exist. We can learn much from Pascal's or Kierkegaard's struggles with the problem of the existence of God, but a philosophy of immanence, including Deleuze's film philosophy and philosophy of art in general, passes to another plane or territory and a different problematic. This plane of immanence places its bets not on a transcendental existence, but rather on thought that begins from the principle of the univocity of Being, and of a world with a single expressive substance. In *What Is Philosophy?*, Deleuze and Guattari write of Pascal or Kierkegaard that there is a secret atheism to the great religious philosophers whose quests are less for metaphysical certainty than the achievement of a certain philosophical serenity. Belief only becomes a genuine concept when it renounces transcendence for immanence, that is, when belief is reconnected to this world instead of projecting it toward another, transcendental world. In Deleuze's account, what Kierkegaard or even Pascal assert in the concept of faith is something that returns humanity's link with the world and with life to us. Hence belief only replaces knowledge when it elicits belief in this world and its future-oriented powers.

Deleuze's ethics, then, is a moral reasoning that wants to give back to us a belief capable of perpetuating life as movement, change, becoming—the eternal recurrence of difference. And rather than yearning for another transcendent or transformed world, we must believe in the body and the flesh, believe in the substance of the world and the world as substance, returning to them their one and unique voice. "We must believe in the body as in the germ of life, a seed that splits the pavement, that is conserved and perpetuated in the holy shroud or mummy's wrappings, and which bears witness to life and to this very world such that it is. We need an ethic or a faith that makes idiots laugh, not a need to believe in something else, but a need to believe in this world, of which fools are a part" (*The Time-Image* 173, 225). This passage signals a modern mutation whereby from Descartes to Dostoevsky the conceptual character of the Fool or Idiot is transformed. In Descartes's version, this represents the private and universal desire of the thinker to want or will the truth, but the new Idiot wants to make of the absurd the highest power of thought—creation. The modern Idiot expresses a utopian and ethical will, one that will never finally accept the verities of History and insists that every victim of history be accounted for and redeemed. The new Idiot, an important motor or motivator of moral perfectionism, wants the world to restore to him what is lost, incomprehensible, or unreasonable.

In *What Is Philosophy?*, this argument is followed by another potentially Wittgensteinian theme: shame as a motif of philosophy. One version of philosophy is based on an ideal of universal agreement to fundamental principles, arrived at through communication and consensus. But in a global milieu dominated by capitalism, one imagines that such a conception of philosophy is easily and thoroughly territorialized by the logic and value of capitalism and the commodity form. Restoring an ethical or moral dimension to philosophy, then, is not based on the quest for consensus and communication as much as on contestation and experimentation. At the same time, philosophy must begin its struggle for thought at the very point where we feel our humanness or lack of it most intensely, which is precisely where we experience the shame of being human. This shame is motivated by our lack of conviction, our paralysis or inaction with respect to life's daily injuries as much as its moral cataclysms, or our inability to sustain belief in this world and its powers of transformation. We experience the shame of being human not only in the extreme situations described by Primo Levi, for example, but also "in insignificant conditions, before the meanness and vulgarity of existence that haunts democracies, before the propagation of these modes of existence and of thought-for-the-market, and before the values, ideals, and opinions of our time. The ignominy of the possibilities of life that we are offered appears from within. We do not feel ourselves outside of our time but continue to undergo shameful compromises with it" (*What Is Philosophy?* 107–108).

The fact that we must continually and shamefully endure and respond to dishonorable compromises with our terms of existence is a powerful Emersonian theme, and thus an interesting bridge back to Cavell. And in this same gesture, Deleuze's desire for philosophy is shown to share much with Wittgenstein's, and thus a possible a philosophy of the humanities as I have portrayed it. Humanity is not something that universally binds us, a quality we all share, but rather the widely shared experience of not living up to our best intentions, or to have failed on a quotidian basis to have been human or to have acted in a responsibly human way. Here the conceptual problem of the posthuman or the Nietzschean superhuman is that the tragedy of being human is not to have fully understood or achieved our humanity. Deleuze's philosophy is thus not a posthuman one. How can one transcend or leave behind something one has not yet achieved or become? And yet we must find strategies for becoming and for responding to daily failures of ethical response and sociability. Here our doubts and lack of conviction or belief may spur us to imagine a future self or a new mode of existence to which we may aspire. (This idea will be one of Cavell's most powerful contributions to ethics and a philosophy of the humanities.) Belief must then be reconnected to the two principles of Deleuze's system. Skepticism is the sign of a thought disconnected from Life that consists of a single substance and a time of constant becoming. But Being and thought are in Life; they speak with a single voice and become in the same time, such that skepticism must be overcome with another will to power, which draws its energy from Life's potential for self-differentiation, and moralism must be overcome by choosing to believe in the ever-renewable possibility of beginning again—eternal recurrence.

13. The Ordinary Necessity of Philosophy

> Philosophy concerns those necessities we cannot, being human, fail to know.
> Except that nothing is more human than to deny them.
>
> —Stanley Cavell, "Aesthetic Problems of Modern Philosophy"

That art may be considered philosophical expression is an important link between Deleuze's and Cavell's interest in film. Like Deleuze, Cavell's cinema books are not studies of film but rather *philosophical* studies—they are works of philosophy first and foremost. Nonetheless, it may also be reasonable to read them as studies of film culture in their deep awareness of how the moving image has penetrated the daily life of the mind and that of being in the twentieth century and beyond. Though they do so in very different ways, both Deleuze and Cavell comprehend cinema as expressing ways of being in the world and of relating to the world such that cinema is already philosophy, and a philosophy intimately connected to our everyday life. Deleuze exemplifies this idea in pairing Henri Bergson's *Matter and Memory* with the early history of cinema. At the moment when philosophy returns to problems of movement and time in relation to thought and the image, the cinematic apparatus emerges neither as an effect of these problems nor in analogy with them. In its own way, it is the aesthetic expression of current and persistent philosophical problems. Nor should one say that Deleuze's thought is simply influenced by cinema. Rather, it is the direct philosophical expression, in the form of concepts and typologies of signs, of problems presented preconceptually in aesthetic form.

In his compelling philosophical and biographical account of Wittgenstein's thought and life, *The Duty of Genius,* Ray Monk recounts Wittgenstein's love not only for pulp detective fiction but also for popular American films, especially Westerns and musicals. No doubt Wittgenstein saw these pursuits as escapes from philosophy. However, as Wittgenstein never commented in writing or in a philosophical context on this love for what might be called the most ordinary of arts, I am led to wonder, philosophically, what is the nature of the philosophy from which so deep a thinker wishes to take flight, and what motivates this escape into the ordinary? Or why would one wish the ordinary to represent a place of escape, out of or into philosophy?

These remarks might also characterize Cavell's deeply original approach to philosophy, wherein the ordinary in all of its manifestations is the expression of a particular stance in or toward modernity. In several strong senses, the wish to escape from the ordinary responds to one of the starkest dilemmas of modern philosophy from the time of Descartes and Locke up through the positivist and analytical strains of the twentieth century. What links these two historical moments is the skeptical desire for certainty—a form of rationality where knowledge (of the world, or of other minds) wishes to suffer no ontological doubts. Ironically, this desire is itself fueled by skeptical doubt, and the incessant return of skepticism and the historically variegated responses to it present a poignant historical lesson: that we may forget the anguish of skepticism, or find temporary relief from it, yet it remains continually with us—the craving for certainty is maintained in the force of doubt. This paradox is a persistent characteristic of the human, or an ordinary state of the human, in at least two ways: it accompanies us daily, and living our daily, ordinary lives in the world and in community is precisely how we exist, often happily, with the dilemmas and doubts that plague us. (This is one of the key lessons of *The Claim of Reason*.)

Here is where Cavell and Deleuze might also locate their greatest differences, in spite of the various claims and concerns that could bring them together. Deleuze's commitment to Spinoza's doctrine of the univocity of Being evades skepticism by weaving human existence into the whole of universal existence. There is much to commend, especially for an environmental politics, in asserting this unbreakable connection to nature and to the universal plane of immanence. But the cinema books and *What Is Philosophy?* show implicitly that Deleuze has not left aside or overcome the existential anguish of skepticism. *What Is Philosophy?* expresses this anxiety in its account of the Other, whom I confront both externally and internally in the division of the self by time; in *The Time-Image*, it is expressed as humanity's disconnection from the world that cinema must restore in faith. In either case, one feels strongly that

Deleuze seeks relief in philosophy through its powers of conceptual innovation fueled by an ontology of time. This is, as it were, a faith in philosophy. For
his part, Cavell draws from Wittgenstein the lesson that for all its attractions,
philosophy will continually fail us if we cannot somehow return it to the ordinary, or make it pass through and return from the ordinary as humanly lived.

Another obvious way of linking Deleuze to Cavell is that in their own unique
ways both share a picture of philosophy as inherently problematic; that is, as
posing its own existence as a problem that must continually be revisited and
rethought. And for both thinkers, the problematic nature of philosophy often
takes the form of ethical questioning. What is the good of philosophy? Why
do philosophical dilemmas of knowledge and value continually trouble us, or
why can we not tolerate the absence of philosophy, no matter how prosaic,
from our lives? These questions do not belong to philosophy alone but rather
are key features of nonphilosophy, especially in our daily existence and in our
encounters with artistic expressiveness. Not that there is an analogy between
philosophy and art; rather, Cavell's career-long project has been to show that
philosophy and art or film are bound and interconnected by sets of common
criteria aimed at justifying our cares for the world, for the self, and for others.
In this way, art and philosophy are brought together as common expressions
of and responses to the dilemmas of skepticism as a peculiar condition of our
philosophical and cultural modernity.

One way of characterizing the unifying threads of Cavell's philosophy,
then, is to consider it a deep meditation on the problem of the modern or of
modernity, not only in philosophy but also as a general condition of present
culture as lived. Whatever problems or questions Cavell turns to seem also to
be a working out of a concept of the modern—in philosophy, in art, but also in
daily life—in all its peculiar temporality. The temporality of modernity is exemplified by what I have already referred to in my discussion of Wittgenstein
as the problem of the human. Cavell's philosophy is (or should be) of central
concern to the humanities because, following Wittgenstein, his aim is not to
define the human or to address the "human condition," but rather to make continually present the dilemma that the human has yet to be achieved. This idea
will eventually lead to the third principal strand of Cavell's philosophy after
the temporality of modernism and the dilemmas of skepticism—perfectionism
as a moral register or expression of the necessity for or aspiration to self-
transformation. From a perfectionist perspective, the human is not what we
are but a condition to be achieved; or better, something that solicits a desire
for becoming human, or for better understanding what it might mean to

achieve the condition of humanity. "Being human is aspiring to being human," Cavell explains in *The Claim of Reason*. "Since it is not aspiring to being the only human, it is an aspiration on behalf of others as well. Then we might say that being human is aspiring to being seen as human."[68] The philosophical desire to become human or to achieve humanity is a continually recurring state aspiring to a possible yet so far unattained future existence, which at the same time wonders, in its present dissatisfaction, to what extent it is continuous or discontinuous with the past. This recurring present preoccupation with a felt discontinuity between past and future, tradition and creation, or between the repetition of habit and the difference of change, is a central feature of Cavell's thoughts on the time of the modern.

This discontinuity may be considered in another way. Of all contemporary philosophers, Cavell comes closest to exemplifying in concept and in action what it means to practice a philosophy of the humanities. This has come about less from the conscious aim of promoting a philosophy of the humanities than as a natural outgrowth of Cavell's career-long concern for the human—in isolation and in community, in its cares and commitments, and in the quest for accord and agreement, partial or not, in inevitable contexts of disagreement. Although greatly influenced by Wittgenstein, Cavell's philosophy is less a philosophical anthropology than a deeply felt ethics. As one of the most original contemporary readers of Wittgenstein, Cavell understood early on, keenly and with consequence, that the later Wittgenstein's appeal to criteria, grammar, language games, perspicuous description, and recounting and reminding was less a perspective on the expressive behavior of others

---

68. *The Claim of Reason: Wittgenstein, Skepticism, Morality, and Tragedy* (Oxford: Oxford University Press, 1979), 399. In sketching an overview of Cavell's philosophical project, I should foreground some of the issues of central concern to him that will be absent from my account. Most important, I will not fully address the depth and complexity of Cavell's critique in *The Claim of Reason* of science's claim to an exclusive and universal mode of rationality, and his defense, through the procedures of ordinary language philosophy, of moral and aesthetic reasoning as ways of exploring the full reach of rational thought, both in the investigation of self and of the self's relation to a community of others. Another important area of concern is Cavell's position on the importance of the practice of criticism, which might contribute to a deeper account of practices of interpretation and evaluation from a philosophical perspective. Of equal importance in accounting for the full spectrum of Cavell's concerns would be his political theory, especially his sympathetic engagement with John Rawls's theory of justice, and how Cavell investigates critically the question of skepticism in Shakespeare's tragedies and romances, and in opera. The best overview of Cavell's work in these respects remains Stephen Mulhall's *Stanley Cavell: Philosophy's Recounting of the Ordinary* (Oxford: Oxford University Press, 1994), a book to which I owe a great debt.

than a thoroughgoing diagnostic and therapeutic examination of one's relationship to self and to others. The threat of skepticism arises here in the iron-
ical acknowledgment that what seams our experience with the world and
with others also separates or divides us as isolated perceptual beings, something which Cavell refers to as an image, picture, or fantasy blocking our relations with the world and a community of others. In the preface to the first
edition of *The World Viewed,* Cavell follows Heidegger in stating "that ours is
an age in which our philosophical grasp of the world fails to reach beyond
our taking and holding views of it, and we call these views metaphysics."[69]
And so a response of philosophy might be giving cause to return to the ordinary
from the metaphysical, just as Wittgenstein wished. In *The Claim of Reason*
Cavell's examination of modes of moral reasoning and aesthetic judgment is
a response to skepticism in that it requires the active presence of others, of
a community with like cares in conversation, and through that dialogue one
establishes not only one's presence in the community but a certain presence
to self, an acknowledgment and recounting of otherwise vague or unacknowledged cares and commitments, woven in new, if fragile, patterns of agreement.

Before examining Cavell's account of modernity and skepticism in greater
depth, I want to sketch out two more issues of central concern to his thought:
the ethical call to philosophy in everyday life, and how, in an American vein,
the call to philosophy seems inevitably linked to our experience of moving
images.

Cavell's writing on film and art, especially the essays, often provides fascinating and encapsulated versions of his broader approach to philosophical
practice. One of his earlier essays on film, "The Thought of Movies," characterizes philosophy as aspiring to learn "to think undistractedly about things
ordinary human beings cannot help thinking about, or anyway cannot help
having occur to them."[70] Foremost among these plaguing questions are the
skeptical dilemmas of deciding whether we can know the world as it is in itself, whether we can really grasp the internal lives of other minds, or whether,
like Descartes before his fire or the characters in *Inception* or *Waking Life,* we
can be certain that we are awake and not dreaming. These epistemological
quandaries are accompanied by evaluative questions concerning the stability

69. *The World Viewed: Reflections on the Ontology of Film,* enlarged ed. (Cambridge: Harvard
University Press, 1979), xxiii.

70. "The Thought of Movies," in *Cavell on Film,* ed. William Rothman (Albany: State University of New York Press, 2005), 92. Originally published in winter 1983 in *The Yale Review.*

of criteria for discerning the good from the bad, the moral from the immoral, or the just from the unjust, and how we might attain a more perfect world. Finally, there are historical dilemmas in wondering to what degree our current values and modes of existence are anchored in tradition or not, and thus whether they should be maintained or superseded. These thoughts present the three principal concerns of Cavell's philosophy—the response to skepticism, moral perfectionism, and the experience of modernity. Cavell continues by remarking that "Such thoughts are instances of that characteristic human willingness to allow questions for itself which it cannot answer with satisfaction. Cynics about philosophy, and perhaps about humanity, will find that questions without answers are empty; dogmatists will claim to have arrived at answers; philosophers after my heart will rather wish to convey the thought that while there may be no satisfying answers to such questions in certain forms, there are, so to speak, directions to answers, ways to think, that are worth the time of your life to discover" ("The Thought of Movies" 92). Philosophy responds to these dilemmas through what I would like to call the aim of concepts, which neither anchor nor represent thought but rather direct or orient it on pathways known and unknown, anticipated and surprising.

Along similar lines, Cavell asks whether the same sensibility that is drawn to and perplexed about philosophy is likewise drawn to and puzzled about movies. An unwavering continuity throughout Cavell's writing on film and philosophy is that for American culture in the twentieth century the movies have been the moral accompaniment to everyday life. Throughout his long career Cavell has insisted that movies have played a role in American culture different from their role in other societies, and that in comparison to Europe, this difference is a function of the historical absence in America of a sustained, public philosophical culture.

At the same time, the craving for thought and ethical examination is no less powerful or ambitious in America than it is in Europe, and so in the absence of a sustained philosophical tradition, America composed its difference in thought or art from whatever portable fragments were culturally at hand. Here Cavell arrives at one of his most controversial yet most appealing propositions: that this absence of a public philosophical culture finds its response at the movies, which at their best inspire, in ordinary encounters, a new cultural ambition of self-thought and self-invention. As the very expression of our modernity, or our modern responses to the world, American film has enacted a democratization of philosophy, where the movies provide a tradition of thought of the ordinary absent from the concerns of academic philosophy, whether European or American. And since American thought was not weighted with the long history of European thought, it was more open and responsive to what the movies might teach us. In the absence of a native philosophical tradition, American public culture lacked the means and vocabulary to explore deep ontological and ethical questions of concern to us all.

According to Cavell, American film found ways to compensate for the lack of a native philosophical tradition by satisfying the ambition of an engaged culture to examine itself publicly. What Cavell often calls film at its best offers, then, three philosophical attractions or invitations: to consider what our fascination with screened worlds expresses ontologically, to assess what film dramatizes as forms of moral reasoning, and finally, to examine how the presence of a community frames our pleasurable engagement with these activities. Perhaps the movies have or had a natural relationship to philosophy not only because the perceptual situation staged by the screening of projected images conditions a certain ontological fascination, but also because an audience was constituted as a temporary yet recurrent community of individuals engaged in a common project of moral reflection in response to the portrayal of lives "pursued by thoughtful, mature people, heavily in conversation with one another about the value of their individual or joint pursuits."[71] Seen from the right perspective, cinema may well be the event where the ancient tradition of philosophical dialogue has found a modern home.

This idea forms the basis of Cavell's later books on comedies of remarriage and melodramas of the unknown woman. The interest of film here is to show it as the ordinary or quotidian expression of the deepest concerns of moral philosophy. And just as Wittgenstein sought to displace metaphysical expression into ordinary language and daily concerns, film brings moral philosophy into the context of quotidian dramatic expression. In the absence of a sustained public philosophical culture, Cavell suggests that these "films are rather to be thought of as differently configuring intellectual and emotional avenues that philosophy is already in exploration of, but which, perhaps, it has cause sometimes to turn from prematurely, particularly in its forms since its professionalization, or academization. . . . The implied claim is that film, the latest of the great arts, shows philosophy to be the often invisible accompaniment of the ordinary lives that film is so apt to capture." (*Cities of Words* 6).

---

71. *Cities of Words: Pedagogical Letters on a Register of Moral Life* (Cambridge, MA: The Belknap Press of Harvard University Press, 2004), 9.

Where contemporary philosophy has reneged on its promise of moral perfectionism, film has responded and compensated, though in the preconceptual manner of all art and sensuous expression. Thus the great project of film philosophy today is not only to help reinvigorate this moral reflection but to heal the rift in philosophy's relation to everyday life by example.

14. "Art now exists in the condition of philosophy"

One of the most fascinating aspects of Cavell's accounts of skepticism and modernism is the implication that over the long term philosophical beliefs and concepts can become the framework for ordinary beliefs about our relations with the world—perhaps something more like structures of feeling in Raymond Williams's sense than a full-blown Foucauldian *episteme.* In any case, such structures are ethical more than epistemological. In this view, the origins of modernism are the origins of skepticism, that is, patterns of thought and senses of the self emerging in early modern Europe, whose first powerful instance is Descartes's *Meditations,* but which are equally and powerfully present in cultural forms such as Shakespeare's tragedies.

Skepticism is not just a problem for philosophers, then, but rather expresses a novel and disturbing situation in which our "natural" relation to the world becomes one of beholding, as if from a distance or in some perceptual withdrawal from the world. One word for such an experience is alienation, though Kierkegaard refers to it as being away, separate, or withdrawn from the world. Cavell is drawn to Heidegger and Wittgenstein, and especially to Emerson and Thoreau, because of their recognition of the power of this condition, as well as their insistence on its ordinariness, or recurrent presentness or presence to us. From Deleuze to Cavell, modernism is portrayed as something like a recurrent existential state of ontological restlessness or uncertainty no less present in philosophy than in culture or art. This condition cannot be submitted to epistemological or ocular proof. No data can be gathered nor any thesis falsified that would ever convince us, or fail to convince us, of the rightness of this perspective; it is a matter of ethical discernment, or more simply, belief. It requires from philosophy, rather, an ethical examination of self, and of myself in relation to others, my form of life, and my encounters with things of value to me, as a practice open to diurnal testing that is in principle unfinished and interminable.

In his earliest essays, Cavell first suggests that modernism is the general (ontological) condition of art, or let us say, artful expression. For this reason there is no essential division between the popular arts, or indeed between existing genres of art. From this perspective, the problem of modernism does not necessarily refer to questions of form or style, but rather to an experience of time or of history where "convention as a whole is now looked upon not as a firm inheritance from the past, but as a continuing improvisation in the face of problems we no longer understand."[72] In modernism the set of relationships linking a practice (in art or philosophy) to its history itself becomes problematic. One relationship to the past can be thought of as continuity in the form of extending and renovating tradition or convention; another can be thought of as a discontinuity or rupture in which the past is overcome or superseded by the absolutely new. Modernism, however, floats in a state of uncertainty, meaning not only that the presence or experience of authentic existence must be questioned and reasserted in every expressive act but also that these assertions find it difficult to place where or when the past appears as a force in the present. (Later, this dilemma reappears in Cavell's account of the ontological perplexities of photography.) After Wittgenstein and Heidegger, Cavell argues that,

> the repudiation of the past has a transformed significance, as though containing the consciousness that history will not go away, except through our perfect acknowledgment of it (in particular, our acknowledgment that it is not past), and that one's own practice and ambition can be identified only against the continuous experience of the past.... But "the past" does not in this context refer simply to the historical past; it refers to one's own past, to what is past, or what has passed, within oneself. One could say that in a modernist situation "past" loses its temporal accent and means anything "not present." Meaning what one says becomes a matter of making one's sense present to oneself.[73]

Making one's sense present to oneself is no doubt the principal act of philosophical practice, especially in ordinary language philosophy; for Cavell, it is also the principal task of both aesthetic and moral expressions. The problem raised by modernism is that the questioning and reassertion of existence is also an acknowledgment that this questioning and reassertion is open and perpetually unfinished. In this way, the ontological uncertainty of art and

---

72. "Music Discomposed," in *Must We Mean What We Say?* (Cambridge: Cambridge University Press, 2002), 201.

73. "Foreword: An Audience for Philosophy," in *Must We Mean What We Say?*, xxxiii.

aesthetic experience recapitulates the ontological uncertainty of the modernist subject. Modernism is thus characterized as

> a moment in which history and its conventions can no longer be taken for granted; . . . the beginning of the moment in which each of the arts becomes its own subject, as if its immediate artistic task is to establish its own existence. The new difficulty which comes to light in the modernist situation is that of maintaining one's belief in one's own enterprise, for the past and the present become problematic together. I believe that philosophy shares the modernist difficulty now everywhere evident in the major arts, the difficulty of making one's present effort become a part of the present history of the enterprise to which one has committed one's mind, such as it is. ("Foreword," *Must We Mean What We Say?* xxxvi)

Modernism is understood here not just as a perspective on art but more broadly as a pervasive cultural condition to which philosophy must respond. What modernism thus signifies is the inability to take for granted the regulation of genres, forms, styles, and practices by ongoing traditions that emits from a kind of groundlessness, or absence of transcendental authority, whereby the relation or continuity of past to present becomes difficult or unclear. This uncertainty with respect to the pressures, demands, or comforts of the past is transmitted into the present as a condition, one wants to say, of the difficult presentness of practice and of artworks themselves. The status of the work— its coming into being or state of Being—is subject to a present, continuous questioning about the fact of its existence, or of its continuing to exist. And this uncertainty and doubt, this self-questioning and self-interrogation, perpetuates itself as a projection into the future in the form of questions about the possibility or impossibility of both creation and interpretation themselves taking place in the absence of an authorizing tradition.

In *Must We Mean What We Say?* convention then becomes less a matter of working with and expanding tradition than of finding strategies for improvised responses to problems we hardly understand, and which confront and detour our present perspectives. In other words, the right of a work to be accepted as art or philosophy can never be taken for granted—this right must be continually earned, and convention and context for given series of works must be continually regenerated through acts of creation and criticism. What might appear at first glance as the interiority or even solipsism of modernism can now be seen as its openness and desire for community, a wish to convert a private conversation into a public one, where an anticipated community feels invited to enter freely into the conversation, no matter how difficult or painful but also joyful, initiated by the difficult presentness of modernist works. What Cavell portrays as the wish for community can also be framed in Deleuze's terms as a work's ethical call to a people who do not yet exist, or setting the conditions for a people to come. Modernist works seek acknowledgment, want to be acknowledged, as does, in the modernist condition, the world, the self in the world, and the self in community. But the world is replete with failed or disappointed desires, and there is no guarantee of present or future acknowledgment. This fact also means that some of the most powerful modernist works, in art or philosophy, may not presently find contexts or communities to interpret, value, or evaluate them. They remain wholly or partly always to be received or to be acknowledged.

I have said that the modernist situation in art or philosophy inspires acts of criticism as well as a desire to be heard and acknowledged. This is why Cavell writes in a late essay that

> I remain grateful to the artwork or artworld objects, as it were, for their still strange interest to me, and particularly, I think, for making me voluble, loosening my tongue, expressing myself. This is also no small matter. On my reading of Wittgenstein's *Investigations*, it is concerned with the human terror of inexpressiveness, of suffocation, alternating with an equal terror of exposure, as if speech threatens to become unable perfectly to refer to objects of my interest or to give expression to my states of being, or else to refer and give expression so fully as to give myself away. It is the version, or threat, of skepticism that I claim Wittgenstein's *Investigations* stakes itself on identifying and dispersing, ceaselessly.[74]

One principal value of art is not just expression, but rather the power of inducing expressiveness, and this power has an ethical force. This is why Cavell asserts that "art now exists in the condition of philosophy" (*The World Viewed* 14). In his discussions of Wittgenstein and Austin, especially in *Must We Mean What We Say?* Cavell argues that in the modernist situation, art responds philosophically to dilemmas of daily existence that philosophy itself has come to ignore. Philosophical dilemmas of knowing and valuing are endemic to daily

---

74. "Crossing Paths," in *Cavell on Film*, 372. This 2002 paper was originally written for a colloquium at Columbia University honoring the work of Arthur Danto.

life, yet philosophy has deserted the diurnal or the temporal, the contingent presentness of modern life, in its quest for a stable and certain image of a known or knowable world; or put more simply, in wishing to know the world with certainty, we lose or become blind to knowledge of ourselves.

For Cavell, our responses to modern art, and its responses to itself as acts of creation, illuminate how the procedures of ordinary language philosophy offer routes for reconnecting the self to world and community by making present the knowledge of self by self. These are means for rediscovering, refining, and deepening our awareness and knowledge of the forms of life we inhabit. Cavell characterizes this procedure as "recounting criteria," or ways of reminding ourselves of "what would we say, or what should we say" in ordinary situations of doubt and disagreement. Routes of consensus often take the form here of projecting new contexts that open previously unforeseen semantic depths and complexities and possibilities of agreement. In asking and answering these questions of ourselves and others, we draw upon capacities of self-knowledge available to any speaker of language in a given form of life. To draw upon or examine one's native competence as an expressive being is also to manifest the criteria regulating expressions or expressiveness. Grammatical investigation then calls upon procedures or practices for displaying, recalling, and exploring these criteria. The value of these practices is that they bring us back to the terms of our alignment with the world by specifying and clarifying what may count as specific matters of fact within the expressive community in which these terms are in play, although as Stephen Mulhall rightly emphasizes, "the nature, extent, and security of those alignments are not determinable in advance of grammatical investigation. In short, ordinary language philoso-phizing is a matter of tapping the resources of the self in a way which will allow the philosopher to recall, explore, and display the nature, extent, and security of her alignments with the world and with the human community."[75]

Therefore, in acquiring and expressing knowledge of ourselves, we also acquire and give expression to knowledge of others. Rather than an interior-ized self confronting the gulf of external objects and minds, in Cavell's per-spective to come to know one's own mind is the path to knowing other minds, to discovering common ground in an interpersonal web of linked and linking criteria, vocabularies, concepts, and grammars of belief. This practice of self-knowing is a way of weaving oneself into a community of others, because to

75. *Stanley Cavell: Philosophy's Recounting of the Ordinary* (Oxford: Oxford University Press, 1994), 19.

acknowledge others is a way of recognizing oneself and opening oneself to acknowledgment by others. As the origin of one powerful strand of skepticism, Cartesian doubt can then be seen as a particular form of solipsism that has forgotten philosophy's more ancient and fundamental concerns with self and community. An innovation of ordinary language philosophy in this respect is its withdrawal from the quest for certainty and the need for universal agreement. Its practices are less concerned with convincing or conviction than with investigating and mapping the possibility of agreement, whole or partial, in a community whose scale and stability cannot be assured either from within or without. Agreement must be continually solicited and negotiated. Yet this process often fails, such that the appeal to the grammar of ordinary language, which we all share, is not just a request for agreement but also an investigation of our quotidian failures of communication and consensus. (Earlier, I characterized this condition as the value of being disagreeable, because disagreement is as important a motivation to philosophy as agreement or achieving conviction.)

The process of trying to communicate with, and to convince or persuade others, is or should also be a process of self-investigation, education, and expression. For Cavell, then, ordinary language philosophy is the quintessentially modern philosophy (or better, the philosophy most prepared to respond to the dilemmas of our modernity), in that its methods or procedures aim at discovering and displaying modes of self-knowledge through which an individual might discover the range and depth of her connections with given communities without relinquishing the right to speak for herself. Nor does such a philosophy expect or require either uniformity or complete agreement among its participants. In each case, its objective is to discover (for myself, for others, within my claim to speak for and to others, and they to me) the web of intersubjective relationships that bind human communities together despite the inevitable facts of disagreement and disagreeableness.

In like manner, the guiding argument of *The Claim of Reason,* in all its depth and complexity, is to demonstrate the variety of ways (in ethics, politics, or aesthetics) in which claims to reason or rationality are not exhausted by methodological monism and scientism's demand to reach agreement on conclusions. And in fact, if philosophy is to become attentive again to daily life, then both moral reasoning and aesthetic judgments might be more appropriate domains for exploring how reason is deployed and debated in human communities than science. Philosophy might be guided by a mistaken view of science, which in its daily practice is less concerned with certainty than with maintaining consensus as to what counts as procedures and protocols that regulate empirical and experimental investigation. (Following his friend Thomas Kuhn, Cavell knows that these procedures are themselves historically contingent.) "If what makes science rational is not the fact of agreement about particular propositions itself," Cavell concludes, "or about the acknowledged modes of arriving at it, but the fact of a *commitment* to certain modes of argument whose very nature is to lead to such agreement, then morality may be rational on exactly the same ground, namely that we commit ourselves to *certain* modes of argument, but now ones which do not lead, in the same ways, and sometimes not at all, to agreement (about a conclusion)" (*The Claim of Reason* 261–262). The humanities need not follow scientific modes of argument nor commit themselves to patterns of logic and agreement through which scientific reason is adjudicated. And in fact, in the humanities both moral reasoning and aesthetic judgment provide a better range and depth of methods and perspectives (call them theories if you like) for investigating how one negotiates situations of rational disagreement without sacrificing respect for the other. Broadly conceived, one might say that for all their messy methodological and multidisciplinary diversity, the humanities provide important laboratories for experimenting with creative procedures of interpretation, evaluation, and recontextualization.

Later, I will examine Cavell's picture of Emersonian perfectionism as exemplifying ordinary moral reasoning in an imperfect democratic society. For the moment, however, I want to look more deeply at Cavell's account of the importance of aesthetic problems for modern philosophy. "Aesthetic Problems of Modern Philosophy" is of course the title of one of the essays in *Must We Mean What We Say?* In the early period of his published work, one of Cavell's main concerns is to restore the claim of reason to both aesthetic judgments and moral debate. One of Cavell's most original strategies is to revisit Kant's examination of the paradoxical quality of aesthetic conversation in the context of ordinary language philosophy: that it requires a disinterested and subjective assessment, as if a conversation of self with self that is both perceptual and affective (Derrida calls this autoaffection), which in turn desires or claims universal assent from all others within range of its hearing. The question can be put another way: Does the absence of universal agreement in aesthetic judgments demonstrate their *lack* of rationality, or alternatively, do they convey another picture *of* rationality? In fact, one of the many accomplishments of *Must We Mean What We Say?* and *The Claim of Reason* is to remap a series of relationships in epistemology wherein aesthetic and moral discussion are investigated and revalued such that criteria of logic and scientism no longer dominate or serve as exclusive models for the rational exercise of thought.

Cavell's aim is to show how the paradox of artful conversation is reasonable. One of Kant's first steps in the *Critique of Judgment* is to observe in sections 7 and 8 of the "Analytic of the Beautiful" that because aesthetic judgments are grounded entirely in the subjective, they can be neither objective, logical, nor theoretical. The nontheoretical character of aesthetic judgments has a precise sense here: such judgments are singular and thus not generalizable, and in addition are unmediated by concepts. Aesthetic judgments also have the peculiar character of asking for universal assent, even if we know that it cannot and will not be granted, at least universally. Does this mean that aesthetic judgments are irrational since we cannot hope for universal consensus and thus risk isolation and ridicule in making them? And what to make of Kant's assertion that aesthetic judgments are without concept, which is a scandal from the point of view of a positivist or analytic conception of philosophy?

At the same time, Cavell takes Kant at his philosophical word but without wishing to dissolve the paradox. For this paradox may be expressive of another power of great human value—the nature of aesthetic judgments is to be arguable, that is, discussable or provoking discussion, as if to say that the capacity for disagreement is also the capacity for conversation and sociability, which is also, one wants to say, a fundamental human capacity.

And there is another paradox to confront in our ordinary practices of expressing aesthetic judgments. One of Wittgenstein's most important and difficult lessons is that at some point reasons are exhaustible. (Recall §217 of the *Philosophical Investigations* where Wittgenstein states: "Once I have exhausted the justifications I have reached bedrock, and my spade is turned. Then I am inclined to say: 'This is simply what I do.'") Or to put it another way, there will be moments when speech loses its force; hence Wittgenstein's frequent appeals to look and to see, which might be an appeal to the other to find their own Idea and own concept or context, since mine seems to be at some point incommunicable. This is a place or situation where reasons fail or find their limits, but in so doing they do not become irrational. In examining the powers of aesthetic and moral judgments Cavell does not seek to replace or overturn claims of scientific knowing. Rather, in his investigation of the limits of the demand for certainty, Cavell finds in the procedures of ordinary language philosophy the bases, no matter how open-ended and contingent, for negotiating rational agreement in whatever domain. In this respect, *Must We Mean What We Say?* and *The Claim of Reason* are two of the great founding texts of a philosophy of the humanities. And in ways both very different from yet similar to Deleuze, Cavell is testing the porous frontiers between philosophy, art, and science, while demonstrating the common ways of thinking and expressing that nonetheless cross between them.

What lessons can be learned, then, about the patterns, procedures, or grammar for reaching agreement in examining our ordinary claims in aesthetic and moral reasoning? In other words, what are the claims of reason expressed in our interpretive and evaluative activities? The first lesson is to value the fact that aesthetic and moral judgments are in principle inconclusive and less open (if at all) to falsification than are scientific claims. Aesthetic judgments are arguable, that is, open to and inviting debate and conflicts of interpretation. What is asked for here is not assent to a conclusion but rather a mutual seeking out of overlapping patterns of understanding and (partial) agreement. What Cavell learns from Kant is that in our enthusiasm for art we may want to ask for universal assent, but we are willing to settle for arriving at and better understanding mutually held contexts—call them patterns or designs— for discerning consensus or agreement, no matter how tentative or fragile. Disagreement may also be valued as the motivation for further conversation. Cavell thus encourages us to recognize pattern and agreement as distinctive features of logic—or better, reasoning—and to recognize that coming to agreement does not necessarily mean assent to inescapable conclusions, but rather only reaching a partial and flexible accord supported by (again partial) consensus in the grammar of aesthetic conversation. And this is also where the subject returns in artful conversation, for "the problem of the critic, as of the artist," Cavell writes, "is not to discount his subjectivity, but to include it; not to overcome it in agreement, but to master it in exemplary ways" ("Aesthetic Problems of Modern Philosophy" 94). Patterns of disagreement can and should be further motivations to self-investigation and the achievement of greater clarity.

The claim to reason in aesthetic judgments therefore presents key features of modes of reasoning in ordinary language. Here empirical evidence is in many cases irrelevant to one's assertions, though some such evidence may support them. Moreover, instances of disagreement are to be commonly expected. If aesthetic conversation lapses into disagreement, consensus will not be achieved by attempting to confirm or disconfirm one or the other's conclusions by collecting new data. Rather, in a spirit of rational accommodation, the conversation starts again in trying to understand why disagreement has arisen, perhaps by imagining novel examples or points of comparison, and then if new points of consensus are found, to try to explain how this agreement has come about and what kinds of grammar support it. In these situations, one often appeals to counterfactual examples that require what Cavell calls projective imagination or projecting a new context. Call this the search for alternatives, or testing through the deployment of imaginative counterexamples the acknowledged and unacknowledged assumptions, grounds, and contexts, or the reasons not fully accounted for underlying every expressive act. There is a comparative and imaginative dimension here as well, in that the "appeal to 'what we should say if . . .' requires that we imagine an example or story, sometimes one more or less similar to events which may happen any day, sometimes one unlike anything we have known" ("Aesthetic Problems of Modern Philosophy" 95). In this process, Cavell writes, "The philosopher appealing to everyday language turns to the reader not to convince him without proof but to get him to prove something, test something against himself. He is saying: Look and find out whether you can see what I see, wish to say what I wish to say. . . . [The] implication is that philosophy, like art, is, and should be, powerless to *prove* its relevance; and that says something about the kind of relevance it wishes to have. All the philosopher, this kind of philosopher, can do is to express, as fully as he can, his world, and attract our undivided attention to our own" (95–96). And in fact, this is all the modernist situation asks of us, whether epistemologically or ethically.

The existential and perceptual uncertainty of modernism and the modern arts is therefore to be valued as demonstrating that achieving certainty is an inappropriate criterion for assessing the reasonableness of aesthetic judgments. For example, in "Music Discomposed," Cavell observes that in the context of modernism the category of the aesthetic has itself become uncertain, raising questions of fraudulence and conviction. In the space of this uncertainty, works of art ask for a certain quality of trust from their viewers, and this request may be betrayed or disappointed. Authenticity cannot be taken for granted or as given—it recurrently requires critical determination that something counts as a work of art and that we are genuinely having an aesthetic experience. Moreover, the process of critical determination is open and contingent—one can never establish with certainty a fixed list of criteria that assure how these judgments can be made and adjudicated.

What modernism insists upon, then, is not the discovery of the object or experience as genuine but rather an awareness that we do not know exactly which is under critical scrutiny: the work or the viewer. Epistemology will not help us here. The critic's job is to persuade or convince, to achieve some confidence that her interlocutor will come to see or experience as she experiences, that one can join her in a special and fragile community of interpreters and valuers. "It matters that others know what I see," Cavell writes, "in a way it does not matter whether they know my tastes. It matters, there is a burden, because unless I can tell what I know, there is a suggestion (and to myself as well) that I do *not* know. But I *do*—what I see is *that* (pointing to the object). But for that to communicate, you have to see it too. Describing one's experience of art is itself a form of art; the burden of describing it is like the burden of producing it. Art is often praised because it brings men together. But it also separates them" ("Music Discomposed" 193).

Cavell follows this argument with the claim that as a form of conduct that affects others, the making of art is subject to the same care and commitments as other forms of human conduct; therefore, it has a powerful ethical dimension, and the same may be said for aesthetic conversations and judgments. Respecting the autonomy of a work of art—its separate and perhaps unknowable and uncertain existence before you—means allowing yourself to be questioned, interrogated, or investigated by it, to be open to it in ways that allow an interpretation in which you yourself, reader, are subject to criticism and change. In any case, one of the great powers of aesthetic sensation is that it is incommunicable. Or rather, every effort to convey such sensations to others rebounds to the subject herself who, in face of the doubts and uncertainties of her interlocutors, including the work itself, must reflexively discover the depth of her conviction and the clarity of her criteria for judgment. "Nothing can show this value to you unless it is discovered in your own experience," Cavell insists, "in the persistent exercise of your own taste, and hence the willingness to challenge your taste as it stands, to form your own artistic conscience, hence nowhere but in the details of your encounters with specific works" ("The Thought of Movies" 93).

In "The Thought of Movies," Cavell reprises his conviction that in the framework of modernism art now exists in the condition of philosophy, as it has always been the condition of philosophy to escape itself. This assertion also connects modernism to the medium of moving images, and indeed film's virtual life of ontological uncertainty, since in modernism it is the condition of art to escape itself; hence, there is also an intimate connection between philosophy and what we experience as our modernity in thought and through artful expression. There is a link here to the temporal condition of the moving image, just as Deleuze so complexly describes it, or as I have characterized it in *The Virtual Life of Film:* the uncertain medium of moving images perhaps exemplifies an art whose temporal condition is to be continually escaping from itself in the expressive condition of becoming and change, thus expressing a duration or temporality commensurate with life, or the world, but also of the self. This is why film is a moving image of skepticism but also a medium of recovery from skepticism.

15. Falling in Love with the World

> I said that one's experience of others puts a seam in experience. Why not consider that experience is endlessly, continuously, seamed? Every thing, and every experience of every different thing, is what it is.
>
> —Stanley Cavell, *The Claim of Reason*

> It is very unhappy, but too late to be helped, the discovery we have made, that we exist.
>
> —Ralph Waldo Emerson, "Experience"

My account of Deleuze's possible contributions to a film philosophy followed upon my sketch of the elements or grammar of a possible philosophy of the humanities. I have already noted that there is an interesting link between Deleuze and Cavell through their common concern with the dilemmas of skepticism and the problem of belief. However, while Deleuze's Spinozan ontology presents a universe or plane of immanence where skepticism should be made irrelevant, in *The Time-Image* his ethical picture of humanity's broken link with the world demonstrates Deleuze's difficulty in accounting for the human dimensions of this dilemma and the possible range of responses to it. A deep though not immediately apparent connection between Cavell and Deleuze might be located precisely at this point. There is a sinuous line along which Cavell's and Deleuze's accounts of ontology complement one another, like two pieces of a puzzle whose pictures portray different worlds that nonetheless fit precisely at their joins. Along this line, Deleuze's ethical demand to restore belief in this world finds itself paired with Cavell's career-long examination of the grammar of acknowledgment and the logic of moral perfectionism. In turn, Cavell's work is exemplary of a philosophy of and for the humanities, particularly in his original attempt to rebalance the concerns of epistemology and ethics. Two principal ideas unite Cavell's philosophical and film work in this respect. Moreover, these are less separate ideas than iterations of the same problem that succeed one another more or less chronologically, namely, the philosophical confrontation with skepticism and the concept of moral perfectionism. One still incompletely answered question here is why film is so important as the companion or exemplification of this confrontation. One clue resides in the title of an important Cavell essay, "What Photography Calls Thinking." What does it mean to say that images or art *think*, or that they respond to philosophical problems as a way of thinking or a style of thought? In the first phase of Cavell's film philosophy, represented by the period surrounding the publication of *The World Viewed*, the responses to this question are ontological and epistemological (at least in the sense of how the experience of modernism conditions our senses of knowing or not). But this ontology refers neither to the medium of art nor to the identity of artworks, but rather to how art expresses our modes of existence or ways of being in the world as a continuous fall into and return from skepticism.

In Cavell's early philosophy, skepticism is also the touchstone for examining and measuring the relationship between philosophy, science, and art. The moment has arrived then to investigate more deeply why the problem of skepticism is of such deep concern for Cavell, and how the definition of this problem and responses to it inform claims to reason in both aesthetics and ethics. This is of course one of the main themes of *The Claim of Reason*. For Cavell the skeptical attitude is one of the foundational characteristics of early modern thought. One might even say that skepticism is the foundation of modern philosophy as an academic discipline, as well as that of the modern scientific attitude.

Descartes is the first protagonist in this story for several reasons. Cartesianism places epistemology as the centerpiece of philosophy, and in so doing makes perception the guarantor of knowledge about the world. At the same time, Descartes knows that human perception is limited and therefore unreliable. One last dilemma must be added to this linking of acts of perceiving to the quest for certainty in knowledge: existence. In the *Meditations*, the instability of knowing is linked to possible failures of perception and judgment that are at once outward and inward directed. Sitting alone before the fire in his study Descartes is lulled into wondering, as we all sometimes are, whether he is awake or dreaming, or into suddenly fearing that the frontiers between these two states are indiscernible or indistinguishable. What makes such thoughts all the more disturbing is that doubts about the existence of the world lead inexorably to doubts about the reliability of the self and its anchoring in a stable, perceptible, and knowable world, as well as about the power of any transcendental authority to assure the universal coherence and meaningfulness of the world. In a strong sense, one could portray Descartes as the founding author of the experience of modernity in its doubled aspect: presenting the self as divided from the world by its capacities for perception and thought, and thus wishing for the self to master both itself and the world, and all the objects in it, by assuring their existence through criteria of certain knowledge—call this method; one might also say, theory. Method functions (as logic will for analytic philosophy) as an asubjective or transsubjective legislator of reason. In the same move, epistemology is removed from the subject, or the subject disappears from epistemology. One might say in this case that reason becomes inhuman. Therefore, one of the principal aims of *The Claim of Reason,* as I have already suggested, is to rebalance epistemology's exclusive claim to rationality with the powers of aesthetic judgment and moral reasoning.

In his quest for the certainty of existence (of self, world, or God) Descartes enacts a series of divisions—of self from world, of mind from body, of transcendental authority absented from the world—whose consequences have persisted for 400 years. Skepticism is another aspect or dimension of modernity, in that the desire for certainty is a response to a perceived precariousness of one's relation to the world, as if there had been a sudden and unexpected dislocation of the subject from the object of knowledge. (Cavell often refers to this experience as the "traumatic event" of the New Science of Copernicus and Galileo, which inspired a new and modern response from philosophy in the work of Bacon, Descartes, and Locke.) The unacknowledged symptom of skepticism, what Cavell sometimes calls the truth of skepticism, is suppressing recognition that it produces the situation it is supposed to overcome. In diverse moments of writing, Cavell describes this condition as the difficulty of making ourselves present to the world, and the world present to us. One should immediately recognize Cavell's characterization of the question of modernism as the difficulty of reconciling presentness and existence as a historical or temporal experience. In its response to skepticism, epistemology creates a new and potentially disquieting situation that Cavell pictures as seeing ourselves as outside the world as a whole. The self is thus constrained to relate to the world as if ontologically distinct from it. Moreover, since perception is optically unreliable, the self or mind is made distinct from the body even if the only way of relating to the world is through the frame or window of perception, as if from an immaterial and partial perspective looking out at different aspects of external objects.

In this situation, the character of the subject and the character of the world are both transformed. The world is fashioned here as what Cavell calls a "generic object"; that is, as something that epistemology can treat in its generality as indistinguishable from all the singular and particular things within the world, or alternatively, where singular things serve pars pro toto as tokens of the world as a knowable object. (This idea is deeply related to Deleuze's account of the cinematographic movement-image's desire to express the Whole of the world, or the world as Whole in relation to a subject capable of perceiving this totality.) In its need to know the world as a complete object, skepticism expresses an anxiety that Cavell presents as "a sense of powerlessness to know the world, or to act upon it; I think it is also working in the existentialist's (or, say, Santayana's) sense of the precariousness and arbitrariness of existence, the utter contingency in the fact that things are as they are" (*The Claim of Reason* 236). In the splitting of the subject from the object of knowledge—and in fact, *creating* subject and object as special categories or components of epistemology—the philosopher promotes a condition that Cavell describes as "one of being sealed off from the world, within the round of one's own experiences, and as one of looking at the world as one object ('outside of us'). The philosopher's experiences of trying to *prove* that it is there is, I will now add, one of trying to establish an absolutely firm connection with that world-object from that sealed position. It is as though, deprived of the ordinary forms of life in which that connection is, and is alone, secured, he is trying to establish it in his immediate consciousness, then and there. (This has its analogues in non-philosophical experience, normal and abnormal)" (238). Later in the book, Cavell asserts yet more forcefully "that *what* skepticism questions or denies my knowledge of *is* the world of objects I inhabit, is the *world*" (448).

These sentences comprise some of Cavell's most direct and succinct descriptions of the dilemma of skepticism. What Cavell then calls the (unacknowledged) truth or moral of skepticism is "that the human creature's basis in the world as a whole, its relation to the world as such, is not that of knowing, anyway not what we think of as knowing. . . . (Then what rootlessness, or curse, made us, let us, think of our basis in this way, accepting from ourselves our offer of knowledge?)" (241). This is Cavell's way of acknowledging Kant's insight that limitations of knowledge are not necessarily failures of knowledge, an implication worked through in different ways in Heidegger and Wittgenstein.

But it is also the case that skeptical doubts are unavoidable; we live with them diurnally. The skeptical misfire is to respond to this doubt only as a problem of epistemology to the exclusion of other kinds of reason and relationality, whether aesthetic, moral, or political. One might also say that the skeptic too strongly wants the world, and so treats it as a generic object, something possess-able in its entirety and totality, rather than as a multiplicity that is relational, contingent, and changing. We need a response to the force of skepticism—though not through certainty or a better epistemology, but rather through a diagnosis or etiology. Driven by the will to truth, the skeptic loses sight of the fact that our desire is a desire for the world, and so loses the world, or at least, loses sight of *this* world in its singularity and contingency, alive, changing, and inhabited by humanity and sociality. What Wittgenstein or Cavell want to return to us is *human* reason, for nothing is more unnatural than the ground-ing of skeptical reason in a kind of naturalism.

One obvious bridge between Cavell's and Deleuze's account of ethics is that both find that the broken link with the world, or the skeptic's crisis of belief and his passion for possessing the world through certain knowledge of it, is death dealing. Call this the original sin of skepticism, where philosophy desires a picture of the world as a static or unchanging and therefore lifeless image. Skepticism imagines the world as a confined and unchanging generic object because only of such imagined objects could we have complete and certain knowledge. (And to obtain this knowledge, one has to imagine a simi-larly confined interiorized subject, also impermeable to change.) Like Deleuze, Cavell is seeking a form of philosophy that will encourage our recovery from skepticism, thus restoring life to the world. However, the way of life or the world is such that the skeptic is doomed to disappointment, and so his quest for certainty is expressed *as* disappointment, in that the aim of achieving and holding certainty of the world's existence means claiming full and uncon-tested possession of the world and of knowledge—an unacknowledged and unattainable desire. In this way, the world's death at the hands of skepticism expresses what might be called the three dimensions of nihilism: the failure to acknowledge the world (as it is, alive and changing); a freezing or fixation of the world as a static and possessable image; and finally, the annihilation of the specificity and value of the world and all the individuated and singular objects and souls within it.

What does it mean instead to acknowledge the world as other, but an other whose existence is both separate from yet necessary to my own? Acknowledging the world's necessity for us means recognizing our interest in it and its attraction for us; acknowledging its separateness means accepting its independence from us by not imposing our interests and needs upon it, but rather by being open to the responses and requests it may solicit. Following Cavell, Stephen Mulhall calls this falling in love with the world on terms of mutuality and equality. In response to the demand of a will to truth that insists upon a single mode or method for knowing, one which regulates rational investigation of all things, both Cavell and Deleuze would agree that thought requires attentiveness to things in the singularity and uniqueness of their existence. This is an appeal for recognizing and acknowledging difference and the uniqueness of singular encounters or events. Or as Cavell puts it toward the end of *The Claim of Reason:*

> But why shouldn't one say that there is a required appropriateness with respect to each breed of thing (object or being); something appropriate for bread, something else for stones, something for large stones that block one's path and something for small smooth stones that can be slung or shied; something for grass, for flowers, for orchards, for forests, for each fish of the sea and each fowl of the air; something for each human contrivance and for each human condition; and, if you like, on up? For each link in the Great Chain of Being there is an appropriate hook of response. I said that one's experience of others puts a seam in experience. Why not consider that experience is endlessly, continuously seamed? Every thing, and every experience of every different thing, is what it is. (441–442)

A seam both separates and unites, of course. It acknowledges that there are frontiers between interiority and exteriority, but also that they are at every point contiguous in our human experience of the world and our relationality with the world and with others. This statement is as close as one can come in Cavell to Deleuze's version of the univocity of Being as *a* life—singular, individuated, and individuating. (It is, moreover, a coherent response to Deleuze's unacknowledged skepticism, or anguish over humanity's disconnection from the world.) To accept and acknowledge the world and our life within it, to understand that we share a life with it, means recalling what we already know—that our experience of separation from the world is part of our shared existence with the world and all the individuated things within it. And we may be called to this recounting at any moment of our existence because it is continually forgotten. This recounting or recalling amounts to a quotidian refinding of difference within repetition as series or iteration—the fact of returning for that which differs—which forcefully contests skepticism's will to repeat the world with its own alienated image. Recovering the world from skepticism means interrupting repetition with difference, and thus Cavell comes strikingly close to Deleuze's own conclusions in *Difference and Repetition*. But in Cavell's view this is more a matter of continually bringing to mind the grammar of relations that bind us to the world, to life, and to others.

This is only half the picture, however. Cavell and Deleuze share a conception of philosophy that seeks to recover itself from Cartesian skeptical dilemmas. To lay claim to my existence, the solitary self-acknowledgment that "I think" is not enough to assert a shared ontology with the world and with others. I must claim my existence, not only by acknowledging it and its relatedness (to the world, to others), but also by *expressing* it, and thereby publicly requesting acknowledgment. Nothing less is meant by participating in a form of life. Because my expressions are anchored in my body and in my life, my expressions display life and expressiveness of an embodied existence, both in me and on earth, as agents in a common world where soul and matter are continuously seamed. Participating in a form of life means drawing from within myself an often unseen or unrecognized knowledge or capacity for knowing—a peculiar form of reflexivity as becoming-other to one's self, of passively allowing oneself to become known by another that thinks within me as the first step toward acknowledgment. Cavell's answer to the question, What is philosophy? seems, then, to respond precisely in many respects to the ethical and existential dilemma expressed so poignantly by Deleuze in *The Time-Image*. Our responsiveness to the world will not be rekindled only by believing again in life and our connection to the world; it also requires that we find strategies for reanimating our deadened or alienated relations with the world and others, and to do so as a daily practice. Acknowledgment, recounting criteria, and assembling reminders thus become practices of declaring and enacting one's existence, and that of other persons and things, as participating in a shared form of life—one we have a responsibility to investigate and to reaffirm anew each day in ways that make us continually responsible for and responsive to the singularity of our expressions and our relations in that form of life.

16. Ontology and Desire, or a Moving Response to Skepticism

> Film's promise of the world's exhibition is the background against which
> it registers absolute isolation: its rooms and cells and pinions hold out
> the world itself.
>
> —Stanley Cavell, *The World Viewed*

In *Elegy for Theory,* I characterized Cavell's *The World Viewed* (1971) and Kracauer's *Theory of Film* (1960) as untimely works, both projecting a vision of (film) philosophy for which there was no appropriate context of reception. Cavell was disappointed, no doubt, by the misunderstandings and confusions generated by *The World Viewed* in philosophy no less than in film studies. A series of essays of the same period—"What Becomes of Things on Film?" (1978), "More of *The World Viewed*," the "Foreword" to the enlarged edition of *The World Viewed* (both 1979), and "What Photography Calls Thinking" (1985)—are meant to respond to these criticisms, though ironically, often not in ways that directly confront Cavell's critics in ways they would like.

With forty years of hindsight, the problems or questions regarding ontology and medium that so troubled Cavell's critics might be obviated if one could rise to the challenge of reading *The World Viewed* against the background of *Must We Mean What We Say?* and *The Claim of Reason.* Even though the latter was published eight years after the first edition of *The World Viewed,* work on *The Claim of Reason,* based on Cavell's 1961 dissertation, was nonetheless his philosophical preoccupation throughout the sixties and into the early seventies. The deep philosophical background so present to Cavell in his first film book is thus probably absent to most of his initial and even subsequent readers.

However, there is another difficulty, perhaps more simply put, which was no less scandalous for readers in film studies and the poststructuralist humanities in the age of Theory and ideology than it was for philosophers working in a postanalytic framework. Cavell's approach to skepticism was not to respond to its epistemological dilemmas but instead to pose skepticism as an ethical question, or rather as a question of evaluating and transforming a mode of existence. To demonstrate the kinship of moral reasoning to epistemology, and not through adjudicating claims of certainty but by demonstrating how they both respond uncertainly to commonly experienced existential crises, would be scandal enough. (Recall that Cavell is not alone here. G. H. Von Wright, Charles Taylor, Richard Rorty, P. M. S. Hacker, Hubert Dreyfus and other important thinkers are all examining similar arguments from their different perspectives.) However, Cavell compounds the problem by connecting it to the domain of aesthetics, most prominently Shakespearean tragedy and romance, classical music and contemporary experimental music, opera, Hollywood comedies and melodramas, and European art films. Moreover, philosophical criticism cannot find its way alone through these dilemmas of knowing and valuing. Rather, Cavell asks us, philosophers and nonphilosophers alike, to acknowledge that the problem of managing one's relation to skepticism is already embedded or expressed in and through art; to put it another way, that the problem is fully immanent to the ontological situation of projected worlds and screened images, as well as the actions and images so deployed there. Here I rediscover in Cavell an intuition or idea that I have been exploring for more than twenty years—that art is always running ahead of philosophy.

In the period coincident with the publication of both *The Claim of Reason* and the second enlarged edition of *The World Viewed* in 1979, Cavell is revisiting and reformulating his arguments about skepticism in ways that subtly and complexly transform the purview of ontological investigation. Ordinarily, ontology is thought of as the question of existence of things, objects, or ideas external to myself. (This modern prejudice would have been unknown to the thinkers of ancient Greece.) One of Cavell's most original contributions to philosophy is to shift the framework of these questions completely, and in ways strangely coincident with Deleuze's philosophy of immanence. Through Cavell's investigations of skepticism, questions of ontology and of examining the best cases for knowing the world and other minds continually return to or fold back onto the subject. The skeptical dilemma only retains its force if the subject continues to *believe* that it is imprisoned by its perception and thus separated from the world and from others. Cavell wants us to understand that when caught by skeptical doubt, we are enthralled by belief or lack of belief, and that epistemology alone cannot give us support or succor. Epistemological or theoretical reason is not reason enough, which is why other strategies must be found for evaluating the hold these beliefs have on us; hence the importance of both moral reasoning and aesthetic judgment in Cavell's larger philosophical perspective. Moral reasoning and aesthetic judgment thus become ways of overcoming the interiority and solipsism of the subject, and of returning us to acknowledgment of the complex web of intersubjective relations that bind us, in every perception and expression, to our forms of life, or rather, to communities that include both the world and all the others in it, in which I myself am an other.

One of the main themes of *The Virtual Life of Film* is that the concept of medium is inseparable from the problem of ontology, but not as a concept of the identity or essence of forms or genres of art. A medium is not simply a passive material or substance; it is equally form, concept, or Idea. Indeed one of the most original arguments of *The World Viewed,* and the source of much misreading and confusion, is that Cavell considers medium as a terrain where works of art establish their modes of existence, and in turn pose questions of existence to us. As I wrote in *The Virtual Life of Film,* a medium is that which mediates—it stands between us and the world (but also confronts us as a world) in ways that return our perceptions to us in the form of thoughtfulness, and sometimes forgetfulness. The whole of Cavell's pioneering and difficult work is marked by a complex phenomenology drawn from Wittgenstein, Thoreau, and Emerson as much as Heidegger, and this phenomenology transforms conceptions of ontology in fascinating ways. Perhaps even Cavell himself did not fully realize at the time that what he had written was less an aesthetic or even a theory of film than a deeply considered work of ethics whose point of attention was a certain kind of emblematic world—the worlds of cinema as projected and screened. *The World Viewed* is a formidable work of aesthetics, and perhaps also of theory, but it is primarily an ethics. This is a powerful bridge to Deleuze, who considers the Image as both an ontological and an ethical concept.

To speak of ontology in reference to a mode of existence for art, as well as our actual or projected modes of existence in relation to art, is already to evoke an ethical reasoning in which relations between object and subject are codetermined, fluid, and suspended from historical or chronological time. Indeed the most powerful aesthetic experiences effect an interruption of time or an opening in temporal experience. Every assertion about medium or automatism in *The World Viewed* is equally a characterization of acts whereby the self engages with *its* forms of identity, where it may come to know itself or project some future self. In glossing Cavell's concept of automatism in *The Virtual Life of Film,* I noted that unlike classical art wherein automatisms function as the renewal and extension of tradition, modernist works provoke in each of their instances the sense of being self-actualizing, of standing alone. It is as if in each act of artmaking the possibility of producing art, and of having an aesthetic experience, has to be reasserted without any promise of success. In this way, the modern work of art embodies an existential condition expressive of our own current mode of existence: in the absence of tradition or any transcendental authority, whether moral or epistemological, the self is provoked to a state of continual self-actualization or invention. What we then seek in cinema, or indeed aesthetic experience, is not the refinding of an essence, but rather the new discovery of our selves, or the discovery of a new self. I said in *The Virtual Life of Film* that a medium, if it is a living one, is continually in a state of self-transformation. In like manner, the force of aesthetic sensation is that of a self discovering another self in a process of new formation.

In this context, Cavell's early definition of cinema as a succession of automatic world projections, which I discuss at length in *The Virtual Life of Film*, also suggests a program of philosophical investigation that links the temporality of modernism to the "movement" or transformative power of the image. *Succession* indicates types and degrees of depicted motion, of course, both within the frame and across continuous or discontinuous series at various scales. Yet this criterion should also be broadened to include the complex temporalities of the image in its states and phases of becoming. (Later, Cavell will refer to the image's powers of becoming as "photogenesis.") *Automatic* designates those aspects of the image that are self-producing independent of a human hand, as well as the absence of people and things so produced on the screen. Call this the inhuman dimension or power of screened worlds, which may also be characterized as the passive intentional power of cinematographic expression. *World* then leads to ontological investigations of the worlds and subjects so made, and the interpenetrating qualities of reality and fantasy experienced through institutional conditions of viewing and response. And finally, *projection* signals the phenomenological conditions of viewing, as if at a remove or distance from the world, as well as the force of analogy in movement and time between the screened world and the profilmic world thus transcribed and projected. Movement, time, and becoming are all complexly linked here, in ways expressive of the unsettled and unsettling force of fantasy and reality (of fantasies of reality, or the reality of fantasy in relations to screened worlds), as well as the passing or becoming of ontological situations thus projected.

In the first phase of Cavell's film philosophy, the problem of ontology does not wish just to account for the existence of the projected world and perception as screened. Rather, Cavell wants to ask, what are the conditions of my current existence that lead me to desire to see and to experience the world in just *this* way, *as* projected and screened? Why does just *this* kind of picturing of the world hold me? What are the sources of its attraction or attractiveness? Cinema itself responds to this question by offering another regime of belief, not necessarily as an escape into fantasy, but rather by offering a condition or situation wherein we might understand more clearly how our views of or on reality are burdened by fantasy. This is neither an escape into or out of fantasy, as if somehow our thoughts, perceptions, and expressions could be disconnected from our desires. The screened world is a perfect emblem of skepticism, as I have already pointed out in *The Virtual Life of Film*, but it also opens to view a range of options for relief from skepticism. And not by bolstering our knowledge of things, not by documenting our certainty of the world either present or past, but by opening to question dilemmas of belief or disbelief framed by a mode of existence that desires these kinds of pictures of the world, or alternatively, by examining the forms of our responsiveness to a world that wants us to experience it as or through moving pictures.

Cavell's version of ontology is transformational. When Cavell asks, in 1978, what becomes of things (or people) on film, he want us to comprehend the world viewed as projected on the screen as a space of transformation, or if you will, becoming. Cavell calls this force of becoming on screen and as image "photogenesis." These transformations do not only count for objects recorded and transformed to the screen but also for the subjects included there. (Indeed as we shall soon see, as transcribed and projected on the screen, people and things enter into a common space of expressive potential.) In his first accounts leading up to *Pursuits of Happiness,* these subjects are ethical exemplars responding to skeptical belief, usually in comic ways, or in fact finding such belief to be comic rather than tragic. In "The Avoidance of Love," Cavell states that in *King Lear,* "Tragedy has moved into the world, and with it the world becomes theatrical" (*Must We Mean What We Say?* 344). Cinema then finds the possibility, perhaps, of detheatricalizing this world, thus undermining skepticism with laughter. The figures of Keaton, Chaplin, or Cary Grant are especially important in this context, not to mention the great actresses of remarriage comedy. Later, Cavell's interest in Emersonian moral perfectionism uncovers new dimensions of immanence where the temporal logic or structure of perfectionism can be seen as fully coincident with certain varieties of cinematographic becoming. Becoming on the screen is a species of (self) transformation, meaning both that it is automatic (or subject to certain automatisms of recording, transcription, and narration) and that it projects reflexively a picture of self responding to pressures of transformation. (Cavell often refers to this process as the ascendancy of actor over character in the cinema.)

Ontology in Cavell's sense is therefore not about an attained existence for either objects or persons that film is then capable of recording, representing, or preserving, nor is it about the preservation or projection of the world as a generic object. The temporal structure of screened worlds and the ethical stakes for our picture of subjectivity so projected are more complex. To understand the concept of ontology as expressing film's relation to reality, and thus fantasy, Cavell asks us to investigate the reality of this relation through moving images as images that move us. What makes cinema an emblem of modernity in the arts or culture is not only that it perfectly expresses the dilemma of skepticism as a structural condition of perception; it also shows that the reality of this condition is inescapably marked by fantasy, and that this condition is in fact escapable.

Take for example Cavell's discussion of the comedy of Buster Keaton in "What Becomes of Things on Film?" Cavell frames his response to Keaton through Heidegger's characterization of the worldhood of the world announcing itself to us, not as a revelation to the subject but rather through the obstinacy of things, which in opposing us expose the limitations of our acts, knowledge, and preoccupations in our encounters and struggles with material objects. The resistance of the world to our actions and will not only circumscribes us as subjects—if we are willing, it also opens us sensuously to so far unrecognized textures and capacities of the world, and to our contingent relationships to it as a space of accidents, which are also unforeseen possibilities. In slapstick comedy, every mischance is a gift and an opportunity for evasion. That this occurs in the time and movements of cinema, Cavell explains, says something about

> the human capacity for sight, or for sensuous awareness generally, something we might express as our condemnation to project, to inhabit, a world that goes essentially beyond the delivery of our senses. . . . I understand Buster Keaton, say in *The General,* to exemplify an acceptance of the enormity of this realization of human limitation, denying neither the abyss that at any time may open before our plans, nor the possibility, despite that open possibility, of living honorably, with good if resigned spirits, and with eternal hope. His capacity for love does not avoid this knowledge, but lives in full view of it. Is he dashing? He is something

rarer; he is undashable. He incorporates both the necessity of wariness in an uncertain world, and also the necessary limits of human awareness; gaze as we may, there is always something behind our backs, room for doubt.[76]

At the same time, these comments are not a defense of stoicism. The personae of Keaton or Chaplin do not ask that we gracefully accept the obstinacy of fate and the world but rather show that human beings are resourcefully capable of pursuing happiness in spite of these limitations—this is not far from Deleuze's ethical demand to exercise the freedom to choose or to recognize the always-open possibility of willed alternatives. Similarly, in "The Thought of Movies," Cavell asks us to recognize "that there are conditions under which opportunities may be discovered again and retaken, that somewhere there is a locale in which a second chance is something one may give oneself" (97). The comic responses of Keaton or Chaplin to the world's contingency and obstinacy are extraordinary manifestations of what any ordinary human being is capable of. Cavell calls this a willingness to care, or to be attentive to the depth of a human capacity for inventiveness and improvisation in seeking out newly imagined alternatives.

Here the link between reality and fantasy in the screened image is especially important. Or rather, it may be characteristic of the automatisms of the screened image that every transcription of the world is also expressive of a desired stance toward the world—the world as we want to see it or desire it to be. The real and the imaginary are not opposed here as genres of cinematographic expression. Rather, they continually flow into and out of one another in the temporality of the projected image and our responses to it. Cavell calls this an alternation between the indicative and subjunctive tenses or moods, or unmarked juxtapositions of reality with some unresolved opposition to reality; Deleuze calls this the indiscernibility of the actual and the virtual, or of the real and the imaginary.

Cavell evokes the term photogenesis to describe the image's peculiar quality of becoming, which is also expressive of "the power of film to materialize and to satisfy (hence to dematerialize and to thwart) human wishes that escape the satisfaction of the world as it stands; as perhaps it will ever, or can ever, in fact stand" ("What Becomes of Things on Film?" 6). To speak of

76. "What Becomes of Things on Film?" in *Cavell on Film*, 3. Originally published in fall 1978 in *Philosophy and Literature*.

ontology here is to address not only or not simply a fact of film, as Cavell might put it, but also to focus on a genetic capacity of the image that needs to be interpreted or evaluated in terms of its qualities of attraction. In the force and quality of their genesis or becoming, the temporality of the world and subjects becoming on film—or in the expressiveness of the image—anticipate the grammar of what Cavell later calls moral perfectionism. Considered retrospectively, this idea is put forward with great clarity in "What Becomes of Things on Film?" when Cavell writes, "That to be human is to have, or to risk having, this capacity to wish; that to be human is to wish, and in particular to wish for a completer identity than one has so far attained; and that such a wish may project a complete world *opposed* to the world one so far shares with others: this is a way of taking up the cause of Shakespearean Romance. . . . In both skepticism and romance, knowledge, call it consciousness as a whole, must go out in order that a better consciousness can come to light" (7).

At various moments in this period of his writing, Cavell repeats that film is a *moving* image of skepticism. To answer the question what becomes of things and people on film means comprehending all the variety and complexity of what "movement" means here. We certainly find cinematographic images to be moving, that is, as inspiring affect or emotion. But they are also unsettling; they make us ontologically unquiet. If film is a moving image of skepticism, it does not so much confirm our subjectivity (as modern, for example) as shake our belief that we know the basis of our conviction in reality. This movement is also transformational. In cutting conviction loose from its moorings, the subject is made vulnerable to pressures of uncertainty, doubt, and self-questioning, and thus open to the possibility of change. And finally, movement is also historical: the passage of skepticism into art or cinema, from the everyday or philosophy into a mode or machine of presentation, may also mean that modernity is changing the terms of its existence, as I already argued in *The Virtual Life of Film*. (Here we pass, perhaps, from an experience of modernity to nostalgia for it, or what Cavell calls losing one's natural relation to art or film.)

The concept of photogenesis plays an interesting role in the first phase of Cavell's thought as a key point of transition from the concerns of ontology to those of perfectionism. For Cavell, photogenesis names one of the principal powers or automatisms of cinematographic presentations, where the transcription and projection of screened worlds enacts transformations whose violence is commensurate with the force of becoming immanent to thought and things on film. The concept of photogenesis is complexly linked here to cinema's specific institutional presentation of the skeptical dilemma. For example, in the foreword to the enlarged edition of *The World Viewed,* Cavell writes that objects projected on the film screen are inherently reflexive or self-referential, meaning first that one is led to wonder about their physical origins in past times and spaces, but also that the quality of their presence on the screen indicates their ineluctable absence. This situation is an emblem of skepticism in that all we need to convince ourselves of the presence of the world is a projected image wherein the world is screened and we are screened from it, as if viewing it from a distance.

Belief in the causal presence of objects on the screen and our surrender of responsibility for that world to film's automatic transcriptions and projections of it are among the satisfactions of skepticism. But the anguish of skepticism is also produced from this situation in two ways, both of which signify a withdrawal or diminution of human agency and autonomy. In viewing this succession of automatic world projections, we are absolved from responsibility for producing views of the world, since another automatic or automatizing (nonhuman) entity has brought them into being. Call this the Platonic view that so worried Jean-Louis Baudry or Christian Metz. Alternatively, in the projected worlds so produced, human beings are also leveled to the plane of immanence of worldly things. In other words, within the space and duration of the cinematographic image people and objects have the same degree and level of expressive potential. Within this space of recorded time and movement, people and objects, events and actions, are absorbed into a common matrix of interdependency that is singular and immanent.

This leveling of beings and things in a common field of expression is one of the most noteworthy characteristics of photogenesis as a significant cinematographic automatism. In his essay "Stanley Cavell on Recognition, Betrayal, and the Photographic Field of Expression,"[77] Richard Moran notes that Cavell characterizes cinematographic expression—call this the image—as a kind of seam in experience, or an ontological link between views and viewing, indeed as a kind of powerful expressive immanence. Because the image takes in the entirety of what exists in the frame and renders all of the elements thus transcribed as equally and uniformly expressive, it enfolds every object, action,

77. Forthcoming in *L'écran de nos pensées* (Paris: Éditions ENS), ed. Elise Domenach.

and individual into a common space and duration, and it does so automatically in ways that supervene human agency.

This observation is one way of characterizing photographic intentionality, or rather, the grammar of intention we evoke in trying to say what the camera does and reveals. The camera creates a zone, Moran suggests after Cavell, where even silence and immobility become expressive, and indeed where objects, themselves silent and immobile, become as expressive as subjects, no matter how moving and voluble. In turn, even the most reticent subject also becomes demonstrative. Cavell refers to this quality as "the camera's knowledge of the metaphysical restlessness of the live body at rest. . . . Under examination by the camera, a human body becomes for its inhabitant a field of betrayal more than a ground of communication, and the camera's further power is manifested as it documents the individual's self-conscious efforts to control the body each time it is conscious of the camera's attention to it."[78]

Moran's observations on photographic expressiveness also clarify what Deleuze tends to call "camera-consciousness." Not that the camera thinks or has an active or reflective self-consciousness in the same way as human minds, but rather that its powers of expressivity are shown as a kind of revelatory intending. There are active powers in the arts of photography and film, of course, through the actions of intentional recording, framing, editing, and narrating. However, in Moran's view, there is also a passive power to cinematographic intentionality. "The camera relates to a human subject, forcing it to reveal itself, not through a kind of *active* power," Moran writes,

> not by interrogation or forcing anything to happen, but rather by its very passivity, by somehow bringing *whatever* is going on in the visual field into the realm of the expressive, the revealing. It is not a matter of forcing the human subject to speak, but rather of creating a space within which either speaking, hesitating, or not speaking at all are all equally forms of expression. . . . Here Cavell's description of the powers of the camera is accented less on the liberatory potential of "giving expression to the inexpressive," than on the inescapability of the expression under the camera's gaze, and on the fact that *what* is thereby revealed is not under the control or understanding of the human subject himself."[79]

78. "What Photography Calls Thinking," in *Cavell on Film*, 126.
79. Moran, 4–5.

In addition, this passive and automatic power does not simply register details of surface and externality; it puts the subject so to speak beside itself in ways whereby the passive expressive intentionality of the camera will always exhaust or overwhelm those of its subjects. Every surface is exposed in the sense that every recorded thing and movement is rendered with the same degree and quality of immanence; it is always "utterly unable *not* to be continuously expressive, to be always giving itself away" (Moran 6). For Cavell, the character of this immanence makes the cinematographic image an emblem of perpetual visibility where in principle nothing can be hidden and all is potentially public and open to view. In a very real sense, Moran concludes, objects and subjects are *exposed* photographically, such that "even the tiniest deflections of one's glance or posture count as part of the manifestation of the self, whether actively or passively. . . . And the interplay between activity and passivity in Cavell's writing, both philosophic and cinematic, helps us to see the dependence of that active power of interrogation on the corresponding power of the camera to hold still, to withdraw from assertion. The forms of expressiveness are inescapable even when not imposed from without, when they are rather the conditions of visibility within the frame" (18–19).

Cavell's characterization of the immanent expressive powers of the image is not a realism, or not only a realism in a limited sense. (This is also a way of saying that when seen from the right perspective Cavell's most abstruse assertions about the cinematic image turn out to be his most precise.) The reality of the condition of cinematic viewing, according to Cavell, is ineluctably marked by fantasy, and in turn fantasy is one of the most powerful components of our experience of reality through cinema. This experience is neither the illusion of reality nor the reality-effect so thoroughly studied by contemporary film theory. Rather, it relates to Cavell's close connection of the skeptical dilemma to the experience of modernity in cinematic viewing, and how that experience conditions our responsiveness to the camera's powers of passive intentionality. There is a powerful reality expressed in this situation, since it is the philosophical background of our daily cultural life in modernity— the experience of cinema is a component of that life and also an expression of it. But the reality of this experience is also permeated by fantasy (of belief or conviction, of a world accessible only through the senses, of a past preserved against time, of a self withdrawn into privacy) as a force of attraction inseparable from our lived reality. In philosophy, this situation is not to be negated, overcome, or deconstructed, but rather acknowledged and evaluated. The challenge of ontological investigation is not to alter our conditions of knowing but rather our conditions of valuing and living. The photographic and cinematic arts have a special role to play here because they embody and replicate the structure of skepticism, and also because they so powerfully inspire a hesitancy or equivocation, which according to Cavell is inherent in the structure of skepticism itself, with respect to skepticism's powers of conviction. In other words, photography both elicits a certain regime of belief and also destabilizes it.

This assertion and destabilization of belief is beautifully expressed in Cavell's statement, early in *The World Viewed,* that "A photograph does not present us with 'likenesses' of things; it presents us, we want to say, with the things themselves. But wanting to say that may well make us ontologically restless" (*The World Viewed* 17). Here Cavell wants to describe the powers of photogenesis simultaneously to affirm belief and inspire doubt, to attract us to the image as confirming the existence of the world through its powers of automatic analogical causation, and at the same time its power to enact a fantasy of the world's presence through its absent existence. This is another way of asserting that the automatic transcription and projection of the world hovers uncertainly between indicative and subjunctive moods, or a copresent belief in the past existence in time of a world preserved and the present projection of a world transformed. We misrecognize photography's hold on us if we gravitate too urgently to one pole or the other. Rather, the truth of the image, if there is one, resides in its uncertainty, contingency, and becoming.

Cavell's concept of automatism is therefore not meant to describe, or not only to describe, the fact of mechanical reproduction; it also wants to account for the powers of attraction or fantasy in relation to images so produced in ways both human and inhuman. Automatism thus manifests a specific kind of desire—the wish to view the world unseen and as if by a self hidden behind perception—and this world must be taken to be *the* world in its totality. This is the modern philosophical wish of skepticism, whose desire for the world as a completely knowable object places it just beyond the reach of our knowing, and so produces a situation where our natural mode of perception is viewing as an invisible and anonymous observer. Here, Cavell explains, "We do not so much look at the world as look *out at* it, from behind the self" (*The World Viewed* 102). This is a precise description of the perceptual and epistemological situation of skepticism, which seems to want to make the self distinct from perception.

In the cinema, this perception appears to be produced independently of the self as an automatic instrumentality. The skeptical attitude thus engenders a peculiar internal division whereby the mind can only assure itself of the possibility of knowledge by treating its own perception as a separate mechanism that intervenes between itself and the world. At the same time, this mode projects an external division separating self from world, whose only points of contact can take place through acts of viewing. Perception thus becomes both a structure of separation between subject and object, mind and world, and also the only pathway through which mind and world can communicate. In thrall of skepticism, Cavell suggests, the only way of establishing connection with the world is through viewing it or having views of it. To wish to view the world itself—as it was in the past or is in the present past—as a complete causally produced object is therefore to wish for the condition of viewing as such but in the passive form of an automatic and instrumentalized perception. In turn, to wish for the condition of viewing as such is to desire a sure connection to the world, but also to hold at bay, unseen and unacknowledged, recognition that this desire is a fantasy of anonymity, privacy, and power over the world. In theatrical cinema, the deepest irony of this situation is that the condition of collective viewing and of shared experience might reinforce our desire for the privacy and anonymity of skepticism. (Perhaps the contemporary proliferation of home viewing and personal data screens might likewise reinforce and expand exponentially an isolation where our only recourse for connecting to the world or to others is through the image and from behind screens. In this ontology we are not alone together, but rather together alone.) Alternatively, philosophical investigation and criticism might be able to release the hold of this fantasy or to let us see the attractions of sociality and a shared mode of existence waiting to be acknowledged beyond it.

17. Automatism and the Declaration of Existence in Time

> Who knows what the human body would expand and flow out to under a
> more genial heaven?
>
> —Henry David Thoreau, Walden

I have been speaking of Cavell's difficult and controversial account of the concept of automatism. At this point in *The World Viewed*, Cavell presents two of the most powerful and elusive arguments in his philosophical oeuvre. One relates to cinema and the other to painting; together they present alternative frameworks for thinking through questions of existence as raised by the concepts of automatism and photogenesis.

Cavell's reasoning is worth examining in detail. One of the key powers of cinematographic automatism is that it relieves the individual of responsibility for viewing, since the screened world produces views automatically with its own (mechanical and inhuman) conditions of causality, projection, and temporality. In this situation, Cavell says somewhat mysteriously that the movies seem "more natural than reality" (*The World Viewed* 102). This statement is rife with irony, but it is also deeply felt. Framed by the long history of skepticism, movies may seem more natural than reality because they reproduce views automatically, and thus reinforce the perceptual and epistemological structure of skepticism as if it were our most familiar and customary option for encountering the world. One is reminded here of Walter Benjamin's observation in "The Work of Art in the Age of Its Technological Reproducibility: Third Version" that "The equipment-free aspect of reality has here become the height of artifice, and the vision of immediate reality the Blue Flower in the land of technology."[80] The intense alienation produced by automated images makes us long for the sight of reality itself, and this may also be a way of agreeing with Benjamin that reality has become denatured within the skeptical culture of modernity.

Alternatively, another power of the movies may be that they alert us to a different view of nature in which objects and subjects are no longer separate and distinct, but rather are embedded and interrelated in a singular and immanent matrix of duration. But here Cavell's argument makes a rather stunning turn. That movies seem more natural than reality is not the sign of escape into fantasy, dream, or illusion so much as a respite from private fantasy and withdrawal into ourselves. Automatism releases us from the task of producing world views. But in automatically reproducing this condition of viewing as a mechanism separate from our selves and actions, we may become alert to the fact that whether experienced with or without projection, the world is already drawn by fantasy. In other words, there are no views of the world unencumbered by our desires, whether singular or collective. It is ever more important to acknowledge and evaluate those desires philosophically so as to understand what kinds of worlds attract us, and either bind or free us. Automatism not only reproduces the conditions of skepticism and the withdrawal of the self behind the anonymous screen of perception; it may also awaken and alert the

---

80. In *Walter Benjamin: Selected Writings*, vol. 4, *1938–1940*, trans. Edmund Jephcott et al., ed. Howard Eiland and Michael W. Jennings (Cambridge, MA: The Belknap Press of Harvard University Press, 2003), 263.

self to other senses of reality and community. "Movies convince us of the world's reality in the only way we have to be convinced," Cavell writes, "without learning to bring the world closer to the heart's desire (which in practice now means learning to stop altering it illegitimately, against itself): by taking views of it" (*The World Viewed* 102).

The density and complexity of these arguments is unwoven in compelling ways in Cavell's 1985 essay, "What Photography Calls Thinking." That we may be convinced of this reality or not is a central fact of its fluctuating existence. Moreover, this instability at the heart of the image is not a matter of representation or illusion, nor can we test this conviction in the framework of epistemology. Rather, it is a matter of ethics, or of an uncertainty or unmooring of our sense of existence expressed as "an impressive range of anxieties centered on, or symptomatized by, our sense of how little we know about what the photographic reveals: that we do not know what our relation to reality is, our complicity in it; that we do not know how or what to feel about those events; that we do not understand the specific transformative powers of the camera, what I have called its original violence; that we cannot anticipate what it will know of us—or show of us" ("What Photography Calls Thinking" 116).

The sense of reality we intuit, or rather inhabit, in relation to a world projected and screened is closely allied to the condition of modernity as Cavell defines it in art or philosophy. "Photography could not have impressed itself so immediately and pervasively on the European (including the American) mind," Cavell writes, "unless that mind had at once recognized in photography a manifestation of something that had already happened to itself. What happened to this mind, as the events are registered in philosophy, is its fall into skepticism, together with its efforts to recover itself, events recorded variously in Descartes and Hume and Kant and Emerson and Nietzsche and Heidegger and Wittgenstein" ("What Photography Calls Thinking" 116). The stakes of philosophical investigation as ethical evaluation are woven into the style of this sentence. Photography is a moving image no less than film; or rather it induces a movement, fluctuation, or sense of transformation that is personal as much as historical or cultural. There is both a fall into skepticism and an effort to recover the self—a diagnosis of illness and suggestion of therapy— expressed in the fact that recognition of our complex and contradictory desires or fantasies in relation to photography make us anxious, or ontologically restless. To the extent that we are in the epistemological thrall of skepticism, the fate of modernity is to relate to the world only by viewing it as if from behind the self. Heidegger diagnoses this withdrawal from the world behind the screen of perception as distance; Thoreau or Emerson refer to the experience as nextness or proximity to the world, which also expresses our separateness from it and each other. But as diagnosed by Cavell, this movement is not only one of withdrawing but also of returning or recovering. Think of movement here as transport, which induces anxieties of dislocation and disorientation, but which also defines arcs of transition toward something else, say a future condition of culture or state of self. Here Cavell's sense of ontology is linked not only to ethics but also to time—the event of photography in Cavell is not so distant from the Event in Deleuze.

Another connection to Deleuze is Cavell's concern with the difficulty and possibilities of thinking. Cavell's title recalls Heidegger's question "Was heißt Denken?"—often translated as "What is called thinking?" but perhaps more powerfully understood as "What calls for thinking?" To ask what a photograph is thinking about is not to attribute consciousness to it but to ask what it knows of itself, or to examine more carefully, as does Richard Moran, its powers of passive intentional expression. When Cavell refers to a text's self-referentiality or self-acknowledgment, and asks what it knows or expects of its viewers or interlocutors, he asks readers to engage in philosophical criticism, not only of the text but also of themselves, thus reinforcing art's call to thinking, and perhaps inspiring artful conversation. To ask what a photograph knows of me is to request a closer examination of how the conditions of photography or film as media in Cavell's sense solicit responsiveness from me, and therefore to investigate the ambiguity, singularity, and strangeness underlying our ordinary experience of such images. In philosophical (self) investigation, the potential derangement or madness of skepticism may be recognized and acknowledged. But this is also a form of evaluation leading, perhaps, to repossession of one's self or possession of a newer self. If film is a *moving* image of skepticism, it is also a point of passage toward something else.

Terms of transport or transformation also suggest creation and self-creation, which is perhaps the central theme of Cavell's treatment of comedies of remarriage and melodramas of the unknown woman. Both genres are exemplary of what Cavell later calls moral perfectionism. And in fact moral perfectionism is meant to describe and account for the (aesthetic) qualities and (ethical) stakes of "movement" or photogenesis in their expressions of fall and return, diagnosis and recovery, leading to new creations of the human. It is an irony, but perhaps a welcome one, that recovery also entails loss. In their peculiar qualities of movement and their capacities to induce movement, photogenesis, transport, and transformation are meant to convey some unsettling varieties of becoming in the image as complex expressions of our experience of time. To be convinced of being present to a past world may lead to nostalgia, but through its powers of ineluctable succession the cinematographic image may also express the incessant passage of time and the transience of life. To be attracted to the past but also caught up in a present that slips from your grasp in every passing instant may leave you distracted and inattentive to the future. Cavell finds such thoughts to be powerfully expressed with "particular lucidity in shots of candid happiness, where the metaphysical transience of such instants marks their subjects with mortal vulnerability" ("What Photography Calls Thinking" 124). But this is only one dimension of film's transport in time, or how it calls for thinking in, of, or through time. Cavell therefore reminds us of his depiction of "a vision of the world viewed—the world as photographed—as the world of my immortality, the world without me, reassuring in the promise that it will survive me, but unsettling in the suggestion that as I stand now the world is already for me a thing of the past, like a dead star. Romantic writers such as Coleridge and Wordsworth and Emerson and Thoreau mean to awaken us to our harboring of such a vision, and to free us from it. Yet our nostalgia deepens. Memory, which should preserve us, is devouring us. We must, as Thoreau put the matter, look another way" (124).

To look another way is to seek out new paths to recovery, or to be present again to one's self by suddenly awakening to the fact that we have forgotten ourselves. It is as if human conduct and human thought continually fail to synchronize with one another—Cavell calls this the condition of a creature whose body and soul do not everywhere fit, which is perhaps the signal discovery of psychoanalysis. The open question, however, is how and why cinematographic thinking might provide philosophical support in aid of recovery.

In his essay on "Behavior," Emerson calls this returning the mind to the living body. In a wonderfully astute and pleasurable reading of Frank Capra's *Mr. Deeds Goes to Town* (1936), Cavell depicts cinematography's attention to thinking as a somatography, or the image's registration and expression of bodily responses to thought in ways unknown or unrecognized by either the body or the self. (This is yet another name for the power of photogenesis and of the camera's passive powers of expressive intentionality.) One of the peculiar powers of the camera is to frame such behaviors, which often remain unknown to the subject and misunderstood by others of his world, in ways where they can finally be acknowledged and evaluated. Deeds is thought insane because of his inexplicably eccentric behavior, one of whose features is renouncing the gifts of inherited capital. In the climactic trial scene, Deeds defends himself not by *explaining* himself, but rather by invoking the criterion of "fidgetiness." Call this the often inexplicable responses of the body to thought, or thought's unsettling of the body, as a shared characteristic of the human. Rather than justifying his eccentricity or singularity, Deeds demonstrates what all present to him share as human creatures: that the presence of thought may render the body speechless but human being is no less thoughtful and expressive. In a wonderful turn, the film refers to this condition as being "pixilated." There is both error and truth in this idiom. The mistaken view of the elderly sisters who bear witness to Deeds's eccentricities is that pixilated means "crazy." Yet in asserting that everyone is pixilated apart from them (thus revealing their fairly deep state of pixilation) they confirm a power of the cinematographic image—it can reveal the presence of thought or thoughtfulness in ways that individuals are often incapable of recognizing in themselves or in others, and it does so through its own attentiveness to everything that moves before the camera and in making movement expressive. One wants to say it gives intelligence to movement.

Before the trial scene, the voluble, sociable, and fidgety Deeds has been reduced to immobility and silence. As the very figure of American communitarianism and civic mindedness, Deeds has withdrawn into himself, perhaps in protest of a community that asks him to account for himself, and which refuses to recognize in him the generosity, honesty, and loyalty, indeed the spirit of criticism, that might be characterized as a kind of American utopianism. There is also something frightening in Deeds's utopianism and his often-violent libertarian moralism, as if the uneven line between democracy and a kind of protofascism was still thinly drawn in 1936. (Twenty years later, Nicholas Ray would explore the darker side of this American madness in *Bigger Than Life*.) Then perhaps the only way to avoid the failure of democracy is to acknowledge our common capacity for pixilation, and to learn to recognize and evaluate whether we have lapsed into real madness or not. Here the camera is meant to help us apprehend, in ways our unaided selves cannot, that soul and body do not everywhere fit. Thoughtful behavior betrays our existence to our selves (the presence of our selves to both mind and body) but not in ways Descartes would find satisfying, nor in such situations would Descartes's proof of existence much compel us. There must be other ways of being and seeming reasonable, and of asserting our claim to existence. To find ways of answering the question, what photography calls thinking thus means considering possibilities for thought and existence that release skepticism's hold on our sense of reality.

In evoking Heidegger, Cavell wishes to convey the idea that what calls for thinking is desire, or rather that the desire to think is essential to the possibility of thinking. Thinking is linked to the human desire for the possible, and for bringing the possible to realization. "Fidgetiness," then, means not so much the unspoken presence of thought as the desire to think and to give expression to thought. Perhaps this is the body's responsiveness to thoughts that it can hardly contain and which it feels compelled to express. For Cavell, this recognition and acknowledgment of the unquiet body, which connects human desire with possibility and realization, captures better and in more prosaic terms what Descartes's *cogito* is meant to prove—the existence of the human or of the possibility of becoming human in spite of the world's denials, or our denials of the world. But here Deeds's impassioned proof is directed less toward the possibilities of knowledge and existence or in proving his own self-possession and sanity than in demonstrating the ethical failure of the community that would judge him. In acknowledging that he has been "away," Deeds wants to awaken his community to the fact that they have all lapsed into that form of pixilation called conformity, in which their own ideals of democratic commons have parted from them, and they are no longer able to recognize the presence of thought to self and thus confirm their existences to themselves and in community. Cavell characterizes this experience as implying that "we are without proof of our existence, that we are, accordingly, in a state of preexistence, as if metaphysically missing persons. . . . But the only difference between their expressed view of the world and Deeds' view is that he does not clearly exempt himself, any more than Thoreau exempts himself, from the madness of the world. Perhaps this is what philosophical authority sounds like" ("What Photography Calls Thinking" 128–129).

Descartes's declaration of existence requires not the presence of thought but rather the ego's exercise of its capacity for thought, and thus Descartes's *cogito* asserts that thinking cannot doubt itself. After Emerson, and later Freud, the proof of thinking is that it cannot be concealed. Yet there is a missing term in this uncanny reversal. Descartes's proof of existence requires the action of a consciousness fully present to itself independently of any body. Not only is thought deprived of its anatomy here, but perhaps thought, and therefore existence, can only occur intermittently, that is, in the action of its exercise, which is all too infrequent. Cavell's portrayal of Emerson suggests another image of thought, one in which thought courses through us continually in the medium of our daily creaturely existence, yet only intermittently becomes present to our selves, or in which consciousness is defined as becoming

again present to self. Existence is never in doubt here, but it is often unacknowledged; we need only to be awakened to the fact.

Cavell says that a reverse field of proof is needed, one responsive to skepticism in ways very different from Cartesianism. Here the camera's passive intentional powers present evidence of another kind of unseen or unconscious
surface—that of our perceptual externality to others. In other words, we are
not a perception hidden by a body, but rather a persistent expressive visibility
at one with the world. Cinema is not the answer to this dilemma as much as
an apposite tool to think with, not only because of its revelatory affinity with
metaphysical restlessness but also because of the ordinariness of its compan-
ionship. I return again here to film's *moving* image of skepticism, not only its
registration but also its promotion of movement into or out of fragile states
of being and becoming. The cinematographic image cannot but produce an
image of change or becoming; we only need to interpret and to evaluate the
forces of becoming it presents to us. And so Cavell concludes that "My idea is
that the invention of the motion picture camera reveals something that has
already happened to us, hence something, when we fail to acknowledge it,
that is knowledge of something fundamental about our existence which we
resist. And the camera also reveals and records that resistance—recall that, in
the course of Deeds' lecture to the court, each time the camera follows his attention to a person's body's motion, that person's reflex is shown to be to attempt to hide the motion. We can think of what the camera reveals as a new
strain either in our obliviousness to our existence, or in a new mode of certainty of it" ("What Photography Calls Thinking" 131).

This is what cinematography calls thinking. No active powers of consciousness need be attributed to the camera here, any more than in Emerson the self
manages to recognize its continual and continuing presence to its body, the
world, or a community of others. The camera's mode of thought is the enact-
ment of perpetual visibility in terms of what I have called, after Moran, its
passive powers of expressive intentionality. Siegfried Kracauer called this
power alienation, or the camera's capacity for capturing and rendering as expressive, and thus humanly interpretable, the flux of existence in time. Time
floods us and overwhelms us; it divides us from ourselves. Yet through its capacity to register this flux and render it expressive, the moving image provides
a new medium for pondering the grounds of our conviction in reality, or what
we believe reality conveys or can convey in the image. "If the price of Descartes's
proof of his existence," Cavell concludes, "was a perpetual recession of the body
(a kind of philosophical counter-Renaissance), the price of an Emersonian

proof of my existence is a perpetual visibility of the self, a theatricality in my presence to others, hence to myself. The camera is an emblem of perpetual visibility. Descartes's self-consciousness thus takes the form of embarrassment" (131).

Skepticism's doubt of existence is the name of this embarrassment. Moreover, photography's powers of automatic analogical causation will not relieve us of this chagrin. (Often enough they are a manifestation of its symptoms.) What the camera recognizes, in helping us examine the fact that we do not yet know in what our conviction in reality relies upon, is that skepticism is not yet overcome—all the camera can do is present to us an image of skepticism moving in an alienated form. This act is not the presentation of a new knowledge, but rather, as Cavell puts it, a registration and revealing of something fundamental about our existence that we resist. At one and the same time, it is both a new variation in our obliviousness to existence and a new mode of certainty in it.

One may wonder here why Cavell's discussions of automatism in *The World Viewed* are placed so close to an excursus on modern painting, by which Cavell principally means the minimalist, abstract, and process-driven art of Jackson Pollock, Frank Stella, Jules Olitski, Morris Louis, and their contemporaries. However, there is a reality to the experience of abstraction that is not so far removed from that of cinematographic transcription. Neither are considered by Cavell to be "representational."[81] Both are deemed to be deeply ethical expressions of and responses to skepticism's division of subject and object, and thus the isolation of the subject in and from the world. (Realist) cinema and (abstract) painting are thus promoted as the two genres or media of art most philosophically characteristic of our modernity, and significantly, in ways that efface distinctions between the popular and elite arts.

The ontology of film declares our distance from the world by automating our views of it, but also by including us in the temporality of succession and

---

81. In "What Photography Calls Thinking," Cavell explains that the strangeness and power of photography derives from the fact that our conventional view of picturing or representing is conditioned by the criterion of semblance or the making of likenesses, that is, as "one thing standing for another, disconnected thing, or one forming a likeness of another" (117). Photography, however, performs another activity: "A representation emphasizes the identity of its subject, hence it may be called a likeness; a photograph emphasizes the existence of its subject, recording it; hence it is that it may be called a transcription" (118). As I argue in *The Virtual Life of Film*, counterintuitive as it may be, this means that a photograph is not a representation—it is less concerned with likenesses in space than with existences in time.

projection—this is a declaration of our presence to past existence. The ontology of minimalist abstraction declares the autonomy of painting as a complete being occupying a specific time and space that confronts us with our own sense (and perhaps our fantasies) of autonomy and independent existence—this is a contingent encounter in an indeterminate shared time of presence. One wants to say that both are declarations of existence, and in their own singular ways, each declare existence in time.

For Cavell, the demands modern painting makes on us are as much ethical as aesthetic, and in contrast to most art criticism, he regards their declarations of existence as art works as less spatial than temporal. Or more precisely, it is not so much the worked space of the canvas that is in question as much as the quality of the spatiotemporal encounters such works solicit as a contingent relation of immanence between work and viewer. Moreover, in following the discussion of automatism in film, the excursus on modern painting powerfully expands and broadens the concept of automatism itself. In adding the example of painting, a discussion that contains some of the most powerful pages in *The World Viewed*, Cavell shows automatism to refer to something deeper and more significant than just technological reproducibility. Automatism is both a productive and a temporal concept that expresses the potentiality of events happening in series. To speak of series, however, is not to evoke redundancy but rather to convey the powers of singularity and contingency in each specific iteration within a series. Paradoxically, what bestows identity on a genre or medium of art is less repetitiveness than the uniqueness of each individual instance, which is produced from within the series yet never identical to it. Although produced from automatisms that color our picture of the evolving form of styles or genres (think here of productive Ideas or concepts, something like Sol LeWitt's "structures"), individual works in the series nonetheless challenge the continuity or coherence of the genre itself. (Here we find again the force of modernism in art.) Automatisms produce work in series, yet each new iteration of the series can swerve or derail the current line of development, or produce unexpected variations in and of it. Series and automatisms evoke the search for the singular, the contingent, and the absolutely new. In this modernism is less a negation of tradition, or a conflict with culture and history, and "more like an effort, along blocked paths and hysterical turnings, to hang on to a thread that leads from a lost center to a world lost" (*The World Viewed* 110). The modernist anxiety of influence is the persistently open question of whether each new work extends the series, or declares its (partial or complete) autonomy from it, or alternatively whether the work is only coherent and meaningful from within the series or in its departures from it. Does the instance vary the series or terminate it?

In Cavell's account, modernist works produce encounters of viewing that are both singular and evanescent, thus recalling Deleuze and Guattari's characterization of sensation as something monumental or durative, yet extremely fragile. In another startling connection, Cavell also invokes a concept familiar to every reader of Deleuze: haecceity, or the fact of singular existence in space and time. Accordingly, the aim of modernism is to free painting from representation and to assert the autonomy of art objects, producing an effect that Cavell calls total thereness. Formally, such effects are accomplished through the flatness and frontality of minimalist paintings as well as through their strategies of self-reference and self-containment. In this way, Cavell suggests, "a painting may acknowledge its frontedness, or its finitude, or its specific thereness—that is, its presentness; and your accepting it will accordingly mean acknowledging *your* frontedness, or directionality, or verticality toward its world, or any world—or your presentness, in its aspect of absolute hereness and of nowness" (*The World Viewed* 110).

One might think that Cavell is veering toward a sense of object and viewer confronting one another as two self-enclosed worlds, and indeed he speaks of such works as being complete without the viewer's presence and in a sense closed to her. But this argument is misunderstood if framed in a formal and spatial perspective rather than an ethical and temporal one. In ways not unlike Deleuze, Cavell writes of such encounters as events where an artwork declares its simultaneity. Simultaneity can be read as complete spatial expression, but also as the contingent and fleeting moment of shared presence in which the viewer encounters the work. The total thereness of the modernist work is thus characterized "as an event of the wholly open. . . . The quality I have in mind might be expressed as openness achieved through instantaneousness—which is a way of characterizing the *candid*" (*The World Viewed* 111).

To be candid is to be frank, open, and sincere, but also to make an image or view without the acknowledgment or awareness of the subject. Children are thought to be candid, hence the clichéd response to abstraction that any child could do it. Such responses withdraw from or repress the challenges of abstraction, and deny its power of generating not only aesthetic responses but also ethical encounters. The candidness of such works derives from the sense that they are free of equipment or *technē,* which is misread as lack of skill or lack of attention to the complex apparatus of producing paintings. But the feeling that this work is free of craft and the artfulness of human hands also evokes "an old wish of romanticism—to imitate not the *look* of nature, but its conditions, the possibilities of knowing nature at all and of locating ourselves in a world. For an old romanticist, these conditions would have presented themselves as nature's power of destruction or healing, or its fertility. For the work of the modernists I have in mind," Cavell continues, "the conditions present themselves as nature's autonomy, self-sufficiency, laws unto themselves" (*The World Viewed* 113).

Here Cavell invokes Wittgenstein's expression in the *Tractatus* of one of the most ineffable qualities of ethical response: "Not *how* the world is, is the mystical, but *that* it is." (6.44). That the world exists, that its existence is intractable in spite of all our words about it and our views of it, that it persists independently of all our doubts and convictions, and that we exist in it on a single plane of immanence and not apart from it, are among the deepest intuitions linking ontology to ethics. Here experience is considered as everywhere and continuously seamed. And these intuitions form a sinuous line that connects Wittgenstein, Cavell, and Deleuze, though each in their different ways with their very different languages and styles of philosophizing. That aesthetic experience can inspire such philosophical intuition is the strongest bridge between Deleuze and Cavell, despite all the other differences that separate them. To restore belief in *this* world, and to turn us away from the interiority, anonymity, and even solipsism of skepticism toward a shared existence with the world (call it nature if you will) and with all the others in it, is one of the greatest tasks of art as well as philosophy. In this framework, Cavell insists that abstraction is not a return to nature as much as a return of it; or perhaps more poignantly, a returning of *us* to *it* as if recognizing or acknowledging our forgotten link or seam with all of existence within a singular ontology. Cavell calls this

the release of nature from our private holds. No doubt such art will not repeal the enclosure acts, but it seeks to annul our spiritual-biological-political accommodations and attachments to enclosure. It reasserts that however we may choose to parcel or not to parcel nature among ourselves, nature is held—we are held by it—only in common. Its declaration of my absence and of nature's survival of me puts me in mind of origins, and shows me that I am astray. It faces me, draws my limits, and discovers my scale; it fronts me, with whatever wall at my back, and gives me horizon and gravity. It reasserts that, in whatever locale I find myself, I am to locate myself. It speaks of terror, but suggests elation—for the shaking of sentiment never got us home, nor the shiver of the picturesque. The faith of this romanticism, overcoming the old, is that we can still be moved to move, that we are free, if we will, to step upon our transport, that nature's absence—or its presence merely to sentiment or mood—is only the history of our turnings from it, in distraction or denial, through history or industry, with words or works. . . . It is not as though we any longer trust or ought so fondly to trust our representations that the absence of them must mean to us the absence of the things represented. Art in the absence of representation could then declare that those earlier approaches to nature had indeed been the making of representations—not merely *of* the world, but *to* it, as appeals or protests. (114)

So perhaps the new romanticism and the new reality of abstract art is not to lodge a protest against nature's distance from us, but rather to declare the terms of our common existence (with nature, with others, and with others and nature on a singular plane of immanence).

The structure of cinematic viewing offers other means for recovering this distance of self from nature or reality. To speak of a succession of automatic world projections is not to sustain an ontology of imprisonment like Plato's cave, but rather to create an interval where attractions of conviction or doubt and of fixation and change may be entertained and evaluated. The automatizing or mechanical reproduction of worldviews may make present before us, and thus available to us, skepticism's conceptual basis—its detachment of perception from our human selves and its isolation of our human minds from one another and from the external world. As I already explained in *The Virtual Life of Film,* that skepticism should reproduce itself in a technology for seeing might mean that it is no longer the ontological air we breathe but rather a passing phase of our philosophical culture. In its very *dispositif* for viewing and encountering the world, cinema presents philosophy's historical dilemma (skepticism's perceptual disjunction from the world) as past, while orienting the modern subject toward a possible future. If, as Cavell argues, the reality that film holds before us is that of our own perceptual condition, then it opens the possibility of once again being present to self or acknowledging how we may again become present to ourselves, in ways similar to the attractions of modern art. (Indeed Cavell's examination of cinema's relation to the fate of skepticism helps clarify a Deleuzian cinematic ethics as faith in this world and its possibilities for change.) For these reasons, film may already be the emblem of skepticism in decline; or rather, perhaps we are confronted with new variations of skepticism in the peculiar monadism of social media. Cinema takes up where philosophy leaves off, as the preconceptual expression of the passage to another way of being. This is why cinema is both a presentation of and withdrawal from skepticism—the almost perfect realization of the form of skeptical perception as a way, paradoxically, of reconnecting us to the world and asserting its existential force as past presence in time. Cinema both presents and replies to the skeptical attitude—the almost perfect realization of skeptical perception is a way, paradoxically, of reconnecting us to the world and asserting its causal presence. The irony of this recognition now is that modernity may no longer characterize our modes of being or of looking, and we must then anticipate something else.

Abstraction enacts this intuition differently but no less powerfully. "Perhaps what we must be faithful to," Cavell concludes, "is our knowledge that distance from nature is no longer represented by perspective, which places us in relation to it, places nature before or away from us, and falsifies our knowledge that we are lost to nature, are absent from it, cannot face it. Then, upon such unpromising ground, an art that reveals without representation may give us perspective. For example, it may show us that a painting must be viewed alone, from the one place one occupies at any time—an acknowledgment not directly that one must view things for oneself, but that one must take them one at a time" (The World Viewed 115). This idea is an expression of the power of series. The modernist declaration of autonomy in space is also an assertion of freedom in time. As I have already argued, the fact of series is not repetition but contingency—the recognition that any new instance produced may exhaust the series or open an entirely novel line of development, thus generating new series, genres, or media.

Here the only ontologically secure fact of modernism, as expressed in minimalist abstraction and our responses to it, is what Cavell calls a declaration of the evanescence of existence in space and time. Thus Cavell explains that "Like a monad, like the world there is, the only fact about these paintings that does not follow analytically from a complete idea of them is that they exist in space and time. Existence in this world, like the existence of the world itself, is the only contingent fact about them. They are themselves, I feel like saying, contingencies, realizations" (The World Viewed 116). Later, what Cavell calls the beauty of minimalism also expresses an experience close in feeling to De-leuze's description of percepts as singular instances related to yet distinct from their forms and materials of expression, and sensation or aesthesis as an effect that is both durative and ephemeral: "the fact about an instance, when it happens, is that it poses a permanent beauty, if we are capable of it. That *this* simultaneity should proffer beauty is a declaration about beauty: that it is no more temporary than the world is; that there is no physical assurance of its permanence; that it is momentary only the way time is, a regime of moments; and that no moment is to dictate its significance to us, if we are to claim autonomy, to become free" (116).

This statement presents an ethics of the Event close in spirit if not in language to Deleuze's own ethics of time as acknowledgment of the freedom to choose nondetermined alternatives. Abstraction presents the possibility of acknowledging and incorporating the Event as an ethical principle, in that the singular contingency of time is irreducible to any presentation of it. Minimalism is thus not a refutation of realism but rather the expression of a new reality, which as expressed above is also the unforeseen passage toward new concepts and new states of existence. Abstraction expresses a new displacement whereby representations fail either to convince us or to assure us of our connection to the world. In cinema, Deleuze calls this the collapse of the sensorimotor connection and a broken link with the world. But this is a sign of skepticism, whereas the promise of abstraction is an overcoming of it. Here the association of reality with representation is posed in a different way, which overcomes

> the representativeness which came between our reality and our art; overcame it by abstraction, abstracting us from the recognitions and engagements and complicities and privileged appeals and protests which distracted us from one another and from the world we have constructed. Attracted from distraction by abstraction. Not catching our attention yet again, but forming it again. Giving us again the capacity for appeal and for protest, for contemplation and for knowledge and praise, by drawing us back from private and empty assertion. These works exist as abstracts of intimacy—declaring our common capacity and need for presentness, for clear separateness and singleness and connection, for horizons and uprightness and frontedness, for the simultaneity of a world, for openness and resolution. They represent existence without assertion; authority without authorization; truth without claim, which you can walk in. It

is out of such a vision that Thoreau in *Walden* ("The Pond in Winter") speaks of nature as silent.

Is the power of representation otherwise irretrievable? Is there no way to declare again the content of nature, not merely its conditions; to speak again from one's plight into the heart of a known community of which one is a known member, not merely speak of the terms on which any human existence is given? "Who knows what the human body would expand and flow out to under a more genial heaven?" (*The World Viewed* 117–118).[82]

The common denominator between Deleuze and Cavell occurs in a grammar of worlding or worldliness—to acknowledge our connection to the world, as a moral connection to the world and to others; to believe again not in a transcendent world, but in this world with its reticence or recalcitrance but also with its powers of change. There is thus both fantasy and reality, expressions of desire and conviction, in the idea that automatic analogical causation brings into being a world that is more powerfully real than our own, or that all its powers of reality derive from our own. There is both anguish and joy in the recognition that both worlds—the one in which we exist and the other that exists before us as screened—powerfully express or make expressible possibilities and dimensions of experience where human actions and beliefs are inseparable from the material life of what I have called the universal plane of immanence. "Then if in relation to objects capable of such self-manifestation human beings are reduced in significance," Cavell writes, "or crushed by the fact of beauty left vacant, perhaps this is because in trying to take dominion over the world, or aestheticizing it (temptations inherent in the making of film, or of any art), they are refusing their participation with it" (*The World Viewed* xvi). The open question, then, is not how better to know these worlds, but how better to live in them through the location and evaluation of appropriate forms of participation.

---

82. The interior citation is from Henry David Thoreau, *Walden* (Mineola, NY: Dover Publications, 1995), 199.

18. Ethical Practices of the Ordinary

> As things stand, love is always the betrayal of love, if it is honest. It is why the
> path of self-knowledge is so ugly, hence so rarely taken, whatever its reputed
> beauties. The knowledge of the self as it is always takes place in the betrayal of
> the self as it was. That is the form of self-revelation, until the self is wholly
> won. Until then, until there is a world in which each can be won, our loyalty to
> ourselves is in doubt, and our loyalty to others is in partialness.
>
> —Stanley Cavell, *The World Viewed*

The cinematographic image makes all of recorded existence expressive; hence there is no such thing as silent film. Ontologically, the image is continually capable of affirming existence, and so are we if only we can return from silence and awaken the self from its state of preexistence. This is why Cavell's Emersonian proof of existence requires a kind of theatricality that reasserts my presence to others, and thus to myself. In other contexts, Cavell calls this conversation, or sometimes, education, as practices contributing to the pursuit of happiness. These are strategies for complementing ontology with ethics, and for rising above mute existence in an effort to construct or rebuild a human community that has failed to sustain itself.

Cavell's investigations of modernity and the quandaries of skepticism are (or should be) of central concern to the humanities because Cavell's aim is not to define the human or to address the "human condition" within modernity, but rather to make continually present the predicament that the human has yet to be achieved. To solicit a desire for becoming human or to better understand what it might mean to achieve the condition of humanity should be key concerns of philosophy. In Cavell's account, the epistemological and ethical framework of modernity was forged historically in a series of blows to human narcissism: the Copernican demonstration that we are not the center of the cosmos; Darwin's discovery that humankind and animals occupy the same continuum; and finally, Freud's investigations of the fact that we are not one with ourselves. Before Wittgenstein, Thoreau best emblematizes the figure who transfigures these dilemmas of alienation or skeptical withdrawal from the world into diurnal possibilities of emergent self-transformation; as Cavell puts it, honoring Thoreau, "the sun is but a *morning* star (there is room for hope); we are indeed animals, and moreover we are still in a larval state, awaiting metamorphosis; we are each of us double and each must learn 'to be beside oneself in a sane sense' (as opposed to our present madness)."[83] In phrases like these, Thoreau and Emerson appear in Cavell's philosophy as conceptual personae able to link the dilemmas of skepticism to an ethical practice of the ordinary. In this context, the project of late Wittgenstein is viewed not as refuting or denying skepticism, but rather as acknowledging, Cavell says, "its permanent role in the human mind, one not to be denied but to be placed (within different historical guises and economies). What this requires, as I read Wittgenstein, is learning to bear up under, and to take back home, the inevitable cracks or leaps of madness that haunt the act of philosophizing and haunt the construction of the world—to take the madness back to our shared home of language, and to take it back not once and for all (for there is no once and for all within life) but each day, in each specific, everyday site of its eruption" ("The Fantastic of Philosophy" 150).

Cavell accepts as a fundamental fact of the human that skeptical doubts cannot be avoided—they return diurnally and so each day we must seek out new responses to them. The lure of skepticism fuels a profoundly human and private dilemma because skepticism fundamentally threatens to barricade us within a self-enclosed and enclosing world. In Cavell's view, this fantasy of isolation can only be kept at bay through the appeal to community and to a certain relationality of the self in its potential (if often failed) intimacy with others. (We shall soon see that Cavell's interest in melodrama and comedy derives from their dramatic expression of problems of privacy and community—of the couple and the impossibility of accepting coupling—as a model for democracy and its continually imperiled status.) The tragedy of skepticism is that it enforces an inhuman isolation—it separates us from human community or sociability and the weave of human responsiveness to and activity in the world. At the same time, to have renounced or overcome skepticism (if this is humanly possible) would be to forego privacy and all protection afforded by my interiority. Perhaps the objective of philosophy, and the human need for it, is not only to form and encourage practices of self-examination but also to assure that there is a continual passage between reflection and communion, privacy and sociability, or, I am tempted to say, between metaphysics and ordinariness. Cavell's answer to the question "What is philosophy?" is responsive, then, to the ethical dilemma of Deleuze's later work, especially on cinema. To believe again in life

---

83. "The Fantastic of Philosophy," in *Cavell on Film*, 149. Originally published in *American Poetry Review* 15, no. 3 (May–June, 1986).

and our connection to the world is not enough. We also need quotidian strategies for reanimating our deadened or alienated relations to the world and to others. Acknowledgment, recounting criteria, and assembling reminders thus become practices of declaring and enacting one's existence and that of other persons and things as participating in a shared form of life, one we have a responsibility to investigate and to reaffirm anew each day in ways that make us continually responsible for, and responsive to, the singularity of our expressions and relations in that form of life.

Both Cavell and Deleuze consider philosophy to have diagnostic and perhaps reparative powers, though their appeals to cinema or art differ in this respect. To understand this difference means looking more closely at Cavell's career-long commitment to ordinary language philosophy as the source of his ethics and as a therapeutic response to skepticism. Moreover, if ordinary expressions are anchored in actual daily practices—our forms of life as lived and language as expressed—and if they offer a range of responses to the dilemmas of skepticism and belief, then philosophy might also turn to other normally encountered nonphilosophical artifacts or expressions for aid in repairing our broken links with the world and with others. This is one way of understanding Cavell's interest in cinema as the moral accompaniment of everyday life, or Deleuze's account of the need of philosophy for nonphilosophy.

Cavell's ontological account of cinema in the early 1970s is already an ethics that investigates and evaluates our modern sense of the self as divided from the world and from other minds by the screen of perception. In the major books that follow *The World Viewed* and *The Claim of Reason,* culminating in *Cities of Words,* the temporality of this epistemological condition is reconsidered more deeply as a question of art and ethical evaluation. The guiding concept here is what Cavell calls moral perfectionism as the nonteleological expression of a desire for change or becoming, which is often precipitated by a sense of existential crisis. In this way, the perfectionist desire for a further, future self, so far unattained, is also a critical intervention in, or interruption of, the temporality or lived time of the ordinary. As the melodramas of the unknown woman will exemplify so poignantly, the desire for transformation often occurs in suffocating conditions, which may be as common as the banality of the ordinary existence of diurnal repetition, a lack of recognition or acceptance that there is a new dawn in every day. What philosophy can try to diagnose and alleviate is a condition wherein our mode of existence is out of sync with our times, which means existing in a present felt as discontinuous with our past and our future, unmoored, disoriented, and uncompassed. Cavell calls this the unarticulated ground on which Nietzsche, or for that matter Emerson, issues his call for the future, for the new day; namely his sickness ("sea-sickness" Nietzsche calls it in the preface to *Human, All Too Human*) in response to the way humankind lives today. He regards himself, while still participating in that way, as having broken with it (he is at sea) and consequently as in a state of convalescence with respect to it, not ready for, not in possession of a context for, a new way; and he knows—it is the state of knowledge in which he writes—that almost all others remain buried in conformity, in an unrelieved routine of ordinariness, the thing Emerson calls conformity, and Nietzsche calls philistinism in the *Untimely Meditations*.[84]

In such comments, Cavell confronts philosophy's recurrent retreat from the ordinary, whose earliest emblem is the human inhabitation of Plato's cave in the *Republic*. Every possibility of transport from this place of capture and constraint is already present there, for those held there are self-captivating. There is an admonition to philosophy here to return to the everyday, to the place where we are held now, to aid us in our navigation of ordinary moral existence.

From the standpoint of perfectionism, our cinematic culture responds to dilemmas of perception and thought through a moral imperative more than an epistemological one. (This attitude, of course, is in stark contrast to the demands of political modernism.) In this respect, the trajectory from ontological to ethical questions in Cavell's thought is exemplary of how he uses cinema to deepen his description of the subjective condition of modernity as itself suspended between a worldly or epistemological domain and a moral domain. In both cases, cinema confronts the problem of skepticism. In the first instance, this is an epistemological disappointment in that we are disconnected from the world by our own subjectivity—all we can know of the world is from behind the screen of our consciousness. The second responds to a moral disappointment in the state of the world or with my current mode of existence. This division is not only formal; it is also, and perhaps primarily, temporal. As Kant posed the problem, the province of understanding, of knowledge of objects and their causal laws, defines the modern scientific attitude whose formidable power derives from making time an independent variable.

---

84. "Philosophy the Day after Tomorrow" (lecture, Einstein Forum, Berlin, November 2000); reprinted in *Cavell on Film*, 325.

What is unknown in the natural world could not become known through the powers of causal reasoning if the rules could change in the course of time. But the problem that so provoked Kant was that intemporal reason was in conflict with moral freedom. To be human is to experience change. So how might philosophy characterize humanity as at once subject of understanding *and* of reason, as subject to causal relations and expressive of moral freedom? Given that as material creatures we are in bondage to the empirical world and its causal laws, philosophy's task is to explain how we are also free to experience and to anticipate change in the projection of future existences.

In Cavell's account, moral perfectionism takes us from the form of skepticism to the possibilities of human change, and to the deeper moral problem of evaluating our contemporary modes of existence and transcending them in anticipation of better future existences. In the first stage, the problem is to overcome my moral despair of ever knowing the world; in the second, my despair of changing it and myself. Thus, Cavell's interest in Emerson (or in Wittgenstein, Nietzsche, or Freud) is to heal this rift in philosophy exemplified by Wittgenstein's disappointment with knowledge as failing to make us better than we are or to give us peace. Alternatively, moral perfectionism begins with this sense of ethical disappointment and ontological restlessness, catching up the modern subject in a desire for self-transformation whose temporality is that of a becoming without finality. "In Emerson's and Thoreau's sense of human existence," Cavell writes, "there is no question of reaching a final state of the soul but only and endlessly taking the next step to what Emerson calls 'an unattained but attainable self'—a self that is always and never ours—a step that turns us not from bad to good, or wrong to right, but from confusion and constriction toward self-knowledge and sociability" (*Cities of Words* 13). This, in fact, is what Cavell means by the pursuit of happiness.

In retrospect, both the problem and form of moral perfectionism seem to have been present already in Cavell's first major works. For example, the lesson Cavell takes from Wittgenstein, even in his earliest accounts, is that philosophy is deeply problematic. Or rather that philosophy lives daily a paradox of wishing to solve problems that in fact it continually creates in the form of skeptical dilemmas posing knowledge against belief. The skeptical desire to overcome the boundaries and finitude of human knowing and expression is pictured as a wish to escape the human, perhaps to become posthuman; Cavell calls this the "predicament of human self-dissatisfaction" ("Crossing Paths" 365). Wittgenstein's discovery was that the skeptical dilemma was neither a result of nor resolvable by recourse to metaphysical or scientific reasoning, but rather, it was an ordinary problem or a problem of the ordinary, which Cavell portrays as

> a drama enacted in philosophy's dissatisfaction with or disappointment with ordinary language, one in which ordinary language both rejects itself and assumes the obligation to come to itself. In this way of looking at things, the "return" to ordinary language is rather seen as a return *of* it, not as to a place of stability, but as of a place of inevitable loss. In particular it is not a place of common sense or shared belief—the thing Emerson calls conformity—but is equally to be understood as an attack on settled beliefs. It is the possibility, or necessity, of this self-dissatisfaction, this battle of the human with itself, that creates the possibility, and necessity, in philosophy, of skepticism. ("Crossing Paths" 365–366)

These lines recall Deleuze and Guattari's emphasis on philosophy's battle with and in *doxa*. Philosophy's continuous struggle, then, is to find ways of unsettling belief, or of changing the conditions of belief, so that we no longer doubt the world and suffer our separation from it but rather embrace its capacity for change and self-differentiation. In a similar way, Wittgenstein was not refuting skepticism but rather diagnosing and evaluating its sources in our everyday and ordinary expressiveness and in our relations with others. In Cavell's account, Wittgenstein's turn to the ordinary comes from the discovery that "human language is such that dissatisfaction with it can never be stilled; the question is not so much whether we can live within our finite means (which those who have respected skepticism have in different ways recommended, from the ancient Greeks to thinkers through Descartes and Hume to such as Bertrand Russell) as whether we can become responsible for our infinite desires" ("Crossing Paths" 366).

To become responsible for our infinite desires is to know how our desires block or release our relation to the world and knowledge of ourselves, hence Cavell's discussions of fantasy and reality in *The World Viewed*. Toward the end of *The World Viewed*, Cavell writes that "to satisfy the wish for the world's exhibition we must be willing to let the world as such appear" (159). Through cinema's automatism, its succession of automatic world projections, perhaps the world is capable of appearing as such but this does not mean that we have released it from our own desires and fantasies of or for it. Nor does it mean that we have acknowledged and evaluated our own fantasies of being lost to self in privacy and anonymity. To free ourselves of fantasy, or to free the world of our fantasies, would require something violent, angst-ridden, and almost impossible: the total exhibition of our selves in complete candor, without concealment or camouflage. Exposing our selves with total and undisguised intelligibility would require the self's betrayal of itself, hence the interest of the passive intentional powers of photogenesis. But this also means that there is not within us only one self to hide or to reveal, and indeed that the mechanism for hiding and revealing, or for dissembling or accounting, is yet another self that speaks in place of my past but also future selves. (Perhaps the fantasy of skepticism is also the fantasy of a self-identical ego untroubled by time's divisions. Yet how could there be self-reflection or consciousness of self without experiencing an internal division of self by self?) Ethically no less than ontologically, we are divided by time as if we lived and thought in two dimensions; hence Deleuze and Cavell's common interest in Kant, and to a certain extent, psychoanalysis. There is the chronological time of the *I* which, from moment to moment, must anchor the self in and against the flow of time as the expression of location, self-indication, and grammatical expression. But there is also the nonchronological dimension of memory in its deepest sense, as the ebb and flow of an immense tidal force that draws on deep and chaotic currents while pitching waves at an uncaring sky. Memory is what catches the ego in undertow and threatens to overwhelm it, but also that which sustains the ego and gives it duration or the capacity to sustain itself in time.

Why would we not wish, then, for an art that fixes the past as sense in time, presents the past as a causal force in the present, and assures me of the world's continuity both by and without my presence? As Cavell writes at the end of *The World Viewed,* a world complete without me is the world of my immortality. However, this is the exact point that requires ethical evaluation, or else we are lost, because a world complete before me, but which is also present without me, is a world that will either confirm my continuing existence or deny it. Skeptical perception is an assertion of power over the world in its totality, but it may also leave me disconnected from the world and thus haunting it as if powerless to change it or myself. So Cavell concludes that "there is reason for me to want the camera to deny the coherence of the world, its coherence as past: to deny that the world is complete without me. But there is equal reason to want it affirmed that the world is coherent without me. That is essential to what I want of immortality: nature's survival of me. It will mean that the present judgment upon me is not yet the last" (*The World Viewed* 160).

In 1971, these are Cavell's last words in *The World Viewed,* at least until he produces the Enlarged Edition eight years later. However, in this extraordinary book I am struck not by the last words but by the last thought before the last. In the penultimate paragraph, Cavell completes his meditation on the perils of total candor of the self. "As things stand," Cavell writes, "love is always the betrayal of love, if it is honest. It is why the path of self-knowledge is so ugly, hence so rarely taken, whatever its reputed beauties. The knowledge of the self as it is always takes place in the betrayal of the self as it was. That is the form of self-revelation, until the self is wholly won. Until then, until there is a world in which each can be won, our loyalty to ourselves is in doubt, and our loyalty to others is in partialness" (*The World Viewed* 160). Acquiring knowledge of self by self is difficult and painful but also comic—a world in which skepticism does not count is comedic, but a world in which skepticism counts too much is ironic or melodramatic. In either case, a transcendental element is indispensable as the motivation for a moral existence—self-disobedience. Transforming the self, if we are capable, means overcoming ourselves in reaching for an as yet unattained mode of existence. This is the time of moral perfectionism.

19. Perfectionism as Self-Disobedience

> The perception or attitude demanded in following this drama is one which demands a continuous attention to what is happening at each here and now, as if everything of significance is happening at this moment, while each thing that happens turns a leaf of time. I think of it as an experience of *continuous presentness*. Its demands are as rigorous as those of any spiritual exercise—to let the past go and to let the future take its time; so that we not allow the past to determine the meaning of what is now happening (something else may have come of it) and that we not anticipate what will come of what has come. Not that anything is possible (though it is) but that we do not know what is, and is not, next.
>
> —Stanley Cavell, "The Avoidance of Love"

In a late lecture on "The Good of Film," Cavell evokes, with forty years' distance, the concluding question of Kracauer's *Theory of Film:* What is the good of film experience? What good can we claim from film (or art, or literature), or what good can or does film offer us? Cavell links perfectionism explicitly here to Foucault's examination of practices of care of the self. But the self only requires care when it is beside itself, that is, when in moments of despair or dissatisfaction the self fissures internally in crises of self-doubt and self-examination.

Deleuze views this as an innate power or capacity of the subject in that the Kantian passive ego lives in every moment its separation from itself through intuition of the pure form of time. It cannot but undergo change and observe itself in the course of transformation—this is the origin of subjectivity in time and as time. In addition, both Deleuze and Cavell are concerned with a similar problem: how does the subject undergo or experience change? However, unlike Deleuze, in Cavell time does not operate as a metaphysical constant but rather as an ethical will that must be continually reenacted because it is continually forgotten.

Moral perfectionism is to Cavell's philosophy what Becoming is to Deleuze. Both concepts require new attention to the force of time in relation to qualities of change and transformation rooted in new and original approaches to Nietzsche's thought. However, this profound link is also a measure of distance between them. Among other things, Deleuze's cinema books present an ethical turn in his philosophy but without a corresponding transformation in his concept of ontology. Deleuze's radical materialism, to which I feel profoundly committed, returns body and mind to the world, makes them one with the world on a single plane of immanence governed by the pure form of time as self-differentiation and universal variation. In a sense, how could we not believe in change and the capacity for (self) transformation, since in Deleuze's philosophy the fundamental intuitions are that the only thing that does not change is the Form of time itself and that what returns eternally is the capacity for self-differing. (Photogenesis is Cavell's analogue for this force of becoming or change in the image.)

At the same time, the philosophical tone of Deleuze's late works is darkened by the effort to sustain a utopian belief in the force of time or difference in the face of all the powers of inertia and resistance marshaled against the subject under late capitalism. However, the pathos pervading Deleuze's later philosophy, in both the cinema books and his work with Guattari, testifies to another unresolved problem: how can this intuition be made humanly livable, or what practices encourage a coming community? In this philosophy without a subject, *The Time-Image* calls for a new place or locus of perception characterized as the *voyant* or seer of modern cinema who can return this intuition to us in the face of all the world's suffering. This seer is itself a kind of conceptual persona who, in response to the universal variation of the movement-image, is capable of transmitting in human form a perception giving the pure form of time as change, and who can show us that it is possible to choose to choose, and to believe again in this world.

The problem is that even Deleuze himself does not seem convinced by this. Or rather one feels somehow that in his philosophical conviction he is still not humanly sustained or satisfied by the ethics he seeks, or that he cannot quite overcome the sense of despair and revolutionary disappointment that pervades his late writing. A clear and active sense of the quality of self-transformation as an active philosophical practice is missing from Deleuze's philosophical constructivism. (In late works and interviews, Deleuze gestures to this practice in Foucault's concept of "subjectivation.") The problem here is how to overcome one's self, to recognize and rid one's self of all that is deadening, inertial, and resistant to change. For example, in his essay "Philosophy the Day after Tomorrow," Cavell examines what is at stake not only in becoming, but in overcoming. Cavell's point of departure is the concluding sentences of Thoreau's *Walden,* which I alluded to earlier: "Only that day dawns to which we are awake. There is more day to dawn. The sun is but a morning star." Thoreau's language echoes Emerson and anticipates Nietzsche, a fact of which Cavell is well aware. But in the acknowledgment that there is more day to dawn, and that in all its blinding brightness the sun is only an anticipation of something in the course of happening that has not yet arrived, Thoreau exhibits an intuition of time and the event that, one wants to say, is Deleuzian. Cavell focuses, however, on the homonym where the sound of mourning is folded into Thoreau's morning star, and thus emphasizes that "every illumination of the world that we have been party to has passed away and is something we must learn to rid ourselves of, to reevaluate. Nietzsche calls this overcoming himself— *Überwinden,* which in Nietzsche's twist of the old prefix *Über-,* would presumably mean to unwind, unscrew, unbind, straighten, release himself. Conquering oneself then becomes a progress of continuing to free oneself, one might say, pardon oneself" ("Philosophy the Day after Tomorrow" 323).

In such accounts, perfectionist practices of becoming, overcoming, and projection are recognized less as a method than as a style or even a kind of dramaturgy or performativity. For example, one of the most remarkable and most criticized features of Cavell's early writing is his eccentric use of the em dash, as if to enact a strange conversation of doubt and disagreement with or within himself. I find these extraordinary moments to enact a sort of philosophical self-disobedience. Perhaps this use of the em dash and a divided voice within his text is Cavell's way of adapting and performing the confessional style of the *Philosophical Investigations,* as if to express an internal division or discord within one's self, a persistent dislocation, doubt, or disagreement that must continually be reckoned with as the price of philosophical continuation.

This practice is an early indicator of the structure of moral perfectionism—an internal division or projected other as the voice of doubt or disagreement, but also of wondering and projecting into new contexts, as a potential transformation of the self, or as a form of self-education. This fracturing of the self recalls Deleuze's version of the Kantian passive ego as the internal division of the self by the Form of time. Alternatively, in the example of Wittgenstein's confessional style, or Cavell's writerly dialogues, the practice of ordinary language philosophy is here deployed as a dialogue of two selves, or between two voices of the same self continually interrogating and questioning one another. No better definition can be found for Deleuze's characterization of intercessors or conceptual personae. Imagine this, then, as an inner deployment of intercessors, or the projection of a philosophical friend real or imagined, who reminds us of, or makes us account for, what we have forgotten or ignored. Ordinary language philosophy wants us to recall this inner capacity, which we all share. It aids in the recovery from skepticism because within the thrall of skepticism's particular will to truth one forgets or loses the human capacity to think of and relate to others and the world as both singular and changing, because skepticism projects a frozen world from which we are divided and so promotes a withdrawal into ourselves. To open ourselves to the autonomy of the world and to others is to ask that our autonomy be acknowledged, and that we be acknowledged as belonging to a shared life. This process is never complete, however. The danger of lapsing back into a nihilistic mood is ever present and thus the need for diagnosis and recovery must be continually reaffirmed as a life-restoring recurrence that contests the life-deadening repetition of skepticism.

In this peculiar form of philosophical dialogue, Cavell restores to the practice of philosophy one of its most ancient and persistent activities: the evaluation of a way of life or mode of existence. And through the concept of moral perfectionism, this book draws a circle that returns to *Elegy for Theory*. The origins of perfectionist discourse and practice are venerable. The first examples are inspired by Socrates's lesson to Euthyphro: that unlike questions of scientific reason, which may be resolved through measurement or further experimentation and the collection of new data, dilemmas that cause hatred and anger must be addressed through forms of evaluative conversation that are in principle interminable. These conversations involve disagreements over what is just or unjust and honorable or dishonorable that involve assessments of moral standing aimed both at myself *and* my interlocutor. And in best cases our own self-assessments of moral standing may evolve as we converse. No single or universal method can govern this process—moral judgments are always contextual and contingent. At the same time, perfectionism always involves an admonition to change your life—or further, to change the mode of existence that limits your life, constraining or circumscribing it with intolerable moral conditions. (In a Deleuzian framework, one might say we are limited by forces that block or suppress acknowledgment that we are free to choose an alternative mode of existence.) In contrast to utilitarian or deontological frameworks for moral reasoning, perfectionism does not seek out common, much less universal, standards for moral evaluation. In every case, the situation of perfectionist discourse will be singular and contextual. However, while the experience of perfectionism is not generalizable, the forms or modes of perfectionist evaluation and transformation have common characteristics. What perfectionism first requires is the often-painful recognition of the need and capacity for change in the desire to seek out what Emerson calls our unattained yet attainable self. But this desire cannot be accomplished alone—it requires an intercessor, friend, or interlocutor, real or imagined. It requires a community (actual or virtual) of at least two to exemplify a process whereby a future self and future form of community can be discovered and aspired to.

Plato's *Republic* offers an early image of perfectionism for philosophy in that ethics is not understood as separate from epistemology, metaphysics, or poetics. Platonic education includes all of these activities in a transcendent journey in which the soul is set upward on a path toward the Good, "one which requires a release, dramatized as a turning away, from its everyday life, a transformation initiated and furthered by a kind of painful conversation with a more advanced figure who sets those who approach him on a path of education" ("The Good of Film" 336–337). Plato's image of perfectionist education is marked by the demands of discipleship and subordination to a sage or master. Cavell, however, turns to Emerson and Thoreau for a more democratic and indeed self-reliant model. The perfectionist admonishment for change thus appears in moments of realization that we are not one with ourselves, at home in our skins, that we are unreachable or unfindable in or by our selves. What is needed here is not a figure of authority, no matter how generous, but rather a philosophical friend or conceptual persona, whether actual or real, in conversation with whom we return to ourselves or become the self we desire to be. Thus Cavell explains that

> The decisive difference of Emerson's outlook from that in Plato's *Republic* is that the soul's journey to itself is not pictured as a continuous path directed upward to a known point of completion but rather as a zigzag of

discontinuous steps following the lead of what Emerson calls my "un-attained but attainable self" (as if there is a sage in each of us), an idea that projects no unique point of arrival but only a willingness for change, directed by specific aspirations that, while rejected, may at unpredictable times return with new power. The path is no more toward incorporation in a given condition of society than it is toward the capacity to judge that condition. The sage in us is what remains after all our social positionings. ("The Good of Film" 337)

Thus in Emerson's essay "Self-Reliance," the friend we are attracted to in conversation is not my model to emulate, but a figure who returns me to my own rejected thoughts so that the process of philosophical engagement becomes a practice of returning or awakening to or within myself. Here education is self-education through a practice that Cavell often refers to as checking one's experience and "subjecting it to examination, and beyond these, of momentarily *stopping,* turning yourself away from whatever your preoccupation and turning your experience away from its expected, habitual track, to find itself, its own track: coming to attention" (*Pursuits of Happiness* 12).

Perfectionism in Socrates or Aristotle requires the presence of a sage or authority confronting you to examine and change your life. A similar appeal to a moral or regulatory authority, conceptual or actual, informs both deonto-logical and utilitarian forms of moral reasoning. In contrast, what Cavell finds so appealing in classic Hollywood cinema, especially the remarriage comedies, is a democratization of perfectionism, which is also given a partic-ular American form. In both cases, the problem of marriage serves as the site or context for working out problems of disagreement and consensus in the pursuit of happiness, and this consensus is unregulated and unregulatable by any standard that does not emerge and evolve from within the community itself. No transcendental or external authority can confirm or disallow this community. As Cavell explains, "A guiding idea of both the comedies, where marriage is accepted, or reaccepted, and of the related melodramas, where marriage is in fact rejected, is that nothing legitimizes or ratifies marriage—not state, or church, or sex, or gender, or children—apart from the willingness for reaffirmation, which is to say, remarriage (the films open or climax with the threat of divorce), and what makes marriage worth reaffirming is a diur-nal devotedness that involves friendship, play, surprise, and mutual educa-tion, all expressed in the pair's mode of conversing with one another, express-ing an intimacy of understanding often incomprehensible to the rest of the world" ("Philosophy the Day After Tomorrow" 324–325). Both dramatically and visually, for Cavell these films are nothing less than a form of philosophical dialogue or dramaturgy, and one open to all that view them, concerning what makes consensus in community worth seeking and struggling for. Marriage stands here for an imagined community of democratic equals, yet at the same time it is not meant to serve as an image of perfected community in microcosm. It is neither the telos of a given social project nor a field of fairness for individual projects. Rather, as a genetic form of community, remarriage comedy figures marriage as the exemplification of a happy enough realization of lives in just enough structure. In *Cities of Words,* Cavell calls this the commitment to pursue "happiness without a concept" (361).

For Cavell, what these comedies dramatize is most obviously the quality of friendship and the necessity for a philosophical friend in working out the evaluation of ethical dilemmas and finding the path toward self-transformation and new creation of the self. Friendship in its highest form expresses a desire to live together, to spend time together, and to find community. Ethical reasoning cannot be born alone in isolated meditation (ethical judgments in principle are not theoretic), but rather must unfold in the context of and in response to a form of life "whose texture is a weave of cares and commitments in which one is bound to become muddled and to need the friendly perception of others in order to find one's way, in which at any time a choice may present itself . . . in pondering which you will have to decide whose view of you is most valuable to you" ("Moral Reasoning" 357). In like manner, Emersonian perfectionism is not a specialized or uncommon activity, but rather a practice of ordinary existence. Or as Cavell often puts it, perfectionism is a philosophy of the everyday.

Another key contrast with Socratic or Platonic perfectionism involves the question of education. Greek perfectionism is in service to a sage or guiding authority figure. But the comedies and melodramas offer an alternative perspective based on mutuality: the dramatic couple or pair function here as a core community, or a genetic ideal of community, who in their discord wish not to learn from one another as teacher and student, but rather to transform in common their conditions of existence. The possibility of transformation must arise in discord and asymmetry, however—the role of the friend here is to inspire me to self-disobedience. In contrast to Greek perfectionism, neither one of this quarreling pair is a youth and each of them has also reached a certain stage of sexual maturity. What brings them together is a quality of attraction whereby they must discover that each is exemplary for the other. Yet there is an inequality of education, say of self-knowledge, between them that their dialogue depends on challenging. Where marriage stands for community, education stands for (self) transformation, and "those who cannot inspire one another to such an education are not married; they do not have the right interest for one another" ("Philosophy the Day After Tomorrow" 325). In remarriage comedy, the idea of marriage as it may be is the projection of a possible or attainable community. (In the derived melodramas, marriage is rejected as given or presented in the films, on the ground that it is the negation of what marriage may be, this community being unattainable in the present world.) In its pursuit of happiness, what this community desires is mutual acknowledgment of equality and similarity of powers and capacities with reciprocal superiority in them, thus suggesting that a precondition for becoming human is to imagine a mode of existence where equal justice is both desirable and possible, and where human beings can aspire to an education equal in rights and possibilities of desire and knowledge.

20. Comedy and Community

> The moral regeneration of mankind will only really commence, when the most fundamental of the social relations is placed under the rule of equal justice, and when human beings learn to cultivate their strongest sympathy with an equal in rights and in cultivation.
>
> —John Stuart Mill, *The Subjection of Women*

> Put otherwise, the achievement of human happiness requires not the perennial and fuller satisfaction of our needs as they stand but the examination and transformation of those needs.
>
> —Stanley Cavell, *Pursuits of Happiness*

The pursuit of happiness is one important dimension or aspect of perfectionism, which is embodied already in Cavell's depiction of remarriage comedy: an open series of works whose core films include *It Happened One Night* (Frank Capra, 1934), *The Awful Truth* (Leo McCarey, 1937), *Bringing Up Baby* (Howard Hawks, 1938), *His Girl Friday* (Howard Hawks, 1940), *The Philadelphia Story* (George Cukor, 1940), *The Lady Eve* (Preston Sturges, 1941), and *Adam's Rib* (George Cukor, 1949). In "The Good of Film," Cavell presents several points of contact between remarriage comedy and perfectionism. One involves the particular kinds of moral problems addressed in and through comedic conversation. Conversations concerning standard moral problems are noticeably absent in these dialogues of questioning and contestation, "quite as if the perplexities of the conditions of ordinary moral life, matters of equality or of the conflict of inclination with duty, or of duty with duty, or of means with ends, pose no intellectual hardships for these people" ("The Good of Film" 338). Perfectionism's attention is usually not focused on headline moral issues such as abortion, capital punishment, or euthanasia, but rather arises in conversations about inattentiveness, contemptuousness, brutality, coldness, cowardice, vanity, thoughtlessness, unimaginativeness, heartlessness, deviousness, and vengefulness, as one soul examines another.

Moral perfectionism is less a method or a theory, then, than a perspective on the value of inevitable human disagreeableness that finds in discord and dissension the potentiality for, and necessity of, entering into moral conversation and ethical self-examination in moments of crisis, confusion, and dissatisfaction with others and oneself. It is a request both from within and from outside myself to examine and to change my way of life. This is not a retreat from politics, much less gender politics, as we shall see. Nor is it the case that great moral dilemmas do not matter to these films. Rather, there is a different point of emphasis whereby perfectionism turns from moral conflict to a kind of ethical examination more deeply rooted in questions of self and community that confront us in local moments of daily life. Thus another important point of contact between remarriage comedy and perfectionism is the importance given to self-transformation, of becoming a new person in support of a new community, through a process of bringing out and making perspicuous and recognizable qualities that were always there. Perfectionism is not about self-betterment, but rather about self-knowledge and evaluation. Perfectionist aspirations arise from the demand to make oneself intelligible, and to make ourselves intelligible to one another, in order to address and redress the daily confusions, conflicts, and misunderstandings that separate us, and in which we deal or are dealt little deaths every day.

In this way, Cavell considers remarriage comedies as philosophical laboratories for examining practices of perfectionist reasoning. These practices are less concerned with influencing courses of action or critiquing social institutions than they are with a conception of ethics that both prepares moments of perfectionist becoming and follows after them, as one soul is confronted with or by another. The prior or preparatory moment involves acts of critical evaluation that question or examine the standing of a moral agent in their judgment of another; what follows is a redrawing and evaluation of the moral framework with which two or more moral agents stage their conflict and try to arrive at consensus. Early in his philosophical career, this was already Cavell's way of responding to the then-dominant emotive theory of ethical judgment, which relied on the expression of feeling to persuade or dissuade the other with respect to given courses of action, as if "there had come upon philosophers thinking of the moral life an amnesia of the fact, or a wish to be free of the fact, that we have claims upon one another, count for one another, matter to one another, sometimes in questionable ways.... One might say that confronting another morally risks one's identity; otherwise one risks moralism" ("The Good of Film" 339).

From a contemporary perspective, having lived and taught in the first American commonwealth to legalize gay marriage, I am struck by the fact that Cavell's focus on the centrality of marriage as a concept, and as an ethical domain for working out questions of perfectionist aspiration, may be less controversial now than it was thirty years ago. Now more than ever, the concept of marriage is targeted as a contested site of community, or a site of contested community, where what counts as public and private business is deployed in conflicts between the law and desire. The lesson to be drawn here is that our image of marriage is unsettled and unsettling, especially as a framework for working through problems of privacy and community, division and consensus, aimed at achieving what John Rawls called good enough justice.

Published in 1981, and following on the heels of *The Claim of Reason, Pursuits of Happiness* deploys a concept of marriage that Cavell explicitly links to his study of skepticism. Whereas one responds to crises of doubt in relation to the world, the other expresses the difficulty of living in community with others, thus weaving an epistemological and an ethical problem into an existential skein. "Two of the fundamental human properties that human societies have been most anxious to limit," Cavell writes,

> are the capacity to relate oneself to the world by knowledge and the capacity to relate oneself to others by marriage. We seem to understand these capacities for relation as constitutive of what we understand by human society, since we attribute to them, if unchecked, the power to destroy the social realm.
>
> If we do not equate human knowledge with the results of science but understand it as the capacity to put one's experience and the world into words, to use language, then the will to knowledge and the will to marriage may be seen to require analogous limitations in order to perform

their work of social constitution, limitations that combat their tendencies to privacy or their fantasies of privacy. (*Pursuits of Happiness* 74)

The regulation of knowledge and that of marriage are thus linked in terms of managing, hence limiting, concepts of the world and of community. It is a striking observation that epistemology and ethics find a point of intersection in the concept of marriage. Yet as Cavell points out, this is a recurrent theme in writers as diverse as Milton, Kant, Hume, Locke, Mill, and Kierkegaard.

The will to manage limits, to constrain or circumscribe and thus isolate, also suggests possibilities for the exercise of freedom and the expression of desire in the world and with others. In his chapter on *It Happened One Night*, "Knowledge as Transgression," Cavell notes in Kantian terms that in contrast to the domain of understanding, where thought and the senses are bound to blind and irrevocable causal laws, moral reasoning requires the possibility of choice, and indeed the acknowledgment and exercise of the human freedom to choose. In this perspective, shared by Cavell and Deleuze, the potentiality for becoming human arises in the self-given freedom of choosing to choose, of exercising choice as a power. While Kant believes we are forever blocked from knowledge of things in themselves, no such limitation constrains the human exercise of moral choice. "In the case of our social life," Cavell explains,

we *do* have a choice over whether the laws of the moral universe, "objective" moral laws, apply to us; which is to say, a choice over whether to apply them, as is implied in their presenting themselves to us as imperatives, matters, as it were, not fully natural to us. This is as we should expect. There is an alternative to moral goodness—moral evil. Moral evil is not merely a matter of falling short of the dictates of the moral law: our sensuous nature indicates to us that for all we know we always fall short. The matter is rather one of choosing evil, of choosing to thwart the very possibility of the moral life. Kant does not say much about this alternative, but I understand it in the following way. One inflection of the moral law is that its necessity and universality are to be viewed as holding in "the realm of ends," which may be thought of as the perfected human community. This realm is also a world "beyond" the world we inhabit, a noumenal realm, open to reason, standing to reason; but I am not fated to be debarred from it as I am from the realm of things-in-themselves, by my sensuous nature; for the perfected human community *can* be achieved, it may at last be experienced, it is in principle presentable. Yet, there is between me and this realm of reason also something that may present itself as a barrier—the fact that I cannot reach this realm *alone*. . . . If the eventual community of humanity is not merely something close to us that we are falling short of, but something closed to us, something debarred, then its nonexistence is due to our willing against it, to the presence of moral evil. This takes moral evil as the will to exempt oneself, to isolate oneself, from the human community. It is a choice of inhumanity, of monstrousness. Then our inability to picture ourselves as debarred from the social, or as debarring it, our drawing a blank here, may express a horror of this possibility, call it a horror of metaphysical privacy, as though picturelessness were a kind of namelessness. (*Pursuits of Happiness* 79)

Skepticism is as much an ethical problem as it is an epistemological one, and to the extent that it encourages (inhuman) isolation, the choice of skepticism toward the existence of others is a choice of moral evil that enforces isolation from others and the world in the exercise of a negative or self-negating freedom. In the first phase of Cavell's philosophy, skepticism poses a deep and disorienting problem of division from the world and difference from others to which philosophy must respond. Acknowledgment of skepticism's powers thus signals the painful recognition that change is necessary, and one's present mode of existence must be transformed. The second phase acknowledges that the pain of self-transformation may yield new forms of desire, or new recognitions of desires present but unexpressed or forgotten. This is why the pursuit of happiness (a striving and not an accomplishment) is not a turning from bad to good, or wrong to right, but rather a movement from occlusion or exclusion and constriction toward self-knowledge and sociability, which indeed requires accepting that this transformation cannot be accomplished alone. It requires acknowledgment of others and of the possibility of a good community, or at least a better one.

Skepticism negates or undermines the possibility of living in a human community with its conclusion that the world is radically unknown to me. Withdrawn into privacy and isolation, I am unknown to myself and to others, and they are unknown to me. "I *must* find a way to put this doubt aside—," Cavell writes in *Cities of Words*, "perhaps through what Pascal calls the taste for distraction, or what Hume depicts as the desire for sociability, or what Kant calls recognizing the necessary limits of human understanding, or what Wittgenstein calls the limits of my language" (426). The pursuit of happiness is therefore another way of expressing the desire for sociability, but also an acknowledgment that a happy, or at least, a good enough compromise with the limits of human understanding of oneself and others may be achieved. In these films, no less than in Cavell's readings of Shakespeare, the quarreling couples of remarriage comedies and the unknown women of melodrama are exemplary of the human capacity to withstand and perhaps even overcome skepticism's doubts concerning commerce with community and the world. And across the two genres, the drama of moral perfectionism addresses a common set of concerns: (re)marriage as the reaffirmation of community, the demand for an education, the need for a philosophical friend, and the metamorphosis of the woman as a new creation of the human.

In the comedies, marriage, or rather remarriage, is an idealized image of an attainable perfectible community. At the same time, the topos of marriage is a figuration of discord and discontent. Part of the general insanity of remarriage comedy, pursuant to its pursuit of happiness, is that the open craving for happiness is a standing test, indeed a threat to social order. Any society that relinquishes or blocks rights of happiness is crazy, and we are reminded of this through the characters' mishaps and misunderstandings, as well as their wild efforts toward recovery pictured as refinding themselves or coming back to themselves.

Here marriage signals a realm of freedom—indeed a Kantian domain of reason and the exercise of moral choice—that demands a transformation of the characters' mode of existence or form of life. Crucially, they are divided. The request for divorce is a demand for freedom. Separation is essential to remarriage comedy because it is an affirmation of choice, to choose to be or to remain married or not. It is an expression of the possibility of freedom in community, which is all that freedom requires—that is, the recurrent possibility of its exercise. Having married the characters now occupy separate worlds, and to reinhabit a joined world will mean suffering transformation, perhaps humiliation. The pursuit of happiness in community is fraught with difficulty, inspiring conflict between the couple and with the worlds they inhabit with others.

The fact that these are comedies of *remarriage* thus projects a complex image of time and transformation. The trajectory of (past) marriage, (present) divorce, and (future) remarriage defines a time of dissent and reaffirmation that figures society as subject to criticism but also to change. "Marriage is always divorce," Cavell writes in *Pursuits of Happiness,* "always entails rupture from something; and since divorce is never final, marriage is always a transgression. (Hence marriage is the central social image of human change, showing why it is and is not metamorphosis.)" (103). Communities can dismantle and rebuild themselves, and do so in the absence of violence, though not conflict, and through the most ordinary of means—the daily (re)negotiation of consent and consensus. Remarriage comedies focalize and dramatize this process, projecting it into an ethical framework; for philosophy, they provide a new concept of marriage. The pair is engaged in a conceptual and experimental journey, where marriage is pictured as an intellectual undertaking, a certain demand for understanding and a willingness to press for an understanding of the conditions of that understanding.

In these terms, a good marriage is a self-generating and self-regulating state that claims for itself the power both to ratify society and to receive ratification from society. But it also maintains the potential to question or threaten the social order and the terms of that ratification. It thus reserves a place from which to judge its society, Cavell claims, in order "to determine for itself (within the couple itself, but by that fact within that fragment of society itself) whether its desires for a world worthy of consent are sufficiently satisfiable within the world as it is given" (*Cities of Words* 76–77). There are no guarantees. This statement thus underscores the moral uncertainty and fragility of perfectionism as exemplified by the couples' unavoidable conflicts and disappointments with one another. The crazy kineticism of these characters presents them as inhabiting a world whose ethical ground is unstable and open to question; they must assess their position in this world, both with respect to one another and to themselves. Nonetheless, the fact that one of them is willing to reform their world, even as they comically test the limits of its intelligibility and desirability, shows their consent to it, no matter how imperfect the world or the conditions of consent. This consent acknowledges that they (and we) are compromised by society's inevitable only partial compliance with the principles of justice. But what remarriage signifies is that the compromise is worth suffering to the extent that society is committed to reforming itself. In these films the ideal of marriage, or rather achieving remarriage, is no doubt utopic as every comedic world must be. But at the same time, this idea is a pragmatic, working image of our prosaic and daily compromises with good enough justice. The problem here is whether one can achieve satisfactory compromise with an other, and whether or to what extent others in community can accept compromise in an imperfect society. And as we shall see in the melodramas of the unknown woman, the demand for compromise can also be powerfully challenged and rejected.

The pursuit of happiness figures, in the image of (re)marriage, the ethical demand for a perfected human community whose medium and form of life is conversation. As a perfectionist ethical practice, conversation aims for an acknowledgment of self and of others that must not only be affirmed but continually reaffirmed. Through the medium of conversation, these comedies invoke the fantasy of the perfected human community, and propose that marriage is our best emblem of eventual community. This is not a figure of marriage as it is, but rather as it may be; that is, an eventuality whose probabilities of success or failure are undecided and undecidable. For these reasons Cavell insists that this fantasy or image suggests "on what may be seen as Kantian and Freudian and Lévi-Straussian grounds, that we cannot know that we are humanly capable of achieving that eventuality, or of so much as achieving a marriage that emblematizes it, since that may itself be achievable only as part of the eventual community" (*Pursuits of Happiness* 152).

Perfectionism in the comedies thus takes the form of the problem of sustaining marriage in the dynamics of conversations where the other is acknowledged as the vehicle for new self-knowledge and a transformation of self; hence the importance of the problem of education and its links to friendship. "The issues the principal pair in these films confront each other with," Cavell explains, "are formulated less well by questions concerning what they ought to do, what it would be best or right for them to do, than by the question of how they shall live their lives, what kind of persons they aspire to be. This aspect or moment of morality—in which a crisis forces an examination of one's life that calls for a transformation or reorienting of it—is the province of what I emphasize as moral perfectionism" (*Cities of Words* 11).

Here conversation becomes the modeling of a mode of existence, where talking together is being together or learning to speak the same language, both socially and sexually. This form of life is the projection of a mode of existence where acknowledging another person, and being acknowledged in turn, is a way of reestablishing intimacy with the world in its dailiness. These diurnal comedies, as Cavell calls them, thus express the particular temporality of moral perfectionism. They conclude not in an anticipated future, "but in a present continuity of before and after; its transformation of a festival into a festivity; its correction not of error but of experience, or of a perspective on experience" (*Pursuits of Happiness* 240). In this, for Cavell remarriage signifies "the two most impressive affirmations known to me of the task of human experience, the acceptance of human relatedness, as the acceptance of repetition. Kierkegaard's study called *Repetition,* which is a study of the possibility of marriage; and

Nietzsche's Eternal Return, the call for which he puts by saying it is high time, a heightening or ascension of time; this is literally *Hochzeit,* German for marriage, with time itself as the ring. As redemption by suffering does not depend on something that has already happened, so redemption by happiness does not depend on something that has yet to happen; both depend on a faith in something that is always happening, day by day" (*Pursuits of Happiness* 241).

 The demand for an education and the centrality of the place of the feminine, both independently and in relation to community, are central features of both remarriage comedies and melodramas. Yet, as demonstrated powerfully in *Brokeback Mountain* (Ang Lee, 2005), heteronormativity need not be the exclusive context for these demands.[85] The urtext for the perfectionist demand for an education as an act of self-disobedience or self-overcoming is Ibsen's *A Doll's House,* where Nora must seek her independence and the completion of her self (re-)creation outside of marriage. Her rebuke to Torvald is that they are not married, that in fact they have never been married, and that he is not the friend with or from whom she might desire or imagine education to a form of life where friendship and mutuality, hence marriage, are standing possibilities. She demands a new imagination of marriage as a space for becoming-other, in a process that Cavell calls education. "This demand for education," Cavell explains, "has to do with the woman's sense that her life asks for some transformation, that she stands in need of creation, or re-creation. I say of this need that it marks a new step in the construction of the human."[86] The perfectionist demand for an education turns on the expression of difference, and in both the comedies and melodramas, problems of gender and the expression of sexual difference are central features of genres whose conflicts also revolve around the suppression and return of the feminine voice. But this voice does not return as it was, as the recovery of a lost or suppressed essence, but rather in the return of new voicing of terms of difference or differentiation as the call for a new possibility of community. Such features call for psychoanalytic interpretation, of course. But one might also say that the suppression

---

85. In *Contesting Tears,* Cavell's "Postscript: To Whom It May Concern" is a fascinating account of the interest of addressing concepts of skepticism, irony, and melodrama in terms that are not heteronormative. I am also grateful in this respect to Ian Polonsky's essay "Contesting Skepticism: *Brokeback Mountain* and the Unknown Human," published in *Cinematic* 4 (2006): 50–54, and more recently a so-far-unpublished essay by Nicholas Mendoza, "Irony, Film, and Queer Identity in Cavell and Edelman."

86. "Ugly Duckling, Funny Butterfly: Bette Davis and "Now, Voyager," *Critical Inquiry* 16, no. 2 (Winter 1990): 216.

of the *human* voice is one of the dangers of skepticism. And in this way, in our culture, or in our modernity as lived, the acknowledgment and recovery of the feminine voice may project some of the most powerful perfectionist paths toward becoming human.

The pursuit of happiness in comedies of remarriage is equally the pursuit of a community of mutually supportive desire. One must desire, or as importantly, one must be free to desire, to belong to just this community, and thus work to desire it and so be desired by or in it. Marriage is therefore one example of the search for a commonwealth of equals who must work out the right ratios of dependence on, and independence from, one another in an exercise of choice regulated neither by duty nor transcendental authority.

One might also call these films, like many related works, comedies of differences of opinion, where ongoing disagreement and dissent arise out of mismatched criteria for assessing what is reasonable or unreasonable to expect from a mutually supportive community of equals. The possibility of misunderstanding is a distinguishing feature of the community in that the central pair of the comedies are often associated or were brought together because of their presumed eccentricity or externality to a more conventional social world. Only these two are capable of really understanding one another because the community they tried to form, and are still trying to form after having renounced it, is misunderstood by the larger society in which they find themselves. They are misunderstood, and yet it is also crucial for the films' projects of education and friendship that they misunderstand one another.

This misunderstanding maps the skeptical problem of knowing or not knowing other minds in a new direction; namely, the question of knowing or not, understanding or misunderstanding, one's sexual other. In these terms, what drives the comedies is not only the mismatch of criteria, and so the potential for misunderstanding, but also an asymmetrical relation of power marked by gender. The central philosophical aim of these films is to examine the problem of community and of human communion and communicativeness. But it is equally important that the films display this problem through the expression of sexual misunderstanding and as the possibility and difficulty of negotiating terms of equality between the sexes. This is why Cavell insists that comedies of remarriage be read as

> a development in the consciousness women hold of themselves as this is developed in its relation to the consciousness men hold of them. . . . Our films may be understood as parables of a phase of the development of

consciousness at which the struggle is for the reciprocity or equality of consciousness between a woman and a man, a study of the conditions under which this fight for recognition (as Hegel put it) or demand for acknowledgment (as I have put it) is a struggle for mutual freedom, especially of the views each holds of the other. This gives the films of our genre a Utopian cast. They harbor a vision which they know cannot fully be domesticated, inhabited, in the world we know. They are romances. Showing us our fantasies, they express the inner agenda of a nation that conceives Utopian longings and commitments for itself. (*Pursuits of Happiness* 17–18)

Another way of thinking about the promise of future mutuality and of addressing and refiguring the asymmetry of gender in the films is to follow through their depiction of the problem of finding or returning to a place of joint habitation, which may also be understood as finding new terms for joining or reconciling private and public life. Marriage, divorce, and remarriage thus become the image of establishing a new public and a new private relation, literally of gaining purchase on a new place, which Cavell describes as "the creation at once of new spaces of communality and of exclusiveness, of a new outside and inside to a life, space expressible by the private ownership of a house, literally an apartment, a place that is part of and apart within a larger habitation. . . . You are also free to understand the economic issue as part, hence as trope, of a more general issue of human happiness, call it the task or the cost of joint inhabitation, an essential requirement of which is the mutual creation of room, the resources for which (economic, spiritual, epistemological, metaphysical, geographical) remain incompletely charted" (*Pursuits of Happiness* 208–209).

The mutual creation of room may also be thought of as the creation of new room, of new placement, hence new ways of considering and refiguring the sexual relation. In the recent past and still current context of theory, the temptation to apply a critical template that reads these films as narratives of the redomestication of women and the management of heteronormative desire is strong. But this would be too easy. Moreover, a symptomatic reading of remarriage comedies might occlude two of the most fundamental and interesting facts about their narrative structure. First, they are primarily concerned with working out a dynamic of mutuality in the recognition and acknowledgment of desire where both sexes have something at stake, where relations of activity and passivity are not often clear, and where desire is not about the finding of an object (it is already found, and lost) but rather, as Freud would say, its refinding, thus suggesting a difference in repetition that cannot be definitively concluded or settled. Among the most essential and disorienting features of remarriage comedy (exemplified best, perhaps, in *Bringing Up Baby*) is that it is impossible to decide whether the man or the woman is the active or passive partner and impossible to know with real significance the difference between the masculine and feminine, or indeed whether concepts of activity and passivity adequately capture the continuum of sexual difference.

Another key feature of remarriage comedies is that marriage is not the conclusion or end of the narrative—marriage neither seals identity nor assures happiness. It is not a point of resolution whose concept can be taken for granted, but functions rather as a site of contestation and debate that aims at the transformation of a concept, marriage becoming remarriage. Perhaps this makes marriage a suspended concept, or a concept that is not free of doubt or uncertainty, and thus must be continually tested. In *Adam's Rib*, for example, marriage is not only subject to debate but is also a concept that can be taken to court, thus turning a private ethical conversation into a public and political one. It is also a film that strikingly investigates a central question of remarriage comedy; that is, whether the man or the woman is the active or passive agent in conflicts of desire and education. *Adam's Rib* plays on the asymmetry of gender relations more than the other films, as is already announced by naming the couple Amanda and Adam. The film is called *Adam's Rib*, but which name and thus position is derived from the other? This phonetic transformation signals how in the course of its plot the film works through different ways of permutating the logic of a field of relations that associates activity and passivity with masculinity and femininity and maleness and femaleness, and all within a debate about the law and what makes private matters of public interest.

A second obvious fact, as I have already suggested, is that the meaning and value of the state of marriage are depicted as contested and undecided; marriage must be open to failure in order for the question of remarriage to present itself through the free exercise of choice and consent. As Cavell astutely points out, Adam's view that marriage is defined contractually and regulated only by law is incoherent. Yet this incoherence clarifies some of the most important criteria in remarriage comedy that philosophy must account for: that divorce and dissent are standing possibilities in any union, and further, that our criteria for knowing what marriage is, or what makes it desirable, are unsettled.

The portrayal of dissenting concepts of marriage as decidable publicly as contract in a court of law signals that there is more than a couple at stake—here again the open play of discord and agreement, of consensus lost and (temporarily?) refound is meant to dramatize the fragility of the democratic social bond and to test its desirability and its possibilities for seeking new forms. These films are less about the return to domesticity and a settlement of active-passive relations along the axis of masculinity and femininity than about the standing possibility of threat or division, indeed the instability, that continually inhabits those relations. And this persistent threat or instability also demonstrates that even in comedy an undercurrent of violence dogs sexual difference. On the one hand, this violence is expressed by what Cavell calls the taint of villainy that mars the male characters—C. K. Dexter Haven's violent ejection of Tracy from their space of common habitation at the beginning of *The Philadelphia Story,* or in *Adam's Rib,* Adam's inability to discern the difference between a slap and a slug and the shading of erotic intimacy into domestic conflict. On the other, violence is also the price of ethical transformation, and of building new terms of existence where the sexual relation may be differently lived. The price of education to this fact is often expressed in situations where the principal pairs together experience a climactic event, suggestive of death or risk of life, that inspires painful change. These events are breaks or detours in the present direction of the characters' lives, which express the fact that progress toward a comic ending requires the exercise of choice as the price of change, and the choice may be painful. Likewise the change.

While there is often an asymmetry of knowledge or desire in these climactic moments, the characters nonetheless live them together and deal with their consequences and draw their conclusions together. The couple educate one another to new terms of existence. This means that the theme of education is strongly tied to mutuality, and that an education happens together or not at all, even if one arrives at understanding or transformation at a pace uneven with the other. But an education to what? Perhaps recognizing the necessity of change and accepting the pain of ethical transformation.

In similar terms, the films' emphases on hunger, thirst, or longing for a different life are thinly veiled expressions of perfectionist desire. In *The Philadelphia Story,* C. K. Dexter Haven calls this longing his "gorgeous thirst," from which he was cured only by finding the right pursuit for his happiness and thus finding or refinding the correct aim of his desire. In *It Happened One Night,* Peter's hunger might be called love, which Cavell describes as

imagining someone hungry for the same things you are yourself hungry for. . . . Since Dexter's praise of alcohol lies in its capacity to open your eyes to yourself, we might think of his thirst as for truth, or for self-knowledge, as well as for [Tracy's] desire, since his implied rebuke to her (that her eyes are closed to her own desire) is that what she could not bear was his thirst for whatever it is the alcohol represented, call this their marriage. He seems pretty clearly, and unapologetically, to be thinking about it still, still thirsting. (His curing himself of his substitute addiction, and moreover curing himself by reading, by an absorption in art, is understandable as the act of self-mastery that has lent him his special powers). (*Pursuits of Happiness* 145)

And indeed what Dexter rebukes Tracy with is her incapacity to accept imperfection or frailty in others, which is not only an inability to accept others, but also to accept her desire for others, or to undertake to help them change, or to undergo change herself. She is called divine, a goddess to be worshipped; what she must become is human through an act of self-disobedience, which will not be achieved without a certain testing of her pride as well as her identity. Thus education takes a particular form in remarriage comedy—that of recognizing and acknowledging desire of and for the other. Here Cavell emphasizes one of the key elements organizing the perfectionist desire for a transfigured form of life: that the obstacles to a happy union "are not complications unknown to the characters that a conclusion can sort out. They have something to learn but it cannot come as news from others. . . . It is not a matter of the reception of new experience but a matter of a new reception of your own experience, an acceptance of its authority as your own" (*Pursuits of Happiness* 240).

New reception of your own experience, and the acknowledgment and acceptance of its power to transform your life, is called perfectionism. One of the conclusions of *Pursuits of Happiness* is that "even in America, the land of the second chance, and of transcendentalist redeemers, the paradox inevitably arises: you cannot change the world (for example, a state of marriage) until the people in it change, and the people cannot change until the world changes" (257). The standing question of remarriage comedy is, how does one undergo change and recognize the necessity of undergoing change in support of the possibility of a new form of life? How does one pass into difference or a state of becoming, a self-overcoming in the creation of a new community? (This is the unanswered question of Deleuze's gestures toward ethical practice.)

The first stage of response is that one cannot undertake this transformation alone. This is why a doubling of identity is so fundamental to remarriage comedy (but also melodramas of the unknown woman), as if one of the parties must project their own conceptual personae to force change in the relationship, or to initiate their partner to a changed relationship, and one that reaffirms the dailiness of friendship, intimacy, and mutual education. In one's care for the other, one must acquire from them an acknowledgment of their rigidity, say their resistance to change and blindness to desire (Tracy in *The Philadelphia Story*) or their fixity in repetition (Jerry's philandering in *The Awful Truth*). This is what education means in remarriage comedy. One tries to force an acknowledgment from the other that they must come to stand for themselves in a relation analogous to that of remarriage to marriage, that is, an overcoming or succeeding of oneself in a perfectionist act of self-disobedience. "Can human beings change?" Cavell asks. "The humor, and the sadness, of remarriage comedies can be said to result from the fact that we have no good answer to that question" (*Pursuits of Happiness* 259). Yet the conditions for undergoing perfectionist change are foreseeable and expressible. Perhaps we only need to act on Nietzsche's request that we inhabit time anew.

21. A Digression on Difference and Interpretation

> Philosophy, which may begin in wonder (thus showing its relation to tragedy), may continue in argument (thus showing its kinship with comedy). Human thinking, falling upon itself in time, is not required of beings exempt from tragedy and comedy.
>
> —Stanley Cavell, *Pursuits of Happiness*

I said that Cavell approaches remarriage comedies and melodramas of the unknown woman as philosophical dialogues, not only as speech or dialectic in confrontation but also as a complex aesthetic structure with its own scenography, narrative arcs, and dramatic space and time. Cavell's critical approach to art, and especially the popular arts, is also powerfully redemptive, though in ways probably best understood in the context of ordinary language philosophy than through the critical perspectives of Benjamin or Kracauer. In *Cities of Words,* Cavell accordingly makes present and perspicuous two principles especially guiding his interest in Hollywood films: "that the concept of art remains powerful enough to contest the idea that human artifacts are homogeneously and with no resistance ideological reflections of their culture; and ... that works with the power of art were regularly, not of course predominantly, produced within the Hollywood studio system" (53–54).

I might rephrase this argument by saying that effects of power are neither homogeneously nor completely and without contradiction deployed throughout a society and its cultural expressions. Nor can the concept of ideology and its critique account for the complete range of relationships of understanding and desire that we enjoy with each other and with works of art, popular or otherwise. I do not wish to undermine or displace the value and importance of ideological criticism here. But I do think that with few exceptions, ideological criticism in the humanities—sometimes called theory—is far too often linked with concepts of totality, negation, and dialectic that are the unexamined conceptual inheritance of Hegelianism. (This was one of the principal lessons of my *Elegy for Theory*.)

This attachment to the absolute—to be inside or outside of ideology, with reference to no criteria of value apart from ideology and its negation—has strong though implicit links to the problematic of skepticism as examined by Cavell. The current interest in ethical assessment and criticism throughout the humanities, and not just in a Cavellian or Deleuzian framework, strongly indicates, I think, that there is more to our complex and contradictory experience of culture than ideology, and, perhaps more controversially, that in philosophy ethics precedes politics. (Perhaps this assertion is no less controversial than the idea, so widely held in the 1970s and after, that theory *is* politics.) As noted at the end of the last section, ethical examination is the best hope for interrupting the circle of confusion that says you cannot change the world until the people in it change, and that people cannot change until the world changes. Or perhaps ethics fully embraces the circle in acknowledging that the possibility and necessity of change is an individual's first step in transforming her or his mode of existence, alone or in the company of others. One may not change without the other. And one must know what one values and does not value in the world before one can ask the world to change. In turn, philosophy must acknowledge that there are more and varied pathways of reason than the one marked by certainty, fallibilism, and "good theory," and in this way it may contribute constructively to the project of theory, whatever we consider it to be. This is tantamount to saying, following von Wright, that the humanities have their own special forms of reasoning, interpreting, and valuing, which remain, perhaps, still to be discovered or recovered and valued.

In contrast to criticism based on the critic's judgments of political blindness and contradiction in the text or in others, moral perfectionism seeks to get beyond a critical perspective that finds everywhere hurtful asymmetries of power and the negation of voice. Perfectionism also provides an alternative to what Cavell calls the moralizing morality of academic moral philosophy, which insists on getting the other to agree to something, to do something, or to believe something that you are persuaded, independently of the conversation, that the other ought to do. (One might find a similar tendency in the association of theory with a politics of identity.) An often unrecognized or unacknowledged question is raised here about the relation of authority to morality or ethical standing—that my judgment of your position occurs without any critical questioning of my authority or right to question you. The worry is that my claim to a right of judgment rests only on some unquestioned transcendental principle, which may blind and deafen me to my own moralizing agenda and isolate and block me from change, when in fact my demand is for you to change. There is no room here for the mutual elaboration of what Charles Taylor calls a language of perspicuous contrast, which is in fact what Cavell calls education. I have already said that perfectionist conversations are singular, contingent, and context bound, and thus without appeal to transcendental authority of reason or morality. Perfectionism requests desire for change, and on this basis provokes a reflexive questioning of what constitutes one's standing in confronting another person with moral questioning. As an alternative to moralizing morality, Cavell reminds us that "in confronting another with whom your fate is, by your lights, bound up (either generally, as another human being, or more specifically by your cares for and commitments to the other, casual, institutional, or permanent), you risk your understanding of the other as of yourself—it is part of the argument you have initiated, or accepted the invitation to enter, to determine whether you have sufficiently appreciated the situation from the other's point of view, and whether you have articulated the ground of your own conviction" (*Cities of Words* 235).

Similar arguments might be raised in any act of criticism, thus linking perfectionism to artful conversation. Here there is another implicit bond of agreement between Cavell and Deleuze (or even Foucault) in that for both the potential for meaning is fully immanent in works of art. Texts already convey all they can possibly convey. From this perspective, producing new readings or recovering latent meanings is less a matter of a symptomology, of knowing better than the text what it says, than a function of readers' own productive acts of misrecognition, acknowledgment, or projective imagination, which continually illuminate or darken new informational foci by bringing new contextual situations and ethical perspectives to critical reading. Reading or interpretation is understood here as listening, as being receptive and open to what the text says, what the other says, and to grant that perhaps they do say what they mean, though perhaps incompletely or inchoately. (They may also be perfectly clear, yet misunderstood. You do not yet speak the same language together, or have the right context for understanding one another. One should be reminded here of Cavell's account of conversation and education in remarriage comedy.) What Cavell calls reading also involves locating and arguing for terms of intelligibility in the text that may in turn provoke a process of reflexively acknowledging and deepening your terms of intelligibility to yourself, and to transmit them in acts of criticism. Our encounters with art and the artful conversations they inspire may lead to perfectionist moments of self-education, in which I grant myself the possibility of change in a new language of perspicuous contrast, or undergo transformation under a new concept. Here philosophy asks us to free ourselves from judgment, or rather, asks us to become less judgmental, and asserts its difference from theory, at least in the forms usually given us in the humanities.

In this framework, an ethical film philosophy again distinguishes itself from film theory. For film philosophy is less interested in producing new knowledge about cinema than in soliciting thought and argument that demonstrate the quotidian importance of the moving image to contemporary ways of being and thinking, and that serve as the accompaniment to the ethical dilemmas of everyday life. Here perfectionism addresses local and daily dilemmas of living together or alone, of conformity or individuality, or of forming a community or standing apart from it. And if Cavell is primarily, though certainly not exclusively, concerned with American film genres, this parallels his lifelong interest in both philosophy's recounting of the ordinary and the possibilities of characterizing a particularly American strain of philosophical activity.

In Cavell's view, the comedies of remarriage discussed in *Pursuits of Happiness* and the melodramas of the unknown woman addressed in *Contesting Tears* stand in relation to one another as different variations of working through the Emersonian problem of self-reliance (which may also be considered in skeptical terms of isolation and existence), though they also share a common grammar for articulating this problem. In *The Claim of Reason*, Cavell suggests that defining the question of the human should be pursued in the discovery or acknowledgment of internal relations that each human being inhabits with others. In the utopic world of the comedies, this binding series of relations is not thought to be present in society as it stands, but rather is expressed through the contests and conversations of the romantic couples who exemplify the as yet unachieved possibilities of human community present in this world. In forming their own world, in declaring its existence, they suggest the possibility of another world present in or next to the one they inhabit and converse in. Their self-reliant reaffirmation of community is the genetic element projecting the possibility of this new world. In the melodramas, however, no matter how deep the isolation and ironic confinement of the heroines, the discovery of self-reliance will require acts of perfectionist self-disobedience where Emersonian qualities of rightful attraction, expressiveness, and joy are undertaken first in relation to one's self.

In asking for a place for film philosophy other than that of ideological criticism, I do not want to say that forceful asymmetries of power and knowledge marked by lines of gender division are unimportant in these films; indeed such asymmetries are central features of their grammar. But if the figuration of marriage is accepted as a genetic form of community, where living together in dissent is a standing possibility, then one must also acknowledge that questions of sexual difference play significant roles, both externally and internally, in the process of change or metamorphosis that these films require and enact. Externally, that little but inescapable difference, as Adam puts it in *Adam's Rib,* fuels conflict and misunderstanding between the couples, but also functions as the price of their achieving freedom and exercising choice; internally, difference is another expression of the fact that division within the self is the price of becoming other than who you are.

Acknowledging division within the self—the self's conflict, or lack of conformity with itself—as preparatory to the possibility of change takes several forms in Cavell's philosophy of film. Through the concept of photogenesis, for example, Cavell illuminates a force of becoming where subjects and things reveal otherwise unrecognized states or possibilities of existence. Change, including ethical transformation, requires reflexivity, recognizing that the other to one's self resides in oneself, or rather that "oneself" may comprise two or more selves (or even a multitude). These are less points of departure than projected images of transformed identity yet to be achieved, as much as past residues of identities overcome.

This reflexivity can also take the form of sexual reflexivity. Cavell suggests that one of the camera's powers of photogenesis is the capacity to reveal the reverse nature of the human subject; in short, that the camera has the power to capture the feminine aspect of masculine physiognomy, and perhaps the masculine aspect of feminine physiognomy. (Remarriage comedy presents this power as expressing the undecidability of whether the man or the woman is the active or passive partner, or whether we can know with real significance the difference between the masculine and feminine, or indeed whether concepts of activity and passivity adequately capture the continuum of sexual difference.) This power is linked to film's powers of passive intentionality—its capacity for revealing thought's expressiveness in the body, thus locating an otherwise nonvisible self. The concept of photogenesis is meant to express the inherent reflexivity of projected subjects and things becoming on screen in the photographic presentation of themselves, a presence that indicates an absence, and perhaps also a past projected toward a future, or some future state of becoming whose direction is often unclear or unrecognized in the present. In *Pursuits of Happiness,* Cavell expands this thought in writing that "I wish to understand as an analogue to this ontological speculation about material objects the speculation about human beings, things with consciousness, that their presence refers to their absent, or invisible, or complementary, sexuality. The reflexiveness of objects harks back, in my mind, to the earlier claim in *The World Viewed* that objects on screen appear as held in the frame of nature, implying the world as a whole. The sexual reflexiveness of human beings would accordingly suggest the individual as expressing humanity as such, what in *The Claim of Reason* I call the internal relation of each human being with all others" (*Pursuits of Happiness* 224–225). This is a point worth repeating: that the reversibility of qualities of activity and passivity along the lines of masculinity and femininity, or maleness and femaleness, does not so much divide gender through criteria of identity and asymmetries of power as affirm human relatedness in a shared if contradictory web of intersubjective relations. Recall Cavell's earlier response to the question of what becomes of things on film. In the image, subjects and things are not only held in the frame of nature (implying the world as a whole, hence a common plane of immanence or existence), those individuated things we call human beings are also shown to exist in a world, in a shared form of life, where each being shares an internal relation with every other being.

22. Perfectionism's Ironic Transport

> Helmer: But to leave your home, your husband, your children! Have you
> thought what people will say? . . . But this is monstrous! Can you neglect your
> most sacred duties? . . . First and foremost you are a wife and mother.
> Nora: I don't believe that any longer. I believe that I am first and foremost a
> human being, like you—or anyway, that I must try to become one.
>
> —Henrik Ibsen, *A Doll's House*

> Skepticism breaks into . . . life, with a surmise that I cannot live with,
> that the world and I and others are radically unknown to me.
>
> —Stanley Cavell, *The Claim to Reason*

Cavell's study of the melodrama of the unknown woman provides some of his
most complex and penetrating insights into the structure of moral perfectionism. Although published fifteen years apart, *Pursuits of Happiness* and *Contesting Tears* are complementary works. (The intervening period was marked
by intensive work on the concept of moral perfectionism perhaps best presented in three books: *In Quest of the Ordinary* [1988], *This New Yet Unap-
proachable America* [1989], and, most importantly, *Conditions Handsome and
Unhandsome* [1990].) *Contesting Tears* shows that there is also a dark side to
perfectionism and the pursuit of happiness. The book returns to themes present earlier in Cavell's discussion of film though not yet set in the context of
moral perfectionism: ethics as the evaluation of a mode of existence that requires contesting and evaluating a community or a form of life; the demand
for an education, apart or alone, in situations that require tests of your own
moral standing no less than those who would befriend you; and film's expression of the power of metamorphosis and the capacity for change, which often
takes the form of a certain reflexivity and the projection of a divided self.

Unlike the comedies, the melodramas explore perfectionism in a mode of
irony that acknowledges the consequences of a life buried in conformity or
consigned to a community blind to or even destructive of the desire for change.
Like remarriage comedy, melodramas of the unknown woman also constitute
an open set, whose exemplary instances include just four films: *Stella Dallas*
(King Vidor, 1937), *Now, Voyager* (Irving Rapper, 1942), *Gaslight* (George Cukor, 1944), and *Letter from an Unknown Woman* (Max Ophuls, 1948). Recall
that the concept of genre as an open set insists on the following principles: that
the coherence of genres is established and continually transformed by critical

reading, and is not set in advance or concluded historically; that the practice of evaluation is itself open, constantly adding or subtracting candidates in a process of critical argumentation aimed at recognizing new formal features in the works, which in turn produce new conceptual possibilities for philosophical investigation; and finally, that the assertion of generic identity projects new contexts for assessing subsequent work. In short, the power of genre is founded through difference in repetition, rather than on a principle of identity, similar to Cavell's discovery of the power of automatism in seriality. In "The Good of Film," for example, Cavell proposes many contemporary candidates for assessment in the context of remarriage comedy, most prominently *Groundhog Day* (Harold Ramis, 1993). Cavell has also examined several recent European films in the context of ethical dramas of unknownness, including *The Marquise of O* (Eric Rohmer, 1976), *A Tale of Winter* (Eric Rohmer, 1992), and *The Captive* (Chantal Akerman, 2000).

As ethical dramas of perfectionism the melodramas of the unknown woman are closer structurally and philosophically to remarriage comedies than they are to proximate versions of melodrama, say the Hollywood women's film. Cavell considers the unknown woman films to be a genre derived from remarriage comedy through a process of negation or inversion, and of turning the comic and affirmative features of the comedies into an ironic mode. Accordingly, what constitutes this group of films as a genre is that they "reveal systematically the threats (of misunderstanding, of violence) that in each of the remarriage comedies dog its happiness" (*Contesting Tears* 83). The genre also continues Cavell's examination of film along the lines of skepticism—if marriage is an image of the domestic, the ordinary, or the everyday, then skepticism's threat to the ordinary may take the form of irony or melodrama. Cavell makes this point in many contexts, including in *The Claim of Reason*. The image of the failed or cursed marriage, or the dissensual community, is accordingly a threat to perfectionism's image of the practice of philosophy as the intimacy of one soul's examination of and by another.

The ironic mode of melodramas of unknownness directly confronts the criteria through which the remarriage comedies pursue their happiness in the formation and reaffirmation of community. The comedies project—through dilemmas of marriage, domesticity, and the social everyday—the problem of maintaining equality between human beings based on Emersonian qualities of rightful attraction, expressiveness, and joy. The melodramas, however, express problems of privacy and qualities of self-reliance that demand such expressiveness first in relation to oneself. Marriage is no longer a standing possibility for the melodramas, or at least it can no longer be valued in the same way. (As in the example of *Gaslight*, it can even be the site of a terrorization of the woman to the point of madness.) Rather than presenting a community in formation, the films examine the problem of a self in need of transformation, not only from joylessness to self-acceptance but also as the assertion of an independent place within a community of equals unbounded by standing concepts of marriage.

The irony of unknownness is key to the ethical dilemmas of the melodramas. Whereas the domestic pairs in the comedies regain acknowledgment of and responsiveness to one another (no matter how temporary, uncertain, or fragile), the ironic conversational mode of the melodramas continually blocks or undermines any communication and social interaction that could permit or advance this acknowledgment and responsiveness. The unknown woman of the melodramas does not share a language with those around her, thus raising the question, in the context of skepticism, of her isolation within her pictured community and therefore from us, the film spectators. This isolation suggests a break or separation in the internal relations binding her to others in a human form of life. In their unknownness to us, and their isolation from the community that surrounds them, the women in these melodramas embody the skeptical dilemmas of a world held at a distance and of a self isolated from other minds, one whose price is voicelessness and a fragile hold on a social, thus human, form of life. Indeed, these are studies of the consequences of an inhuman existence, all the more horrific because of its setting in the domestic or the ordinary. How is recovery possible? If skepticism is held at bay through acknowledgment, sociability, and conversation, then the unknown women of the melodramas must find adequate partners in dialogue and education; they are in need of a philosophical friend even if, as in the case of *Now, Voyager*, that friend is transcended or becomes irrelevant.

In these films, the solution to inhuman isolation is not found necessarily or only in others, especially the men in the films, but rather more forcefully from within the protagonist herself through the discovery of a new mode of self-reliance. In Stephen Mulhall's account, what the melodramas express is "a mode of metamorphosis which is a route towards a new or original integrity that can be (at least provisionally) achieved in isolation—a personal change without social interchange" (*Philosophy's Recounting of the Ordinary* 239). In the context of moral perfectionism, the melodrama of the unknown woman amplifies the ethical problem of self creation or re-creation, as if discovering or constructing within oneself a new conceptual persona as a route toward self-disobedience. And to the extent that this process involves the recovery of her voice, hence language in a new form of life, this new creation of the woman is linked to a new imagination of the human. What these women show us are the stakes of aiming toward perfectionist paths for becoming human, and the high price of failing to recover from inhuman isolation. The route out of irony toward self-reliance can thus be thought of as "involving a relation between two selves," Mulhall explains,

> or rather two states of her self: condemned by the world of her film to a mode of existence in which she at best haunts the world, she stakes her life on her capacity to envision a further state of her self which it is within her power to realize or enact. She permits this vision of an unknown but knowable future self to attract her away from her present self, to initiate her self-transformation, her refusal of her world and its conditions—to initiate and maintain her refusal to conform. Thus the melodrama of self-reliance involves a doubleness within the self, a capacity for self-transcendence which amounts to a movement from one state of the self to another, an avoidance of fixation or repetition and an openness to the unknown future. (242–243)

I have called this capacity perfectionism as self-disobedience. Since it is also a revolt against a standing community of conformity, suffocating and resistant to change, self-disobedience becomes civic disobedience—a contestation of the community as it stands, and sometimes, the imagination of a community to come, perhaps a new and more human form of existence.

As an image of community, the problem of marriage remains central to the grammar of these melodramas, though in the form of negation rather than affirmation or reaffirmation. These women are sisters of Ibsen's Nora, who rejects marriage as the mode of existence in which a new life, say a newly won human life, can be discovered. Understood in a perfectionist context, here the woman seeks her unattained but attainable self otherwise than in marriage, whose opportunities and promise of community have proven to be destructive for her. It turns out that the partner to whom she was drawn as a way of sharing her fantasies of transcendence of the everyday was one capable only of inspiring fantasies, not acting on them. Accordingly, she must leave children and husband behind on the ground that there is no marriage between them

because he is not the individual with whom a mutual education is possible—
she must set out from her current habitation to find an education and a new
mode of existence.

As a possible route to creating a new and original integrity, marriage is contested and even transcended in these films. Yet as Cavell points out, "The route
to this alternative integrity is still creation, or what I might call metamorphosis—
some radical, astonishing, one may say melodramatic change of the woman,
say of her identity. But this change must take place outside the process of a
mode of conversation with a man (of course, since such a conversation would
constitute marriage)" (*Contesting Tears* 6). Considering that the two genres
run parallel to one another historically, one may presume a standing conversation between them on the concept of marriage. And indeed what the melodramas bring forth in stark clarity is the topos of marriage as a site of contestation or failed consensus where the pursuit of happiness is fraught with risk.

We have arrived at the central (perfectionist) question that binds the two
genres in a common grammar: How is change possible, or better, how is *human* change possible? To the extent that these films are considered media of
art (neither Cavell nor I have any doubts on this matter, though perhaps it remains for you to discover this for yourself), the question of becoming on film,
how the concept of becoming is projected in film—its automatisms, its elements or forms, its genres—must now be connected, philosophically, to the
perfectionist problems of self-reliance defined as self-disobedience, of aversion to conformity, and of overcoming one's fixed or stagnated self as a recovery of human existence. In *Contesting Tears* Cavell asks, "Does, for example,
the moving picture do its work by fixation or by metamorphosis? Here we
need to think about change or difference in connection with concepts of identity and of repetition, in Kierkegaard's, Nietzsche's, and Freud's senses, invoked in *Pursuits of Happiness*" (141). No doubt, to think of difference in identity through Kierkegaard, Nietzsche, or Freud suggests another unfinished
conversation with Deleuze. Still, the main issue here is that in their deployment and expression of concepts of transfiguration and transvaluation, the
moral of the melodramas of the unknown woman—or better, what they construct and convey from and through the medium of film—is that one of the
powers of photogenesis is to express the transformation of fixation *as* metamorphosis, to show that subjects do become, or become-other, on film. This is
one of film's most powerful affinities with perfectionism.

Interpreting and evaluating our given terms of existence and their possibilities for transformation is a key task of perfectionism. In like manner, the

problem of existence—or rather, the will to recover from a problematic existence—is a key element linking perfectionism to what Cavell calls the underlying myth of melodramas of the unknown woman where "a woman achieves existence (or fails to), or establishes her right to existence in the form of a metamorphosis (or fails to), apart from or beyond satisfaction by marriage (of a certain kind) and with the presence of her mother and of her children, where something in her language must be as traumatic in her case as the conversation of marriage is for her comedic sisters—perhaps it will be an aria of divorce, from husband, lover, mother, or child" (*Contesting Tears* 88). Marriage and family play important roles in these films, though often perverse ones, as do relations between parent and child, which often image the temporal possibility of extending the past into the future, either ironically as identity (eternal recurrence of the past in the present), or hopefully as difference (being reborn into a transformed world). (There can be utopia in the melodramas no less than the comedies.)

The shared grammar of marriage also signals important criteria of contrast with the remarriage comedies. With the exception of the heroine of *Gaslight*, the woman is shown to be a mother, or as in the case of *Now, Voyager*, she assumes the role of a (revised) mother. In any case, she is often shown in relation to a child. The woman is also presented in relation to or in fateful separation from her mother, who haunts her present psychologically. Lastly, the woman's desire is in conflict with the law, sometimes represented by an authoritarian father. If her father (or a father figure, sometimes a husband) is present, he is never on the side of desire, but rather stands for the prohibition of desire. *Now, Voyager* plays an interesting variation on this element, in that Charlotte's desire is blocked and suppressed by a tyrannical matriarch, who has absorbed the dead father's powers of prohibition.

I want to speak soon of the temporality of these melodramas in contrast to the time of comedy. But *Now, Voyager* raises another set of problems, often less clearly set out or articulated in the other films. The image of the impossible or failed marriage is intimately linked to the perfectionist logic of this film. In turn, ironic impediments to marriage, or at least a certain standing idea of marriage, unfold in stages through the narrative as variations on questions of identity and existence, of giving in to conformity or finding new possibilities of self-disobedience and self-reliance, of who can be a friend in this dilemma and for how long. Problems of identity and sexual difference are raised in every case around these questions, and with interesting consequences.

My thought is that the power of *Now, Voyager* derives from its critically savvy remapping of concepts of gender and class difference in pictured society as it stands. A central argument of the film is that names or predicates do not define existence; or put another way, existentially, the community of Vale is not set in stone. The rainswept boundary stone in the film's opening shot is also a signpost to an altered form of community, where the terms that constitute a family named Vale—call this a view of the domestic—must be transformed. The narrative arc of the film clearly unfolds along divisions that separate the world of women from the world of men. The Vale home is, significantly, a world where men are absent, apart from a manservant. Initially, the world of women is the world of Charlotte's isolation, almost to the point of madness, as signified by the locked room where she attempts to protect some form of privacy against her mother's authoritarian control. Doctor Jaquith is brought into this world by Charlotte's sister-in-law and niece, both of whom return later in the film at significant moments as friends and markers of change. Jaquith will also escort her out of this world, first to his country clinic, Cascades, whose name suggests not only a poetics of falling gently but also a process of displacement in series, and then by recommending an ocean voyage. Connected by an image of water, hence rebirth, both Cascades and the setting of ocean liners are significant topoi in the film. To be on a boat is to be "at sea" but also to be in transport; the linking of the two is important to the film's perfectionist narrative.

As shown in flashback, Charlotte's first failed "marriage" takes place at sea with the handsome young radio operator, Leslie Trotter. The discovery of their secret romance also initiates the increasing isolation of Charlotte by her mother. The film then progresses through a series of failed attempts to marry. Jerry, whom Charlotte meets on the trip after her first stay at Cascades, makes no secret of the fact that he is married with two daughters, one of whom, the younger Christina, will become Charlotte's fateful double. Jerry, like Jaquith, is pictured as a philosophical friend and a key agent enabling Charlotte's transformation and her education to a new form of life. Jerry encourages and enables Charlotte's play with image and transformation as she tries on the identity of Renée Beauchamp, and finally christens her Camille, the lady of the Camellias. Camellias will be the secret image of their shared past together, as well as a sign of Charlotte's unmarried "idiosyncrasy," as she calls it.

However, Jerry also presents an image (literally a photograph) of a failed or unhappy marriage. His sickly and demanding wife isolates him, no less than Charlotte is isolated by her mother; his only hope for the future is an introverted and unhappy child, unwanted by her mother. Of course, there are not one but two family photographs exchanged in the film: one of Jerry's wife and daughters, the other of the imposing Vale clan with Charlotte on the margin on the right, the spinster aunt, the "fat lady with the heavy eyebrows and all the hair." Two photographs and two families, both of which offer an image of a stultifying past still active in the present. Together they also present the possibility of still-undecided choice in two family domains: that Renée-Charlotte-Camille might be able to take a step into a revised future is still not a standing possibility for Jerry's daughter, Christina.

And here is another irony of the film. What Charlotte refinds with Jerry is the possibility of marriage. On returning home, to reestablish her new identity through the discovery that that she is no longer afraid, especially of her mother, she must now again confront the fact of marriage in the person of Elliot Livingston, a notable Bostonian from her own social caste. This would be a marriage of conventionality and conformity, as the film makes clear by reintroducing Jerry into the plot. What Charlotte and Jerry discovered together is what makes for a happy marriage. Elliot is a fine man, though lacking Jerry's sense of humor, sense of beauty, and sense of play. Elliot, alternatively, is incapable of being her friend, or not like this—he cannot teach her to be loving and affectionate as Jerry did. In the meantime, Jerry has taken his own step into a revised future. One may say that he has been educated by Charlotte's example, and so becomes the architect he always wanted to be, that he was meant to be. But this is not enough to make a marriage. The most powerful irony lies here. In the world of the film, aristocratic Boston, ethically Jerry and Charlotte cannot marry. Yet through her past with Jerry, Charlotte has discovered what might make a good marriage, and must now acknowledge, again ethically, that she cannot create this world with Elliot—there is no possibility of further education, hence change, with him. The narrative of the film is littered with images of failed marriage. Or if there are happy marriages, like that of Charlotte's sister-in-law, husbands never seem to be present. Is a marriage only happy in the absence of a husband? How unhappy or happy is this thought? This is not funny, but it is also perhaps not bad. These are all marriages ruled by a transcendental principle of conventionality and conformity. To prevent falling into tragedy, a revised vision of family, of community, must be discovered and constructed.

Before returning to the concept of marriage as contested and transfigured in this film, I want to pursue one last digression briefly. I said that the narrative unfolds along a line that separates a world of women, say the darkened

Vale matriarchy, and a world of men. The masculine is first given in the film as an image of care and concern in the character of Jaquith, and then as romance in the figures of Leslie and Jerry, both significantly discovered at sea. What kinds of men are these? If we care to divide masculinity from femininity along the lines of activity and passivity, Leslie and Jerry are rather limp and indecisive figures, as Elliot will be later. At the same time, each represents poles of attraction and desire in the film: Leslie is the site of fantasy and impossible romance, literally found in books; Jerry presents the possibility of the good but unattainable marriage; Elliot represents the sign of possible marriage, though perhaps not good enough, since this path leads to a life of predictable conformity. In Nietzsche's terms, these are passive men capable only of marshaling reactive forces; they are incapable of imagining, encouraging, or undergoing further change. Apart from Jaquith, to whom I will return later, it is mostly women in the film who support and encourage care and transformation. That Jerry is capable of being a true friend to Charlotte shows that there is something like an active femininity in him, signified perhaps by his European accent and manners. Alternatively, the fact that Charlotte's mother has replaced her father in the form of a lonely, repressive, and domineering tyrant shows that a woman can exercise an active masculine power, though in this case through a kind of destructive and passive aggressivity that reduces her to bedridden stillness. In this film, the criteria defining masculinity and femininity, activity and passivity, or what defines a home, family, marriage, who is a child and who is a parent, are all distorted and out of joint. What ironic self-reliance will mean in Charlotte's case is that new perfectionist terms of identity must be created, wherein a new creation of the woman becomes the source of a revised vision of family and community. We will come back to this.

Perfectionism asks for the capacity to change, and accordingly projects an image or concept of time. Here again the melodramas invert or negate the structure of the comedies. In contrast to the comedies, with their openness to inventiveness and a revised future, in the melodramas time is frozen in the past, resistant to change or exchange, and this stultifying past is compulsively active in the present. The comedies have short and rather unified and linear time spans—from less than twenty-four hours to a few days or weeks—whereas the arc of action in the melodramas is more extended (sometimes including a span of many years) and elliptical. Often the past deforms the present as an irrepressible force of return that takes the form of temporal reversals and recursions. The best-known examples are no doubt given in the complex narrative time of *Letter from an Unknown Woman*. In the remarriage

comedies, repetition or recurrence signify invention, improvisation, and openness to change. Melodramatic time in a film like *Letter* is self-enclosing and
loops back on itself in death-dealing repetitiveness. Finally, the melodramas
tend to conclude where they begin, opening and closing in the same house—as
if to insist upon the difficulty of undergoing change, but also more positively,
as a sign of possibility for transforming the domestic. If the ending is to avoid a
complete acquiescence to irony, a form of difference in repetition must transcend or overcome the eternal return of past unhappiness in anticipation of an
attainable better, future life. In fact, *Now, Voyager* is the only member of the
genre that clearly depicts an attainable revised future; in *Stella Dallas* there is
also the suggestion of a step into a new existence, but one not yet visionable or
imaginable by the film.

In a similar way, the past is not a place of shared happiness, but rather a site
of blockage, failure, and unredeemed desire, which takes the form of isolation
and voicelessness. (*Letter from an Unknown Woman* varies and amplifies this
idea: the woman's voice guides that narrative as the recovery of a lost memory.
But this voice is not only the resurgence of a lost past, it also comes from a
woman lost to life and thus signifies the unavoidability of death for Stefan, as
well as his acceptance of this fate.) In the comedies, perfectionism is deployed
in playful and confrontational conversation in which the romantic pairs try to
discover whether they can indeed define new terms of existence together based
on mutuality. In the melodramas, the place of conversation is transformed
and negated. It is no longer an improvisational and intimate battle of wits, but
rather an isolating struggle with irony and misunderstanding: "not a clearing
of communication," Cavell writes in *Cities of Words*, "but a darkening of it"
(109). Communication and conversation are everywhere undercut by irony,
and at various levels—dialogue, image composition, and camera movement—
making of irony a pervasive expressive mode in these films.

The problems of time and transformation, of repetition and difference, raise
again the question of sexual difference. A taint of villainy in the men is part of
the shared grammar of the comedies and melodramas, especially in the working out of themes of conversation and education. In *Contesting Tears*, Cavell
directly confronts the moral cloud that hangs over the woman's demand for
an education—whether in Ibsen or more specifically, remarriage comedies—
with respect to the difficulty of their relations with men. From what place or
desire does the woman's need of creation, re-creation, or new creation come
from? "Does creation from, even by, the man somehow entail creation *for* the
man, say for his use and pleasure and pride?" Cavell asks. "If not, how does

the woman attain independence; how does she complete, as it were, her creation?" (*Contesting Tears* 116).

If the comedies end in new creation or re-creation, this is not only a transformation of identity but also an expression of belief in the possibility of creating and inhabiting a renewed form of life in which terms of difference may (must) be reconfigured or remapped. Comic endings believe in the possibility of changing one's self, and of helping others to change, in situations where one does not so much risk autonomy or independence as bet on the possibility of achieving a new condition or grammar for autonomy. (And the aim of such transformations is neither the recovery of a lost essence nor the discovery of a new one. Here autonomy means the acquisition of new agency and new terms of existence.) That happiness may be pursued in a transformed world is the heterocosmic image of remarriage comedy. The ironic image of the melodramas, however, expresses the risks of autonomy as a return to and revaluation of self-reliance, because the promise of happiness may not be enough—its compromises may not be worth the price of pain of transformation. That a taint of villainy mars the image of masculinity in remarriage comedy thus acknowledges the presence of a background of pain marring relations between the sexes. As Cavell explains, in the comedies it is as if "maleness, or rather masculinity, has been defined, or deformed in our culture. The implication is that the woman's creation will be completed, furthered, only with the man's. The derived melodrama will then be expected to ask where the woman gets the power to demand the man's transformation, which is to say, where she gets the power to transcend his standing. The melodrama signaled in the tainted male of the comedies suggests that there is a structure of unhappiness that the happiness of the comedies is lucky to escape, even temporarily, even (and always partially by happenstance) partially" (*Contesting Tears* 116–117).

In the melodramas of the unknown woman, the affirmative mode of the comedies is inverted as if to acknowledge and to make perspicuous the undercurrent of violence to which the women are often submitted. The potential for suffering, and for suffering alienation, is not hidden by these films whose structure of irony resolutely focuses on a feminine subject blocked and damaged by life under patriarchy. Of the four films, *Gaslight* is the most extreme example of a near-absolute negation of the remarriage genre, in that marriage is depicted as a mode of existence that the man constructs as the very scene of skepticism and madness, in which the woman is isolated, deprived of a voice, and made to see herself as an object of madness and horror. *Gaslight*'s scene of madness is an almost pure expression of the moral cynicism to which perfectionism must respond. As if to amplify the ironic tone of these dramas, the male characters are often depicted either as extreme manifestations of the skeptical personality or, even when portrayed sympathetically, as fixed in their identity and incapable of recognizing the capacity for change or the possibility of constructing new terms of existence with the women. It may well be that the perfectionist need for transformation is literally incomprehensible to the man in these dramas, and that unlike the remarriage comedies, at some point mutual understanding is no longer possible between the woman and the man. In other words, there is no possibility of a mutual education, and thus the validity and legitimacy of marriage are undermined.

In the ironic mode, Cavell suggests that the first perfectionist step occurs in recognition that "the initial onset of self-knowledge is the reality for the first time of being known, being acknowledged in her difference, as if until then her existence had been denied—suffered the polite skepticism of everyday life" ("Philosophy the Day After Tomorrow" 329). One of the deep ironies of these films is the recognition that moral cynicism (related to what Cavell earlier called moral evil) is a motivator of perfectionist desire for change. Another name for this moral darkness or obscurity is what Emerson called conformity—the perpetual sense of having assumed a false position in society without anyone having exactly placed you there, or without you yourself realizing that you have acquiesced to this compromised position. The acknowledgment of moral cynicism may thus be a moment preparatory to perfectionist self-examination. "A mark of this stage," Cavell writes in *Cities of Words,* "is a sense of obscurity, to yourself as well as to others, one expression of which is a sense of compromise, of being asked to settle too soon for the world as it is, a perplexity in relating yourself to what you find unacceptable in your world, without knowing what you can be held responsible for" (23).

The irony of this situation expresses itself in a recognition of voicelessness, of lacking language or concept with which to make one's self intelligible to one's self or to others, as if the power to imagine the possibility of becoming other requires the invention of a new language. This felt lack of language or concept distinguishes perfectionism from both teleological and deontological conceptions of moral reasoning. Based on a concept of the good, teleological theories evaluate the consequences or ends for which actions are taken. As expressed in the utilitarianism of Hume, Bentham, or Mill, moral theories define a rational society as one that attempts pragmatically to maximize the amount of good present and available in a given society for those governed by it. Deontological theories are based on concepts of right and the correctness of motives rather than consequences. Exemplified by Kant's categorical imperative, these theories give priority to concepts of justice and duty that outweigh individual desires, and define society by fundamental principles of justice that neither governments nor individuals may infringe. Both approaches assume a subject capable of recognizing and accepting a concept of the good, or of expressing and conforming to a categorical imperative. However, the perfectionist desire for change is motivated by the intuition that the present world and existing terms of language fail me, that I am not one with myself, and that my conformity to their terms of existence is both false and damaging. Both I and the world need to change, and new criteria must be found to attune my relationship to the world and to others. Accordingly, perfectionism is not an alternative to utilitarianism and Kantianism, but rather a response to the intuition of being left out of their sway and of finding no solace in their concepts. It is a response to a secret melancholy, as Emerson says, where either you or the world is wrong.

As exemplified in *Now, Voyager,* the melodramas often depict the woman in two states of her life, set years apart—a state of innocence and a state of experience. One could also say that this temporal distance marks a transition from conformity to self-reliance, or from a sense of obscurity to herself (as well as to others) to the voicing of the possibility of a revised world because a new perspective has been found from which to contest the limitations of this world. Finding a voice also signifies a recovery from isolation, or from enforced terms of skepticism, whereby the woman discovers her power to contest and transcend the man's moral standing and to demand his transformation in a revised world, if he is capable. (The closing of *Now, Voyager,* to which I will return, is exemplary of this situation.)

To be placed in position to judge the world is to decide whether or how we accept or resist conformity in or with that world. In "Self-Reliance," Emerson calls this practice the aversion of conformity. To live in conformity to a given state, whether existential or governmental, is to accept its usurpation of your voice, to let it speak you and thus render you voiceless. Cavell considers this a form of madness; it is at least a relinquishing of one's own claim to reason. The ethical response to this situation is not to radically reject this world or to turn your back to it. How does one escape a world? With a characteristic Emersonian twist of meaning, acting in aversion to society does not only mean turning away from conformity but also directly confronting it. Cavell calls this a process of deconformity, where one's aversion to conformity also means standing next to it, being beside it as if being beside oneself or some former state of self.

Here Cavell repeats Thoreau's definition of thinking as being beside oneself in a sane sense, as if we were continually vacillating between madness and sanity. Thinking in conformity, then, would be being beside oneself in despair of the possibility of change or of turning in a new direction, as if facing a forever frozen mirror image of one's identity.

In *Now, Voyager*, Charlotte Vale dramatically (I would say aversively) confronts such images more than once. One of the lessons of *Now, Voyager* is that the temporal path of perfectionism is complex. At their first lunch together on shore, Jerry expresses fascination (and perhaps expresses our fascination) with Charlotte's unknownness. He says that he wishes he understood her. After he leaves Charlotte alone at the table, she reflects that "he wishes he understood me." There is a cut to an over-the-shoulder shot that tracks in to Charlotte's image doubled in a nearby window. The angle reverses again to show Charlotte's look at herself, and then changing to a new angle, shows more clearly what the spectator sees of Charlotte as she repeats with a self-ironizing emphasis: "He wishes."

What does he wish? Or what does Jerry desire of Charlotte's fragile identity, and what in turn does she desire in response to his wish? In this simple series of shots, Charlotte recognizes Jerry's attraction to her unknownness, which the film also marks as a reflexive moment of isolation in which she acknowledges her sense of obscurity to herself. And in this moment, the film suggests that Charlotte also intuits new terms for her own desire. Perhaps this is a desire for further transformation, for taking a next step in the transition from Charlotte to Renée and Camille. But Jerry's desire for her, fueled by the mystery of her identity, is not congruent with her own desire. The otherness she now discovers within herself is, in my interpretation, the discovery of a new power to become other. And if she discovers new desire in herself, it is not a desire to conform further to Jerry's fantasy of her. She will, to some extent, want to become known to him, at least as far as he is capable of knowing her. In this series of images she is confronting a sense of obscurity to herself. At the same time, she is discovering a new person, a projection of one future version of herself, as if confronting her unknownness to herself with a new concept of identity.

He wishes, but so does she (as if her wish was folded into and out of his). The perfectionist structure within remarriage comedies and melodramas of the unknown woman depicts a journey to a new form of life as a turning from conformity and the achievement of new possibilities of choice and self-reliance. Cavell calls this "a journey, or path, or step, from haunting the world to existing in it; which may be expressed as the asserting of one's *cogito ergo sum,* one's own 'I think, therefore I am,' call it the power to think for oneself, to judge the world, to acquire—as Nora puts it at the end of *A Doll's House*—one's own experience of the world" (*Contesting Tears* 220). Charlotte takes a new step toward an Emersonian discovery of self-reliance in seeing how the criteria marking her difference from others open onto a new discovery of difference within her self. In this present time of transformation, Charlotte's present self confronts a reflection of a future self, already emergent in the present as if her present past began on her ocean voyage rather than in a life of isolation in the Vale mansion.

Very soon the film presents other means of temporal comparison. First there is Jerry's presentation of his family photograph (an image wherein he is significantly absent or absented), which is the image of past unhappy love that he carries with him on the present voyage. A brief time later, Charlotte will reciprocate, offering a photograph of the imposing Vale clan as evidence of why she does not have a high opinion of herself. The significance of this repetition lies in the fact that while Jerry is absent, unlocated in his scene of domesticity, Charlotte is visible yet unrecognized or unknown in hers. "Who's the fat lady with the heavy eyebrows and all the hair?" Jerry asks. At first Charlotte hesitates. She is embarrassed that Jerry has introduced her to his friends as "Camille Beauchamp." (Significantly, as named by Jerry she is no longer Renée and not yet the newly transformed Charlotte.) As always in the ironic mode, Jerry is half-wrong, yet half-right about many things. He mistakes Charlotte's mother for her grandmother, but judges the mother to have a strong character. Charlotte's response to his question is to offer a cascade of ironic predicates to identify this image: a spinster aunt, then, "I am the fat lady," and finally, "I'm Aunt Charlotte and I've been ill." Charlotte both is and is not these nominations; or rather, they are the background of past pain against which new identity is forming, or emerging from a structure of irony.

There is another photograph, however, that serves as the background of this scene of confession. Behind Charlotte and Jerry is an obvious back projection of a beautiful seascape at night, sparkling with reflected moonlight. This film is marked by its rapid rotation between registers of romance and melodramatic irony. What interests me more are the temporal dislocations presented by this mise-en-scène, which is at once ironic and romantic. Charlotte is unfixed along a line of becoming, where she must come to terms with a past that is already behind her—her present past, the way she lives now, is the present of the ocean voyage with Jerry. Significantly, it is obviously finite; it will come to a scheduled end, no matter how many times delayed. At the same time, this rather clichéd image of the moonlit sea is the background for this time of transformation. Is it ironic? No doubt it is utopic. It suggests the possibility of an awakening of desire that may urge Charlotte along her perfectionist path, where the series Charlotte–Renée Beauchamp–Camille enacts displacements in the series spinster–aunt–fat lady with hair–Charlotte who has been ill. But like all phases of perfectionist becoming, it is only one world, one finite world, and it too must be overcome, for all its attractions. Romance suggests the possibility of marriage, yet we already know that marriage is impossible for Charlotte and Jerry. Charlotte must look another way.

What is Charlotte doing when she faces her image in the window and also turns from it, facing us in an image of self-absorption? She is thoughtful, reflective. Is it too much to say that she is here confronting herself in aversion to (past) conformity as one of her first steps to self-reliance? In his lecture on Emerson's "Aversive Thinking" in *Conditions Handsome and Unhandsome*, Cavell reconsiders the place of thought in relation to moral perfectionism and its desire for change. In the framework of my elegy for theory, this may be another way of reasserting the primacy of ethics in philosophy. Cavell presents Emerson's sense of thinking as a process characterized by acts of transfiguration and conversion. One might say that there is no thinking without becoming, as if thinking yourself into a new form of life. Aversive thinking requires that difference be enacted as constitutive of a twofold becoming. As I have already written, it requires facing conformity, facing up to it or perhaps facing it down, in order to turn away from or to look another way, indeed to look *for* another way. (Need I say that this is a variation on Deleuze's ethical demand to choose to choose?)

Conformity is the name of Emerson's distaste for moralism, or moral cynicism, which is often given expression as a "disgust with or disdain for the present state of things so complete as to require not merely a reform, but a call for a transformation of things, and before all a transformation of the self. . . . We must become averse to this conformity," Cavell says, "which means convert from it, which means transform our conformity, as if we are to be born (again). How does our self-consciousness—which now expresses itself as shame, or let us say embarrassment—make us something other than human?"[87] Aversion

---

87. "Aversive Thinking: Emersonian Representations in Heidegger and Nietzsche," in *Conditions Handsome and Unhandsome: The Constitution of Emersonian Perfectionism* (La Salle, IL: Open Court, 1990), 46–47.

arises in crises of identity, but its power lies in the free exercise of moral choice. Moral cynicism refuses the human capacity for change and thus blocks or debars us from choosing a moral life or from taking active responsibility for our forms of life, instead of acting automatically or out of habit. Accordingly, embarrassment takes the form of ironic recognition that we have or had already chosen a life of conformity, and thus renounced the possibility of exercising moral freedom. "That debarment or embarrassment is for Emerson, as for Kant," Cavell emphasizes, "a state other than the human, since it lacks the humanly defining fact of freedom" (48). In Emersonian terms, I want to say that here Charlotte is discovering her "genius," that is, discovering within herself (as if another self) the capacity for self-examination and self-criticism, of being freed to take the next step in self-overcoming toward her as yet unattained attainable self. Call this a philosophy of the human based on the capacity to claim the freedom to exercise moral thought and moral choice. In *Now, Voyager,* this is another version of what photography calls thinking.

I have said that Charlotte is thoughtful. Or it might be better to ask, what sort of thoughtfulness opens these images photogenetically to artful conversation? The brief series wherein Charlotte confronts her doubled image in the window comprises a rotation of perspective, Charlotte seeing and being seen from various angles as if facing and turning from different facets of identity where she is newly theatricalized. The concluding image is one that we, viewers, have of her in her isolation and thoughtfulness. Here Bette Davis showcases a power for conveying what Cavell calls in *The World Viewed* the opacity of self-consciousness. To present self-consciousness in the condition of opacity is to claim or to express existence as a sign or surface presented outwardly to others—it is a way of existing for others, and also of presenting acknowledgment and acceptance of the limitedness of others' views of oneself.

What is Jerry's wish, and what is hers? With her beauty and her irony, what Davis conveys artfully throughout the film is that the claim of existence—the new assertion of existence or the assertion of new terms of existence—remains somehow uncertain or intangible no matter how powerful its outward manifestations. Cavell calls this the quality of unknownness. In *The World Viewed,* Cavell links the quality of unknownness to a photogenic capacity of film whose discovery marks the acknowledgment of another power of the medium of film. There are subjects for film, indeed subjects in film, that demand physiognomies that are not simply unknown, "but whose point, whose essence, is *that* they are unknown. Not just any unknown face will do; it must be one which, when screened, conveys unknownness; and this first of all means that it conveys privacy—an individual soul's aliveness or deadness to itself. A natural reason for a director's requirement of this quality is that his film is itself about unknownness, about the fact and causes of separateness or isolation or integrity or outlawry" (*The World Viewed* 181). That a soul is thus placed—isolated, imaged, and framed—might yield new knowledge of another link between the time of moral perfectionism and the time of becoming on film. Cavell calls this the discovery at any moment of "the endless contingency of the individual human's placement in the world, as though nothing could be more unanticipated than one's existence itself, always in placement" (181).

The endless contingency of individual human placement in the world is a fair characterization of the thought of moral perfectionism. The contingency of identity also reprises another element of grammar shared between remarriage comedy and melodramas of unknownness. As if anticipating his later book, Cavell observes in *Pursuits of Happiness* that remarriage comedies often engage in philosophical conversations about comedy and romance, as if a goal of these films were to consider reflexively their own grammar and conditions of possibility. To examine their own conditions of possibility while testing the concept of marriage also raises a deeper metaphysical problem, which Cavell defines as "the problem and the concept of identity—either in the form of what becomes of an individual, or of what has become of two individuals. On film this metaphysical issue is more explicitly conducted through the concept of difference—either the difference between men and women, or between innocence and experience, or between one person and another, or between one circumstance and another—all emblematized by the difference, hence the sameness, between a marriage and a remarriage" (55).

I have discussed at length how the question of difference is articulated in the shared grammar of gender asymmetry in the two genres. Now another possible difference emerges in the possibility and impossibility of marriage. Irony supplants comedy here because the unknown woman of the melodramas must judge whether the concept of marriage is worth the price of compromise (with the world of men, but also with the world), or whether it must be revised or rejected. Indeed she must decide whether to renounce her privacy, her unknownness, fully, or rather to embrace irony as a form of identity. Is the desire for romance or for marriage worth the price of compromise, or must a different form of life be imagined and aspired to, no matter its cost? These women derive their power to judge the world from their aversion to conformity. There is a deeply painful and unromantic side to unknownness. One may be unknown because one has been reduced to a state of isolation and voicelessness, unrecognized and unacknowledged by others, as if dispossessed of the capacity of speech and held in a state of pre-existence apart from the internal relations that bind each human to others. "Then what is wanting," Cavell responds, "—if marriage is to be reconceived, or let's say human attraction—is for the other to see our separate existence, to acknowledge its separateness, a reasonable condition for a ceremony of union. Then the opening knowledge of the human is conceived as the experience of being unknown. To reach that absence is not the work of a moment" (*Contesting Tears* 22).

We are closer now to understanding the multiple valences of Charlotte's wish. (Does this make her any less unknown?) In a first act of self-reliance, she has understood that she is unknown, especially to her self, and she has imagined the possibility of a new existence apart from that self. Here self-reliance takes the form of self-education, say an education in the philosophical art of self-fashioning. This possibility may have occurred because she is finally learning to see herself as Jerry sees her. His interest in her or attraction to her is inspired by her unknownness, in which he perhaps recognizes his own unrealized capacity for becoming. No happy conclusion is assured, though this film may be able to reimagine concepts of identity and marriage just enough to reach a new compromise in its vision of happiness. At the same time, Bette Davis's physical power for expressing privacy—active knowledge of her unknowability—is a claim of personal freedom in this film, no matter how limited or fragile. Through the exercise of this power she becomes more than the various predicates that would define and limit her identity: Vale, spinster, fat lady, Aunt Charlotte who has been ill. Like her sisters of privacy and unknownness, Garbo or Dietrich, Davis is able to convey in this and other films not only images of love, fate, or irony, but also, and more importantly, of chance and choice in a declaration of singularity and freedom.

The opacity of self-consciousness and the quality of unknownness are thus linked to the deeper philosophical problem of the films, which is to examine the irony of human existence as such. Charlotte's facing of her own transformed image and the voicing of her wish to comprehend her own unknownness as passing through and emerging from an other ("He wishes") are powerful aesthetic expressions of this irony. Perhaps it can be said that she claims Jerry's wish as her own, acknowledging and voicing its irony as the expression of a newly active feminine difference. Human existence is ironic because the capacity for undergoing change, for the self to think existence as a power of change, means acknowledging that the self is not one. In this context, the

opacity of self-consciousness recognizes the division of the self as still whatever the world sees—of how the world sees or has seen one's self—and at the
same time knows the self to not be or to never have been identical to that outward image. To be capable of undergoing change means being capable of an
internal division whereby identity can be beside itself, to separate from and
leave behind a prior yet still unforgotten self. In her capacity for thoughtfulness, for reflexivity and metamorphosis, Charlotte shows that she is and is not
what she is or has become; in his incapacity for self-education and change, Jerry
is not what he is not nor can ever become. The irony of perfectionist transformation is that the copresence of past identity with present becoming means
that simultaneously "Every single description of the self that is true is false,
is in a word, or a name, ironic" (Contesting Tears 134–135). And ironically,
change would not be possible if this were not the case. Identity must yield to
difference.

Cavell recognizes in Emersonian perfectionism the self's desire and capacity
for change, which comes from recognizing that the self can neither be whole
nor at rest—Thoreau calls this the self's answerability to itself, its neighboring
of itself. One of the deepest and most painful ethical dilemmas we can experience, then, is that we have become incapable of undergoing change. There is a
diagnostic side to Emerson, of which Nietzsche was well aware, that begins in
my awareness of the self as lost, frozen, or fixated, and thus in need of regen-
eration or rebirth. This is a first philosophical step toward recovering from
skepticism (what Wittgenstein would call a Gedankenweg), but a step without
conclusion or clear direction. It is a step taken not once but rather on an open
path in a continuing process of becoming from one stage or state of the self to
another. Each state is itself an achievement of new terms of existence; yet if
change is to occur each must eventually give way to new experience. The perfectionist practice of refinding the truth of oneself, or the humanity in oneself, is a journey whose first step is discovering that one is lost to the world, as
if buried in a fantasy of skepticism. And rather than sinking into despair, perfectionist desire refuses this society to seek another more humane or cultured
state of society and the self. If the truth these women find within themselves is
the irony of human existence, then what they have discovered is a capacity of
the human for becoming human, as if living in conformity means that all
of us only haunt existence or persist in a state of preexistence. The isolation of
unknownness is painful, just as the doubts of skepticism and the fantasy
of finally putting doubt to rest are painful. Another dimension of this irony,

then, would be expressed in the incapacity to enact one's aversion to conformity, and thus to be incapable of overcoming one's self in the imagination of new terms for existence. Call this irony as blindness to difference. (In *The Claim of Reason* Cavell terms this condition "soul-blindness.") This is one aspect of moral cynicism and a negation of human freedom, which in accepting isolation also negates the possibility of community.

To enact aversion to conformity is to interrupt repetition with difference, to take a step out of that fateful circle and to enlarge the diameter of experience. This perfectionist step is exemplified in Cavell's original reading of the conclusion to *Stella Dallas*. In one reading of this film, the ambition of the proletarian protagonist to overcome herself or to aspire to a better class (through, as it turns out, an unhappy marriage) is continually thwarted, marking irony as embarrassment. Stella's absence from her daughter Laurel's wedding to a young and wealthy husband, her withdrawal from that social space to view it at a distance, from the outside, framed and screened by a brilliantly lit living room window, is often interpreted as sacrifice and a renunciation of ambition. It is worth noting that a condition of this marriage has been Stella's granting of a divorce to Stephen Dallas, Laurel's father, so that he might marry the more prominent and refined Helen, his now-widowed original fiancée. The wedding is taking place in Helen and Stephen's home, the site of their newly won upper-class domesticity, and significantly, it is Helen who stages the scene, the wedding movie as it were, by insisting that the curtains remain open. Helen stages an image of happiness for Stella, as if in a movie, but what is the nature of this happiness?

In Cavell's reading, Stella learns that the world her daughter desires—of desire bound by law and church, of exclusiveness and belonging; in short, conformity—is not to her taste. This world is given to Stella as an image—indeed a screened image, an image from which she is screened—yet in ecstasy she turns away from it. Turns away from what, or in favor of what direction of new transport? "May we imagine," Cavell asks, "that we have here some Emersonian/Thoreauvian image of what Nietzsche will call the pain of individuation, of the passion Thoreau builds *Walden* to find, expressed as his scandalous pun on mo(u)rning, the transfiguration of mourning as grief into morning as dawning and ecstasy?" (*Contesting Tears* 212). This is a happy enough image of aspiring to another world, unseen yet perhaps just adjacent to the frame of this image of existence, where happiness may be pursued alone and outside of marriage. The world from which she is debarred is not her home. She must find another.

In this Stella is sister to Nora in *A Doll's House* in the sense that any future one might imagine for her is less important than the fact that she has a future, yet to be imagined and inhabited. In turning toward this world, facing it, she turns away from a mode of existence that she has discovered is not to her taste. At the same time, in Cavell's reading,

> In fancying Stella walking away as one continuation of Nora walking out, there is the additional moment to consider of her walking toward us. Again a house is turned away from, one that for a woman contains (self-) destructive illusion, or a way of illusory perception she had taken as reality, a way allegorized as a perception of the film screen. The mother's gaze she has received from such a screen replaces that of the screen she had identified with the world of the man she married. The ratifying of her insistence on her own taste, that is, of her taking on the thinking of her own existence, the announcing of her *cogito ergo sum,* happened without—as in Descartes's presenting of it, it happens without—yet knowing who she is who is proving her existence. (*Contesting Tears* 219)

At the end of *Stella Dallas,* we discover the variable senses of what tears contest. Are they tears of protest and of the joy of discovery and pain left behind, and do they then contest what tears are usually taken to mean in melodrama? The promise of Stella's transport, away from the screen and past the edge of her current existence, is an artful expression of the fact that repetition can also take the form, as Cavell suggests, of the promise of return as unpredictable reincarnation.

Rereading Linda Williams's interpretation of the film in her essay "Something Else Besides a Mother," Cavell writes that in these melodramas, "the woman's problem is not one of not belonging but one of belonging, only on the wrong terms; unlike the exile, the woman is not between two different cultures but is at odds with the one in which she was born and is roughly in the process of transfiguring into one that does not exist, one as it were still in confinement" (*Contesting Tears* 213). Perfectionism may also want to say that she is in the process of transfiguring this world into one that does not *yet* exist. Along these lines, Stephen Mulhall interprets Emersonian perfectionism as having a political dimension whereby the unknown women of melodrama confront and contest a society that fails to acknowledge them and their autonomy: "these women both instantiate a mode of self-reliance which amounts to a visible withdrawal from their society, a refusal of its conformity which functions as a rebuke to their fellow citizens in the name of an unknown but attainable state of each individual and consequently of society as a whole. And what these terms highlight is the political dimension of self-reliance, the implication that individuals who enact a proof of their own existence and so overcome skepticism can be thought of as engaging in a species of civil disobedience, an act that democratic society should not only permit but honour" (*Philosophy's Recounting of the Ordinary* 265). The self-disobedience of perfectionism is also an expression of civil disobedience in which the irony of identity is given another turn. Here and now in the present, we are all there is of the human or what can be expected from the human, and it is lacking; "we are not what we are meant to be," Cavell writes in *Cities of Words,* "not what the human expects of itself" (210).

The promise of return, indeed of the time of difference and eternal recurrence, and of unpredictable reincarnation, opens onto a practice of ethics that is as fundamental to Cavell's philosophy as it is to Deleuze's. To locate the expression of this ethical practice as a power immanent to cinematographic expression, and in a genre that requires the transfiguration and transvaluation of the woman's image and the refinding of the active voicing of her existence in new terms, is thus a significant discovery. If indeed one can link the new creation of the woman to the creation of the human, then philosophy has been discovered or rediscovered in an unanticipated domain, one that makes philosophy immanent to an art of lasting public power. The new creation of the woman as a new creation of the human is therefore not only a transfiguration of her own terms of existence; it also suggests a grammar for the aspiration to transform human existence, or whatever part of existence might define the human. In this, perfectionism recognizes Nietzsche's call for an untimely philosophy, in contradiction to and in contest with the present, where "culture is the child of each individual's self-knowledge and dissatisfaction with himself. Anyone who believes in culture is thereby saying: 'I see above me something higher and more human than I am; let everyone help me to attain it, as I will help everyone who knows and suffers as I do.'"[88]

In the melodrama of the unknown woman, there is something that the woman may give to the man—a form of education, as if introducing him to a new culture of difference, if he is willing to listen or to look, and this lesson is conveyed precisely by her unknownness. Perhaps it can be called an educa-

---

88. "Schopenhauer as Educator," in *Untimely Meditations,* ed. Daniel Breazeale, trans. R. J. Hollingdale (Cambridge: Cambridge University Press, 1997), 162.

tion in the passion for time. What I call the lesson of a passion for time draws upon the photogenetic powers of the moving image, whereby the automatic transcription and projection of the world hovers uncertainly between indicative and subjunctive moods, or a copresent belief of the past existence in time of a world preserved and the present projection of a world transformed. To say that a joyful passion for life is linked to the acceptance of transience, to the ability to mourn and thus transcend past time, means acknowledging becoming and change as forces integral to the possibilities of human identity. These ideas provide a new context for understanding the place of the feminine in both the comedies and the melodramas, which often figure a splitting or doubling of the projected presence of the women in the film, as if these characters held a greater share of knowledge or acknowledgment of a self-given capacity for transformation whether playful or ironic. This particular feature is perhaps best exemplified by Barbara Stanwyck's portrayal of Jean/Eve in *The Lady Eve* and Irene Dunne's Lucy/Dixie Bell in *The Awful Truth*. "For this we require a new creation of woman," Cavell writes in *Pursuits of Happiness*, "call it a creation of the new woman; and what the problems of identification broached in these films seem to my mind to suggest is that this creation is a metaphysical enterprise, exacting a reconception of the world. How could it not? It is a new step in the creation of the human. The happiness in these comedies is honorable because they raise the right issues; they end in undermining and in madcap and in headaches because there is, as yet at least, no envisioned settlement for these issues" (65).

Both genres share a grammar wherein the feminine conveys a new active concept of identity, which is marked by a structure of irony and aversion to conformity whose genealogy leads back to Nora in *A Doll's House*. What the woman must undergo is a metamorphosis, a painful acquisition of new identity, one in which the past is neither negated nor forgotten but rather exists alongside new terms of identity as if they were always present within her, yet for a time unavailable or inaccessible. Another form of irony then is recognition of a divided or divisible identity, one of which is isolated, voiceless and unknown—in short, cocooned. In this structure, old lives are not forgotten but ever remain as a past to be reckoned with. Current standing is fragile and subject to decay or revision, and the newly achieved voice is ironic because it knows that at any moment it may be reduced again to silence. This voicing of the irony of existence is an image of Cavell's career-long depiction of the human as expressed in a skeptically inspired condition that rotates wildly between the terror of absolute isolation and inexpressiveness on the one hand, and anxieties of absolute and unconditioned exposure on the other. Irony is the condition of the present and of recurrently possible conditionings of the future. In contrast to the comedies, only a compromised future is possible, if one is possible at all.

Cavell also notes that in contrast to the comedies, the painful journey to transformation takes place in a world where the mother is present, as is a child who spiritually if not biologically belongs to the protagonist. I think of the presence of the child as the projection of a so far unredeemed future. This is indeed the case in *Now, Voyager*. But this dramatic constellation has other meanings as well, as it seems to project new terms or conditions of identity. The woman is neither the mother, nor the child, nor biologically (call this the past's terms of transition) mother to the child. And if she also refuses to become or to be wife to a man, the pre-given lines of domestic identity are transformed. Jaquith's friendship no less than Jerry's is surely essential to Charlotte's perfectionist voyage of identity. Jaquith helps her discover her autonomy. In turn she must declare and protect this autonomy in relation to Jerry, and also preserve her new autonomy as a standing possibility for Jerry's daughter to take her own perfectionist step toward a revised future. The ethical power or possibility that Charlotte must preserve is that of the power to choose, to select and affirm lines to future selves that are so far undetermined by present possibilities weighted with a deadening past.

Accordingly, not only marriage but also motherhood is placed into question by this film. Or rather, considering the stultifying and oppressive powers of both Charlotte's mother and Jerry's wife, the terms of existence defined by motherhood must be transformed no less than those of marriage. For a child to be raised, to be given the power to become, she needs a new woman—that is, a newly created or recreated woman—who is something else besides a mother, to quote *Stella Dallas*. One might call this one woman's revolt against a certain tyrannical image of women. This revolt is not only an act of self-disobedience but also a transformation of the terms of consent by which parents are given the power to govern children, hence the power to control the future governed. Cavell notes that this image of consent is a fairly explicit reference to Locke's *Second Treatise of Government*:

> Now the significance I draw from the way this grown daughter contests the authority over her—a woman who has everything money can buy and that position can secure—is that the legitimacy of the social order in which she is to participate is determined (to the extent to which it can be

determined) by her consent, by whether she, in her state of freedom, finds that she wants the balance of renunciation and security the present constitution of society affords her. The price is madly high: the life of desire (outside the price of marriage) is one of irony, of enforced transcendence, and of romance as creating "cads," a name Charlotte and Jerry each claim for themselves. It turns out in Locke's *Second Treatise* that the existence of consent, hence of the social order, may be no easier to be clear about and establish than, as in Descartes's *Meditations*, the existence of a finite other proved to be. In linking the position of a woman's voice (hence her individual existence) with the constitution of consent (hence the existence of the social order), the film offers a sort of explanation about why we remain studiedly unclear about both.

That Charlotte consents in the moments we conclude with—and for her own reasons—is clear enough. That she would consent under altered conditions is unknowable. A good enough or just enough society—one that recognizes her say in it—will recognize this fact of, this threat in, or measure by, the woman's unknownness. (*Contesting Tears* 147–148)

This argument leads, again, to asking how are we to interpret the sense of ending in these films. Cavell notes that the melodramas solicit our tears and our recognition of sacrifice. At the same time he asks: "But is it that the women in them are sacrificing themselves to the sad necessities of a world they are forced to accept? Or isn't it rather that the women are claiming the right to judge a world as second-rate that enforces this sacrifice; to refuse, transcend, its proposal of second-rate sadness?" (*Contesting Tears* 127). The tears that mark the conclusion to *Now, Voyager* are not Charlotte's acknowledgment that she can expect nothing more of life with Jerry but rather that she expects a different, better life. To the extent that he is incapable of educating himself to this life, perhaps the tears are for him. Cavell reads Charlotte's words thus: "The fat lady with all the hair is eternally grateful. Yet having saved me from the exclusions of that fate, without denying that it was mine, allowing my metamorphosis, you cannot (I assume) be saved yourself. So these tears are from what the world calls an old maid, and they are tears for you, for your limitations, as well as for me and for mine. I assume, that is (correct me if I am wrong), that you cannot aspire to anything more from me" (*Contesting Tears* 132). At the end of *Now, Voyager*, Charlotte no longer occupies the same level of spiritual existence as Jerry. He has been transcended, left behind in conformity and conventionality.

Can the man practice an active passion for time? In the comedies the perfectionist pair take a step together into the future; in the melodramas the man is psychically fixated and it is the woman alone who seeks change and permits herself metamorphosis. Gender asymmetry is figured differently here. With respect to remarriage comedy, the reversibility or malleability of the network of relations mapping activity and passivity onto masculinity and femininity is reformulated. In melodramas of the unknown woman the man is often incapable of undergoing or even recognizing change. (The character of Stefan in *Letter from an Unknown Woman* is the emblem of this figure of masculinity as stuck in time, blind and impervious to change.) Only the woman is capable of shedding the frozen past that has entrapped her in a cocoon of irony and privacy, and thus taking an active step into a revised future.

Yet part of *Now, Voyager*'s revised vision of happiness is that men can develop an ear for the irony of identity, acknowledging and accepting its powers and passions. Before drawing completely to a close, the film reintroduces Doctor Jaquith to Charlotte's home in the company of Jerry—it is in fact a home that is now hers—a move whereby the film draws a contrast between the couple Charlotte-Jaquith and Charlotte-Jerry. Jaquith is able to inhabit this revised site of domesticity in ways that Jerry cannot. As Cavell describes it: "What these two discover together, looking like a couple well along in marriage, is that she is unknown—that the various names and labels that have been applied to her (another pervasive theme of the film) are none of them who she is. That this is a desirable therapeutic result I would like to maintain from a philosophical point of view of what the self is, something which no set of predicates can in principle exhaust, indeed something to which, as Heidegger takes *Being and Time* to demonstrate, no predicate applies, in the way predicates apply to objects. This idea of the self—always and never my possession, always to be discovered—is fundamental to the idea of perfectionism." (*Cities of Words* 245).

Recall, then, the conclusion to *Now, Voyager*. Charlotte and Charlotte's moral universe have never been more unknown to Jerry. And indeed, despite the love she still has for him, she embraces her own moral standing in their relationship by confronting him with the worst accusations possible—pretentiousness, piousness, conventionality—because in fact, he unknowingly wants to remove the gift of freedom and the power of choice from her by refusing to let her, as he sees it, sacrifice her life for Tina's.

Jerry finally accepts the limits of their relationship and Charlotte's freedom to continue building the life she has chosen, which includes caring for Tina and being something else besides a mother. The emblem of this acceptance is one of the most quoted lines in the history of American cinema. When Jerry asks Charlotte if she will be happy, she replies, "Oh, Jerry, don't let's ask for the moon. We have the stars." The end of *Now, Voyager* is sometimes considered to be incoherent. Yet this incoherence, which is rather a lack in understanding of what is perfectly clear, should be embraced as precisely in tune with the moral logic of the film. The ending is only incoherent from the point of view of the man in his ethical failure to comprehend the necessity of change and the attraction of a future society. Here the failure of the man is a failure of self-disobedience and of becoming human, and a failure to understand that he has lost or relinquished all power, especially the power of change. In contrast to the comedies, the man has not learned a perfectionist passion for time. Nor can he enter a community based on the comedies' respect for the daily reaffirmation of difference, of time as creation and ever-present becoming in a revision of the domestic or the ordinary, where in Cavell's terms, "the respect for difference demands responsiveness, specificity of response to the unforeseen, the perhaps uncategorized, say an improvisation of vision" (*Contesting Tears* 135).

Another difference that demands respect is the woman's capacity for metamorphosis, self-disobedience, and self-overcoming. Yet another is acceptance of the heterocosmic difference expressed in her vision of a transformed society, indeed a society where terms of friendship and marriage are themselves projected differently. The presence of Jerry and Jaquith in the denouement of the film is equally important for the narrative and philosophical arc of *Now, Voyager*. Both emblematize the possibility of relation whereby marriage is contested as a standing possibility, but differently. Jerry signifies marriage as it presently stands, and thus offers no vision of marriage as a transformed relation— one might think of this as a vision of marriage with romance but without desire or further becoming. As Cavell puts it, Charlotte and Jerry might have a child together, but Charlotte and Jaquith have a life and a future together on terms of equality. In the penultimate images of the film, they form not just an implied couple but a whole community, one founded on mutuality in education and care and in the desire to construct new terms for life. They are building a community of care for others. There is a positive irony here; Charlotte has found happiness in marriage, but in so doing she has transformed the concept of marriage and produced new terms for existence within marriage.

What does it mean, then, to relinquish the moon for the stars? Perhaps the moon is a sign of romance foregone, but having the stars is to possess the means for new navigation. The stars thus become guides for new departures, new arrivals, and new becomings. "So to begin with," Cavell writes, "we have the stars as Bette Davis is a star, hence we have images of independence to aspire to, individuality to the point, if necessary, of undeciphered idiosyncrasy.

Further, we have stars as Emerson and Thoreau had them, as signs of a romance with the universe, a mutual confidence with it, taking one's productive habitation on earth; signs of possibility, a world to think" (*Contesting Tears* 137–138).

Signs of possibility and a world to think are apt characterizations, as good as any, for whatever happiness philosophy can bring to human existence.

23. An Elegy for Theory

> **Éloge.** *n. m.* (1580: lat. *elogium,* pris au sens gr. *eulogia*). 1. Discours pour célébrer qqn. ou qqch. *Éloge funèbre, académique. Éloge d'un saint.*
>
> —*Le Petit Robert*

> Philosophy, as I understand it, is indeed outrageous, inherently so. It seeks to disquiet the foundations of our lives and to offer us in recompense nothing better than itself—and this on the basis of no expert knowledge, of nothing closed to the ordinary human being, once, that is to say, that being lets himself or herself be informed by the process and ambition of philosophy.
>
> —Stanley Cavell, *Pursuits of Happiness*

I would have preferred to title this project *Éloge de la théorie,* for in composing an elegy for theory I have kept in mind the subtle variations present in French. Combining the English sense of both eulogy and elegy, and something more besides, an *éloge* can be both praise song and funeral chant, panegyric and *chanson d'adieu.* (In addition, it conveys the second meaning of a legal judgment expressed in someone's favor.) If you feel I have been indecisive or unnecessarily subtle in my assessments of the prospects and future of theory, this is perhaps because it is necessary to explore critically the full range of emotions it inspires. Certainly I think the enterprise of theory is still a worthy one. Yet why in contemporary critical discourse are there so few left to praise and none to love it?

This question is still unanswered. Your work is long, and yet having reached the end of this journey, I feel we are left with no clear definition of theory, or even Theory, and no sense of whether we should embrace or contest it.
If one accepts my argument about discontinuity and retrojection in genealogies of theories as set out in *Elegy for Theory,* then the idea of theory as a potentially unified or unifiable concept is chimerical. The variable senses of theory

can only be located pragmatically, as contingent and historically positioned practices. Indeed our idea that Theory could represent a genre of critical discourse for the humanities, falling somewhere between criticism and philosophy, is fairly new, arising only in the 1960s. The goal of my two books could never have been to produce a stable conceptual definition and defense or criticism of theory or Theory. The best one can do in the framework I have offered is to delineate and examine the variety of language games in which concepts of theory have been deployed, and in grasping their overlaps, uneven edges, tectonic shifts, and contested borders, to consider theory as an open set. When examined genealogically, "theory" can only be presented as what Wittgenstein calls an intermediate case. There is a virtual life of theory no less powerful or elusive than that of film. We will never settle on a satisfactory definition of theory, even though one of the attractions of theory may be to demand just this satisfaction from us.

We still hold a picture of theory in our minds as an orderly image well composed and contained in a beautiful frame. It is rather a wild mountainside, densely forested and overgrown with prickly vegetation. So let us produce a natural history of theory, no matter how disorderly, clearing back the brambles to discover the eccentric paths—call them rhizomes—twisting over and through the concept. Or even a geology of theory where one finds a tangle of superimposed layers from different ages in exposed crevices and cracks, discolored and bleeding one into the other while still preserving something of their distinctiveness. There is still a picture, or series of pictures here, though it will take genealogy's tactful eye and sensitive hand to draw it out. And in making our way along this mountainside, in good weather or bad, we may find ourselves emerging out of theory onto the landscape of philosophy.

Nevertheless, just as Wittgenstein approaches and critiques the notion of absolute value by assembling and testing the variety of language games in which concepts of ethics are deployed, can we not settle on some idea of theory, and thus achieve some consensus regarding its senses and its range of activities?

We turn to or from theory with ease, though often without critical acknowledgment and interrogation of its multiple provenances and lines of descent. I have tried to make a full account of theory's long and complex genealogy, to feel its weight and density completely, and to plunge unafraid into its tangle of meanings and practices. One of my principal motivations for undertaking such a long and arduous journey was to demonstrate how theory returns across the history of philosophy and continually remakes itself as a rival to philosophy. From the standpoints of ethics and epistemology there are many disputed borders between theory and philosophy, and the territories they contest are themselves continually shifting and evolving.

Yet perhaps one frontier, no matter how elusive, could be drawn in this way. Theory is often driven by a desire for certain or secure knowledge, no matter how quixotic the quest. In its latest space or location of contestation, the academic practice of Theory is a curious mix of structuralist and poststructuralist arguments. While poststructuralism sought to counter the positivist and scientific pretensions of structuralism, nonetheless a certain specter of truth refused to be exorcised. In the age of Theory this will to truth was sustained in an epistemology of identity that persisted in locating truth, the truth of the subject, and the subject's access to truth in the essence-granting experience of an asymmetrical relation to power. At the same time, theory and philosophy often meet in interesting ways in poststructuralism, especially in a line that runs through Kristeva, Barthes, Derrida, Foucault, Lyotard, and Deleuze. Kristeva and Barthes, especially, approach theory as a turning of the subject upon herself, or a concept's turn upon itself, in the form of a critical division and asymmetry within the subject that projects future relations to knowledge and to self.

The desire for philosophy, however, is expressed only in what might be characterized as persistent existential crisis. "What is philosophy?" is the intractable and insistent question to which every philosophy worth its salt returns. In *Contesting Tears,* Cavell observes that this might be the only question to which philosophy is really bound. And regardless of its historically contingent forms, to cease caring about the practice and existence of philosophy is to abandon it recklessly to logic, science, politics, or religion.

Here it would seem that an open or incomplete notion of the practice(s) of philosophy is now turning around your vision of theory as an open set.
Our senses of theory cannot be resolved into a continuous picture. Theory's genealogical lines are contested, discontinuous, variable, and retrojecting; once examined genealogically, they begin to unravel like so many multicolored and differently textured threads falling from a tangled skein. By contrast, in spite of the variability of its forms, contexts, and methods, the practice of philosophy displays relative continuity. (This is one of the most compelling lessons

of Pierre Hadot's work, among others.) This is the final irony or paradox of this book, and the reason why a life in philosophy requires an elegy for theory.

Perhaps the moment has finally arrived to state clearly that despite their jagged and irregular borders, and all of the seams or edges that both link and separate them like the ocean meeting the land, both reaching over and withdrawing from it, philosophy is not theory. Philosophy may overlap with and link to many problems of theory, yet for me it remains distinct from theory as a practice.

One way to characterize theory might be as an activity wherein experience is converted into thought, and so made expressible and communicable to others. Along these lines one might also say that theory is outward directed while philosophy is inward directed. Theory's primary activity is explanation. Theories designate or refer to an object, which they hope to describe completely and whose effects they wish to account for or explain. In its generality, this definition counts as much for the criticism of art as it does for investigations of the natural world. Alternatively, in turning to art and other forms of human inventiveness, philosophy expresses knowledge of our selves and our relations with others. Art provokes in philosophy self-referring inquiries and evaluations of our ways of being and styles of existence. Here interpretation and evaluation are always turning one over the other as mutually amplifying activities. This is why I refer to philosophy as artful conversation. The style of philosophical expression is ontological and moral or ethical more than it is epistemological. And in turn, philosophy is a practice of styling the self and of projecting a world, no matter how unattainable, where that self might find new expression.

You still leave many questions unanswered, and you have also strayed very far from standing conceptions of film and media study. Does philosophy belong in the critical and historical study of film, not to mention literature or art? Do we need philosophy to give us better theories, or even to teach us to live without theory?
I can put the idea more radically in an example. Film theories are "about" film—they take or even construct films as objects of knowledge. They propose explanatory concepts to examine what film is (and these concepts will give us many competing definitions) and to explain its logics and effects. Here one presumes the empirical existence and history of the object and its effects, and the activities of theory are dependent on our sense of this object.

Alternatively, philosophy turns to film to examine and clarify problems and concepts that are of concern to philosophy. Paradoxically, this means that a (film) philosophy is not necessarily a part of film studies; rather, it belongs to philosophy alone. Philosophy explains nothing "about" film. However, it might have a lot to say about why and how film and the arts matter to us, why we value them, and how we try to make sense of ourselves and the world with and through them. It may even want to examine our "theories" of film to test their conditions of sense. However, I do not seek in philosophy a model for theorizing, for the straightforward reason that for me philosophy is not theory and does not propose theories. Its domain and activities lay elsewhere.

If a philosophical reading returns to film or literary studies some fact or insight regarding the nature or history of the medium and its meanings, it is in the form of a gift. Here philosophy overlaps with or contributes to theory, perhaps, but it does not become, for all that, a theory of film or art or literature. Perhaps we should reserve "theory" for epistemological inquiries into the nature of things, matters, and causes. Theory would be epistemological and empirical, then, in diverse and open senses of the concept. Still, there is a point where philosophy and theory touch or find a common join: where in examining an object we also evaluate the conditions and styles of knowing, limits as well as possibilities, that confront us in efforts, successful or not, toward knowing.

If there is any continuity to my work of the past thirty years (and I hope that there is), it has been to probe and test the conceptual foundations of what we say about film or the arts. Here there is a second task for theory, one which borders on philosophy, and which Kant calls "critique" as an activity that tests the limits and possibilities of our knowledge. This second task of theory can come into conflict with the first to the extent it makes us aware that we are constantly creating our objects, or at least the forms of their intelligibility and value; thus they do not preexist our conceptual characterizations, but are always relative to them. (This is perhaps one of the greatest lessons of Althusser that 1970s film studies neglected to absorb.) Philosophy is ill served, though, when its self-image is based on establishing conditions of truth, or judgments of truth and falsity. It is better served in casting epistemology not in matters of science but in questions of ethics: What do we want from truth? What powers does the will to truth serve, and what world would it make in its image? This activity is evaluative. Ethical (self) investigations and the ethical evaluation of epistemology—the will behind styles of thought—are two of the domains proper to philosophy.

And now comes a third turning. There is conceptual critique but also conceptual creation and innovation. This is what really interests me in Deleuze or

Cavell. Here philosophy engages art in order to aid the further creation or clarification of concepts. As philosophers, when we turn to film we come back to philosophy.

Are Deleuze and Cavell theorists or philosophers?
Well, a bit of both. Cavell reads films very closely and I think he has made a significant and undervalued contribution to the problem of defining genres. That is a real theoretical contribution. And Deleuze has helped us to understand films in a host of new ways. But it is almost always the case that this theoretical work in both thinkers is geared toward moving forward larger and more general philosophical problems. Is this kind of philosophical work only metaphysical or speculative? No, because our engagements with the world, both moral and epistemological, are oriented by the concepts we inhabit and deploy pragmatically. And we can only understand those engagements, and possibly transform them, by reflexively practicing conceptual critique and conceptual innovation. In our artful conversations, film and other forms of art often help this reflection in profound ways, but in so doing, we are usually philosophizing, not theorizing.

Your question puts into focus something I have been thinking about for a long time. Am I really a "film theorist"? In my career have I ever presented something resembling a film theory, generalizable concepts or arguments that explain something about the nature and effect of film? In some of my early essays, perhaps, but I think in none of my books. And if this activity is not theoretical, then how do I describe what has driven me to write the books that I have written? "Working in philosophy," writes Wittgenstein in *Culture and Value,* "is really more a working on oneself. On one's own interpretation. On one's way of seeing things. (And what one expects of them.)" I have yet to find a better characterization of philosophical investigation.

I believe your emphases on interpretation and evaluation are too strong. Can one not make knowledge claims without any larger epistemological or ethical commitments?
How can one make knowledge claims without commitment to an ethical perspective that would give them value and provide criteria for what makes them reasonable or not? What my vision of philosophy teaches us is that adherence to a domain of reason is marked by an existential choice. In any case,

one should have a sense of what one values in knowing if knowledge claims are to be worth something. This is why Charles Taylor insists that evaluating import ascriptions is vital to assessments of our claims to reason and their potentially transformative effects for good or ill. At the same time, it is crucial to evaluate and continually critique the senses of theory or philosophy to which we find ourselves attracted. It is equally important to clearly acknowledge that the senses of theory to which we feel epistemologically allied are wrapped into uses of language and forms of life that we value and express discursively, and which in turn are framed and conditioned by history. You might see here, then, why ethical evaluation is so important to me. In philosophy, and perhaps even "theory," I believe that the separation of epistemological questions from ethical ones is a dangerous business. And I think it is impossible to make a claim to knowledge outside of an implicit or explicit sense of what we value in knowledge and how we go about seeking it.

I can put the question in another way. In "Traveling Theory" Edward Said notes the obvious yet always incompletely learned fact that no reading is neutral or innocent. Every interpretation arises in the context of some guiding concept or idea, however implicit or unconscious. No matter how open or ambiguous, such conceptual frameworks guide interpretation and sense making, and we can call these frameworks theory. Another feature of theory is that it is invariably incomplete because, happily, conceptual understanding can never exhaust the interest of everyday life and experience for us. This observation is important, since aspirations to systematicity, continuity, homogeneity, completeness, and universality are among the most persistent qualities of what one might call theory's truth games; likewise their force of retrojection in each new appearing. Nevertheless, theory travels in time no less than space, and each one of its displacements yields new mutations of sense, enlarging or constricting its potential for generating new ideas or for connecting to new areas of interest. Displacements in context also mean that theories are continually translated and retranslated in both literal and abstract senses—their "language" can be deformed and refashioned, leading to renewal or decline. All of which is to say that in spite of its retrojecting tendencies, theory has no sense nor power in the absence of history.

Perhaps this is another way of asserting thought's relation to time and philosophy's relation to history or genealogy. Is not historical thinking a real alternative to theory or philosophy?

This intuition is also incompletely learned. Why do we resist fully embracing the fact that thought is time bound? I think of this as a piercing of theory by history, which subjects the internal structure of concepts to a certain violence that loosens the connections among its components, holding them open, fragmenting them, or producing irregular spaces where new and foreign genetic materials sometimes settle and blossom. To attend fully to the force of history in theory or philosophy requires attention to detail and sensitivity to context as well as receptiveness to time. Said calls this "critical consciousness," which is one of his most powerful yet least-remarked-upon concepts. Critical consciousness is not a rival to theory. (Neither is philosophy a rival to theory, to my mind.) Indeed critical consciousness is close to what Nietzsche calls genealogy. It is something like the conscience of philosophy or theory, or an ethical will that encourages critical thought to evaluate the displacement and mutation of concepts in time and place in constant recognition that sense and value are relational and contextual.

Would critical consciousness be an act of theory or philosophy?
Said characterizes critical consciousness as a spatial sense or faculty for measuring and assessing the situatedness of theory and its incompleteness in any given situation. Theories emerge, persist, mutate, or decline in response to specific and often unrepeatable historical forces in concrete circumstances. Investigating the historical senses of theory or mapping its genealogies, then, does not only mean restoring or deepening knowledge of a theory's provenance but also critically assessing the singularity of its appearances. The singularity of a theory's historical displacements also shows that no theory exhausts, or is itself exhausted by, its original or subsequent locations.

But what happens to the association of theory with politics here, or perhaps more precisely, the critique of ideology? Or in fact the relation of theory or philosophy to practices lived and suffered?
Said says that above all "critical consciousness is awareness of the resistances to theory, reactions to it elicited by those concrete experiences or interpretations with which it is in conflict."[89] One might even say that theories "decline" grammatically and genealogically in or through forces of resistance. In this

89. Edward W. Said, "Traveling Theory," in *The World, the Text, and the Critic* (Cambridge, MA: Harvard University Press, 1983), 242.

sense, every theory is a grid of selection and omission, produced in conflict and productive of dissensus. Genealogy as critical consciousness not only restores a sense of the historical conflicts in which theories are born and to which they respond, it is also the critic's job, as Said puts it, "to provide resistances to theory, to open it up toward historical reality, toward society, toward human needs and interests, to point up those concrete instances drawn from everyday reality that lie outside or just beyond the interpretive area necessarily designated in advance and thereafter circumscribed by every theory" ("Traveling Theory" 241–242). In this critical consciousness is a third domain, distinct from both theory and philosophy yet overlapping with them. Indeed, one of the attractions of the kind of philosophy I care about in figures as diverse as Wittgenstein, Foucault, Derrida, Deleuze, Lyotard, or Cavell is its critical capacity—the desire for philosophy is incited in the very conditions that oppose or resist thought. For Cavell, this critical capacity defines the difficulty of philosophy as well as its particular strength, which Cavell himself characterizes as receiving "inspiration for taking thought from the very conditions that oppose thought, as if the will to thought were as imperative as the will to health and to freedom" (*Pursuits of Happiness* 42). The possibility of thinking, or better critical thinking, should also be a potential pursuit of happiness, and thus part of the daily practice of the good city.

Of course, one must also take account of the resistance to philosophy, which has often occurred from within philosophy itself. Our vision of philosophy today (primarily academic philosophy) is a also a picture transposed retroactively on the whole history of philosophy. And philosophy's vision of itself (primarily analytic philosophy) is one that wants to stand apart from this history in its attachments to abstract reason as an activity and a form of life that belittles matters of value, say art or ethics, as "metaphysical." The critical stance of analytic philosophy is one wherein the whole history of philosophy must be accepted or rejected, and critiqued, only from within the framework of analytic philosophy and its own claim to reason. Here again, we must reclaim or try to imagine what is continuous, as well as discontinuous, in a life called philosophy. Analytic philosophy is too small an island, or too low a hill, for surveying the continent of philosophy. (In any case, its gaze is turned in the wrong direction.) If Kant is the great turning point in philosophy—its modernization or modernity, hence its institutionalization in the university—then Kant's reading of Hume, Rousseau, Descartes, Spinoza, and Leibniz accomplishes a violent double gesture. These thinkers enter a history of philosophy as academic philosophy in the form of the creation of systems and their critiques—an Oedipal line of father killing. But in so doing, other lines of descent, other conceptions and genealogies of philosophy are suppressed. And this includes the classical philosophers, who taught in academies but were not academics, and for whom philosophy had a different role with respect to the polis. Think again here of Emerson's and Thoreau's or Nietzsche's wish to recover or heal philosophy, thus freeing it from its professionalization.

I am curious now about what interpretation means in this context. Is interpretation an intermediary practice where we pass from theory to philosophy?

You have led me to understand that interpretation has a special sense for philosophy. The central question that binds Deleuze's and Cavell's conception of philosophy in something like a common grammar is: How is change possible, or better, how is *human* change possible? In this context, the need for interpretation often begins in confrontation with an internal and external division. Foucault calls this a confrontation with the Outside (of self or of thought; in any case something completely alien to the world I currently inhabit). For Deleuze my internal or external relation to time is something that divides me like an alien force. In other terms, the need for interpretation arises in the experience of unknownness—of others' unknownness to me or my unknownness to myself—and in this interpretability also takes account of my capacity for being unknown to others. The difficulty of being unknown is a quality that we all share, or a form of life we inhabit in common as humans. And only in acknowledging this commonality can we avoid skepticism and violence by entering into interpretation, no matter how difficult or unsure.

This is also why the dilemmas of skepticism are as much ethical as epistemological. My explicit promotion of philosophy, and hesitant withdrawal from theory, is inspired in important ways by Cavell's attempts to moderate problems of epistemology as raised by skepticism's persistent claims on us. In this way, the will to theory may be reframed in terms of the skeptical tendency to want too much from knowledge of the external world, or of other minds. *The Claim to Reason* might thus be read as an attempt to curb the immoderate desire of epistemology to require certainty in all domains, when in fact there is not one standard of knowing or rationality for all things, especially human thoughts, actions, and creativity. In contrast to theory, philosophy embraces this uncertainty, no matter how disorienting or alarming, as a path toward change and for its possibilities of a life examined and reexamined in oneself and with a community of others. This is why Cavell insists that what opens us to possible knowledge of the human, or of discovering the internal relation of each human being with all others, is the experience of being unknown to myself and to others. The perfectionist practice of refinding the truth of oneself, or the humanity in oneself, is a journey whose first step is discovering that one is lost to the world, as if buried in a fantasy of skepticism. The call to interpret in philosophy is inspired by this fundamental insight. Fueled by the attraction of certain knowledge, the temptation of skepticism is the fantasy of possessing absolute knowledge of the world, of self, or of others. But the will to interpret, the desire to interpret, arises from the experience of confronting the human limitations of knowing oneself or others.

Cavell's insistence, following Wittgenstein, that dilemmas of skepticism are irresolvable is therefore a way of acknowledging the absence of totality in knowing, despite the fascination and terror inspired by the unknowability of others and despite philosophy's insistent craving for certainty. A feature of human life might then be that human behavior is less to be explained than interpreted. Philosophy should encourage us to embrace the facts that we are interpretable and that we have the capacity for becoming known to ourselves and to others, no matter how uncertain or fragile we consider this knowledge to be.

In this perspective, interpretation may indeed be an activity wherein we pass from theory to philosophy. Questions of interpretation only arise with respect to beings we perceive to be capable of expressive behavior despite all their ostensible differences from us, and consequently in the belief that miscomprehension can give way to comprehension. In these situations of otherness, we need "passing theories," as Donald Davidson might say, to ferret out patterns of similarity and difference wherein we can make ourselves understood by one another. And in so doing we not only comprehend but also create what Taylor calls new languages of perspicuous contrast. In this way, there is a virtuous circle wherein miscomprehension, theory, and interpretation turn around one another. There is value in being disagreeable, as I have said, because we can only come to terms with human potentialities for sociability and concord through discord and disagreement. The pursuit of happiness through marriage must always pass through divorce.

Another way of thinking through this question is to imagine the strange style of Wittgenstein's *Philosophical Investigations* as vacillating between theory and philosophy, like turning between two incommensurable pictures in aspect seeing. Theory arises in situations of doubt and hesitancy where one feels the need to chance an explanation, or to make a guess in confidence that new discovery of some missing piece of information will solve the riddle once and for all. That is one way of seeking conviction or certainty. Subsequently, if Wittgenstein finds that philosophy is not theory, or that theory is little help to philosophy, this also means that nothing is deferred in philosophical problems—there is nothing to look for or wait for that is not already present before us or available to us. Everything one needs for philosophical investigation is present or "open to view" in the forms of life we inhabit and practice. Call these human expressive resources, or in short, culture. And if we are in a state of disagreement, there is no standard or measure to which we can appeal that is external to this form of life. Strangely, it is as if there is no content to philosophy—no theses, no syllogisms, nothing to believe or to take another's word for, no explanation to accept on condition that further evidence or data will prove it with certainty. This is less a sense of philosophy's criticism of theory or disdain for theory than an acknowledgment that philosophy is not theory, or that philosophy speaks or writes or shows from a place that is not theoretical. A shift of perspective is enacted here whereby I cannot prove philosophy or give evidence for philosophical assertions apart from inspiring a form of examination or investigation that begins with—in—my self, and your self as well as mine. The desire for philosophy only arises and moves—but also declines and disappears—in an internal relation with one's own thinking, a process of interpretation that begins with self-interpretation.

It may also simply be the case that acts of interpretation are unavoidable in any mode of inquiry we undertake, whether as scientists or humanists. Interpretation is integral to sense making and value assessing in all its varieties. Interpretive acts also frequently produce acts of creation, thus producing new situations and frameworks for understanding. In such cases, there is both a transformation of the conceptual contexts in which inquiry and understanding take place and also a subjective transformation of the interpreting agents. In this perspective, there is no separation of an object from a subject of knowledge, and thus the ascription or creation of sense will also involve a corresponding self-interpretation and transformation. Such arguments are aimed at preserving a space for the humanities in the face of an ever-expanding instrumental and technological reason. But they also profoundly challenge any strict division separating the humanities and the sciences. Perhaps the basis or fundamental context of a philosophy of the humanities is this: not to be engaged in the discovery of new knowledge, but rather in the creation or establishment (experimentation) of novel modes of knowledge that place in new contexts both our possible knowledge of self and the self's relations to a community of others. The focal point of a philosophy of the humanities, then, is to assert and evaluate the place, function, and importance of the human subject with respect to these activities of interpretation, creation, inquiry, and understanding. However, as both Cavell and Foucault warn in their different ways, the creation of a new mode of knowledge may equally be that of a new mode of ignorance. The task of philosophical criticism is unending.

Does this mean that we have "found" philosophy more certainly than theory?
The power of this question only makes sense in the context of perfectionism and the perfectionist embrace of becoming other, and becoming other in thought. The philosophy most meaningful to me asks that we acknowledge that being and thought are incommensurable, and that this incommensurability is a force that divides thought from itself and pitches it toward new thinking, if we do not instead fall into darkness and confusion. Thought has no telos apart from the pitch of thinking, and the sage is wise only in theory since wisdom is the emblem of an attainable yet always unattained state. Therefore, the commitment to philosophy means that one can never become a philosopher or finally attain a state of wisdom. There are only steps to be taken without finality toward each new thought or new term of existence, and each step is uncertain and unbalanced, guided only by the projection of a desired future self, one which is attainable but for which there is no guarantee of achievement, for there is always another step to be taken.

As I wrote earlier, in the long view the two critical tasks of philosophy are to interrogate the bases, grounds, and frameworks wherein reasons are given and defended—not only to constrain them when they are unreasonable but also to expand and ramify them in the production of new frameworks, contexts, and concepts—and to evaluate the axiological commitments that frame or structure our forms of reason giving. To claim to know is always to value certain ways of knowing, and to value is to project a world commensurate with the forms of reason one aspires to define and develop in conceptual expression. Since the time of Socrates, philosophy has always been finding its way (because the desire for philosophy arises from the distress of being lost) by way of these two compass points. And in this way, perfectionism has been a recurrent presence in the will to philosophy as the emblem of a desire for change and for becoming other, which leads us to seek out new terms of existence by fully interrogating, sometimes to the point of madness, our disappointments with life as it stands.

Perhaps, then, philosophy is the practice of a virtual life, of embracing becoming and perfectionist aspirations to new and as yet undiscovered terms of existence.

In the prologue to *Cities of Words,* Cavell reprises Thoreau's lament that "There are nowadays professors of philosophy, but not philosophers. Yet it is admirable to profess because it was once admirable to live." How well Thoreau foresaw the difficult life of philosophy in the twentieth and twenty-first centuries. If one must compose an elegy for theory, let us hope it awakens a new life for philosophy in the current millennium.

At the same time, it is a delicious irony that at the beginning of the last century, Hugo Münsterberg, arguably the first film theorist, was in fact a philosopher who grasped completely that the new medium of moving images asks both ontological and ethical questions of us. And so it is most fitting that as film bows from the stage of history, it leaves us with our thoughts and returns us to philosophy. After a one-hundred-year history, what becomes of theory? Philosophy.

Films still entertain and move us, but they also move us to thought.

ACKNOWLEDGMENTS

To acknowledge is to take account of one's philosophical friends, without whom thinking could not take place. I am fortunate in having many such interlocutors and critics whose contributions to this project have been immeasurable.

Lindsay Waters, Executive Editor for the Humanities at Harvard University Press, has been unwavering in his support for this project, which grew in scale and ambition beyond either of our expectations. I remain deeply grateful for his encouragement, advice, and above all, patience. A few courageous friends undertook the task of reading large sections of the manuscript, providing invaluable advice. James Chandler provided many helpful suggestions for structuring the project, as did anonymous readers for Harvard University Press. Among the other dear friends and colleagues who shared their work, ideas, and criticisms were Dudley Andrew, Homi Bhabha, Dominique Bluher, Karl-Alfred and Eliane Bluher, Rosi Braidotti, Sarah Childress, Stephen Greenblatt, Martin Jay, Paola Marrati, Toril Moi, Richard Moran, Richard Neer, Geoffrey Nowell-Smith, Brian Price, Robert Ray, Diana Sorensen, Megan Sutherland, and Justin Weir. The ever-extraordinary Renée Pastel provided invaluable editorial help, verifying citations, reviewing translations, and copyediting with her usual precision and thoughtfulness.

Many of my arguments were honed in response to challenging audiences at invited lectures and conferences at the University of California, Los Angeles, the "Waking Life" conference in Berlin, the Chinese University of Hong Kong and Hong Kong Shue Yan University, the New School for Social Research, the University of Edinburgh, the Laboratory for Advanced Research on Film and Philosophy, Instituto de Filosofia da Linguagem, New University of Lisbon, Internationales Kolleg für Kulturtechnikforschung und Medienphilosophie, Bauhaus-Universität, Weimar, the Centre for the Humanities at Utrecht University, the University of Chicago, and at the Shulman Seminar Lecture at Yale University. I remain deeply beholden to the staff, colleagues, and fellows who shared with me one of the most extraordinary and fertile semesters of my career at the Internationales Kolleg für Kulturtechnikforschung und Medienphilosophie in Weimar, including the generous and brilliant codirectors of the Institute, Lorenz Engell and Bernhard Siegert.

Portions of Sections 7 and 8 appeared as "Of which we cannot speak . . . : philosophy and the humanities," in *Zeitschrift für Medien-und Kulturforschung Heft* 2 (Autumn 2011); portions of Section 12 appeared as "The World, Time," in *Afterimages of Gilles Deleuze's Film Philosophy*, ed. D. N. Rodowick (Minneapolis: University of Minnesota Press, 2009), 97–114, and are reproduced here with the permission of the publisher. I wish to thank the editors of these publications for their attentive comments and suggestions, and for their kind permission to reprint this material here. I also wish to thank the editors of *Sites* and *Critical Inquiry* for their comments and suggestions, and for allowing me the opportunity to develop themes and topics discussed here in earlier articles: "'Art now exists in the condition of philosophy,'" *Sites: The Journal of 20th-Century/Contemporary French Studies* 16:2 (March 2012); and "The Value of Being Disagreeable," *Critical Inquiry* 39:3 (Spring 2013).

My debt to my undergraduate and graduate students at Harvard University is ongoing. Both *Elegy for Theory* and *Philosophy's Artful Conversation* were shaped in influential and unforeseen ways by students in several iterations of my seminar on Philosophy and Film, including the fall 2004 seminar on "Post-Theory," the fall 2007 seminar on "The Film Philosophy of Stanley Cavell," wherein Stanley generously played a crucial and personal role, and finally and perhaps most importantly, my spring 2012 seminar on "Deleuze and Cavell." I conclude then with expressing heartfelt thanks, again, to Stanley Cavell for a lifetime of generosity in philosophy.

INDEX